SMASH AND GRAB

ANNEXATION OF SIKKIM

SUNANDA K. DATTA-RAY

First published by Vikas Publications in 1984

Revised edition published by Tranquebar, an imprint of westland ltd, in 2013

Published by Westland Non-Fiction, an imprint of Westland Books, a division of Nasadiya Technologies Private Limited, in 2025

No. 269/2B, First Floor, 'Irai Arul', Vimalraj Street, Nethaji Nagar, Alapakkam Main Road, Maduravoyal, Chennai 600095

ISBN: 9789360455583

10 9 8 7 6 5 4 3 2 1

Typeset by FourWords Inc.

Printed at Manipal Technologies Limited, Manipal

In memory of

JUNGKHYANG

Who believed
to the end

CONTENTS

INTRODUCTION vii

PREFACE TO FIRST EDITION xxxi

PROLOGUE xxxv

Chapter 1
SMASH AND GRAB 1

Chapter 2
BELGIUM OF ASIA 23

Chapter 3
SEPARATE BUT TOGETHER 57

Chapter 4
BURRA KOTHI 81

Chapter 5
WAR OF NERVES 102

Chapter 6
EIGHTFOLD WAY 119

Chapter 7
SPIDER'S WEB 140

Chapter 8
POISED IN TIME 157

Chapter 9
SHORTER LEASH 183

Chapter 10
VOTE FOR FREEDOM 200

Chapter 11
THE BIRTHDAY PARTY 217

Chapter 12
FOOT IN THE DOOR 249

Chapter 13
DEATH WARRANT 273

Chapter 14
AGAINST THE LAW 306

Chapter 15
WINNER TAKES ALL 332

Chapter 16
LAST-DITCH STAND 359

Chapter 17
THUMB IMPRESSION 379

APPENDICES 416

INDEX 419

INTRODUCTION

Many readers assumed this book was banned as soon as it appeared in 1984. Even NDTV's anchor said so when introducing me in *The Big Fight* programme. Given the title, which quotes the twelfth Chogyal of Sikkim, Palden Thondup Namgyal, the conclusion was not unexpected. It was strengthened when *Smash and Grab: Annexation of Sikkim* disappeared from view just as its revelations were beginning to attract attention.

A ban would have been clumsy. As it happened, Gurbachan Singh, the last political officer in Gangtok and Sikkim's de facto overlord, filed a defamation suit against me demanding enormous damages. Normally, defamation has to be proved before the courts take any action. Proving can take months, even years. In my case, the Delhi High Court issued an order at the first hearing, forbidding sale of the book until the case had been settled. A contempt charge was piled on that when Gurbachan Singh produced a cash memo from a shop in some small town which had sold a copy. The matter was resolved only when the eminent jurist, Soli Sorabjee, representing me in a generous act of friendship, persuaded the prosecuting lawyers to accept an out-of-court settlement entailing an apology (Appendix A) but no money. The sales ban was lifted but the publisher claimed he had no copies left to sell. He wasn't interested in reprinting either.

Neat, you might say. What J.N. (Mani) Dixit, the former head of India's foreign office who died suddenly in 2005 soon after Manmohan Singh appointed him national security adviser, told me much later made it seem neater still. 'South Block was very worried about what you might come out with,' he said one day over lunch in his bungalow in Gurgaon. 'The defamation suit was a godsend!' Apparently, Gurbachan Singh's colleagues in the external affairs ministry and the prime minister's office, both housed in South Block, had made a point of playing on his wounded vanity. Whether they did or not, the suit was as effective as a ban without laying the government open to the charge of censorship. South Block was even more relieved when the matter was settled out of court. That averted an embarrassing public discussion of actions that were legally and morally questionable.

Dixit was one of the few in the know. Among those to be taken in by official propaganda was Daniel Patrick Moynihan, the American ambassador who cultivated a viceregal presence. His Wikileaks Cable1973NEWDE04127_b exonerated New Delhi of stirring up trouble or contemplating annexation. 'Indians will probably prefer to preserve the existing treaty relationship', he wrote on 10 April 1973, in response to State Department inquiries. Two days later, Moynihan approvingly cited (Cable 1973NEWDE04291_b) the report of 'an experienced American official now posted in Europe who was vacationing in Sikkim during the current unrest'.

> The official believes that the demonstrations by the Nepalese-Sikkimese majority against the Chogyal's regime, which favoured the indigenous minority, were spontaneous, appeared to be non-violent, (and) were not induced by the Indian government... India does not plan to incorporate Sikkim within India.

Indian officials who took pride in planning and executing the operation would have split their sides laughing. They can't be ignored because just as my last book, *Looking East to Look West:*

Lee Kuan Yew's Mission India, highlighted the most constructive aspect of Indian diplomacy, *Smash and Grab* is the only account of the militarism, deceit and betrayal that policymakers are also capable of. Happily, that dark side of India's Asian strategy has not been repeated. But the reminder may still be necessary.

Despite the courtroom drama, writing the book was relatively uncomplicated compared to the reporting that preceded it. Since I had some knowledge of the Himalayan region, N.J. Nanporia, my editor at *The Statesman*, asked me to go up to Gangtok when the disturbances broke out in April 1973. He also advised caution. 'That Chogyal fellow has money here, you know!' Nanporia added, tapping his desk. He was never into social niceties unlike the paper's managing director, C.R. Irani, with whom he had an uneasy relationship. Irani had asked the Chogyal for a loan. Canny in small things, the Chogyal examined the paper's accounts and decided against risking his own money. Instead, he instructed the State Bank of Sikkim to provide the funds. The bank advanced ₹ 300,000 but refused when Irani wanted more.

The tension between Irani and Nanporia was a much greater nuisance than any expectations the Chogyal might have entertained for bailing *The Statesman* out of its perennial financial crises. With his strong Swatantra Party loyalties, Irani projected himself as the lone crusader battling Indira Gandhi's pro-Soviet dictatorship. Sikkim was another stick with which to beat her. He was also gratified to hob-nob with royalty, especially the Chogyal's grander relatives in Bhutan. Queen Kesang Wangchuck, wife of the third Druk gyalpo, King Jigme Dorje Wangchuck, was the Chogyal's first cousin. The connection gave Irani a social edge over his cousin, Nani A. Palkhivala, who had plucked him out of an obscure insurance company and made him managing director of *The Statesman* even without any experience of newspapers.

Irani badgered me to 'expose' Indira Gandhi. Nanporia urged prudence. My reports in *The Statesman* and *The Observer* in London (I was the paper's South Asia correspondent) must have reflected these conflicting directives, for *The Observer* placed no constraints on what I wrote. Readers who noticed inconsistencies blamed Indian censorship. At that stage the pressures emanated mainly from the tussle in Statesman House.

That doesn't mean there was no official obstruction. As described in the book, the Indian military once blocked a tunnel so that I couldn't reach Gangtok in time to see the Sikkim legislature's Indian presiding officer coerce timid Sikkimese legislators into signing their country's death warrant. There was a sequel. A buzz in the newspaper world soon afterwards gloated that the external affairs ministry had given the lie to a story in *The Observer* claiming I 'was prevented from leaving the country and from filing' my report on Sikkim. Katyayani Shankar Bajpai, Gurbachan Singh's predecessor as PO, from whom I sought an explanation, said, 'Ask your friend Karma!' He meant Karma Topden, the Chogyal's former deputy secretary (also intelligence chief and chief of protocol), who then represented Sikkim in Calcutta. He later became a member of the Rajya Sabha and India's ambassador to Mongolia.

Karma was a close friend and didn't need any persuasion to tell me all. The Gyalmo, the Chogyal's American second wife, the former Hope Cooke, had called to tell him of the legislative coup and how I was prevented from reporting it. Karma dutifully telephoned the news to the Chogyal's son, Crown Prince Tenzing, a Cambridge undergraduate. He had passed it on to *The Observer*. Unfamiliar with Himalayan geography, the paper thought the blocked tunnel had prevented me from leaving India for Sikkim. It was an innocent mistake in this Gangtok-Calcutta-Cambridge-London game of Chinese whispers. The interesting discovery for me was that telephone lines—of the palace in Gangtok, Karma's in Calcutta, and possibly mine too—were tapped. Sitting in Gangtok's India House, built as Britain's first China-watching post, the PO could listen in on all our conversations.

Bajpai advised me to insist on a retraction in *The Observer.* I wrote a stronger letter than called for so that South Block didn't have any excuse to accuse me of misrepresentation. *The Observer* published my rebuttal in full. The Indian high commission's propaganda sheet in London gleefully reproduced both it and the offending report under the heading '*Observer*'s Fiction and Fact' (Appendix B). That didn't deter the Hon. David Astor, editor of *The Observer*, from sending me his 'personal congratulations and thanks for the really magnificent reporting ...' My report 'had every virtue—it was factual, detailed, enterprising, fair-minded and, I am sure, extremely courageous' he wrote, adding, 'You deserve high praise for your devotion to the duty of reporting what happens.' Astor predicted my reports would 'appear in the history books' because I was 'more-or-less alone in witnessing and communicating the essential story'. He didn't know the power of official patronage in India. Nor that Indian historians, being also candidates for preferment, weren't going to risk their prospects for inconvenient truth.

Paradoxically, most senior Indian functionaries, including the last two POs and the coercive presiding officer, were never anything but charming to me personally. When a transport strike paralysed traffic between Bagdogra airport and Gangtok, Bajpai invited me to hitch a ride for the six-hour journey in the jeep he sent down for the diplomatic bag. His juniors were not so affable. A Sikh first secretary in particular never failed to get in a snide remark about my Sikkimese contacts, contriving to make them sound subversive. One afternoon, when the Chogyal had agreed to receive me for a private briefing, I found the palace surrounded by Indian troops whose commanding officer refused to let me through. I went to India House where Bajpai was in a huddle with high-ranking military men. Murmuring something about Nepalese terrorists sneaking into the palace to assassinate the Chogyal, he said 'We can't take any chances with the old man's life' as if I was likely to bump him off! But he ordered the first secretary to give me a military vehicle to get past the Indian cordon. It was an opportunity for the man to get in another jibe. 'Why don't you take that!' he sneered, pointing to the PO's Mercedes as soon as Bajpai's back was turned. He later told journalists I had appealed to him for military protection. Worse than the untruth was the implication that he had saved me from attack by Sikkimese democrats who were incensed by my reports!

I shall never know what was noted in the official files. Since I enjoyed no government favours, the usual pattern of withdrawing them as punishment was not possible. But authority made its displeasure known. The Federal German embassy was forced to withdraw an invitation for me to visit Germany. Then, Irani's nominee as editor after the independent-minded Nanporia had been eased out, refused, at South Block's bidding, to let me cover the 1976 non-aligned nations summit conference in Colombo. Much to everyone's chagrin, I went all the same for *The Observer* after Astor made it clear to India's high commissioner in London that petty harassment over passport and visa would have to stop. The next editor was obliged to be present when I interviewed Rajiv Gandhi for a new *Statesman* supplement. Gandhi had already agreed to the interview, but his powerful media adviser, H.Y. Sharada Prasad, telephoned the editor to warn the interview would not otherwise be allowed as I 'had a record'.

None of this matches up to the imprisonment Dipankar Chakrabarti, editor of a small provincial Bengali monthly, *Aneek*, and his colleague, Sukanta Raha, suffered for publishing an editorial titled 'India's annexation of Sikkim' in a special issue of April–May 1975. They were arrested under the Defence of India Rules, and an additional sessions judge refused them bail on the grounds that the article 'seems to be calculated to prejudice the minds of the people against the territorial integrity of the Union of India.' A Marxist might have attributed the difference in the government's responses to *Aneek* and me to 'class justice'... or injustice. Sachin Chaudhuri, the distinguished lawyer and parliamentarian who became India's finance minister (1965–'67), anticipated my problems. 'You've been a good friend to the Chogyal,' he commented after reading the book. 'But in the process you may not have been a good friend to yourself!' There's consolation in the comment by Nari Rustomji of the Indian Civil Service that *Smash and Grab* shows the author is 'as true a friend of Sikkim as he is a good patriot of his own country'.

There being no conflict between the two positions, a new edition twenty-eight years later should not make me an even worse friend to myself. With *Smash and Grab* long out of print, people with an interest in Himalayan affairs cannot be denied an honest alternative to the 'manufactured consent' of the official version. They must also be saved from a pirated edition that closely resembles the original. Pirated is not perhaps the right word since this clandestine product is also the handiwork of the publisher who formally returned the copyright to me on 16 February 2000. He said he was not interested in another edition (Appendix C). I was all the more surprised suddenly to discover he had surreptitiously flooded the market with a new paperback.

• • •

Telling the story again does not mean a u-turn is possible, or even desirable, in history's one-way street. My Sikkimese friends have made their peace with destiny. On the whole, they have profited from it. Today's Sikkim is far more vibrant than the sleepy kingdom I knew. Everything is bigger, if not always better. Sikkim's first economic plan, spanning the seven years from 1954 to 1961 had an outlay of only ₹ 32.4 million. The 2011–'12 plan boasted a ₹ 14,000-million budget. This is in addition to the money New Delhi pours into the state for roads and power plants, special development under the Seven Sisters (as the north-eastern states are called) budget, and for disaster relief. The military invests massively in border defence. Expenditure on this scale is bound to yield results. Rajiv Gandhi's calculation that only 15 per cent of development funds reach the target also means Sikkim's 607,688 people are making money hand over fist. They enjoy the additional benefit of subsidised essential commodities like fuel. Those with 'Sikkim Subject' cards (meaning they or their ancestors were bona fide residents of the kingdom) pay no income tax.

It's boom time in this little corner of the Himalayas. Many development projects that the Chogyal mooted but New Delhi shot down then are in full swing now. But it's progress without the stabilising ballast that tradition provides. Land prices have shot up. Peasants who made a killing selling their holdings are setting new records in ostentatious consumerism. A young farmer who traded in his field for the most flamboyant motorbike also hired a driver to support the prestige of affluence. Easy come, easy go. Some become bankrupt. Others are reduced to nervous wrecks. One feckless youth now tills the land his fathers owned. A gift racket to launder black money followed the excise scam that created many millionaires. The innocent Sikkimese did not think of exploiting the absence of any excise duty in the Chogyal's time. But the shrewd Indian businessmen who flooded Gangtok after the annexation were quick to grasp they could make a killing from duty-free goods. All they needed was an address in Sikkim, a front man and a dummy company. Soon, greed overcame prudence. Factories elsewhere in India began rolling out manufactures stamped 'Made in Sikkim'. The exchequer is believed to have lost ₹ 3,500 million on account of evaded tobacco duty alone.

Old distinctions of birth and rank as well as traditional cultural supports are dissolving in this upsurge of new wealth. Christian evangelists have never had it so good. Construction is booming. Travel restrictions that kept foreigners out have been relaxed. Indian Airlines' ancient Dakotas no longer monopolise the air route to Bagdogra. Helicopters ferry passengers to the Burtuk helipad in Sikkim. A ropeway whirls visitors above Gangtok. An aerotropolis is coming up at Pakyong. Trekking tours compete with orchid and rhododendron displays, exhibitions, talks and seminars. The once moribund Namgyal Institute of Tibetology hums with activity. Even the agitation against hydroelectricity projects (no fewer than twenty-nine in north Sikkim alone) speaks of social dynamism. The one dump of a hostelry of the 1960s long ago gave way to a galaxy of hotels, spas and resorts.

Gangtok has become a throbbing business and tourist centre with packed cafés, a busy walkway and one of India's few casinos. The Chogyal's youngest son and daughter by Gyalmo Hope have made a major contribution to the modernist image. Prince Palden, a successful investment banker in New York, has married into the Sikkimese aristocracy and built a magnificent mansion in Gangtok that he visits regularly. Princess Hope Leezum and her husband, a Sikkimese nobleman in the police force, live in Gangtok where she runs a thriving tourist business. Few look back with nostalgia. But no one can afford to ignore the interlinked historical processes that converted a kingdom under India's protection into the twenty-second state of the Indian republic. The disappearance of the old Sikkim was not the end of the Himalayan story. It was the beginning.

• • •

The twentieth century was a time of tectonic change along the 1,500-mile sweep of the mountains Kalidasa called a gigantic measuring rod striding the earth from ocean to ocean. Mao Tse-tung's 'liberation' of Tibet (from whom? wondered a bemused Jawaharlal Nehru) in the north destroyed a traditional buffer state, converted a monastic backwater into a military base to project power into South Asia, and brought the world's two most populous nations, both nuclear-armed, face to face across the Himalayas. It also created the 'Tibetan question.' A diaspora of more than 100,000 Tibetans gives unrest a global dimension. To the south, some 700,000 Nepalese spilling out of their homeland every year are challenging borders and demanding political recognition of their ethnicity. Not for nothing did British writers call these border marches 'the Asian Balkans' and 'the Belgium of Asia'.

Bhutan, the Dragon kingdom, is the region's success story. Sole survivor of the five monarchies that once nestled in the Himalayas, it is a newcomer in royal circles. Sikkim and Bhutan were bracketed together for a long time. Both were Buddhist kingdoms, their royal families closely related. They faced similar challenges from India, China and Nepal. But they were temperamentally different, and some believe their fortunes illustrate the difference personality can make to diplomacy. That is true only up to a point. Personal equations seldom counter legal and political factors. The Chogyal's ineptness or the Gyalmo's zeal in furthering her husband's aspirations might have irritated New Delhi but would not in themselves have sanctioned intervention. Neither would the machinations of the chief minister, Kazi Lendhup Dorji, better known as 'L.D. Kazi', have made this possible. Even the virulent propaganda against the Chogyal launched by Kazi's European wife, who exulted in styling herself 'Kazini Saheba Elisa-Maria Dorji Khangsarpa of Chakung', was more rumbustious than decisive.

What really mattered was a substantive political difference between the seemingly identical kingdoms. The fourth Druk gyalpo, King Jigme Singye Wangchuck, now referred to with irreverent affection as K4, put his finger on this crucial factor. 'Sikkim didn't have the same treaty,' he reminded me laconically on the eve of his coronation in 1974. He was then only nineteen but wise beyond his years.

King Jigme's astute observation contradicted the illusion that official publications like *Bhutan and Sikkim* (May 1968) nurtured. Even the British blurred differences. After signing the treaty of Punakha with the first Druk gyalpo on 8 January 1910, Sir Charles Bell, the PO with additional responsibility in those days for Bhutan and Tibet, cabled back ecstatically: 'By one o'clock the signing and sealing of the Treaty were over and Bhutan was incorporated in the British Empire.' As Nirmala Das points out in *The Dragon Country*, 'one cannot deny that Bhutan became a subservient state of the British and the latter interpreted the treaty of Punakha as it suited them'.

Smaller Sikkim actually seemed grander and more modern then. The chogyals were an ancient dynasty when Ugyen Wangchuck became the first Druk gyalpo on 17 December 1907. Their elaborate court rituals were modelled on Manchu protocol. They were educated by Western governesses and tutors and were fluent in English. Sikkim had a settled system of revenue collection, an administrative hierarchy, written records, roads, and inspection bungalows for touring officials. Bhutan's planning process was launched in 1961 with a ₹ 170-million Five-year Plan when Sikkim's First Plan was ending.

However, Sikkim was India's protectorate. The treaty signed on 5 December 1950 may have been of questionable validity since India refused to register it with the United Nations but it gave India control of the kingdom's external relations, defence and communications. A dos-and-don'ts letter from Harishwar Dayal, the first Indian PO, further restricted the durbar's freedom while the Indian army virtually took over his kingdom's northern and eastern districts bordering China. All this is fleshed out in *Smash and Grab*, which is basically the story of how the last Chogyal's efforts to win a greater measure of independence played into the hands of RAW, the Research and Analysis Wing of the cabinet, as India's external intelligence service is called.

Bhutan only agreed under Article 2 of the treaty signed on 8 August 1949 'to be guided by the advice of India' in conducting its foreign policy. After a while even this seemed irksome to the Bhutanese. India's defeat at China's hands in 1962 emboldened them to ask for a new treaty. Finding New Delhi unresponsive, the Bhutanese sent an aide memoire saying they interpreted Article 2 to mean Bhutan was free to seek India's advice on any matter it chose but was also free not to accept the advice given. New Delhi did not reply but realised the need for flexibility. Queen Kesang's cosmopolitan Dorji siblings, then the power behind the Dragon throne, were always a step ahead.

Taking back the government after her brother, Prime Minister Jigmie Dorji, was mysteriously murdered in April 1964, King Jigme Dorje endeared himself to New Delhi. He established his democratic credentials with a law making the monarchy subject to a three-yearly vote of confidence. He ensured South Block's cooperation by engaging a senior Indian diplomat to represent Bhutan at the United Nations and steer it through to full membership. Indira Gandhi was immensely gratified when he toured Bangladesh refugee camps. Bhutan was the first country after India to recognise the infant republic.

K4, who succeeded to the throne in 1972, brilliantly accomplished the seemingly irreconcilable feats of both moving closer to India while also pushing farther on the road to complete independence. He anticipated the future by ending a century of royal absolutism and foisting a democratic constitution on his somewhat bewildered subjects. He also convinced New Delhi through prolonged track-two negotiations that Article 2 of the India–Bhutan treaty was impracticable and would give a handle to India's enemies (read China). Instead of 'advice', a new Article 2 in the treaty of peace and friendship in perpetuity which replaced the 1949 treaty on 8 February 2007 spoke of 'abiding ties of close friendship and cooperation.' It committed both governments to not allowing their territory to be used 'for activities harmful to the national security and interests of the other'. Bhutanese dissidents could no longer operate from north Bengal. More important, China, the kingdom's only other neighbour, was denied a foothold in Bhutan.

China is as much Banquo's ghost in Indo-Bhutanese ties as it was in Indo-Sikkimese relations. India had previously represented Bhutan in negotiations with China, but was excluded when Sino-Bhutanese talks to discuss the undemarcated 470-km border began in 1984. Twenty rounds of negotiations appear to have eliminated most differences but though Bhutan's sovereign status and United Nations membership limit India's options, the Bhutanese remain mindful of Indian sensitivities. They have so far resisted Chinese pressure to enter into formal diplomatic relations and publicly sign a border agreement. A stable new Bhutan had come into being by 2008 when K4's eldest son, twenty-eight-year-old Jigme Khesar Namgyel Wangchuk, was crowned fifth Druk gyalpo (K5). Mark of New Delhi's high esteem for a country that claims to be India's only reliable friend in South Asia, K5 was the chief guest at the dazzling parade when India celebrated her sixty-fourth Republic Day in 2013.

The new Bhutan was much better able to tackle the historical challenge of Nepalese immigration that destroyed the old Sikkim. While Bhutan and Sikkim were cultural fragments of Buddhist Central Asia spilling into South Asia, race, language and religion made Nepal a South Asian island in Central Asia. Now Nepal is a republic in turmoil and the entire sub-Himalayan tract from Meghalaya in the east to Uttarkhand in the west bears witness to the restless Nepalese quest for better living conditions. It is part of modern Nepalese mythology that they have always occupied these hills. True, their armies overran some areas from time to time. But the census records quoted here show most Nepalese are relatively recent arrivals.

Sikkim did not have a single Nepalese in 1873. By the time the agitation erupted a century later they accounted for three-quarters of the population. Calculating it would be easier to manage Hindu economic refugees with a natural affinity to India than Mongolian Buddhists with Central Asian ties, the British sponsored migration. Self-serving but shortsighted Sikkimese nobles—notably Kazi's kinsmen, Phodong Lama and Khangsa Dewan— supported them in return for bribes from the migrants. About 225,000 of today's 300,000 registered 'Sikkim Subjects' are ethnic Nepalese. Another 35,000 Nepalese probably have fake certificates. Sikkim's Tibeto-Buddhist ethic has been watered down, and indigenes complain of existing on sufferance. Kazi once chided me for not speaking Nepalese. 'It's the language of the people,' he said.

Ironically, the Sikkimese Nepalese are most worried today about their future. When Nar Bahadur Bhandari, the first ethnic Nepalese chief minister, declared Sikkim had merged but would not be submerged, he was expressing his fear of West Bengal's better educated, politically more articulate and physically more active Nepalese who have reinvented themselves as Gorkha. Darjeeling, rechristened Gorkhaland, the second feather in the Nepalese cap, is on its way to becoming India's second Nepalese-majority state at the time of writing. Not many Gorkha leaders know—or care—that Gangtok leased Darjeeling to the East India Company in 1835 and asked for its return in 1947, sending a copy of the memorandum to the International Court of Justice at The Hague. New Delhi ignored the application. As Gangtok's *Himalayan Guardian* reported in January 2013, Gorkha militancy has provoked a new loyalist National Sikkimese Bhutia Organisation to claim Bhutan's Ha and Ammo valleys, the Illam region of Nepal, the Chumbi valley in Tibet, a slice of Bihar and, of course, Darjeeling.

Bhutan's astute rulers did not miss the writing on the demography wall. They noted that the revolt against the Chogyal was a Nepalese affair to which Kazi lent a semblance of Sikkimese respectability. They saw how easily RAW officials manipulated ethnic Nepalese opinion. K4's first response to the crisis in Sikkim was to repeal his father's much-praised law on the confidence vote. He then turned his attention to ensuring that foreigners didn't also swamp Bhutan.

Unlike Sikkim, Bhutan does not share a frontier with Nepal. The Nepalese didn't begin to move there until 1900 when the Bhutanese government recruited labourers (*tangyas*) to work the tropical forests in the extreme west which the indigenous Drukpa disliked. They were allowed to stay on as tenant-farmers and more than 12,000 ethnic Nepalese were granted citizenship under the 1958 Nationality Law after Bhutan's first countrywide census in 1988. Another census seven years later, assisted by the United Nations Population Fund, recorded 125,336 working foreigners. Most were illegal migrants who had taken advantage of Bhutan's porous borders, empty spaces, planned growth and \$425 per capita GNP against Nepal's \$160 and India's \$350.

'Those who entered Bhutan after 1958 and acquired citizenship, land and property illegally are not Bhutanese citizens and cannot be accepted as such under our citizenship laws,' the government warned to justify the evictions that followed. But the ethnic Nepalese who were there in 1958 'and their descendants are genuine Bhutanese citizens'. Drukpa officials meticulously avoid the word Nepalese. 'We call them Lhotshampa, Southern Bhutanese' King Jigme Singye Wangchuck told me. It is thought the Bhutanese term will make assimilation psychologically easier. Druk dignitaries admit privately that Lhotshampas constitute a much higher share of the population than the officially acknowledged 20 per cent. How Bhutan tackled the threat and the ensuing refugee problem is no part of the Sikkim story. Ogyen Thinley Dorjee is.

• • •

Many regard the personable young seventeenth Karmapa Lama, head of Buddhism's Karma Kagyu sect and representative of the world's oldest unbroken line of succession through reincarnation, as the Dalai Lama's natural heir. The future of this potential world leader of the Tibetan and Buddhist communities is inextricably linked with that of Sikkim where Rangjung Rigpe Dorje, the sixteenth Karmapa Lama who fled Tibet with the Dalai Lama and died in 1981, established the gated red and white Rumtek Dharma Chakra Centre. It adjoins Sikkim's ancient Rumtek monastery and is the new seat of the Karmapas. It is also the global headquarters of Karma Kagyu Buddhists.

Ogyen Thinley Dorjee was born in 1985 in a nomad family in eastern Tibet. He was identified as the reincarnate in 1992, and installed in the traditional seat of the lineage at Tsurphu near Lhasa. The Dalai Lama recognised his status. The Chinese hailed him as a 'Living Buddha', the Communist regime's term for high incarnations. When he escaped from Tsurphu and arrived at the Dalai Lama's headquarters in Dharamsala early one January morning in 2000, he at once became a complication in India's domestic politics. Though New Delhi granted him official refugee status, it doesn't appear to know quite what to make of him. The foreigners who visit India to worship at his feet, the thousands of dollars they offer in homage, the worldwide network of fervently loyal Karma Kagyu centres and the many invitations to address congregations in Europe and America feed into Indian paranoia about the outside world. Other contenders for his throne take care to fan instinctive suspicion of a possible Chinese plant.

The vast majority of Buddhists believe, however, that allowing the young Karmapa to assume the duties of his lineage would solve many future problems. The disappearance in 1995 of Gedhun Choekyi Nyima whom the Dalai Lama had recognised as the Panchen Lama and his substitution by

China's nominee warns of Beijing's strategy of controlling Tibet through its traditional institutions. An even more ignominious, acrimonious and divisive succession struggle is likely if the Chinese try to impose their protégé on Tibetans as the next Dalai Lama.

Pawan Kumar Chamling, Sikkim's ethnic Nepalese chief minister, has repeatedly asked New Delhi to let the Karmapa Lama take over Rumtek. The heads of Sikkim's sixty-four monasteries and the leaders of all the political parties in the state back the demand. The Sikkim Pradesh Congress Committee even made the Karmapa's return an election plank in 2004. But the Indian government keeps him like a prisoner of state at the small Gyuto monastery near the Dalai Lama's headquarters in Dharamsala. He cannot step out of Gyuto without official permission. Although New Delhi has allowed him to visit the United States, it will not, for some unexplained reason, permit him to accept invitations from Karma Kagyu centres in Europe. Within India, he cannot set foot on Sikkimese soil. The nearest he was allowed was Mirik in Darjeeling district, just across the border with Sikkim. Thousands of devout Sikkimese flocked to Mirik where he presided over a mammoth public rally.

Thirty-seven years after the annexation, New Delhi still finds it necessary to be more circumspect about Sikkim than any other part of India. Perhaps this is because, contrary to public belief, China has not explicitly recognised Sikkim as an Indian state. India acknowledged Chinese sovereignty over Tibet in the 2003 *Declaration on Principles for Relations and Comprehensive Cooperation between India and China.* But, as an American scholar, David Scott, points out in his essay, *Sino-Indian Territorial Issues: The 'Razor's Edge?'*, 'the text shows a one-way agreement, one-way obligations and one-way concessions'. Complacent Indian commentators cite China's acceptance of a border trade post at Nathu-la as recognition of Indian sovereignty over Sikkim. Scott warns 'that was implied rather than explicit, de facto rather then de jure.' As if to bear out his doubts, China contested Indian control of the 2.1-sq-km Finger Area tract in northern Sikkim five years after the *Declaration*.

That might explain the confusing and contradictory explanations still trotted out for the actions this book describes. The democracy version is peddled at the popular level as the most appealing. Sympathetic Westerners are told that border defence had to be consolidated against China's military build-up in Tibet. Hints are dropped—without substantiation—that the Chogyal was in secret cahoots with the Chinese. That's what Shankar Bajpai seemed to suggest as we strolled through the National Palace Museum during a visit to Taiwan in 1990. 'Do you really think we could have allowed the Chogyal to get away with things?' he suddenly asked, apropos of nothing and without elaborating what dreadful 'things' the monarch hoped to get away with. According to N.N. Jha, a former lieutenant-governor of the Andaman and Nicobar Islands, the Chogyal's meeting with the Chinese ambassador at King Birendra's coronation was the last straw. 'I was there and I had to report it to New Delhi,' he says. It wasn't a mere ambassador the Chogyal met in Kathmandu: what cooked his goose according to P.N. Dhar, Indira Gandhi's principal secretary, in *Indira Gandhi, the 'Emergency' and Indian Democracy*, was an encounter there with China's vice-premier, Chin-hsi Liu.

Another bizarre version surfaced at the packed luncheon meeting at New Delhi's Oberoi Hotel in April 2011 when the Aspen Institute launched *Looking East to Look West: Lee Kuan Yew's Mission India*. A man introduced himself as V.K. Mathur, son-in-law of Bipin Bihari Lal, the kingdom of Sikkim's last chief executive who became the first governor after annexation. Mathur had something important to tell me but could do so only in private. We met the next day at the India International Centre where he whispered in the strictest confidence what, according to him, very few people knew: 'Hope was a CIA agent!' Having dropped his bombshell, Lal's son-in-law sat back and stared at me with an exultant 'now-what-do-you-make-of-that!' look.

Actually, the CIA canard was whispered from the moment the Chogyal's interest in an unknown young American woman became known. I never believed it because it was obvious that despite his reputation for philandering, the Chogyal was deeply in love with Hope. It was clear, too, she was no giddy socialite: she had studied Buddhism and Tibetan culture, and had great hopes of realising his ambition for a prosperous sovereign Sikkim. But the twenty-three-year-old American marrying a much older widowed Mongolian king felt isolated and persecuted in an alien setting. American diplomats in New Delhi were not particularly sympathetic. A senior member of the embassy there habitually let his voice drop to a breathless whisper in mocking imitation of her speaking style whenever her name came up in conversation. But when I was going up in 1973, a kindly Peter Burleigh in the American consulate in Calcutta (who nearly forty years later twice acted as American ambassador to India) asked me to inquire if she wanted anything. 'Cheesecake!' Hope exclaimed when I passed on the message. She then thought better of it and sent me a note saying it was a joke. *Smash and Grab* may have added to her discomfort. In July 1997 she compressed her complaints into a closely typed seven-page note. Much of it is personal trivia. But she does say at the end that what she misses 'overall in the account is analysis.' This introduction is partly an attempt to answer that charge.

The book reflected the general perception at the time. It didn't mean to question Hope's personal credentials. She had returned to the United States when I began my researches. There was no means of knowing that some of her most controversial moves were made at her husband's direction or that she drew on her own funds to keep the household going. I have decided, therefore, to leave the narrative as it is. It would be improper to change it without corroboration, which is no longer possible. In any case, Hope has very capably defended her position in her most readable autobiography, *Time Change.*

It came as no surprise to the Sikkimese when Dhar's memoirs confirmed that RAW's R.N. Kao personally supervised all the seemingly spontaneous events that led to the annexation. 'Under Kao's overall guidance, the RAW team helped the pro-democracy leaders build up their organisation and make their weight felt in the politics of Sikkim,' Dhar writes with measured candour. 'This process had started several months before the storm broke in April 1973.' In short, RAW set the revolutionary ball rolling before Kazi and the Nepalese mob knew they were revolting. The reason? China's conquest of Tibet had made Sikkim 'an area of geo-strategic importance overnight'.

I read Dhar's revelations with some disquiet. I never met Kao. It surprised me, therefore, when Sellappan Rama Nathan, Singapore's former intelligence chief, former executive chairman of the newspaper group that published the *Straits Times,* and the island-state's sixth president, told me Kao had strongly recommended me for a senior job in Singapore. It didn't happen then. Kao was dead and Nathan no longer headed the newspaper group by the time I joined it as editorial consultant. It was my independent decision to go to Singapore after a stint at the East-West Center in Honolulu when my editorship of *The Statesman* was usurped. But Nathan's disclosure intrigued me. Though Singapore's former president insisted Kao had stressed and highly praised my journalistic abilities, I wondered if the recommendation was another ploy like the blocked tunnel to keep me out of Sikkim.

Nothing is impossible. It was the Great Game all over again. Kazi, Kazini, the Gyalmo and even the Chogyal were pawns on the chessboard of Asian power politics. India had decided to absorb Sikkim for reasons that had little to do with the local players. The turbulent events described in the book and the tumultuous personalities that held the stage were incidental to that steely purpose.

• • •

I had started revising *Smash and Grab* when out of the blue arrived an e-mail that seemed as wildly improbable as Kazini's tales of exotic places and exalted people. I still don't know how much of it to take seriously. The author of this astounding message, apparently from some remote Scottish village, claimed Kazini as her very own 'Gran'. According to Claire M. Jordan, Kazini's son Roderick (Rory) Denis Edward Langford Rae had once courted her mother, now eighty-three. He had left Britain unaware his girlfriend was pregnant. The world knew Rory, product of Ampleforth, the famous Roman Catholic public school, and Oxford, as an executive of the Indian Tea Association in North Bengal. The woman who claims to be his daughter savours a far more sensational version.

In her telling, Rory was soldier, civil servant and spy, fluent in several Chinese dialects, and involved in hush-hush Sino-Indian border talks in Arunachal Pradesh when he died in 1965. He was then thirty-eight. Claire says there 'was something dodgy' about the end. The death certificate places it in Dibrugarh town in Assam. But the Assamese police told her mother 'he died at Dum Duma, fifty miles from Dibrugarh and most famous for having a military airbase there'. His 'body was flown back to Dum Duma and a car accident faked to conceal the fact that a British government agent was involved in the (Sino-Indian) dispute'.

Reading with mounting wonder a thriller that might have come from John Le Carre's pen, I asked myself why Kazini needed to invoke such distant celebrities as Kemal Ataturk and Field-Marshal Carl Gustaf Mannerheim when she had all the excitement right in her own family, born of her own womb. If Rory had lived adventurously, his daughter seemed determined not to lag too far behind. Claire says she was trained as a biological scientist to rehabilitate (joke?) sick or injured hedgehogs. Those prickly creatures aren't her only specialty. She proudly claims to be one of the world's few authorities on the proper care and handling of orphaned ship rats! She has worked as a secretary on Britain's *Daily Telegraph* newspaper, been a computer programmer and data analyst for the National Health Service, and owned a small occult shop. Her accomplishments don't end there. She runs a discussion group on the Net 'which dissects the Harry Potter books in immense, forensic detail'; has 'won a couple of quite major prizes for poetry'; and is working on a science fiction novel. The only weakness—apart from poverty—this versatile woman admits is linguistic. Unlike Kazini who indicated she was fluent in several European languages, Claire 'can't get much further with foreign languages than *Je ne parle pas Francais*'. The local council pays her 'a pittance' to stay home and help her arthritic mother. Lest anyone doubt her tale, Claire silences sceptics by saying she finds lying physically painful because she has a strong mania for accurate data.

Claire's version paints Kazini as a far humbler being than the European grande dame she made herself out to be. That she was plain Ethel Maud and not Elisa-Maria I knew already from the Macdonald sisters who ran Kalimpong's Himalayan Hotel. According to Claire her maiden name was Shirran and she was born in Doune, Perthshire, Scotland in January 1904, in a family of farm labourers of mixed English, Southern Irish and Scottish stock. Claire seems much impressed by Kazini's father's rank of Regimental Quartermaster Sergeant in the Black Watch regiment which was 'only one step below Regimental Sergeant Major which is the most senior NCO there is.' She was not to know that in the class-conscious Indian cantonments where Shirran served (two of his daughters were born there) he would have been shown the servants' door.

No wonder Kazini, who knew better, went to such lengths to replace her real background with dazzling invention. Being without formal education except for a stint of secretarial training, she relied only on her intelligence, charm and ambition to weave a fantasy world. Her first husband, Claire's grandfather, Bertram Langford Denis Rae, was an Anglo-Burmese (with Karen, Shan and Chinese blood) policeman in Burma. He was 'a war hero and a part-time British government spy'. George Orwell, then Eric Blair and also in the police, was supposed to be a friend. Bertram and Kazini divorced in 1940.

I might have treated Claire's tale with even greater reserve than Kazini's flights of fancy had it not been for Sangharakshita with whom she put me in touch. Born Dennis Lingwood, Sangharakshita is an English Buddhist monk who had lived in India for twenty years, fourteen of them (1950–1964) in Kalimpong. Our paths never crossed but I gather from his racy memoirs, *Precious Teachers: Indian Memoirs of an English Buddhist*, which he kindly sent me, that we had some common acquaintances, Kazini among them. Sangharakshita who obviously knew her far better found her as eccentric and obsessive as I remember, but also more human. She confessed to him her distaste for India and Indians and preference for Pakistan and Pakistanis, which she wouldn't dream of revealing to an Indian journalist whose help she sought.

Sangharakshita's account explained Kazini's reticence about her son. Unable to imagine her as a mother, he was not surprised when she told him 'she had no maternal feelings and was quite indifferent to her son'. Rory's death 'had not affected her in the slightest' she assured him 'in a tone, and with an air, that suggested the event was of absolutely no interest to her.' If so, she was even better at dissimulation than I thought. For she responded on 19 April 1965 to my letter of condolence after Rory's death with fulsome praise for him and me. 'I am only sorry that you did not meet, for you would have liked each other tremendously... he was so like you, frank, humorous, brilliant and honest... he was a man, like yourself, who could walk with beggars and kings' she typed on her personal writing paper, signing 'Kazini' with her usual flourish.

Claire wasn't the only surprise to crawl out of the woodwork. When excerpts from *Smash and Grab* appeared in several publications, a man called Narinder Kawlra turned up to say Kazini was his aunt. She had been married to his uncle, Barkat Narain, director of India's health services. He remembered her as 'an affectionate and loving lady'. There was a sequel. Kazini descended on Sachin Chaudhuri, who was holidaying in Kalimpong, with a heavily annotated copy of the book under her arm. She had never admitted to a third marriage, she said, and my mention of the health services director was greatly embarrassing. She wanted to sue for defamation. By way of replying, Chaudhuri told her a well-known story about a leading Calcutta barrister and MP whose stock response (in a colloquial mix of English and Bengali) whenever defamation was mentioned was 'Defamation is all right but first prove the "famation"!' Kazini didn't sue but wrote viciously abusive fictitious letters to the newspapers.

Sangharakshita says he realised even in the 1950s that Sikkim was doomed. 'India's shadow had fallen across Sikkim' and 'sooner or later, by one means or another, Sikkim would be absorbed into the Indian Union and lose its separate identity'.

A tale so full of colourful personalities and political drama is certainly worth re-telling.

SUNANDA K. DATTA-RAY
Calcutta, 15 June 2013

PREFACE

This is not the story of the Chogyal's life. Only he could have written that. Nor does it pretend to be a comprehensive account of Sikkim's Buddhist polity. It is an observer's chronicle of a recent passage in the subcontinent's history. Describing what happened, and how, will not change the present or future. But it may serve some purpose if, in truly recounting how law, usage and promises were ruthlessly set aside to destroy one of the last surviving fragments of a cultural empire that once straddled the heart of Central Asia, it also reveals the dangerous ease with which public opinion can be whipped up into chauvinistic acquisitiveness.

Governments the world over sometimes take morally indefensible action to protect national interests. But seldom are such measures clothed in the righteousness that seemed to sanctify every excess in Sikkim. So successful was the propaganda that no one in India deemed it necessary even to question the official picture of an enslaved people struggling against a tyrannical king. Nor did anyone think of asking at the end of the painful saga when the king had unceremoniously been removed and the kingdom ceased to exist, whether the Sikkimese had gained any freedom under an Indian governor who was far more powerful and autocratic than the Chogyal had ever been.

He may have been an evil oppressor. His subjects may have had every reason to revolt against the throne. But even if, for argument's sake, we accept these postulations, they do not justify outside intervention to extinguish a country's identity. Only two Indians, S. Dutta Chowdhury, the police commissioner, and Tarachand Hariomal, the judge, sustained faith in Indian justice.

We tend to forget that when the British left the subcontinent in 1947, they wiped the state clean of all traces of colonial political and administrative arrangements. They explicitly refused to transfer paramount authority over the princes to the new government in New Delhi. In the case of Sikkim, there was no paramountcy: it was an independent kingdom in a treaty relationship with British India. When the treaty was annulled and British India had ceased to exist, tiny, vulnerable Sikkim was as much a sovereign nation as India herself. An independent Sikkim placed itself under India's protection in 1950, entrusting only certain aspects of its governance to New Delhi while retaining the essence of sovereign authority in Gangtok. Whatever we may think of the Sikkim durbar or of the Chogyal, who was ill-served at the end by sycophantic advisers, grasping relatives and meddlesome lawyers, the fact of juridical parity cannot be gainsaid. Even if the British had been masters of Sikkim, India could not claim to exercise their imperial prerogative.

This book has been inordinately delayed. It was started when the 1975 coup was still fresh in the public mind, and would have been completed long ago but for a series of domestic interventions. But time does not alter basic principles. Delay is of even less consequence in this instance because earlier publication would have had as little practical impact. The odds are that any contradiction of the official version will be denounced as further evidence of the ingenious Chogyal's ability to expound his case even after death.

It would have been difficult to write this account if he and his sons had not generously placed their records at my disposal, allowing me access to a great deal of unpublished correspondence with the political officer and chief executive in Gangtok, and with the Indian government in New Delhi. The late Crown Prince Tenzing enthusiastically supported my labours; his younger brother, Prince Wangchuck Namgyal, now the thirteenth Denzong Chogyal in the eyes of legitimists though he is lost in meditation somewhere in the jungles of Nepal or Bhutan, continued with information and assistance.

Nor would I have appreciated the personal flavour of Sikkimese politics but for the exuberance of Kazini Elisa-Maria Dorji Khangsarpa of Chakung, to give her the full honorific she so revels in. Kazini never failed to enliven my holidays in Kalimpong with titillating descriptions of people and events, all of which bore the unmistakable stamp of her vividly imaginative personality. It was a matter of deep regret to me when she decided some time in 1975 that my sympathy for Sikkim made me uncomfortable company.

Many others—members of the royal family, civil servants, politicians and diplomats—helped in almost equal measure. At some time or other during the last two decades and more, I have discussed the situation with almost every one of the actors who play some part in this story. Even those who might appear in a less than favourable light—and this cannot be helped, for their actions, not my personal relationships, shape the tale—were always ready to hold forth on the subject.

Kayatyani Shankar Bajpai was never anything but warmly hospitable, as was his successor, Gurbachan Singh, the last of the proconsuls. B.S. Das must have been one of the most easily accessible administrators ever sent to Gangtok. I drew a blank only with Bipin Bihari Lal. But then, I was not the only one. Even Kazi Lendhup Dorji, the first chief minister, without whose collusion Sikkim would never have been absorbed, stood in awe of Lal's abrasive tongue and overbearing demeanour. Lal treated the Chogyal like dirt.

Nearer home, my thanks are due to D.P. Simpson for typing the preliminary draft, and to Mrs Mercy Sam who spent many laborious hours painstakingly making the almost illegibly corrected manuscript presentable for the publishers.

It needs to be added that my account may seem to rely rather heavily on Sikkimese sources. The fault lies entirely with the Indian authorities who responded to the simplest queries with evasion or propaganda. When I asked the Lok Sabha secretariat to confirm M.C. Chagla's reported clarification in Parliament of Sikkim's separate status, the secretariat evasively referred me to the external affairs ministry. In public, New Delhi still clings to the defence that it merely responded to spontaneous local developments. Privately, Indian officials hint vaguely at the Chogyal's intrigues and the Chinese threat. But no specific allegation was ever made, leave alone substantiated. Even Das's admirably candid description of his tenure does not go beyond suggesting that the Chogyal's desire for revision of the 1950 treaty and recognition of his country's status were somehow an intolerable affront to New Delhi's dignity.

The absence of any credible Indian explanation, coupled with all that I saw and heard while reporting the story, conveyed its own lesson. The Chogyal would undoubtedly have been acclaimed as a freedom fighter if he had been engaged with the Americans, British or French; he became a conspiring monster only because he had the misfortune to be pitted against democratic, anti-colonial India. To be pro-Sikkimese was to be anti-Indian.

The Sikkim durbar, as it then existed, was amateurish, overly trusting and incorrigibly timid. Some of its luminaries were always more careful of private interests than of their national cause. It totally lacked the resources to cope with a crisis of this magnitude. Ultimate irony, it was never able to abandon faith in Indira Gandhi's innate sense of justice, or in the sanctity of legal commitments. But, at least, it had nothing to hide.

SUNANDA K. DATTA-RAY
1983

Prologue

'Palden Thomdup Namgyal, Chogyal of Sikkim, died more of a broken heart than of throat cancer.'

The Voice of Sikkim,
5 February 1982.

'If India believes that it is a democracy, if it believes in the democratic principles of Panchsheel, I think it should do justice to us.'

Prince Wangchuck Namgyal,
Sunday, 18-24 April 1982.

A tubby little man in a grey lounge suit bustled into the crowded drawing-room and bowed low before the carved and gilded table, *choksey* in Sikkimese, behind which Prince Wangchuck Namgyal sat. Placing yet another *khada* (the white scarf symbolising purity that is presented on all ceremonial occasions) on the already overflowing heap, he folded his hands and murmured: 'We hereby recognise you as the Thirteenth consecrated Chogyal of Sikkim.'

The wheel had turned full circle. The man in the grey suit, Bhim Bahadur Gurung, was an ethnic Nepalese politician and prominent among the *batisey chor* (thirty-two thieves) of Kazi Lendup Dorji's party, a leading architect of the throne's dissolution and the kingdom's destruction. In the distant past, Gurung had enthusiastically defended his king's demand for independence, but he had recanted his loyalty to become one of New Delhi's most loyal adherents in Sikkimese politics. As speaker of the assembly before the 1979 elections, and as legislative leader of Ram Chandra Poudyal's opposition Congress (Revolutionary) Party afterwards, Gurung had not allowed any memory of national loyalty to influence his actions.

There were more surprises in store. Beyond the gilt trellis of the palace windows echoed the haunting strains of *Dela Jong Sil Lee Gee Yang Chagpa Chilo*—Why Is Denzong Blooming So Fresh and Beautiful?—the national anthem no one had dared sing for nearly a decade. The singing had continued for hours as an endless stream of ragged peasants, men and women, tramped over hill and valley for days to reach the palace. They filed before the prince to measure the ground three times with their bodies in token of submission to his sovereignty; not the abbreviated homage of bowing from the waist, fingertips touching the ground three times, but the full-length prostration with knees, palms and forehead flat on the carpet. This was the *kowtow* of imperial China. Bhutiya-Lepchas call the obeisance *cha*, and the Nepalese *dok*. It is India's *sastanga-pranam*. Each visitor added to the pile of khadas before Wangchuck until his pale bespectacled face, wan from the strain of living in public for days on end, could barely be seen. The array of silver sacramental dishes holding rice, millets, butter tea, *chhang* (millets fermented in hot water) and other auspicious symbols, laid out before his seat under the drawing-room's enormous and priceless *thankas* (religious scroll paintings mounted on antique brocade and watered silks) had disappeared long since.

As the last notes of the anthem faded into the silence of the Himalayas, there rose a more militant throb: hundreds of feet stamping round and round the palace to the resonance of 'Long Live Denzong Chogyal!' Bhim Bahadur Gurung produced his final trump to that defiant accompaniment: a sheet of court paper with a one-rupee stamp, on which was typed:

> On the Nineteenth day of February, Year Nineteen Hundred and Eighty-two, Tibetan calendar Chya-Jya and Chu-Khy, the people of Sikkim have decided to offer traditional scarf to the Thirteenth consecrated Chogyal of Sikkim, Tobgyal Wangchuck Tenzing Namgyal, at the Tsuk-la-khang of Gangtok at 3.00 pm.

There were minor inaccuracies. The presentation was in the palace and not the Tsuk-la-khang chapel royal, a square double-storey building with a gleaming yellow roof across the lawns, where the Chogyal's coffin had lain in state for nineteen days. It was late in the evening after the funeral, and the shadows were closing in, when Gurung was finally able to edge into the seemingly unending queue. The prince's correct names are Tenzing Topgyal Wangchuk Sisum Namgyal. But the mistakes passed unnoticed. What everyone talked of was the incontrovertible fact that thirteen men in public life had invited India's wrath with that affirmation of loyalty.

Gurung and two others represented the Congress (Revolutionary) Party in the legislative assembly. Dugo Bhutia, once active in Nar Bahadur Khatiawara's militant Youth Congress, sat as an independent member. Six signatories were legislators from the chief minister's own Congress (Indira) Party. The three others enjoyed less formal political prominence. P.B. Subba, president of the Tsong Association, had shared Nar Bahadur Bhandari's imprisonment during the Emergency. Rinchen Wangdi, an impetuous young aristocrat married to the Chogyal's niece, had recently been won over by Kazi Lendhup Dorji's devious and mischievous appeal to Bhutiya-Lepcha youth to stand up and fight for their rights against Sikkim's ethnic majority. Finally, Sonam Yongda, the Sikkim Guards captain who had paid dearly for his patriotism, and returned to the monastery whence he began. Clad in the lama's maroon, Yongda acted as general secretary of the Lhadi Tsokpa, the monks' body.

For them and for 30,000 others, the death of one chogyal was the birth of another. The mantle of monarchy had fallen on twenty-nine-year-old Wangchuck, educated at St Paul's school in Darjeeling, and Harrow in England, with an honours degree from the Ealing School of Business in London, and nearly three years of working experience in the Heinz factory in England, which had put him off baked beans and tinned soup for life. 'The succession is automatic,' said the prince, realising only too acutely that no matter how softly he spoke, every word was clearly audible in New Delhi. The reserved young man, with no previous experience of responsibility or a public role, had almost overnight acquired confidence and maturity.

Prince Wangchuck dismissed a coronation as an unnecessary state ceremony. 'It is for the people to accept and acknowledge me as the new chogyal, and you can see for yourself the support I have been shown by the people,' he told reporters. The monks of Pemayangtse (the sublime perfect lotus) monastery had already formally recognised him as the *gyalpo* (king) who upholds the *chhos* (righteousness), hence chogyal. Their recognition had a special significance for Lhatsun Chempo, the monastery's founder, had consecrated his ancestor Phuntsog Namgyal 'ruler of the southern slopes' 341 years earlier. That was enough for the Sikkimese, Buddhist Bhutiya-Lepchas and Hindu Nepalese alike. The khada, symbol of purity, token of allegiance, solemnised their acceptance of a new king. No mute gesture could be more expressive.

Gangtok was swathed in khadas. An American woman, Buddhist and bull-fighter, had even brought back the scarf that the Chogyal had placed in the private altar of her French chateau. Reverently, she laid it on his bier. A cord strung between a scarlet and gold lacquered pillar and the heavy droop of a brocade banner in the Tsuk-la-khang was piled high with skimpy strips of gauze offered by the poor. Villagers who had come unprepared could buy a scarf for a rupee. Superior fabric cost five rupees. The money helped to pay for invocations by more than 300 lamas in the capital alone during the forty-nine days of mourning; prayers that testified to the profound faith of a king who had only his religion to sustain him during eight lonely years of humiliation and persecution.

Once there were ivory lengths of watered silk from China. But the Nathu-la trade had been cut off many years ago. Proud clans like the Martam Topdens, Rhenock Tashis and the Densapas of Barmiok still treasure bolts of antique Chinese silk carefully preserved in aromatic herbs, but most have to be content with the glossy manufacture of Indian factories. As Karma Topden told curious reporters at Dum Dum airport, Sikkim received everything, from khadas to constitutions, readymade from India!

The ritual survives from a time when Denzong, the rice bowl, called Sukhim, or happy house, by Tsong refugees, was a fragment of a vast spiritual empire that extended from Ladakh to Arunachal Pradesh, from the Mongolian steppes down to the Ganges plains. Though Bhutan is also a child of that disappearing civilisation, a certain sturdy individualism separates the martial Druk race from the heartland of Tibetan culture. Ladakh, where still survive the descendants of Tibet's ancient kings, was more nearly related to the Tibetan founthead. But Sikkim was the closest of all, seeking Lhasa's guidance in its worship, social customs and political institutions.

Immigration has so heavily diluted that ethos that the last census revealed that Bhutiya-Lepchas, now reduced to being a protected tribe in their own homeland, constitute less than 24 per cent of the population. Hindu settlers from Nepal and India comprise the overwhelming majority. Therein lay the country's weakness: the vulnerable Achilles' heel through which the Chogyal was wounded and brought low. His durbar could not stand up to the onslaught of manipulated ethnic strife.

But the Great Leveller also heals. There could have been no more inspiring embodiment of racial integration than Khatiawara, the rebel politician who had once vowed to gorge on the Chogyal's blood, making the strenuous ascent to the royal cremation ground as his private act of expiation. His gesture was just as dramatic as Gurung's testament. More expectedly, Sikkim's young chief minister, Nar Bahadur Bhandari, afflicted by a painful back ever since the Indian police beat him up in 1975, waved away his official jeep, also to follow the cortége on foot. Pressed by Darjeeling to take more immigrants, Bhandari retorted that Sikkim had merged but would not be submerged.

• • •

It was the passing of an age. Slowly, the procession of monks and mourners climbed the windswept heights of Lukshyama cradled in a distant ring of snowcapped peaks. A richly caparisoned riderless pony preceded the coffin as the Chogyal's own Mercedes had done on the drive from Gangtok's Libing helipad to the Tsuk-la-khang. Wangchuck led the royal mourners. His sister Yangchen and her English husband, Simon Abraham, his half-brother and half-sister, children of the Chogyal's American second wife, Hope Cooke, walked with him. Upright young Palden, uncanny in his striking resemblance to the dead crown prince, stocky little Hope Leezum, phlegmatic as any Tibetan.

It took four hours to cover the distance of about six miles, the final lap steeply up a stone and boulder-strewn bridle path to the last resting place of the Namgyals. Thousands of grieving Sikkimese already waited there. The metal trident of Apa Sahib Pant's Hanuman temple shone down from above. Indian soldiers worked noisy pneumatic drills in clearances below, and the old mule track to Tibet meandered away through the mountain ranges. Thick grass covered the slope and a tree with a curiously hollow bole provided a perch for hundreds of spectators.

Three *chortens* (receptacles for offerings) in which relics, or sometimes prayers, are enshrined, on a higher ridge marked the cremation sites of Sir Tashi Namgyal, the eleventh chogyal, and of his parents, the hare-lipped Thutob Namgyal and his domineering Tibetan gyalmo, Yeshi Dolma. There were two newer stupas lower down, for Sangey Deki, the Chogyal's beautiful first wife who died in 1956, and Crown Prince Tenzing, killed in 1978 when his Mercedes, swerving to avoid a truck speeding up the hill, was hurtled into the ravine below Deorali. The vigorous young crown prince was only twenty-eight, glowing with robust health, when he perished so cruelly. Tragedy seems to dog all first-born heirs to the Sikkimese throne.

They brought his battered body here to be burned by his mother's memorial. The two chortens stand side by side, the cube for earth, the orb for water, and the cone for fire, each topped by the wooden finial of a crescent and circle signifying air and ether. They were modest monuments, testifying to the humility of a dynasty that had never sought the ostentatious grandeur of India's maharajas, relying only on native dignity and public loyalty. Now, the Chogyal too followed that doleful route. A small new stupa awaited his body, its whitewash still damp from the rains. His permanent memorial was to be in Tashiding (the elevated central glory) monastery built in 1716 whose sacred Thongwa Rangtrol chorten promises nirvana at sight. As a high incarnate lama, the Chogyal was entitled to share this honour with two of Sikkim's most revered ecclesiastics, Jamyang Khentse Rimpoche and Gyaten Rimpoche.

It was the end of a tragically star-crossed life. Posterity may one day be able to explain why—and the precise moment when—fate turned against Palden Thondup Namgyal, the twelfth consecrated Denzong chogyal. Few men can have known such extremes of fortune. Sir Tashi's second son was recognised at birth as an incarnate of the eighth chogyal, Sidkeong Tulku, and through him, of a legendary king of Tibet, as well as the monk, Aen-Tul Karma Rinchen of the Kargyu-pa sect of Kham. In his person, therefore, the Chogyal united the Nyingma-pa sect, to which the royal family belongs, and the more widespread Karma Kargyu sect, one of the earliest branches of the Kargyu-pa school of Mahayana Buddhism, which acknowledges the young Ogyen Trinley Dorje as its seventeenth Gyalwang Karmapa. The Dalai Lama had identified the Chogyal's early mentor, Linghu Rimpoche, from the monastery of that name near Gyantse, as an incarnation of Lhatsun Chempo.

He was elected president of the Mahabodhi Society of India and invited to Buddhist conferences in Burma, Japan and Cambodia. Jawaharlal Nehru sent him on a delicate mission to Lhasa as New Delhi's confidential envoy. He led India's delegation to a Moscow conference of Orientalists. Britain admitted him to the Order of the British Empire; France created him a Commandre de L'Ordre de l'Etoile Noire; and India made him a Padma Vibhushan. He was an honorary major-general in the Indian army and colonel-in-chief of the Eighth Gurkhas. Nehru was paternally fond of the active and imaginative prince so bubbling with enthusiasm for his country. Diplomats and academics admired his illuminating discourses on Himalayan fauna or the religious rituals and political traditions of the border marches. Even the humblest caller enjoyed his hospitality. He was fêted in European capitals and the USA; an admiring world regarded him as the beau ideal of an enlightened executive monarch. The international glitterati flocked to Gangtok for his second marriage to an attractive, well-connected and very young American heiress who seemed anxious to identify with Sikkim and its culture. The world regarded it as a fairytale romance.

Sikkim's transformation from a primitive mountain principality into a modern nation was due entirely to the Chogyal's vision and effort. A streamlined administration, thrusting economic plans, an impartial system of justice, and a finely balanced political dispensation that reconciled tradition with democratic aspirations were the lasting achievements of his reign. Roads, bridges, industry, modern farming, schools and hospitals bore witness to his efforts. His career blossomed between the late 1940s and the middle 1960s. They were the most fruitful years of his life. The Chogyal was ambitious even then, but it was admitted that his ambitions were all for his people's welfare. Those who met him during those years of fulfilment paid tribute to his gentle charm, classical Tibetan scholarship, progressive administrative ideas, and scientific interest in contemporary forms of advance. They also recognised in him a staunch ally of India's democratic leadership.

Suspicion set in only when the kingdom seemed likely to break out of the strict limits laid down by the protector; when economic growth and social awareness coalesced in a political awakening that threatened to take Sikkim out on a tide beyond the reach of New Delhi's control. The Chogyal did not try to hold back the nascent forces gathering in his country. He saw the new impulses that provoked unreasonable fear and hostility, strong enough to eventually overwhelm him and his ideas, as the natural culmination of the process that India had helped him to start. No man should be pilloried for seeking freedom, he pleaded, but he pleaded in vain. His tactical failure was to allow detractors to portray the higher status he sought for Sikkim as personal, not national, ambition. The propaganda might not have been possible if the Chogyal had ensured that more ordinary Sikkimese—especially the Nepalese majority—understood and shared his aspirations. By failing to take enough Nepalese officials and politicians into his confidence, or to give them the sense of authority they craved in their adopted land, he allowed propagandists to project him as only a feudal Bhutiya-Lepcha chief.

And so he was publicly reviled and rejected in the closing years of his reign, depicted as a tyrant and a monster, painted as India's implacable foe, and the enemy the Nepalese had to overthrow. The sad, shy man with his gentle ways and embarrassing stammer, his soft speech and quiet thoughtfulness, was lost to view under an avalanche of abuse. The ludicrously unreal image that emerged was of a sinister racist schemer who exploited the Nepalese poor, squandered the kingdom's revenues and Delhi's development assistance on his own extravagances, conspired with India's enemies, and relentlessly pursued his wanton pleasures amidst the smoking ruins of his country. It was a cruel and wicked distortion. But it served its purpose. Sikkimese, especially Nepalese, officials who had earlier striven for his patronage, carefully shunned the palace. Indians who had been flattered to claim royalty's acquaintance would no longer risk communication with the deposed ruler. The American woman he had raised to the throne, who had offered so many irritants in Gangtok's uneasy relations with New Delhi, dragged him through the US courts over her financial settlement and custody of their children, even disputing their right to visit their father in Sikkim, until the union, disastrous for king and country, ended in divorce. It was too late by then for the severance to help his blighted career.

Tenzing's untimely death was the final blow. He was Sikkim's vibrant young hope. The Deorali accident extinguished the faint glimmer that all that the Chogyal had so ceaselessly striven for would one day be vindicated through his son's restoration. The triumphs of earlier years were forgotten in the lonely twilight of the shabby genteel palace. But his bold experiment of blending the best in Sikkim's past with the demands of emerging nationhood did not deserve to fail, just as this son of Khampa princes did not deserve to forfeit the promise and goodwill with which he had set out.

• • •

The cremation was the end of a pilgrimage, the fall of the last outpost of a civilisation whose totems had carefully been preserved in an alien ambience. Central Asia's influence was evident in the chain of khadas attached to the bier, its other end held by a lama who preceded the pall-bearers. It was a relic of the Chinese *hurin-fan*, the soul's banner. The yellow umbrella over the coffin (yellow being royalty's colour in the antique rituals of the Ch'ing court) and the full-length prostrations with which wave upon wave of subjects, rediscovering their allegiance in a moment of sorrowful clarity, bade farewell to their departed king and paid homage to his successor also reflected Sikkim's roots in the Asian heartland.

Matrimonial pacts reinforced the old alliance. Aware of the ethnic divide that had toppled his father, Crown Prince Tenzing used to joke he would take two wives, a Bhutiya-Lepcha and a Nepalese. Otherwise, Sikkim was cocooned in the minority's cultural past. The Chogyal's mother and first wife were Tibetan. Two of his sisters had married into the Lhasa aristocracy. His younger brother's wife had been chosen from the Dalai Lama's exiled entourage in Dharamsala. The Densapas of Barmiok and the Tashis of Rhenock followed the precedent. Even Kazi's richly endowed first wife had originally been married to one of the Panda Tsang brothers, warlords of the Kham marches. More to blame than anyone else for the kingdom's disappearance, Kazi was busily lobbying in New Delhi on the day that Sikkim nursed its grief. But everyone else was there to acknowledge that the siege was over. The garrison had capitulated. A nation's umbilical cord had been cut.

Tashiding and Pemayangtse are obvious expressions of Sikkim's connection with Tibet. The Nyingma-pa sect reveres the Mindolling monastery, which had reared Lhatsun Chempo. The Kargyu-pa faith is rooted in Tolung, north-west of Lhasa. These tokens of the past dominated the day as the Chogyal made his last journey with far greater pomp and pageantry than he had ever done in life.

Indira Gandhi's government had his body flown back from New York to New Delhi. It laid on an air force Avro to transport the coffin to Bagdogra, and an MI-8 helicopter for the last lap to Gangtok. With the generosity of which she was personally capable, she promised that India would pay the cost of the funeral and agreed to full ceremonial honours and official mourning. Gangtok had already spontaneously responded with a 500-member citizens' committee under Sonam Tshering, the veteran Speaker. Bhandari had made it clear that his government looked on the cremation as a national occasion. 'He had suffered a great deal and was quite ill. He was a sensitive man with concern for his state,' Mrs Gandhi announced with unconscious mockery, though still doggedly talking of 'Shri Palden Thondup Namgyal'. New Delhi's governor of Sikkim, Homi Taleyarkhan, echoed his prime minister to praise 'Namgyal-ji' as a 'highly polished and refined gentleman'. India's President, home minister and army chief sent condolences. Nihar Ranjan Laskar, a junior minister in Mrs Gandhi's cabinet, flew into Gangtok to represent her government at the funeral.

With so many pious protestations to mark the death of the man they had robbed and ruined, Kazi too managed dutifully to produce a khada and tell the press: 'I may have battled against him, but Sikkim is the poorer by his death.'

The irony of these attentions was not lost on the Chogyal's friends and family. 'I shall never forget the time when they took Jungkhyang' (the customary honorific by which he was known) 'aside at Bagdogra and subjected him to a thorough body search,' recalled son-in-law Simon Abraham. It was not the Chogyal's only taste of petty persecution. They took away his distinctive car number plates, removed the Namgyal name from institutions he had founded and fostered, and turned away friends who wanted to call on him. They forbade him the use of airport VIP lounges so that he had to queue with his suitcases like other passengers, refused to let him go abroad, and seized most of his property. Taleyarkhan would not even let him accompany Palden, Hope Leezum and an American school friend holidaying in Sikkim on a trekking expedition in the West just a few months before his death.

Surveillance was most harsh during the 1975–'77 Emergency. Very few people could see him then; a formidable circle of intelligence officials always surrounded him on visits to Calcutta or New Delhi. They kept constant watch at the door of his Wood Street flat, drove dinner guests away from his table in the Grand Hotel, and set up a watching post when he ate in the Calcutta Club. The Chogyal was a prisoner even during that tormented crisis when, goaded beyond endurance, he took an overdose of sleeping pills.

My mother was allowed to ask him to dinner just after that nightmare ordeal in 1976. But the police descended on us in frightening force half an hour earlier to search the house and question the servants. Livid with fury when told that a young West German diplomat and his wife, who were leaving Calcutta and whom the Chogyal had met before, had also been invited, they threatened not to allow him to get out of the car if the Germans did not leave at once. Rather than compound difficulties, the Germans left voluntarily without dinner, and the Chogyal was allowed to come in. It was a dismal evening. The principal jailer, a special branch inspector, demanded that the Chogyal should not be out of his sight for a moment, not even to use the lavatory. He refused to eat with us but sat at a distance muttering dark imprecations and glowering at the despondent ruler, clearly taking a venomous delight in being as obtrusive and unpleasant as possible. Such torment was a feature of the Chogyal's daily existence.

This harrowing vigilance was relaxed when Morarji Desai's Janata party came to power. 'I had maintained that the merger was undesirable and I maintain that,' announced the new prime minister. But Desai's morality never rose above political convenience, and he bluntly told the Chogyal that he would not undo what had already been done. Such courage as Desai had ebbed away when his mild disapproval of the annexation, confided to the *New York Times*, provoked a furore in India's press and parliament. But Desai offered generous compensation, and Charan Singh, then his home minister, promised to make the Chogyal governor of an important state if only he would endorse Sikkim's absorption into India. The Chogyal thanked them politely and declined the offer, not caring to explain that his conscience would not allow him to swear to uphold India's constitution. The solemn bond of his own coronation oath sustained him in his impecunious isolation. 'He lived always for Sikkim,' says Wangchuck.

There was a resurgence of hope in October 1979 when Kazi and his men, by then sailing under the Janata flag of convenience—for their politics changed with every shift in New Delhi—were roundly trounced in all thirty-two Sikkimese constituencies. The election was a spectacular victory for Bhandari's Janata Parishad. Denied recognition as a formal party, deprived of its familiar voting symbol, and handicapped by all manner of other crippling restrictions imposed by Bipin Bihari Lal, as governor, and India's election commission, the Janata Parishad nevertheless swept the polls. 'We have always said and we still say that the manner of Sikkim's merger with India was not legal and constitutional,' said Lal Bahadur Basnet, the winner from Gangtok and deputy speaker in the new assembly. But the chief minister prudently rationalised that open defiance would mean dismissal and strengthen New Delhi's stranglehold through the constitutional device of President's Rule. The limited autonomy he was able to secure for the Sikkimese was preferable to that.

Even this muted freedom did not long survive Mrs Gandhi's return to power in 1980. The new Indian government again picked up Kazi, ready to lend himself to any stratagem to regain office. Rather than be outmanoeuvred, a panicky Bhandari merged his party with Mrs Gandhi's Congress.

Some of the old restrictions were reimposed, at least during the Chogyal's trips to India. My wife and I again received a police visit when he dined at our flat in the summer of 1981, and a leading but acquiescent newspaper published a planted story about the Chogyal's ominous meetings in Calcutta. He was able to shrug off persecution with resignation, and even wit. When security men invaded his taxi in New Delhi, he gently suggested that if they were inviting themselves to share the journey, they might also consider sharing the fare.

Bhandari couldn't influence events in Calcutta or Delhi but he made life in Gangtok easier. Princess Yangchen's wedding in 1979 was almost a state occasion, government departments and employees helping out with the arrangements. He attended the ceremony in the palace and presented a khada to the dethroned and dispossessed Chogyal whom he called 'the first gentleman of Sikkim'. All the officials who had once basked in royal favour flocked back to court then. The Chogyal welcomed them back without a trace of recrimination; indeed, with something of his former wistful charm.

He had few illusions left and had ceased to expect anyone to place patriotism above prospects. For himself, short of money, obliged to beg favours of people whom he looked on as usurpers, forced to travel on an ordinary Indian passport, still hemmed in by all kinds of niggling little restraints, and frequently having to suffer Lal's rude outbursts, the knowledge that he could be a free and rich man if only he acquiesced in the annexation must have been a source of considerable private solace.

The Chogyal had very little interest left in what was happening, or even in himself. Often, he would be sunk in gloom for hours on end. He could hardly eat because of a painful throat when we stayed with him in Gangtok in July 1981. It was probably pharyngitis he said, possibly something worse, not seeming to care much. It was too late by September when he was finally persuaded to go to New York and able to coax some foreign exchange out of the Indian government. The Sloan-Kettering Cancer Center doctors were hopeful to start with. He wrote to me in October to say that though the tumour had shrunk under chemotherapy, an operation would cost him his voice. 'So I will be dumb until I learn to speak anew which takes about six months, but I cannot stay here that long. Hence you are likely to meet a dumb man when you see me next!'

• • •

They brought his body back instead, embalmed in the lotus position as befits an incarnate lama, the *dorjee* (thunderbolt) in his right hand and the bell in his left. He was sealed in an upright coffin wrapped in the kingdom's forgotten flag that had for years flown only in the palace and the terrace of his Calcutta flat. Rain, sleet, and snow had scourged the land ever since the cortége arrived; the unusually inclement weather betokened Sikkim's pain, they said. It also signified the restlessness of an anguished soul that found peace as elusive after death as it had in life.

The coffin was placed in the Tsuk-la-khang where a policeman with a black armband stood at each corner, head bowed over his rifle. The rapidly mounting piles of khadas had to be cleared away every so often. Dozens of butter lamps twinkled under the ornately embellished ceiling as lamas chanted the liturgy, cymbals clashed, and bells tinkled. The deep notes of a thigh-bone trumpet and the resounding throb of leather drums—beaten by Tsongs ever since the reign of Chador Namgyal, the third chogyal—rose above the incantations.

They served his dinner on a tray exactly as he had always had it in the palace, replete with wine glass and a poignantly familiar little stone sauce jar. Prince Wangchuk stood erect on the high seat where his father had sat in frosted brocade and fur hat during Yanchen's glittering wedding, as the congregation burst into the lost strains of the national anthem. If anything was more moving, it was the beseeching plaint of *Om Mane Padma Hum*, the powerful resonance of hundreds of voices pleading for compassion. Many broke down and wept as they paid their last respects. Gentle and dignified, Ashi Kesang, Queen-Mother of Bhutan, his first cousin and a devout Buddhist, bent her head on the polished wooden floor before the altar. Sikkim's now moderately loyal assembly, which in Kazi's time had churlishly refused to acknowledge Tenzing's death, mourned the man who had 'lost his kingdom but gained a martyr's halo'.

The heavens cleared two days before the funeral. It was in the cold, dry sharpness of dawn that the coffin was brought out and placed in an appliqué tent. The soul had found its haven, all proclaimed. Some gave praise to monks credited with miraculous control of the weather. More khadas, more full-length prostrations, a sadly rousing farewell by the Sikkim police, and then, after they had circled the chapel royal three times with the coffin, Wangchuck and the other pall-bearers set out for the hills—a vast, slowly surging sea of humanity. Old women festooned in turquoise jewellery whirled their prayer-wheels in endless rotation, lamas counted their beads in silent prayer, young children clutched the red and white national flags that policemen tried to snatch away. Bhandari and Khatiawara, yesterday's bitter enemies, walked side by side in the union of bereavement. Nepalese peasants, Bhutiya-Lepcha patriarchs, civil servants and traders, politicians and shopkeepers, everyone grasped that an era in history was over.

The fire was kindled in the chorten on Lukshyama some five hours later under clear azure skies. The faithful counted seven vultures—the Chogyal's guardian bird—circling protectively above.

In the solemn magnificence, the like of which Sikkim will never see again, intruded pathetic gestures of honour emulated from the West. The Chogyal had all his life craved the contemporary trappings of sovereignty, not for personal grandeur, for he was an utterly simple man, but in recognition of his country's status. They were there in his death in profligate abundance: flags at half-mast, mourning bands of black, the *Dead March* in Handel's *Saul*, bugles blowing the *Last Post* through the hills, guards of honour with drawn swords, and three crackling salvos. But the Eighth Gurkhas, of which he was colonel-in-chief, and the army in which he held the rank of major-general, were conspicuously absent. If Laskar was present in a Congress minister's regulation black coat and trousers, Taleyarkhan, who had begrudged foreign exchange during the Chogyal's last fatal illness in New York, was resplendent in a flamboyant scarlet-lined cape and hood of vivid blue, thickly covered in braided embroidery. He scampered round like an excited child at a party, gaily taking photographs like any casual tourist at a fun fair.

Marks of official favour prompted more surprise than gratification. Not because these same agencies had hounded the Chogyal to the day of his death, but because alien formality means less in the Himalayas than their own timeless ceremonial. There can be no improvement on the eloquent language of the khada. It can be used to brutal purpose as when Pende Ongmu, the third chogyal's scheming sister, was murdered with a scarf stuffed down her throat. It can also be the instrument of devastating reproof. When, under New Delhi's stern command, some of the frightened signatories asked Wangchuck to return the document recognising his accession, the prince said he would also return their khadas. The request wasn't repeated.

A khada is spread out for felicitations, such as Wangchuck received in acknowledgement of his kingship. It is tightly bunched for condolence and often wound round a wad of notes to help with funerary expenses, its fringed edges neatly tucked in. It is presented then with butter, rice and chhang. Sometimes it is pleated into a fan, then flung out to stream away, and caught deftly from below before the floating silk flutters down. Traditionally, chogyals do not return the scarves of inferiors. They do not even touch them. A subject's khada is placed on a table as an offering to the throne, though a genial ruler may drape it round the giver's neck—never put it into his hands—in blessing. A person of equal rank, or someone who stands a shade higher, receives another scarf in return, the exchange symbolising trust and goodwill. Even then, the level at which hands are held can convey all kinds of meaning.

A seemingly simple gesture is in fact governed by elaborate protocol that often baffles the outsider. In public, the Dalai Lama would produce a scarf in exchange for the Chogyal's, deferring to the latter's spiritual and temporal position. In private, he might return the Sikkimese ruler's khada with his blessings and place it round his neck. Usage is not always synonymous with etiquette; compulsions of custom and courtesy add to complexity.

The Sikkimese were charmed in the 1960s by the grace and meticulousness with which Mrs Gandhi appeared to have mastered the nuances of this ritual. But times change, and tact and politeness vanished after 1975. 'She strides down the receiving line snatching away our khadas without even looking at the giver,' grumbled the old Densapa chieftain whose Lepcha ancestors held Denzong long before Khye-Bumsa, the first Bhutiya king, came out of Kham in the thirteenth century. Himself the soul of politeness, Barmiok Kazi could think of no offence more grave than ungraciousness.

Khye-Bumsa's descendant was even more punctilious in treating all comers as equals. Sikkimese peasants, Indian officials and their wives, visitors from abroad, stood at the Kagyet or Phanglabsol dances in the palace grounds, nervously clutching their little bundles of white cloth. For each there was a smile, a greeting, some word of personal inquiry. Each scarf was accepted with murmured thanks, held for a moment, then gently placed back in the giver's hands, no matter how lowly his station. So much was this egalitarian reciprocity a constant feature of the Chogyal's personal style that even senior Sikkimese officials, well versed in court rites, did not always realise that he was breaking with custom to bridge the gap in status. Protocol impinged on his innate kindness only when high-born Tibetans, with their insistence on Lhasa's rigid etiquette, were present in the palace.

•••

In all the years that I knew the Chogyal, I never got round to presenting him with a khada. Our first encounter in 1960, when I had taken a taxi up from Kalimpong as a tourist and wandered curiously into the palace to find him sipping tea and poring over files on a carpet in the garden, was far too casual for ceremony even if I had known the drill. Later, ceremony would have grated on friendship. An opportunity arose, or so I thought, when the Chogyal came down to Calcutta for our wedding reception. But he explained that bride and bridegroom take precedence on that one day and that he could accept no scarf from us. It was his privilege to give. First, a khada for my mother as hostess; then two round our necks; finally, two more over our outstretched palms. A rich haul of five lengths of silk, and none to give back.

The omission of twenty-two years was repaired on 19 February 1982. As the shadows closed in on Lukshyama hill, and clouds of black smoke billowed out of the whitewashed chorten within which smouldered the funeral pyre, I offered my first—and last—khada to the Chogyal.

CHAPTER

1

SMASH AND GRAB

'If we bring a small country like Sikkim within our fold by using force, it would be like killing a fly with a bullet.'

JAWAHARLAL NEHRU,
The Statesman, 3 June 1960.

'I have no words when (the) Indian army was sent today in a surprise attack on Sikkim Guards who are less than 300-strong and were trained, equipped and officered by (the) Indian army who looked upon each other as comrades... This is a most treacherous and black day in the history of democratic India in solving the survival of our little country by use of arms.'

The CHOGYAL to INDIRA GANDHI,
9 April 1975.

Gangtok was buzzing with rumour. Many Sikkimese feared that Chinese troops, guarding the Nathu-la exit into Tibet about forty-five miles to the north-east, were about to attack. Others whispered that Mrs Indira Gandhi's India, commanding the plains to the south and bound by treaty to protect Sikkim, was determined to teach the Himalayan kingdom a lesson. Relations between protector and protectorate had been strained for two years. The quarrel was avidly discussed in the bazaar, where they stripped it down to its bare bones over cups of butter tea and long draughts of chhang. Nothing remains secret in Gangtok. Everyone knew that fifty-two-year-old Palden Thondup Namgyal, the twelfth consecrated Chogyal of Sikkim, had incurred the hostility of India's all-powerful prime minister and that her agencies were using disgruntled elements among Sikkim's Nepalese majority to achieve India's purpose.

Tension reached a high pitch as the sleepy little town, strung out at an altitude of nearly 6,000 feet, woke up to unaccustomed military frenzy on Tuesday, 8 April 1975. Gangtok might have been preparing for war. Indian soldiers in full battle order manoeuvered trucks, jeeps, radio cars with tags on their aerials and ambulances through the dizzily winding roads of the normally placid capital. Assault ladders were dragged to the hilltop, where in all its doll's house serenity, stood the royal palace: a cream stone bungalow encrusted with scarlet and blue mythological beasts. With a painted roof and ornately framed windows, it was set in a gravel surround among three acres of terraced gardens. Mobilisation on this scale had never been seen in Gangtok, though India had also flexed its military muscles in 1949 to intimidate the Chogyal's father, Sir Tashi Namgyal, into signing a treaty.

The Chogyal was sipping tea under a blue and white appliqué tent by the vegetable patch behind the palace, when they told him of the troop movements. Nearby was a cushioned swing; tubular steel chairs lay scattered about him; emblazoned Tibetan rugs covered the green. Over the tent drooped Sikkim's thickly embroidered royal standard—the eight auspicious symbols of Buddhism caught in a circle of protective flame. Wind and rain had bleached the flag until the emblem was barely visible. The stout pole was scarred with age. But it was a unique standard, not raised anywhere else in the kingdom. All other masts flew the national flag, a field of white for purity enclosed in a border of crimson strength and holding in its heart the yellow eight-spoked wheel of righteousness.

The tent was one of several garden retreats that allowed the Chogyal to receive officials and public delegations in an atmosphere of relaxed informality, his family surrounding him. The site also offered a good view of the hill outside the palace. A flimsy railing edged the lawn near where he sat. Below it, the long drive sloped away to a triple gateway with sentry boxes on either side, and a yellow upturned roof. The road beyond is called the Ridge. It is a straight carriageway flanked by sidewalks fringed with flower beds. Descending from it on the right were the barracks of the Sikkim Guards, and further along on the left a colonial building called White Hall, used as a club for civilian officers. In the middle of the Ridge stands a circular pavilion, after which the road stretches to Mintokgang (blossom-crowned hilltop), a bungalow that belonged to the palace but was then occupied by Sikkim's Indian chief executive, Bipin Bihari Lal.

The road bifurcated at Mintokgang, the left sweeping up to India House, seat of New Delhi's representative, the political officer, or PO, as everyone called him. On the right, it rose steeply through straggling bustees, past the Enchey monastery about a mile to the north, to Tagongteng plateau where Sikkim's hereditary noblemen, the Kazis, are cremated. Above it lay Bhot-lha-solsa, the Tibetan prayer grounds, and, even higher, the sacred mountain known to Buddhists as Lukshyama and venerated by Hindus as Hanuman Tok. Sir Tashi and his parents were cremated there; three white chortens rearing out of the leech-infested bushes mark the sites. The Chogyal's guru, who lived alone in a small hut, was for many years the only living being in this wilderness; now the area crawls with Indian soldiers whose camps and sentry boxes stretch along the road. This is the old trade route to Tibet, a disused mule track now meandering away into a lost horizon.

Viewed from the Rumtek (our lady has left) monastery, twelve miles across the valley, the entire hill resembles a crouching elephant. The palace stands on the beast's head, Mintokgang on the nape of its neck, which is the Ridge, and the royal cremation ground on the higher swell of its haunches.

'They told me troops were pouring down the hill from Enchey to command the Ridge,' said the Chogyal. The Indian army had taken over Tagongteng and set up positions on the old Tibet road. Medium machine-guns had been placed at Bhotlha-solsa, and eighty-one-millimetre mortars looked grimly down from the heights above Mintokgang. A battery of artillery monopolised Lukshyama. The palace was the obvious target, its only exit—the Ridge—cut off.

'Friends in the bazaar said the guns were pointed at the palace,' recalls Captain Roland Christopher Chhetri, a Presbyterian officer in the Sikkim Guards. Chhetri's father had been a junior commissioned officer in the British Indian Gurkhas; his mother was an indigenous Lepcha of ancient family. He himself had been trained in the Indian Military Academy in Dehra Dun and was seconded for two years to an Indian paratroop battalion. Chhetri had many friends among the 25,000 Indian soldiers who had been stationed in Sikkim ever since the 1950s when Jawaharlal Nehru and Chou En-lai fell out over the Himalayan border. His Indian contacts told Chhetri that the army was only preparing for a routine exercise.

That was also the bland explanation when the Chogyal telephoned India House. Sardar Gurbachan Singh, the PO, suavely assured him that there was no cause for alarm. 'It's only a military exercise, Your Highness,' he burbled. 'A dry run without ammunition.'

Within forty-eight hours—at about 12.45 in the afternoon of Wednesday, 9 April—an entire Indian brigade swung into action against the unsuspecting ruler of a state that was under New Delhi's protection. The meticulously planned offensive included simultaneous assaults from three directions. 'The First Paratroopers, Thirteenth Jammu and Kashmir Militia, and

Sixteenth Jats attacked the palace, with an artillery brigade in support, and the Seventeenth Mountain Division standing by,' says Captain Chhetri. 'About 5,000 men had been mobilised.'

But first, a clumsy attempt was made to lure the Chogyal away. Gurbachan Singh telephoned him early on that fateful Wednesday, apologised profusely for the short notice and explained he had forgotten to read a high-priority telex message from the Indian government that had arrived late the previous evening. Mrs Gandhi wanted to see the ruler in New Delhi on Thursday morning. There was no time to lose. He would have to set out at once. The journey from Gangtok is neither short nor easy. There is first a six-hour drive down to Bagdogra in the West Bengal plains to catch the forty-five-minute flight to Calcutta; then a tedious wait of several hours in Calcutta for the night flight to Delhi. To cut it short, the PO offered an Alouette army helicopter for the first lap to Bagdogra.

The Chogyal explained he would need to take his trusted secretary, Jigdal Densapa, and his legal adviser, Yale-trained Maharajkumari Bhuvanesh Kumari, one of the Maharaja of Patiala's daughters, who was staying in the palace. Singh felt that three would be too many for an Alouette, whereupon the Chogyal suggested that a second Alouette be provided. Singh then demurred at a woman travelling in military aircraft; the army would never allow it, he said, though India House had no objection. The Chogyal at once telephoned Mountain Division headquarters and talked to the GOC, Major-General Harbhajan Singh Kullar, who readily agreed to fly the maharajkumari. When told that the military had agreed, the PO apologised that the second Alouette was being serviced and would not be available. So it went on, conversation after conversation over the telephone, until the Chogyal 'asked for one of those big Soviet helicopters, MI-4s, I think', as he told me. Again Singh prevaricated, eventually explaining that none of them was free.

So the Chogyal agreed to fly alone, though considerably surprised at this sudden imperious summons from a woman who had many times before kept him cooling his heels in New Delhi's Ashok Hotel before condescending to a meeting. But the sense of impending disaster in Gangtok left him little choice. He was also perhaps flattered by the urgency of her invitation, and anxious to grasp at any straw and make any gesture that might placate Mrs Gandhi. Densapa was asked to report to the palace at once, the drivers told to get the Mercedes ready, and an ADC sent across the lawns to the Tsuk-la-khang royal chapel to consult the lamas on the precise moment when the party should set out. The palace was plunged into a flurry of sorting out papers and packing. The Chogyal's stenographer had not yet arrived, but he himself sat down at a typewriter and hammered out a letter to the PO which expressed a nagging sense of unease:

> Since I am asked to go to Delhi to meet the Prime Minister of India tomorrow morning, I am leaving as per your arrangements. However, I have reports of bazaar talks that there is to be a concerted organised demonstration to storm the palace and the Sikkim Guards from today. It is also rumoured that this is likely to bring in Indian army intervention. I am sure that these are not correct and would request you to please ensure that nothing untoward happens during my absence in Delhi.

He still could not bring himself to believe that the army would directly he involved in any form of aggression. 'We never dreamt that India would attack us. After all, the Sikkim Guards were trained and armed by Delhi. We looked on the Indian Army as our comrades and gurus.' The Chogyal enjoyed military company and believed he had a good rapport with India's brasshats. As an honorary major-general in the Indian Army and colonel-in-chief of the Eighth Gurkhas, he was a regular visitor to army messes and even more frequently entertained Indian officers at the palace. Field Marshal Sam

Maneckshaw was a particular friend. The Chogyal also believed them when Indian officers assured him that even if political relations soured, the military would prevent New Delhi from doing anything drastic. His faith in the army's goodwill was complete.

Two hours after the note had been sent round to India House, around 9.30 in the morning, Singh was back on the line to cancel the appointment with the prime minister as abruptly as it had been made. He pleaded that the Bagdogra–Calcutta flight was fully booked. 'I thought it funny because there's always a VIP quota on this plane,' reflected the Chogyal who had never had difficulty getting a seat, even at the last moment. He later understood that the meeting with Mrs Gandhi was only a blind. They were anxious to get him out of the way in case the Sikkim Guards, getting wind of what was afoot, took up defensive positions. 'When they discovered that we were quite unprepared, they didn't bother.'

The Sikkim Guards were a tough little fighting force, recruited from sturdy peasant lads, mainly Nepalese Magars, in their late teens or early twenties. They were dedicated to their monarch and proud to wear his uniform, worthy descendants of the soldiers who had fought the British in the nineteenth century and of the brigade of about 5,000 men that Sikkim raised during World War II. They were proud cousins, too, of some 2,000 Sikkimese volunteers in the Indian army. A succession of Indian officers had done their job well. Not only did they impart skills and discipline to raw recruits, but by themselves always wearing the ankle-length *kho* (*baku* in Nepalese) that is the kingdom's national dress, they stressed the force's Sikkimese identity. Young men like Chhetri had been trained and commissioned in India to eventually take over the command. It was probably the kingdom's only *truly* Sikkimese—neither exclusively Nepalese nor Bhutiya-Lepcha—institution.

But the Guards were not at their best in 1975. Constantly attacked by the chief minister, Kazi Lendhup Dorji, falsely accused of wounding another Congress legislator, Ram Chandra Poudyal, and of all kinds of murderous conspiracies, resented by Gurbachan Singh and Lal, criticised by New Delhi and harried in the Indian press, morale was understandably low. Though the Chogyal had never used the Guards in any civil disturbance, and the force had given valuable assistance to the Indian army in the 1965 conflict with China, they were projected as a feudal ruler's private thugs. In one of his many haughty ultimatums to the palace, the PO demanded that guardsmen should be withdrawn from sentry duty at the homes of the Chogyal's mother, the aged Gyalum, and of his brother and sister.

Nor did the latest batch of seconded Indian officers contribute anything to esprit de corps. The total strength in 1975 was four officers and 272 men; of them, the commandant, Lieutenant-Colonel Kishen Singh Gurung, the adjutant, Major R.K. Jagota, another officer, four JCOs and sixty-one men were Indian. Unlike earlier deputationists, they were not integrated with the force, choosing to remain at an emotional distance from their Sikkimese comrades. Of the rest, 25 per cent had reported sick, 10 per cent were on leave, and 10 per cent were non-combatants. Yet, even this rump force provided the throne with a more effective shield than any of the pacts and treaties to which New Delhi was party. Without exception, the guardsmen were ready to lay down their lives for king and country. They comprised the Chogyal's praetorian guard.

The force was under the Chogyal's exclusive command. It said so in two agreements that he had signed with India in 1973, the leaders of Sikkim's three political parties also being signatories to the second. Both explicitly recognised that 'the palace establishment and the Sikkim Guards will remain directly under the Chogyal'. India, represented by Gurbachan Singh, had no authority over it. Neither had the Sikkim administration under Lal and Kazi.

But the Guards had just been deprived of the leadership of one of the most passionate adherents of the nationalist cause. Like Chhetri, Captain Sonam Yongda too had passed out with distinction from the Indian Military Academy and had trained for more than a year with an Indian Gurkha regiment. The son of a senior lama at Pemayangtse monastery, where he himself had also been ordained, Yongda came of sturdy Bhutiya stock. His home was near Yoksam, scene of the first chogyal's anointing. He was a devout Buddhist and unflinchingly loyal.

The Indian Central Reserve Police suddenly arrested Yongda early in the morning of 7 April and thrust him into jail. They allowed him to petition Gangtok's Central Court for release the next day, but before the application could be heard he was whisked off to Gyalzing in the west. There the captain submitted another petition to the district magistrate, but again the CRP took him under custody to the southern town of Namche. All that his captors told Yongda was that, acting under the Chogyal's orders, he had engaged a man called Sonam Tshering—a very common name in Sikkim, Bhutan and Darjeeling—to assassinate Kazi and the Youth Congress president, Nar Bahadur Khatiawara. The captain angrily denied the plot, but was not questioned. Nor was he ever charged. The unsubstantiated verbal accusation was only an excuse to put him away.

But in Gangtok, the chief executive briefed reporters with more lurid details. According to Lal, Yongda had signed a statement implicating the ruler. He had admitted in it to providing the hired killer with an army service pistol with seven spent and two live bullets as well as ₹ 600. The Indian government spokesmen in New Delhi embellished the story to add that the confession accused both the Chogyal and Sikkim's auditor-general, Madan Mohan Rasaily, of 'masterminding' a series of arson and looting outrages in addition to murder. When I asked to see the statement, Lal promised it would be released in Gangtok the next day: it was then on its way from

Gyalzing. It never was released. No one ever saw it. Yongda admits to signing only two documents, both petitions complaining of unlawful arrest and wrongful confinement. He did not even know of the alleged confession until 22 April when the Gangtok Central Court ordered the police to release him on bail. It was a short-lived reprieve, for the Bhutiya captain was at once taken into military custody.

His imprisonment had been carefully timed and planned. With Yongda behind bars, the Sikkim Guards were deprived of the only officer who could have forged commitment and fervour into resistance. Failing him, the burden of leadership devolved on the engaging young Chhetri, who could not match the older man's resolution or perspicacity. Those who played this masterstroke had shrewdly gambled on the temperamental difference between the two captains. Yongda's clan attachment to the Namgyal dynasty and his faith in the kingdom's religious identity made him acutely conscious of the throne's importance if Sikkim were to survive as a separate entity. Though also utterly devoted to the Chogyal, Chhetri was just a cheerful young soldier, happiest playing volleyball with his men or singing lilting Nepalese melodies on picnics in the hills. Possibly because of his Gurkha father, his mother's Lepcha heritage and even his Christianity, Chhetri didn't have the Bhutiya Buddhist captain's intense political commitment.

But even the virtually leaderless Guards provided a bulwark against annihilation. Captain Chhetri may have been young, carefree and uninvolved, but he had taken a soldier's oath. The Chogyal's two elder sons were his friends and playmates. Both he and his men had to be immobilised before the Chogyal's sacerdotal office could be touched.

The burden of the arrangements for the journey—before it was cancelled—fell on Chhetri, who was down in the Guards area, below the Ridge, arranging for the royal escort. Colonel Gurung should have seen off the ruler, but pleaded an urgent summons from the Indian army's divisional headquarters. 'He asked me to present a khada for him and make his apologies,' says Chhetri. 'I think he was warned.'

The captain had other reasons for unease. An Indian havildar clerk, whom he had ordered to make out contingent bills three days earlier, had shrugged and mumbled something about it being pointless. Chhetri had also intercepted strange looks and heard echoes of enigmatic remarks. All the Indians on deputation were behaving secretively. Most of them had stopped doing any work. They merely smiled mysteriously when told to get on with their tasks. The sudden rush of leave applications was equally bewildering.

Troubled, but unable to pinpoint the cause of his misgivings, Chhetri began to lock up just after noon on 9 April. Since the Chogyal was not leaving, he had no more work that day. In any case, the barracks always shut down for maintenance on Wednesday afternoons. None of the Indians was to be seen as the captain finished his tasks and went to his quarters where his young wife waited with lunch. 'I took off my belt and cap, and then, some instinct made me look up through the window.' At once his nameless fears crystallised into a sharp comprehension of danger.

Two rows of men in CRP uniform stood on the Ridge above. Bowling down the road from India House was a steady stream of one-ton military trucks and jeeps with lowered hoods. Soldiers in battle fatigues crammed the vehicles. The convoy stopped at the pavilion, where men poured out to begin the advance. One file doubled towards the triple gateway. The other branched off to clamber down the ravine into the Guards area from where Chhetri watched in horrified disbelief. 'I heard the charge order covering fire from Bhot-lha-solsa about 800 yards from the palace gates.' He couldn't believe his ears.

• • •

They were no less incredulous within the twenty-room palace, where the Chogyal, showing little sign of the constant strain he was under, conferred with Crown Prince Tenzing, his twenty-five-year-old heir. Tenzing was a handsome and ebullient youth, popular among the ordinary townsfolk, and increasingly viewed as the one person who might be able to bring together Sikkim's king and disgruntled Nepalese politicians. Realising his son's public appeal, the Chogyal had lately begun to rely on the young man's advice. They had drawn closer together since the Gyalmo (formerly Hope Cooke), the Chogyal's American consort, had returned to New York the previous year.

Densapa had also joined them, bringing a suitcase just in case he had to accompany his master to New Delhi. So had Rasaily. The palace staff consisted of two young civilian ADCs and about sixteen servants, including two or three ageing women. They were under Emil Manuel, the Goan housekeeper whose habitual black suit and lugubrious expression concealed an acid wit.

No house could have been less prepared for a siege. The Guards did not even have live ammunition. Trenches dug during the 1973 riots had long ago been filled in. The sandbags that then lined the drive had all been kicked aside. There should have been two non-commissioned officers and six men at the gates. Instead, just an NCO and one guardsman kept casual watch.

Servants and master were aghast as they huddled by the lawn railings, taking turns to peer through a pair of binoculars. 'Guns pointed directly at the palace from only about 600 yards away,' said the Chogyal. 'When they saw us watching, they swung the guns sideways.' Infantrymen marched down the mule track. As they emerged on the Ridge, they began running along the pavements on either side. The Chogyal wondered why they did not use the road. 'It still did not enter my head that the palace could be attacked. But I was beginning to feel apprehensive for the first time.'

A sudden burst of machine-gun fire broke the tense silence. 'The column on the north under a Sikh NCO had reached the gates and fired at the sentries. I couldn't see it all but realised they were trying to take over the two sentry boxes. The eastern column opened fire on the quarterguard.'

The action was brisk and bloody. It was also entirely one-sided. One of the two sentries, Basant Kumar Chhetri, only nineteen, levelled his rifle at the attackers, but did not live to pull the trigger. He was shot in the chest and killed in the first volley. His eighteen-year-old comrade, Nima Sherpa, stumbled out of the guardroom in surprise and was at once hit in the right arm. It had later to be amputated. When Naik Lal Bahadur Limbu, who was at lunch in his billet, came out to see what the noise was all about, he too was caught in the fire, but escaped unhurt. It was all over in less than three minutes, a numbing nightmare, macabre and bizarre.

'There was no ultimatum to lay down arms. No formal surrender either. It was just a smash-and-grab raid,' the Chogyal mused afterwards.

Nothing made sense to Roland Chettri who looked on in wonder and dismay. 'We were not at war with India. They were our protectors. We had done nothing wrong. Why should they attack our king's palace and wound and kill our men?'

The press were later told that the Sikkim Guards had been asked through a loudspeaker to lay down their arms and that, instead of doing so, had opened fire so that the Indian army had to retaliate in self-defence. The defenders vehemently deny this version. 'Had we been given even that much warning, we would first have taken a few lives!' exploded a bitter young guardsman. But the most convincing refutation of India's official line came from the PO's wife two days later. I had asked why the Sikkim Guards weren't asked to surrender. 'You can't know the Chogyal at all if you think he would have responded to an ultimatum!' Mrs Gurbachan Singh snapped before her husband could reply. 'Surprise was the only way of taking the palace!' she added. The PO, whom I had known in Europe, quickly intervened, 'But darling, he knows the Chogyal much better than we do,' he warned. The outspoken Sardarni was silenced. The indiscretion was not repeated.

The Chogyal was too dazed at the beginning to understand what was happening. But the crackle of gunfire sent him running into the ADC's cottage from where he dialled India House. 'What the hell do you think you're doing?' he demanded, and the PO, for once flustered and at a loss for words, jabbered incoherently and shoved the receiver at General Kullar, who was with him.

'Sir, your men must lay down their arms and surrender,' demanded the general, though not in a disrespectful tone.

'I must go and talk to them.'

'All right, but you must come alone, unarmed, and speak to them only in Hindi because our chaps don't understand your language.'

The phone rang as soon as it was replaced. Captain Chhetri reported that the quarterguard was under fire. His commandant was still mysteriously absent. Another Indian officer, the adjutant, and Major B. Tsering, a Sikkimese, were also missing. The area had been stormed. Lance Naik Man Bahadur Lepcha had been shot in the leg. Indian soldiers were searching every house in the nearby Tatangchen bustee where palace servants and the married guardsmen's families lived. Most of the men had been rounded up at lunch in the canteen and placed under close guard.

It was left to the young Guards officer to defend his country and save the honour of his regiment. But there was no panic. Remembering his military manual, Chhetri suggested mustering the few guardsmen who had still not been caught to form a defensive perimeter. It was a daring and courageous plan in the face of formidably superior power, but the Indian operator manning Gangtok's telephone exchange intervened before the Chogyal could respond to such a desperate last-ditch stand. There was a click and the line went dead. It was just past one in the afternoon.

Unable to get orders and refusing to yield, Chhetri tried to make his way to Colonel Gurung's house in a last attempt to explain to the commandant that his men expected loyalty and leadership. But Indian soldiers were watching the house. They also kept guard over the officers' mess. The Indian army was everywhere. In the distance, the captain could see his guardsmen lined up in the football field with their hands above their heads like criminals. Many had been resting and were in their underclothes. Suddenly, a rifle shot sounded from the direction of the mess. As the bullet whistled past his head, Chhetri leapt into a dry ditch about twenty feet below and began running, crouching low. He did not stop until he had placed at least 200 yards between himself and the quarterguard. He must have waited in the undergrowth for more than an hour before a bugle sang out the cease-fire.

There was no clear idea in his mind except a resolve not to be caught. He hoped to hide somewhere until nightfall, then slip out of Gangtok and take to the mountains. So the captain edged his way through the straggly jungle to the home of Ashoke Tsering, a leading National Party politician whom he could trust. Chhetri expected temporary sanctuary, some explanation of the day's baffling events, and mature advice.

He found his wife there. An Indian soldier had driven her to Tsering's house in an army jeep. Tearfully, Mrs Chhetri explained that their house had been ransacked and was under guard. She had little food and no money; the Army wouldn't allow her to go to any of their friends. The Chhetris had two daughters, aged two-and-a-half years and a year, and the young woman was hysterical with fear. She pleaded with her husband to return. The Indians had promised her they would be well looked after if she could persuade the captain to give himself up. Otherwise the entire family would be harassed. Unable to resist his wife's entreaties, Chhetri went back to his own house to find a crowd outside the front door and two Indian officers lounging in his sitting room. Laughing and chatting with them, though bereft of belt and cap, presumably in token of his nominally captive state, was the elusive Colonel Gurung, the Sikkim Guards' Indian commandant. He had abandoned his post and left his men to fend for themselves. It was a cruel awakening for Chettri to find his superior so clearly ranged with the enemy. He had not till then consciously thought of the colonel as a foreigner with political allegiances that transcended his military honour and his responsibility to his command.

'Where the hell have you been?' one of the Indians burst out angrily. But the Guards captain cut him short: 'Talk to me properly as one officer to another.' Gurung intervened to say with patronising jocularity that it was all part of the game. 'It's the funniest game I ever saw!' retorted Chhetri. His commandant was not abashed.

One more scene of betrayal remained to be enacted. When all the Sikkimese soldiers had been assembled, an Indian officer played to them a recorded message from Kazi, urging surrender. The chief minister promised that no one would be dismissed, yet assured them of honourable re-employment. The prisoners listened in contemptuous silence.

They were kept under watch until midnight when they were herded into trucks and driven out of Gangtok. Chettri noticed that none of the sixty-eight Indian deputationists accompanied them. The convoy headed south, and people in Singtam, an hour's drive from the capital, recall how the night was filled with song as the vehicles hurtled through the deserted marketplace. The swelling strains of the national anthem, *Dela Sil Lee Gee Yang Chagpa Chilo* (Sikkim, May It Always Be Blooming) and the livelier melody of *Teesta-Rungeet* spoke of defiance. Lal had banned both tunes. 'We will come back,' they yelled from the speeding trucks. 'We will come back one day and demand justice.'

The convoy passed on, not stopping until it reached Sirwani, some twenty miles to the southeast. The guardsmen were told it was only a transit camp; they would not be detained there for more than four or five days. But hope faded as they entered Sirwani's forbidding outer perimeter of barbed wire under the watchful eyes of the Ninth Madras Regiment. Arms at the ready, soldiers manned the barrier. The Sikkimese were stripped naked in the pitiless glare of spotlights, searched and individually questioned before being thrust through a second cordon, again with hands above their heads like prisoners in a concentration camp. 'We have orders to shoot if you try to run away,' coldly warned the commandant who boasted he had guarded Pakistani prisoners after the 1971 Bangladesh war. The register described Sirwani as the Sikkim Guards Prison Camp. Captain Yongda joined them there about two weeks later, suffering with the rest for four months the full humiliation of an enemy force captured in ignominious defeat.

The world was only told that the Chogyal's palace guards had peacefully been disarmed. Casualties were never mentioned.

• • •

Disarming the Guards didn't take more than twenty minutes. The Chogyal could not see the action from his garden post, but he had begun to guess something of what was happening in the quarterguard. More alert to what might follow, Tenzing, meanwhile, set about collecting whatever firearms there were in the palace. There was no armoury. Individual pieces, most of them old and rusty, had to be brought together from attic and cellar. There were eighteen in all: eight .303 rifles left over from World Wars I and II, several hunting rifles and shotguns that had been presented by visiting potentates, two or three broken-down carbines, and three sub-machine-guns. Somewhat foolishly, the crown prince buried some of the weapons in a flower-bed. He had no plan in mind, save an instinctive desire to prevent the family's arms being confiscated.

The operation was probably watched, for a little later Colonel Sudharshan Singh of the First Paratroopers stalked up the drive with about a dozen soldiers and, without even saluting the Chogyal, demanded that all firearms should be handed over. He had brought a metal detector and knew exactly where to look. The Chogyal tried to plead that private weapons were not part of the Guards outfit, but the explanation was brushed aside. All eighteen pieces—including the few that had been hidden—were taken away. They were never returned. They are probably displayed today as trophies of war in some Indian army mess or, more likely, adorn the private collection of one of the senior Indian officers.

After searching the house, Colonel Singh wanted to inspect the grounds, and, to snap out of the paralysis that seemed to grip him, the Chogyal climbed into the driver's seat of a jeep and himself drove his uninvited guests around the lawns. What he saw was chilling. Indian soldiers with Sterling sub-machine-guns and seven-millimetre self-loading rifles were stationed every fifty yards along the paths. 'It was gradually sinking in that it was the end of everything. Sikkim was lost and I was a prisoner.'

But there were no recriminations when he received an apologetic and deferential General Kullar in the back garden tent. Curtly ordering his escort not to approach, the general walked up alone to the defeated monarch and came smartly to the salute. 'Sir, you are my senior general,' he said. 'What am I to say? I am very sorry for what has happened. I have been trying to avoid this for the last year. But the PO and Lal worked on Delhi and I was overruled.'

The Chogyal understood. He was not surprised to learn later that the brigade commander of his own regiment, the Eighth Gurkhas, Brigadier Dipender Singh, Dippy to his many Sikkimese friends, had queried his orders. Apparently, he agreed to carry them out only when warned that a less sympathetic officer would be far more ruthless. Lieutenant-General J.F.R. (Jake) Jacob, Eastern Command's GOC-in-C, was also subsequently to claim that his moderating influence had averted greater bloodshed. The civilian intelligence officials who planned the attack would probably have been happier if the Chogyal had fallen.

His own safety did not then worry the ruler. His thoughts were for those who had risked their lives for him and the country. The Chogyal asked that the guardsmen be treated with the courtesy due to soldiers who had acquitted themselves bravely in battle, and that the Sikkim Guards colours be marched up to the palace with the proper escort of an officer. 'We'll give you not just an officer but a full contingent,' was General Kullar's generous promise. It was not kept.

In contrast with the Chogyal's dignified restraint, his legal advisor Bhuvanesh Kumari petulantly exclaimed, 'I suppose this means another medal for you, General?' Kullar ignored the taunt. But Major Arjun Katoch of the First Paratroopers was, in fact, awarded the Seva medal.

The Chogyal's self-control broke only when Gurbachan Singh breezed into the library that afternoon. Hope had furnished the room with fitted bookshelves along all the walls, deep leather sofas from Heal's in London, transparent Perspex chairs and pendant lights in wicker shades. Autographed photographs of Indian dignitaries in crested silver frames thickly covered the one expanse of wall that was free of books. The carpet was cluttered with chess and Scrabble pieces, magazines, and family photographs that were being sorted out. It was a comfortable lived-in room. The PO was brimming with solicitude as he paid a surprise visit, but his host was livid.

'You have the bloody g-g-gumption to show your face here after what you've done...' blazed the Chogyal, red in the face, his stammer becoming more pronounced as it always did under stress.

'If you want me to leave, I will,' was the stolid reply.

'Please do.'

Gurbachan Singh turned on his heel and walked out.

• • •

The palace had become a prison. No one could leave or enter. The telephones were all dead. But attacked, abused, immobilised and isolated, the Chogyal still retained a sense of kingly obligation. He was at the mercy of his country's sworn protector, but that was only one more betrayal in a life that had been tragically star-crossed. He was yet to bear a far greater burden of grief. Many of the men he had trusted most had in the end preferred reward to loyalty; the wife he still loved had packed her bags and gone as soon as the queenship she had hankered for had lost its savour. The Chogyal's relations with his family, even with his mother, were more dutiful than affectionate. Many of his relatives sponged on him. Indian politicians and civil servants who frequently enjoyed his generous hospitality thought nothing of running him down the moment they returned to Delhi. Intimacy he lacked, and also genuine companionship. His position condemned him to loneliness. Even Tenzing was sometimes persuaded to wonder if his father had not jeopardised his rightful inheritance. The clash of arms within his compound only added to the disappointments of the sad, shy man who had known so little satisfaction in private life or public career. But self-pity was not allowed to impinge on what he still saw as his function as anointed king.

When the last of his visitors had gone, the Chogyal changed from bush shirt and slacks into the crisp khaki of colonel-in-chief of the Sikkim Guards. Tenzing did not know his father's purpose, but still unnerved by the shattering experience they had both shared, sought a part in it. The Chogyal refused. 'He had just received a captaincy in the Guards, and the whole force was under arrest. I didn't want to give them the chance of seizing him too!' he told me later. The crown prince had to stay back as his father set out on his last lonely mission.

The Chogyal himself did not know what to expect as, fending off anxious retainers, he walked across the gravel and turned left into the drive. A small chorten stood among the flowering bushes and behind it were the palace garages under which the Dalai Lama's gold had been buried for safety after the historic flight from Tibet. As he strode down the slope to the gates, the Chogyal saw that the tarmac streamed with blood. He did not know why, for the triple archway was not fully visible from the lawns. No one had mentioned fatalities. He thought that the Guards had only surrendered to superior firepower. The PO had volunteered no details. Neither had General Kullar.

The posse of Indian soldiers who had taken up position at the gates looked on curiously, but would not reply to questions. Perhaps they had instructions not to. Wanting to ask Gurbachan Singh what exactly had happened, the Chogyal remembered there was a battered old field telephone in one of the sentry boxes. Only when he swung aside its door did he stumble on Basant Kumar Chhetri's rigid corpse. Someone—probably an Indian soldier moved by fellow-feeling for another's valour—had draped the body with the Sikkimese flag. Patches of blood stained the coarse white fabric.

The Chogyal was curtly to be refused permission to attend the young guardsman's funeral. The national flag was soon debased into a personal totem for Kazi and his ministers, gracing their cars and bungalows, until it was proscribed altogether. But it was sadly appropriate that before it was so degraded, the flag should perform a final duty as shroud for a brave young defender. It was apposite too that his master's last kingly observance was to honour the sacrifice of a Nepalese Hindu who had given his life to protect the Buddhist Bhutiya-Lepcha kingdom.

There, under the arches of the gateway, in full view of generals and jawans of the conquering army, the Chogyal knelt down to dip the forefinger of his right hand in the dead guardsman's congealing blood. He then smeared it on his own forehead.

Afterwards, the Chogyal could not explain why he did it. It was an instinctive gesture. But in making it, he momentarily shed the present to revert to the most valiant of his legendary ancestors, the mighty Khye-Bumsa, 'the superior of ten thousand heroes'. Khye-Bumsa was the first Tibetan prince to make his way into Sikkim in the thirteenth century when he swore blood brotherhood and eternal friendship with Thekong-tek, chief of the indigenous Lepchas. Kabi, just north of Gangtok, where the pact was sealed, is still the most poignant of Sikkim's many places of pilgrimage. It enshrines a hallowed memory.

Hushed into awe, watchers well understood the significance of the Chogyal's action. Such rituals are familiar to all ancient civilisations. It was an act of homage to the dead. It was also a solemn vow to avenge a pointless murder.

CHAPTER

2

Belgium of Asia

'What is this Sikhim that it should become the Belgium of Asia?'

H.H. Risley,
Gazetteer of Sikhim, 1894.

'Sikkim is an Independent State whose territory comprises some 3,600 square miles of country, wedged in between larger Independent States of Nepal and Bhutan, which occupy that large strip of country immediately under the great range of the Himalaya mountains to the north of Bengal and the North-West Provinces of India.'

Captain H.A. Iggulden,
The 2nd Battalion Derbyshire Regiment in the Sikkim Expedition of 1888.

Predators have always harried the Chogyal's domains. His ancestors had no less trouble with China, Tibet, Nepal, Bhutan and Britain's rising power in India. If the country survived these vicissitudes, it was by repeatedly coming to terms with covetous neighbours, absorbing new influences, and adjusting to conditions beyond shrinking borders.

The earliest settlers were Captain Chhetri's mother's people whose roots have been variously traced to eastern Tibet, to some remote corner of Assam, and to a lost tribe from South-east Asia. The Lepchas called themselves the Rong-pa, ravine folk, and knew their homeland as Denzong, rice bowl, which is still the official Sikkimese name for Sikkim. The Tibetan version of this was Bree-me-jong, rice country, used by the Jesuit priest, Ippolito Desideri, who reached Lhasa by way of Leh in 1716.

The Lepcha name was commonly used until Limbu settlers, also known as Tsongs, arrived from the Limbuana region, now in Nepal. These wanderers, originally from Tibet's Tsang-po valley, christened their new homeland Sukhim—happy home—because the tranquillity of uncharted mountains and virgin valleys slumbering between turbulent Nepal and ferocious Bhutan offered peaceful sanctuary. Sukhim was corrupted to Sikkim.

It was an extensive country then, considerably bigger even than Captain Iggulden's description, encompassing parts of Nepal, Bhutan, Tibet and India. The kingdom swept south into the plains to include the northern marches of Bihar, West Bengal, and what is now Bangladesh. Its boundaries were the Arun river in the west, the Taigon pass in the east, and Kishengunj in Purnea district in the south.

Little remains of that expansive past. Taking advantage of internal weakness, greedy neighbours gnawed away at Sikkim's territory until only 2,818 square miles were left. Among the Densapa papers are records relating to Naxalbari in West Bengal, notorious for giving birth to the Maoist rebellion, which once lay within the family estates. Pink pearls that a Raja of Jalpaiguri gave in lieu of the land rent he collected for the Gangtok durbar are studded in the Gyalum's twin-peaked ceremonial head-dress. The Chumbi valley with its ruins of the Sikkimese royal family's old summer palace has been lost to China. Substantial slices of territory to the east and west were carved out by Bhutan and Nepal, some of it passing to British India which steadily pushed north until Sikkim was deprived of all access to the plains.

British chroniclers treat the kingdom's early traditions with predictable scepticism. But the Sikkimese believe that a Namgyal ancestor, King Indrabodhi, once ruled what is now the Indian state of Himachal Pradesh. From him was descended Tibet's first king, Neh-Thi-Tsenpo (born *circa* 416 BC) who in turn fathered the Minyak dynasty, which reigned over Kham in eastern Tibet in the ninth century. The mighty Khye-Bumsa is believed to have been an offspring of this line. Another branch eventually found its way to Ladakh where Tibet's ancient royal family survives to this day in greatly reduced circumstances.

After Khye-Bumsa died in the Chumbi valley, his third son, Mipon Rab or 'leader of men', crossed the mountains to take up residence near Gangtok where he was acknowledged chieftain. He was succeeded by Guru Tashi, so called because he was born while the Tashi-rubne (a festival of good luck) rituals were being performed. In time, Guru Tashi's great-grandson, Phuntsog Namgyal, was consecrated as the first king of Sikkim.

Modern history begins with this monarch who was born in 1604 and anointed thirty-eight years later. Phuntsog shifted the capital to Yoksam which was more central and because the Yatung valley had lost its importance. He also laid the foundations of a centralised administration by dividing the country into twelve districts (*dzongs*) each under a Lepcha *dzongpon* (governor) and appointed twelve of his Bhutiya braves as *kalons* (ministers). They were the ancestors of today's hereditary noblemen who were later known by the Nepalese title of *kazi*. The term was probably derived from the Arab *qadi* or magistrate and introduced by India's Muslim rulers. Among themselves, kazis still address each other by the traditional Sikkimese title of *yap-la*, wives and daughters being *chum-la*.

Phuntsog's appointments were astutely calculated to reconcile indigenous Lepchas to the Bhutiya conquerors. Both groups enjoyed equal rank at court. But many of the twenty-four original clans are extinct. Only twelve kazis were listed in

1899. A later *Gazetteer of India* mentions twenty-one. Today, there must be several hundred Bhutiya-Lepchas (the two communities were bracketed together for convenience) who flaunt the title. Many of these claims are spurious. Others claim descent through illegitimate offspring or through daughters. The Chakung title used by Lendhup Dorji, and so grandly embellished by his British wife, actually died out long ago. No kazis have been created in recent times, though Rai Bahadur Lobzang Chhoden was recognised as one after he had satisfied the durbar of his rightful title to the Lingmo estate.

Jigdal Densapa's father, Rai Bahadur Tashi Dahdul Densapa of Barmiok, whose honorific of Athing-La gives him precedence over all other noblemen, is probably the premier Lepcha kazi today. Athing-La is chief of the Barfungpa (flowing from on high) clan which traces a semi-divine lineage to Thekong-tek, the Lepcha ruler. The modern surname of Densapa is derived from Den-chap or regent because a member of the family governed in the ruler's place whenever the latter was away in Tibet. Athing-La cuts a magnificent figure on state occasions in his brocade kho, single turquoise earring dangling from the left ear, plaited hair wound about his head, the whole impressive ensemble topped by a felt hat. The Metternich of Sikkim, he was Sir Tashi's secretary and advised his son on constitutional matters until Bhutan borrowed his services to guide the Dragon Kingdom's emergence into modern planning. Prominent among the surviving Bhutiya kazis is young Paljor Tashi of Rhenock, Penjola to all Gangtok, whose father, Tse-ten Tashi, was an accomplished photographer and a renowned botanist, with an extensive collection of Himalayan orchids. Tse-ten succeeded Athing La as Sir Tashi's secretary. Penjola was himself the Chogyal's assistant secretary and married his royal master's half-sister, Lhanzin-la. The Barmiok and Rhenock kazis followed the fashion set by the Namgyals and usually sought brides in Tibet.

Not only was Phuntsog Namgyal responsible for creating an hereditary nobility, but the circumstances of his elevation led to future political ambiguity. It is said that three Tibetan lamas—Lhatsun Chempo, Sempah Chempo and Rigdsin Chempo (the three superior ones)—met at Yoksam in the middle of the seventeenth century to convert Sikkim to Buddhism. 'Here are we three lamas in a new and irreligious country,' said Lhatsun Chempo. 'We must have a dispenser of gifts (king) to rule the country on our behalf.' Men of god being no less ambitious than laymen, Rigdsin at once proposed himself, being heir to a celebrated governor. Sempah promptly disputed the claim because he was of royal birth. Lhatsun then intervened, 'In the prophecy of Guru Rimpoche it is written that four noble brothers shall meet in Sikkim and arrange for its government. We are three of these come from the north, west and south. Towards the east, it is written, there is at this epoch a man named Phuntsog, a descendant of brave ancestors of Kham in eastern Tibet. According, therefore, to the prophecy of the guru, we should find him.'[1]

Phuntsog was given Lhatsun Chempo's family name of Namgyal and invested with the title of chogyal or the gyalpo (king) who upholds the chhos (righteousness). The Dalai Lama sent greetings to the 'ruler of the sacred land of the southern slopes' and presented the first chogyal with Guru Rimpoche's mitre and a valuable sand image.

Possibly because of this source of the first king's title, Lhasa always claimed certain rights over Sikkim. Desideri endorsed the view when he wrote of the 'provinces' of Phari, Sikkim, Haldibari and Purnea under the kingdom of Tibet and therefore 'subject to the emperor of China'. Tsugphud Namgyal, the seventh chogyal, submitted all his disputes with Lhasa to the Chinese *amban* (resident) at the Dalai Lama's court. In 1873 the amban wrote to the ninth chogyal, Thutob Namgyal, blaming him for building roads that had facilitated British intrusion, and ordering him in the name of the emperor that 'the Peling Sahibs (British) should not be allowed to cross the frontier'. Thutob Namgyal was more specifically forbidden to allow John Ware Edgar, Darjeeling's deputy commissioner, access to Tibet through Sikkim. Apparently accepting his subordinate position, the ninth chogyal received a Chinese button of rank, and in 1880 executed a document promising that 'in good and evil we will not leave the shelter of the feet of China and Tibet'.

Relations were never as simple or clear-cut as the implied three-tier—China–Tibet–Sikkim—hierarchy implied. Tibet's constitutional ties with China were not a constant factor, and might have been resolved differently if the Dalai Lama had been able to stand up to Mao Tse-tung. A distinction should also be drawn between Lhasa's ecclesiastical jurisdiction over Sikkim which the Sikkimese did not dispute, at least at that stage, and periodic pretensions to temporal authority which the Gangtok durbar usually rejected. Tibet's attempts to assert its claims fluctuated from reign to reign, determined by the durbar's strength and by the state of its relations with Nepal, Bhutan and—increasingly—British India.

There was little sign of actual Tibetan control and none of any Chinese authority. Neither country ever tried seriously to enforce its will on the Sikkimese. The British looked on Thutob Namgyal as 'a man of indolent disposition, whose inclination was to live in retirement and aloof from the worries and the government of his little state'. They thought too that he was entirely under the thumb of his mother and his second wife, both Tibetans. But the ruler was probably more astute than people imagined. Menaced by British India, he sought to preserve his independence through alliances with regimes that he understood and could cope with.

He had cause for nervousness. Powerful neighbours had whittled away chips of his country ever since 1703 when the Deb Raja of Bhutan suddenly opened hostilities. Though some land was regained with Tibet's help, Kalimpong was lost. So was south-eastern Sikkim which had been heavily colonised by the Bhutanese. Gyurmed Namgyal, the fourth chogyal, had been forced to cede Limbuana, Elam, and Topzong to Nepal. The Gorkhas invaded again in 1788, took over the southern districts and occupied Rabdentse, then the royal capital. Under Prithvi Narayan Shah, who united Nepal, Gorkha armies constantly harried the peaceful Buddhist kingdom to seize slaves and cattle. Magar risings in Sikkim and further border skirmishes with Bhutan added to the pressure. Sikkim might altogether have collapsed if Tibet had not repeatedly come to its rescue.

It was as much to put an end to Lhasa's influence south of the Himalayas as to call a halt to Nepal's eastward expansion that the British finally intervened. Both reasons were, however, subordinated to the compulsions of commerce: British India was determined to open a trade route through Sikkim to Tibet.[2] Edgar's expedition and the mission to Sikkim and the Tibetan frontier, that Colman Macaulay of the Bengal Civil Service led in 1884, sought to achieve this end. Neutralisation of Sikkim was seen as the policy's first imperative.

Hence, the treaty of Titalya, signed on 10 February 1817, after the conclusion of the 1814-'16 Anglo-Gorkha war. This first Anglo-Sikkimese agreement transferred 'in full sovereignty to the Sikkimputtee Rajah, his heirs or successors, all the hilly or mountainous country situated to the eastward of the Mechi river and to the westward of the Teesta river, formerly possessed and occupied by the Rajah of Nepal'. It also specified that 'the Honourable East India Company guarantees to the Sikkimputtee Rajah and his successors the full and peaceable possession of the tract of hilly country specified in the first Article of the present agreement'.

Britain's gains were considerable. Kathmandu's gratitude was ensured since large tracts of Sikkimese territory were left under Nepalese control. At the same time, the company acquired Debgong and Titalya which the Gorkhas had earlier annexed from Sikkim. Formal relations with the ruler of a strategically placed country wedged between India, Tibet,

Nepal and Bhutan encouraged hopes of future gains. But no suzerain rights were claimed in the treaty which continued to govern relations between Britain and Sikkim for the next forty-four years.

Meanwhile, another quarrel was brewing. When one of the durbar's leading Lepcha ministers was murdered in 1826, about 800 of his followers fled to Nepal from where they were incited to lead regular raiding parties into western Sikkim. Tsugphud Namgyal appealed to the Company for assistance, and Lord William Bentinck sent J.W. Grant, commercial resident at Malda, and Captain George William Aylmer Lloyd, commander of the British frontier force at Titalya, to investigate. Instead of doing so, they reported that Darjeeling's climate would be ideal for a sanatorium. But when the question of asking for its cession was raised at the council in Calcutta, Sir Charles Metcalfe, then acting governor-general, firmly opposed making demands on the chogyal.

The matter might have rested there if another Lepcha incursion had not taken Lloyd to Tumlong in February 1835. When the captain appeared at court, Tsugphud Namyal complained that the British were illegally collecting taxes in Sikkim's Morung district. He also asked for the restoration of Debgong. Lloyd countered by demanding Darjeeling. Believing this to be the Company's price for conceding his demands, the chogyal made out a deed of gift and entrusted it to the Sikkimese officials escorting Lloyd to the border. Their strict instructions were not to part with the document until the British had kept their side of what Tsugphud Namgyal was convinced was a bargain.

It is not clear how Captain Lloyd managed to examine the deed: the Sikkimese officials accompanying him may have been bullied or bribed like so many of the last Chogyal's courtiers. The upshot was that having read the deed, Lloyd felt it was not sufficiently binding. He drafted another document, backdated to 1 February, and sent it back to Tumlong where the durbar was located. Tsugphud Namgyal readily ratified it in the belief that Darjeeling would be transferred only after his claims in respect of Morung and Debgong had been met.

However, the Company turned down the Sikkimese requests, and Metcalfe ordered Lloyd not to press for Darjeeling since the ruler was not 'cordially disposed to cede it'. Much to everyone's surprise, the captain then produced the deed of cession from his pocket, adding for good measure that Tsugphud 'makes the grant freely, mentions no conditions whatsoever and seems to regret that he has been misunderstood'. Even the scrupulous Metcalfe saw no reason to reject such munificence, and 'all the land south of the Great Rungeet river, east of the Balasun, Kahil and Little Rungeet rivers, and west of the Rungpo and Mahanandi rivers' became India's. Four months later, Tsugphud Namgyal was sent a double-barrelled gun, a rifle, twenty yards of red broadcloth, and four shawls, two superior and two inferior, as tokens of British gratitude.

Sikkim was outraged. Insult was added to injury in 1841 when, after repeated representations, the British finally and grudgingly agreed to pay an annual rent of ₹ 3,000 for territory acquired by trickery. Even this was payable only from the date of the announcement. Tsugphud Namgyal demanded seven years' back rent while making it plain that he expected far more generous compensation. Not until five years later was the rent doubled. It was raised to ₹ 9,000 in 1868 and, eventually in 1874, to ₹ 12,000.

Tibet's reaction worried Tsugphud Namgyal even more than the loss of territory. The Dalai Lama was content to leave Sikkim alone so long as it provided an effective barrier for Tibet's jealously guarded solitude. But the vigour with which the Company set about clearing and developing the territory it had gained provoked fears of invasion. The hill station gave the British a foothold in the heart of Sikkim's territory that could also be used as a launching pad for the long dreamt-of trade route to Lhasa. The Tibetans feared that guns might follow merchandise. It is said that when the mountainside was being blasted to lay a road, a percipient old Tibetan thoughtfully remarked to Darjeeling's deputy commissioner: 'Sahib, the sound of that powder is heard in Lhasa!' Tibet punished Tsugphud Namgyal for exposing it to this threat by stopping his annual presents, restricting his visits to the Chumbi valley to once in eight years, and cancelling Sikkim's grazing rights across the border.

Resentment continued to simmer even in 1849 when the superintendent of Darjeeling, Dr A. Campbell, and Joseph Hooker, an English botanist, insisted on travelling in Sikkim in spite of the chogyal's lack of enthusiasm. The visit was more actively resented by his minister, Dunya Namguay (the British called him 'Pagla dewan', the mad dewan) who had married Tsugphud Namgyal's daughter and wanted nothing to do with the British. But ignoring hints, the two men rode to the Tibetan border near Chola pass where they were turned back by a posse of Tibetan horsemen. Returning to Sikkim, Hooker and Campbell were roughly seized by the dewan's men. According to Sikkimese lore, Campbell, who was bound hand and foot, began yelling 'Hooker! Hooker! The savages are murdering me!', whereupon one of his captors ordered: 'If he wants a hookah, let him have one!' The unfortunate superintendent was forced to the ground and Dunya Namguay's own hookah thrust into his mouth and held there for a considerable time.

The unwelcome guests were allowed to return only when news arrived that the Company was sending up an English regiment and three guns preceded by 300 Bhagalpore Rangers. But the offence to British prestige could not so easily be forgiven. The Company stopped paying rent for Darjeeling. It also annexed the entire Morung district (Terai) and a large portion of the middle hills, 'the whole southern part of Sikkim, between the Great Rungeet and the plains of India, and from Nepal on the west to the Bhutan frontier and the Teesta river on the east'.

Tsugphud Namgyal's original deed was for an enclave of about thirty miles by six miles. Nowhere was it wider than ten miles. The site was entirely surrounded by the chogyal's domains, entry and exit being restricted to a narrow path. Now, in one ruthless stroke, the Company seized 640 square miles, made Darjeeling contiguous to Purnea and Rangpur in Bengal, and carried the Crown's jurisdiction right into the heart of the Himalayas.

Official British policy still sought to avoid provocations that might force Sikkim into Tibet's arms. But the Company was also looking for an opportunity to consolidate its influence. That came when the Sikkimese led another slaving expedition into Darjeeling. There was also the matter of Campbell's wounded honour, which had been further injured when the Guards repulsed the large body of troops that he personally led into Sikkim in 1860. Using slabs of stone as shields, the Sikkimese crushed to death some men of the Derbyshires at an encounter at Rinchinpong, forcing the rest to flee. The expedition did not last for more than a few weeks, its confused retreat being gloated over by Dunya Namguay who had set up camp on Namche hill, not three hours' march from the site. British accounts gloss over the defeat. One of the few official references to it is the subsequent demand that the durbar restore 'all public property which was abandoned by the detachment of British troops at Rinchinpong' which suggests a hasty flight. But Rinchinpong graces the Sikkim Guards' list of battle honours.

The setback only whetted the appetite for revenge. Another force of about 1,800 men was assembled under Lieutenant-Colonel J.C. Gawler, with Ashely Eden as special commissioner, and sent into Sikkim in 1861. Tsugphud Namgyal being away in Chumbi, his son, Sidkeong, was forced to sue for peace. China and Tibet did not go to Sikkim's help; but neither did Nepal's Jung Bahadur take advantage of the conflict to take another bite at Sikkimese territory. The Titalya treaty was revoked and a new treaty of 'friendship and alliance with the British Government' entered into at Tumlong on 28 March 1861, by which time Sidkeong Namgyal had ascended the throne. This arrangement continued to govern Sikkim's relations with India until 1950.

The twenty-three-clause document confirmed that 'the whole of the Sikkim territory now in the occupation of British forces is restored to the Maharajah of Sikkim, and there shall henceforth be peace and amity between the two states'. It drew clear political, jurisdictional and economic lines between British India and the chogyal's kingdom, while also recognising the separate status of the Crown's subjects and of those who owed allegiance to the durbar.

Articles 8 and 9 of the treaty referred to Sikkim as a 'country'. Article 16 acknowledged that 'the subjects of Sikkim may transport themselves without let or hindrance to any country to which they may wish to remove'. The ruler's right to offer sanctuary to 'subjects of other countries' was also recognised. Article 18 acknowledged that the chogyal was entitled to raise an army, and under Article 22, he could post an accredited envoy in Darjeeling. There was no question of Sikkim being a protectorate, leave alone a part of India.

The informal insistence that Dunya Namguay, feared as the real obstacle to the extension of the Crown's influence, should be expelled to Chumbi was a more formidable demonstration of British India's might. With the quixotic candour of their island race, the British described their adversary as 'a man of considerable strength of character and real ability, a quality so rare in these parts'. Edgar thought him 'a man of great mental and bodily activity, and an unusually quick intelligence. The dewan showed a great eagerness for information, and a rare insight in grasping the meaning of subjects quite outside his own experience.'[3] These were precisely the qualities the British admired most, but would not tolerate in people whom they looked upon as ethnic inferiors. It had been much easier to bully Tsugphud Namgyal with his hare-lip. The capable Dunya Namguay had to go.

In spite of such coercion, the Tumlong treaty did not convert Sikkim into a feudatory. Helpless the ruler might be, but he remained sovereign. The obvious physical disparity between the signatories was understandably reflected in the agreement's more restrictive clauses, and in British India's subsequent attitude; but the document was a full-fledged treaty between equals as understood in international law. It did not disturb legal parity between India and Sikkim. This official view was expressed by several writers who described Darjeeling and its environs as 'British Sikkim' and the chogyal's kingdom as 'Independent Sikkim'. Among them was Sir Richard Temple who wrote: 'The small political area in the Himalayas called Sikkim by Europeans, and variously Dinjing, Dijang, and Lho by its inhabitants, is divided into two parts, known as British and Independent Sikkim... Independent Sikkim lies to the north of Darjeeling district.'[4] The distinction is significant. Not only did it recognise the chogyal's sovereignty in Sikkim, it also admitted that the area seized by the East India Company remained under his de jure authority. The notion was to spell trouble for independent India.

Taking advantage of the treaty, the British built the Darjeeling–Jelap-la road. It made the durbar uneasy, and worried Lhasa even more. The pro-Tibet party at the Sikkmese court gained the upper hand; secret negotiations were resumed with the Dalai Lama and ambans; and Thutob Namgyal, who had succeeded Sidkeong, refused a summons to go to Darjeeling to explain his conduct. Lord Randolph Churchill's plan to send a commercial mission under Macaulay to Lhasa in 1885-'86 evoked even greater resentment. Though the proposal was dropped, about 300 Tibetan soldiers marched thirteen miles across the border, fortified a position astride the new road, and stopped all trade. Thutob Namgyal seemed to acquiesce in Tibetan aggressiveness, and China turned a deaf ear to British protests.

There followed the only major engagement that the British ever fought in Sikkim. The Sikkim Field Force, as it was called, was formed from the Mountain Artillery, Derbyshire Infantry, the Pioneers, Bengal Infantry, a Gorkha regiment, and the Bengal Sappers and Miners—six guns and about 2,500 men. The Tibetans brought up further reinforcements, and there were a number of desultory encounters around Lingtu, Gnatong and Rinchengong. The Tibetan army was finally pushed back through Jelap-la in September 1888, and the Derbyshires poured into Chumbi to ransack the chogyal's palace. It was 'a large three-storeyed rambling building... rich with valuable and curious china, costly arms, and all sorts of quaint curiosities'. The royal family never again occupied it though they sometimes stopped at the ruins on their visits to Chumbi. The crumbling tombs of British soldiers can still be seen around Fort Graham near Lingtu.

The campaign over, Thutob Namgyal was arrested and sent back to Tumlong under surveillance. His was a singularly unlucky reign. The king was 'kept in solitary confinement, like an ordinary prisoner for thirteen days, when even food and water could be had only after repeated requests'. The British accused him of using forced labour, ordered him to leave Rabdentse and set up house in Gangtok. They also wanted him to send for his elder son, Tchoda, who was reluctant to leave Tibet. Claude White, the first PO who reached Gangtok in 1889, lectured the ruler on 'the importance of obeying the order of the government' and warned his self-willed consort, Yishey Dolma, of the 'very serious' consequences of defiance. When Thutob Namgyal and his gyalmo tried to escape into Tibet with nine followers, they were caught in Nepal, brought back to Sikkim and imprisoned in Ging, Darjeeling and Kurseong. They were allowed twenty servants and a pension of ₹ 500.

The chogyal received his sentence in silence, but Yishey Dolma flew into a rage. 'They had come into opposition with the British Government,' wrote the PO, 'and from an exaggerated idea of the importance of Tibet and China, and with no conception or understanding of our ways, they had run against a mighty power to their hurt and consequent suffering'.[5] Thutob Namgyal refused to speak to Claude White or even to open his mouth in the Englishman's presence. Tashi Namgyal, his third son, was born in captivity which lasted for two and a half years.

This display of Britain's might did not affect Sikkim's legal position. The talks that Sir Mortimer Durand, the foreign secretary, opened with the Chinese amban, Sheng Tai, at Christmas in 1888 collapsed in the new year because Sheng Tai would not agree to surrender Lhasa's claims to suzerainty over Sikkim. He insisted that 'no marked separation existed formerly between Tibet and Sikkim' and that Tibetans looked on the kingdom as an extension of their own country.

The Manchu envoy could not, however, hold out when negotiations shifted from Chumbi to Calcutta, where Lord Lansdowne, the viceroy, himself presented Britain's case. The celestial empire was in no position to resist such high-powered pressure. Sheng Tai was also under the influence of J.H. Hart, a British officer in the Chinese customs who acted as his secretary. The Anglo-Chinese convention of 1890 announced: 'It is admitted that the British Government whose protectorate over the Sikkim state is hereby recognised, has direct and exclusive control over the internal administration and foreign relations of the state, and except through and with the permission of the British Government, neither the ruler of the state nor any of its officers shall have official relations of any kind, formal or informal, with any other Government.'

It was an exhaustive statement of control without consulting either of the two principals—Sikkim and Tibet. The Tibetans protested vociferously and let it be known they did not recognise an agreement to which they were not a party. Sikkim also rejected the Anglo-Chinese convention as well as the boundaries it stipulated, and clung to its title to the Chumbi valley ('a dagger aimed at the heart of India', Sir Charles Bell called it) which the British gifted to China. As far as Tibet and Sikkim were concerned, the self-styled Kaiser-i-Hind (as Queen Victoria was proclaimed) and the tottering Son of Heaven might as well have agreed between themselves that Germany had no right to the moon.

Legally, the convention was of doubtful worth. In practical terms, it was irrelevant, for the exercise of British power mattered far more than fudged legality. With or without the benefit of Chinese acknowledgement of British protection, the viceroy would have done as he pleased in the Himalayas. It was an age when all Asia deferred to the white man. Even the celestial emperor did not dare disobey. Lesser eminences like the sovereigns of Thailand or Afghanistan were treated like petty dependents. The Denzong chogyal could not hope for greater freedom than subservient rulers of much bigger countries. The degree of autonomy enjoyed by a monarch was measured by the needs of British imperialism. Risley explicitly stated these compulsions: 'Once let our hold be relaxed, and Sikkim would become the Alsatia of the eastern Himalayas, and such a state of things would react most formidably on the security of life and property in the great European settlement of Darjeeling.'[6]

Hence the insistence on control. Although Sikkim was officially governed by the maharajah-in-council, the ruler was in exile or imprisonment, and the PO took all decisions. This state of affairs continued while Thutob Namgyal lived. He was succeeded by his second son, Sidkeong Tulku, because the elder son, Tchoda, refused to return from Tibet where he ruled the small principality of Taring. The new chogyal had been to Oxford, and the British expected him to be amenable. But precisely because of his relatively modern upbringing, he proved even more intractable than his father. As crown prince, Sidkeong Tulku had administered Sikkim's forests, monasteries, and schools with enlightened zeal. As chogyal, he abolished jail sentences for unpaid debts, reformed the system of land tenure, tried to compel monasteries to accept responsibility for social welfare, and banned Indian and Nepalese settlers. Anxious to strengthen the kingdom's Asian contacts, he suggested marrying first a Japanese bride and then a Burmese princess.

India Office was alarmed. Throughout the East, the British encouraged ignorant and orthodox potentates who preferred sybaritic indulgence to responsible statecraft. In perpetuating their own autocracies, such rulers also protected paramountcy. Sidkeong Tulku was a rare exception, and it may have been no accident that when he unaccountably fell ill in December 1914, the British physician brought in by the PO 'administrated a heavy transfusion of brandy and put him under a number of blankets; at the same time a fire was kept beneath his bed'.[7] The dangerously innovative chogyal was dead within the hour, having reigned just eight months.

William Montgomery McGovern, who visited Gangtok eight or nine years later, recounts how the PO consolidated his authority after Sidkeong Tulku's half-brother, Tashi Namgyal, a young man with defective vision, succeeded to the throne. He was provided with an English 'personal assistant', at this time a British non-commissioned officer. Later, there were Anglo-Indian clerks from the New Delhi secretariat. 'He is nominally a servant of the native ruler, and in theory can be engaged and dismissed by him, but in practice he holds his post at the pleasure of the Political Officer.'[8] Sir Tashi could not disregard the recommendations of an official who combined the functions of secretary, adviser and administrative superintendent.

In spite of these severe restrictions, Sir William Lee-Warner of the political department defined Sikkim's relationship with the Crown as a 'subordinate alliance'. British Indian ties with the much bigger, richer and more powerful Mysore state were 'protective and subsidiary'.[9] In view of later Indian claims that Sikkim was one of the least significant of the 'native states', some of the differences are worth noting. The British government did not have to approve the succession in Sikkim as it did for the grandest Indian princes whose coronations had no validity until the viceroy's representative read out the *sanad* or patent of recognition. Nor were Sikkimese chogyals called upon to swear loyalty to the Crown as many exalted maharajahs had to do. When the Indian Statutory Commission described Sikkim as an Indian state not situated within the boundaries of any province, it was, in the opinion of Mohammed Hidayatullah, the Supreme Court chief justice who became India's vice-president, 'no more than a geographical description since Sikkim and Bhutan enjoyed a special status in international law'.[10]

A separate, if short-lived system of coinage also underlined Sikkimese sovereignty. Minting began when a Newar landlord, Laxmidas Pradhan, leased a tract of land on the Rungeet river, cleared the jungle, and brought in Magars and Kamis to work copper deposits at Pachekhani, Bhotangkhani and Tukhani. He also engaged shroffs from Darjeeling, paying them between ₹ 12 and ₹ 20 a month. The coins were inscribed in Devanagri *Sri Sri Sri Sikkimpati Maharaj* on one side and *Sri Sri Sri Sikkim Sarkar* on the other. Though the coinage enjoyed Thutob Namgyal's approval, many of the more superstitious Bhutiya kazis feared that exploitation of the treasures of the earth would be visited by sickness of men and cattle, and by crop failure. The experiment lasted for only two years; it was discontinued in 1885 when Darjeeling's deputy commissioner refused to allow durbar currency to circulate in British territory.[11]

Another crucial difference between Sikkim and even the biggest and richest of the Indian states was that the latter categorically handed over responsibility for defence and foreign relations to the Indian government. Sikkim did no such thing.

While undertaking that its entire military force should join and aid British troops when employed in the hills, it retained the right to raise and use the army for its own defence. The exercise of foreign relations was certainly circumscribed by the necessity of obtaining British permission for the durbar's initiatives, but it still remained within Sikkimese competence, and did not pass to the Indian government as in the case of, say, Baroda or Hyderabad.

It was a delicate position. Sikkim was constitutionally sovereign, but subordinate in practice. The kingdom lay outside British jurisdiction, and official maps showed it a pale green while Indian states where painted yellow. Moreover, the viceroys who regularly descended in triumph on the Indian rulers did not appear in Gangtok until 1934 when Lord Linlithgow paid the first viceregal visit. Relations with Sikkim were handled by the external affairs department while the home (political) department looked after internal principalities. This was not merely a matter of convenience because Kashmir and Manipur, both border states like Sikkim, were firmly under the political department.

'With regard to Sikkim,' summed up Dr B.V. Keskar, deputy minister for external affairs, 'in many matters it is controlled by the Government of India, but in many matters it stands independently, not exactly as a state within India. It is something between a state in India and an independent state.' Nehru didn't regard Sikkim as a part of India either. 'Bhutan is in a sense an independent state under the protection of India,' he informed Parliament. 'Sikkim is in a sense an independent state but different from the other...' Later he told George Patterson: 'I don't like to use the word "protectorate", but it [Sikkim] is more definitely within the Indian sphere of help, etc., [than Bhutan].'[12]

It was a unique situation, defying easy definition. The only parallels can be found in British colonial history. Sikkim stood in much the same relation to India as self-governing entities—

the kingdom of Tonga, for instance—did to Britain. The legal position was never clouded. The map in earlier editions of V.P. Menon's masterly and authoritative work, *The Story of the Integration of the Indian States*, shows exactly the same blank white space for Sikkim as for the two wings of Pakistan, Tibet, Bhutan and Nepal. India's international boundary runs through Rangpo on the Sikkim–West Bengal frontier where there was (and still is) a checkpost. It is revealing that the authorities found it necessary to tamper with the map in later editions. Despite this retrospective cartographical aggression, they couldn't touch Menon's text, which does not mention Sikkim at all as an Indian state.

The lay mind may have been confused because the chogyal was addressed as His Highness the Maharaja. He was granted a salute of fifteen guns, and was nominated to that golden morgue of history, the Narendra Mahal, or chamber of princes.

There was no logic in these marks of distinction. The Titalya treaty describes the chogyal as Raja. In the treaty of Tumlong he is arbitrarily promoted to Maharaja which is also how the Sultan of Johore in distant Malaya was styled. The Sikkimese ruler's true title (chogyal) was unknown to the British who capriciously used whatever designation was handy and with which they had become familiar. If honorifics are anything to go by, the Nawab of the Carnatic must have been a very superior personage since there can still be seen in Madras's Fort St George a letter dated 14 March 1794 from Lord Cornwallis to 'His Kingship the Nabob Omdatul Omrah', no less. Even the kings of Afghanistan and Nepal never merited more than 'Highness'. And, the *Imperial Gazetteer* included the world's only surviving Hindu kingdom among India's 693 princely states.

In the arrogance of their conquering glory, the British were convinced that any Oriental potentate would be flattered by the boom of saluting British guns... or a gun. The king of Nepal and the sultan of Zanzibar (nineteen guns), and the king of Bhutan, sultan of Muscat and the governors of French Pondicherry and Portuguese Goa (seventeen) also figured in the viceregal table of precedence. A galaxy of other international rulers followed the chogyal in this list. The sheikhs of Bahrain, Kuwait, Muhammerah and Qatar came and went to seven salvos. Five roared in welcome for Abu Dhabi's ruler. Lesser luminaries like the chiefs of Ajman, Dubai, Ras-al-Kheima, Sharjah, and Umm-ul-Qawain were dismissed with the fleeting salute of three casual pips. Socially, it may have been a tremendous achievement to move to the thunder of cannon. Politically, the honour meant nothing, for most of Asia already lay at Britain's feet.

The Narendra Mahal was another whimsy. Lord Reading made it clear at the inaugural session in 1922 that the chamber was an advisory and consultative body with no executive functions. 'Attendance at the meeting will always be voluntary,' he stressed, 'and no pressure will be applied to those who prefer to stay away'. Sir Tashi realised after the opening ceremony that he did not belong to the bejewelled throng of nawabs and maharajas who, for all their fabulous wealth, occupied their thrones by courtesy of the Crown. Some states had actually been created by the British. The Duke of Connaught, who represented King Edward VII at the first meeting, emphasized that the chamber was not a subordinate institution of the Indian government. It could discuss matters relating to the entire British empire. Membership would not affect the sanctity of individual treaties or impair a ruler's freedom of action. In short, the Narendra Mahal was totally without constitutional or any other kind of significance.

• • •

In practice, the durbar's powers were gradually eroded as much by British Indian assertiveness as by internal weaknesses. The latter were often a product of the former. Indeed, as the

Sikkimese emerged from feudalism, they were encouraged to squabble among themselves and to look beyond the king to India's British rulers. Two factors gave impetus to this process: the position of the kazis and Nepalese immigration.

The first was a gradual transformation of Phuntsog Namgyal's administrative system. The twenty-four dzongpons and kalons he created had specific functions that were discernible even in the late nineteenth century when Edgar reported that 'the Guntuck Kazi is one of the most influential officials in Sikkim, and there are more than eight hundred homesteads on the lands which are under his charge.' He went on: 'There are twelve kazis in Sikkim, and several other officers of various names exercise jurisdiction over specific tracts of lands. Each of these officers assesses the revenue payable by all the people settled on the lands within his jurisdiction, and as far as I can make out, keeps the greater portion for himself, paying over to the Rajah a certain fixed contribution. At the same time, he has no proprietary right in the lands, though the kazis have at least a kind of hereditary title to their office. The kazis and other officers exercise limited civil and criminal jurisdiction within the lands the revenue of which they collect, all important cases being referred to the Rajah...'[13]

As the years passed and the ruler's own authority diminished, the kazi institution also became more and more nebulous. While the disparity between birth and actual functions or position made many kazis dissatisfied, the exercise of such powers as they still enjoyed aroused wider complaints. The sixty-seven *illaka* courts over which they presided were by no means impeccable; the land-lease arrangement militated against peasants; and the *kalobari* system of forced labour resulted in considerable hardship. Less tangible privileges like the right of entrée to Pemayangtse monastery, access to the ruler, and a place on the council of state, setting kazis apart from others, were also resented

When Claude White reached Gangtok, the principal kazis were bibulous old gentlemen of some charm but no particular ability or experience. He described them as being 'of very little account; belonging to the old school, not caring much for anything that went on and given to getting very drunk; but notwithstanding they were good-natured and ready to do anything that was wanted of them to the best of their ability.'[14]

Their subsequent resuscitation owed much to British patronage. Confronted with truculent monarchs who instinctively looked to Tibet and China, the Crown sought allies among courtiers. The British in Darjeeling were always in touch with discontented noblemen, and in 1873 Edgar had sounded out some kazis on forming a council that would in effect control the king's actions. Claude White implemented the plan, largely through the help of the two Khangsarpa brothers, Phodang Lama and Khangsa Dewan, from whom Lendhup Dorji claims descent. They were the leading members of the nominated council which acted as a rubber-stamp for whatever White, its president, decreed. The council set aside the absent Tchoda's claims and nominated his younger brother, Sidkeong Tulku, as Thutob Namgyal's heir. Another prominent collaborator, Tseepa Lama, who had interpreted for Hooker and Campbell and accompanied Ashley Eden to Bhutan in 1864, was Sir Richard Temple's protégé. He was rewarded with a tract of 75,000 acres near Darjeeling. Tendook Paljor, who managed this estate and helped the British military expedition in 1888, received costly gifts and the title of raja. They were nominated the chogyal's *vakeels*, or representatives, in British India.

Others who similarly helped the British were appointed to the council, encouraged to send their children to school in Darjeeling, and provided with opportunities for amassing wealth. New money supported ancient rank. The kazis took over the Tibet trade when the road was opened, converted paddy fields to cardamom which yielded a much higher income, and became contractors for numerous lucrative public works. Such enterprise continued into recent times. Lendhup Dorji profitably ran taxis from Kalimpong and a busy petrol pump in Gangtok.

With the advantage of birth strengthened by successful commercial ventures, the kazis were able to monopolise the administration as it was expanded and streamlined.

The consolidation inevitably led to friction. Commoners too acquired wealth in the twentieth century, but felt they were kept down because of birth. Since the throne was the fount of all honour, their resentment against kazis found expression in criticism of the king who was seen to protect the social structure. Relations may have been strained between the durbar and ambitious nobles who really served the PO, but ordinary Sikkimese lumped them together as what was later (and elsewhere) dubbed 'the establishment'.

Illustrative of the complex was the history of Katuk Lama Chankapa, a non-kazi whose family had been hereditary keepers of a Gangtok monastery and who spent five years in Lhasa with the British mission. He left Sikkim because he could not abide the class hierarchy, and joined the Indian Frontier Administrative Service in which he did well. Chankapa returned to Sikkim after retiring as commissioner of Himachal Pradesh and contested the 1974 elections against Lendhup Dorji's Congress. Though an independent candidate, he supported the durbar in that crucial test, but told me that even loyal Bhutiya-Lepcha courtiers had voted for his Congress opponent who was a kazi. They preferred one of their own to a man of proven ability though plebeian birth.

The term *kazi-pazi*, once much in use, explained the dichotomy. It expressed the tension and animosity between the two classes that gradually soured Sikkimese life. No aristocrat would soil his hands then in the rough-and-tumble of politics. National Party politicians like Sonam Tshering, Netuk Tsering and Martam Topden were all commoners. They were loyal to the throne and personally devoted to the Chogyal, but it rankled with them that the institution for which they fought always looked with more favour on aristocrats who contributed far less to public life.

Martam Topden's perceptive elder son understood that sense of injustice. One of the Chogyal's most intelligent and efficient officers, Karma Topden, graduated in social science from Manchester University, trained at the Wakefield Detective College in England and was seconded for a time to the Hereford County Police. He had been one of the palace ADCs before going to England. On returning, he joined the Sikkim police and, in time, became deputy secretary to the Chogyal, his chef de protocol and also, though this was supposed to be a secret, head of an infant intelligence service. Young Topden's education at St Joseph's, the Jesuit boarding school in Darjeeling, the years he spent abroad and his marriage into British county society—his wife was the great-grand-daughter of a Scots earl—gave him a cosmopolitan breadth of vision and a certain social ease. He also enjoyed power in the durbar for the Chogyal could appreciate merit and loyalty even outside the charmed circle of kazis. True, Karma reported to Jigdal Densapa of Barmiok, but Penjola (Paljor Tashi, kazi of Rhenock and husband of the Chogyal's half-sister) reported to him as assistant secretary in the palace secretariat.

Karma's ambivalent attitude to the durbar hierarchy—he always held the ruler in affectionate respect—may have derived from his mother who was as independent as his father was obedient. The Topden matriarch had brushed against the kazi-pazi syndrome early in her husband's career. Being married to an important politician, she was invited to accompany the Gyalum to Lhasa for a double royal event. They were to bring back the Chogyal's bride and deliver one of his sisters to her Tibetan spouse. Condemned by protocol to following the entourage on foot, Mrs Topden defiantly broke away from the Gyalum's party, privately hired a horse and braved the hazards of riding alone to Lhasa. Karma, too, would wryly recall that visiting kazi homes as a young boy, he was served tea in a cup without a saucer. The full complement was reserved for lineage.

Class conflict was compounded by the far more serious ethnic exclusiveness of Lho-Mon-Tsong-sum, traditional land of the Lepchas, Bhutiyas and Tsongs. The Nepalese had no place in it. In any case, Tsugphud Namgyal had forbidden immigration. When Edgar visited the kingdom, its population comprised 2,500 Lepchas, 1,500 Bhutiyas, and 1,000 Tsongs. There wasn't a single Nepalese. But Tseepa Lama, nominally one of the durbar's vakeels in Darjeeling but really in British pay, quietly began to encourage infiltration. He was helped by Lasso Athing, Khangsa Dewan and Phodang Lama, who were all suspected of taking handsome bribes from settlers. They were also paid by rich Newar traders led by the firm of Laxmidas Brothers, while Claude White blessed this dilution of Sikkim's racial and cultural identity. He had spent a year in Nepal before taking up his job in Gangtok, and regarded Bhutiyas and Lepchas as 'lazy and unthrifty'. The PO justified immigration on the grounds that 'the unenterprising aborigines would not respond to the strong inducements held out to them to open up this new land'. The increased population of 59,014 in 1901 did not reflect a suddenly high birth rate.

White's administrative report for 1905-'06 boasts of his success: 'Immigration from Nepal is steadily increasing and is encouraged by all classes as the Nepalese ryot is hardworking and thrifty as a rule, pays his taxes regularly and at the same time is a law-abiding and intelligent settler.' The PO regretted in 1910-'11 that 'immigration from Nepal continues but not on as large a scale as formerly'. But it was gratifying that, because of the influx, a 49.4 per cent rise had pushed up the population to 88,248. White recorded in 1906 that 'in the interests of the state and of the Lepchas themselves, the reserves north of Gangtok should be thrown open to Nepalese settlers'.

Despite the PO's claim about the local response, the Sikkimese did not take kindly to the invasion. Edgar noted the reluctance of the kazis to admit Nepalese settlers because 'they distrusted and dreaded all Paharias'. Lieutenant-Colonel

L.A. Waddell of the Indian Medical Service, who went to Tibet with the Younghusband expedition, recorded that 'the Sikkimese accompanying me considered that this (immigration) was a great grievance to their people'.

Led by a Densapa ancestor, Dalam Athing, and Tarching Lama of Pemayangtse, a group of orthodox nobles and clergymen tried to resist the influx with force. They made three attempts to evict immigrants but could not cope with the guile of the Khangsarpa brothers. Colonies of Nepalese sprouted in Chakung and Rhenock, in the latter place in the teeth of the Rhenock kazi's objections. Civil war followed, with the Barmiok and Rhenock kazis aided by Pemayangtse lamas determined to send back all immigrants. Pitted against these traditionalists but blest by the British, Khangsa Dewan and Phodang Lama desecrated the Yangang monastery and looted the royal palace at Tumlong.

The immigration lobby eventually obtained its objective by fraud. About this time the Lhadi Medi—Sikkim's ancient Parliament of Elders—met in Kalimpong and adopted a resolution banning settlers. The document was sealed with Thutob Namgyal's insignia to be presented to the British. But the Khangsarpas obtained the ruler's seal and added above it in Tibetan 'according to the governor's desire I promise to abide by the policy of allowing the Gorkhalese to settle in uninhabited and wastelands of Sikkim'. Hearing of the forgery, an alarmed Thutob Namgyal journeyed to Kalimpong in 1878 to plead with Ashley Eden that the interpolation did not have his authority. But all he obtained was the assurance that the Nepalese would be confined to the south, and that they would never be allowed to hold any office of state or even village headship.

In outlining the British case for immigration, Risley also acknowledged with refreshing candour the chogyal's reasons for opposing it:

> Most of all will our position be strengthened by the change which is insensibly but steadily taking place in the

> composition of the population of Sikkim. The Lepchas are rapidly dying out; while from the west, the industrious Newars and Goorkas of Nepal are pressing forward to clear and cultivate large areas of unoccupied land on which the European tea-planters of Darjeeling have already cast longing eyes. The influx of these hereditary enemies of Tibet is our surest guarantee against a revival of Tibetan influence. Here also religion will play a leading part. In Sikkim, as in India, Hinduism will assuredly cast out Buddhism, and the praying-wheel of the lama will give place to the sacrificial implements of the Brahman. The land will follow the creed; the Tibetan proprietors will gradually be dispossessed, and will betake themselves to the petty trade for which they have an undeniable aptitude.
>
> Thus race and religion, the prime movers of the Asiatic world, will settle the Sikkim difficulty for us, in their own ways.[15]

He could hardly have been more prophetic. Inspired by expectations of a better living, the flood of Nepalese felt little allegiance to the country or its government. Their gratitude was reserved for the British who had helped their migration. So successful was the policy that the 1967 census revealed 59,705 Nepalese plus another 3,778 members of the Hindu lower castes from Nepal who were enumerated separately. There were only 18,014 Bhutiya-Lepchas and 4,548 Tsongs. When Sikkim went to the polls in 1979, 134,000 Nepalese accounted for an overwhelming majority of voters. Claude White's policy had triumphed. Sikkim's Tibeto-Buddhist ethic had been watered down and the indigenous people reduced to a minority existing on sufferance.

All this helped to consolidate de facto British authority. Sir Olaf Caroe, formerly external affairs secretary, had this in mind when he claimed in a letter to the *Daily Telegraph* newspaper in London in 1974 that 'for decades prior to 1947

Sikkim had been a part of India, its external frontier a sector of India's frontier'. Caroe's testimony cannot, however, be treated as legally conclusive since he has been accused in another context of falsifying the records of the 1914 Simla conference, withdrawing the original Volume XIV of Sir Charles Aitchison's *A Collection of Treaties, Engagements and Sanads Relating to India and Neighbouring Countries*, and substituting it with a new volume printed in 1938 but with the 1929 imprint line. The object of this ingenious fraud was to push out British India's frontiers in the north-east (now Arunachal Pradesh) at Tibet's expense. An imperial adventurer like him would regard possession as nine-tenths, or more, of the law.

But de jure authority still rested in the durbar. Even if, for argument's sake, Sikkim was a feudatory of the Crown, the bond was liquidated on 15 August 1947. London's views were adequately stated by the British Cabinet Mission whose memorandum of 16 May 1946 (reiterated by the British government on 3 June 1947) explained that 'paramountcy can neither be retained by the British Crown nor transferred to the new Government [of India]'. About three weeks before Independence, Lord Louis Mountbatten assured the Indian princes that dominion status meant that 'the states have complete freedom—technically and legally they are independent'. He was clarifying Section 7 of the Indian Independence Act which read:

> The suzerainty of His Majesty over the Indian states lapses, and with it, all treaties and agreements in force at the date of the passing of this Act between His Majesty and the rulers of Indian states, all obligations of His Majesty existing at that date towards Indian states or the rulers thereof, and all powers, rights, authority, or jurisdiction exercisable by His Majesty at that date or in relation to Indian states by treaty, grant, usage, sufferance or otherwise.

British India didn't claim paramountcy over Sikkim. But Britain did unilaterally repudiate the treaty of Tumlong. The Crown's rights were neither given to, nor claimed by, successor governments in India and Pakistan. Hidayatullah's view that 'each princely state became an independent and sovereign state in international law since the paramountcy of the Crown lapsed' echoed Indian court decisions that each state became 'an independent and sovereign state in the full sense of international law'. They lost that sovereignty only by executing instruments of accession and merger agreements.

Sikkim did neither. Nor did India expect it. The Denzong kingdom was not included in the scheme of states or in the scheme of mergers. It was excluded from the definition of the Indian Union in the constitutional schedule that was then being drafted. Replying to questions on 9 March 1949, Nehru told the Constituent Assembly:

> Sikkim has not acceded. The question in that shape has not arisen. All the matters are pending and are under consideration. The present position is that the old relations of Sikkim and Bhutan with the Government of India continue. What exactly the future relations will be is a matter for consideration between Sikkim, Bhutan and the Government of India.

Those were anxious days in Gangtok. The Sikkimese had lost contact with traditional allies in the north. China was engulfed in chaos, torn between a corrupt and inefficient Kuomintang and the Communist insurrection that was gathering momentum. Tibet had been left far behind by the march of time. It was also beleaguered by its own efforts to wrest independence from the Chinese. But in spite of domestic preoccupations, the Dalai Lama's administration was not prepared to surrender what it saw as its rights south of the Himalayan watershed.

Lhasa had never accepted the 1890 convention between Britain and China. On the contrary, it actively displayed its hostility to British claims under it. Lord Elgin complained to Kwei Huan, the amban, on 9 August 1894 that Tibetans had occupied Sikkimese territory near Giaogong. Claude White's boundary pillars at Jelap-la, Donkhya-la and Donchuk-la were demolished the following year and the number plaques removed. The Khampa dzongpon regularly led his men across a border that Tibet did not recognise. British attempts to demarcate the frontier on the ground were frustrated, and Tibetans would have no part in the trade marts that the 1893 regulations provided for. In fact, the Younghusband expedition was launched mainly because Lhasa denied that Britain's treaties with China had any application in Tibetan territory. Tibetans resisted the expedition as much as they could. The Dalai Lama fled the Potala. Since the remaining members of his government accepted British terms only under duress, Lhasa felt entitled to repudiate them when the opportunity arose.

That happened when India became independent. On 16 October 1947, Lhasa cabled New Delhi with a request for the restoration of a wide swathe of territory from Ladakh to Assam and including Sikkim.

Logically, the Sikkimese should have been tempted to side with Tibet. The Namgyals had a host of relatives in Tibet. The Gyalum's family, the Ragashars, were so exalted that they did not need a title and were said to be the only family with unbroken descent in the male line since Tibet was created. They enjoyed the unique privilege of honouring their dead with silver effigies. The Gyalum's father had been captain for life of the Dalai Lama's bodyguard. Two of the Chogyal's beautiful sisters, Princesses Coo Coo La (Pema Tsedeun Yapshi Pheunkhang) and Kula (Pema Choki Yapshi Yuthok) had married important Tibetan dignitaries, members respectively of the families of the eleventh and eighth Dalai Lamas. There is a fascinating account of the Pheunkhang family's priceless embroidered saddle rugs made on their own estate in Gyantse in *Of Wood and Loom: The Tradition of Tibetan Rugs*, by Trinley Chodrak and Kesang Tashi. The Chogyal's father-in-law, Yapshi Samdup Phodrang, of the clan of the seventh Dalai Lama, still lived in Lhasa. There were also the rajas of Taring, descendants of Sir Tashi's eldest brother Tchoda, who had stayed on in Tibet. The Barmiok and Rhenock kazis had matrimonial connections in Tibet.

There were persuasive institutional reasons, too, for looking north. 'In religion, in politics and in social matters,' wrote Percy Brown, historian of the Himalayan countries, 'the people of Sikkim have been guided by the authorities of Lhasa, and all the institutions of the state were based largely on those of Tibet. The Sikkim Buddhists refer to the Dalai Lama on all important secular matters, and the aristocracy, having allied themselves matrimonially with Tibetan families, have accordingly vested interests in the larger country.'[16]

• • •

Emotional attachment was buttressed by sound practical reasons. Sikkim, like Bhutan, owned several attractive enclaves in Tibet. Sohar (the resting place of the patron lama), was perhaps the most important, but there was Taring too, and Chumbi with its palace and the two ancient monasteries of Bhakcham and Kirungtsal, administrated by a Sikkimese headman designated Chumbi Adow. There were also about 150 square miles covering Chokar, Teling, and Nyentse under Doptha's administrative jurisdiction. The Phari Kutsap, as the durbar's representative was called, administered this tract. The Doptha-pas regularly and freely travelled to Gangtok to pay homage to the ruler and deposit their land revenues in the durbar treasury. In addition to being exempt from Tibetan land rent and customs levies on wool, salt and other items, Doptha-pas were not subject to military service or forced labour in Tibet. They enjoyed grazing rights in northern Sikkim.

• • •

The exact nature of the durbar's authority over these enclaves has been disputed. Some British writers believe Lhasa recognised Gangtok's sovereignty over them. The official Indian view is that the enclaves were the royal family's personal estates. Chumbi was always a bone of contention and passed out of the durbar's effective management when the Tibetans prevented the Sikkimese delegate from reaching Phari in time for an arbitration hearing, whereupon the amban delivered an ex parte judgment in Lhasa's favour. The durbar demanded restitution after the Younghusband expedition, and Sidkeong Tulku pressed the British to take up Chumbi's status at the Simla convention of 1914. But Sir Charles Bell, the PO, overruled him. The British would not tolerate any change in the 1890 convention.

• • •

These were strong temptations for Sikkim to affirm the older northern alliance. But they belonged to the past. There was also a future to be shaped. Sikkim's Nepalese population, Britain's debilitating legacy, extended a strong pull on the durbar. The kazi-pazi tension was threatening to erupt into unrest. The Chogyal wanted stability and the opportunity to develop his country's resources and revive its suppressed nationhood. He expected the restoration of lost territory, development aid, and guidance towards political viability. Nehru's philosophy had made a deep impression on him. 'We are not hostile to any country and we do not want to meddle in other people's affairs,' the Indian leader had promised. 'Every nation should be free to choose the path it considers best.' Inspired by that hope, the Chogyal turned his back on ancestral but decadent Tibet to meet the future in partnership with renascent India.

REFERENCES

1. V.H. Coelho, *Sikkim and Bhutan* (Vikas, New Delhi, 1971).
2. Colman Macaulay, *Report of a Mission to Sikkim and the Tibetan Frontier 1884* (Bengal Secretariat Press, Calcutta, 1885).
3. J. Ware Edgar, *Report on a Visit to Sikkim and the Tibetan Frontier*, 1873 (Bengal Secretariat Press, Calcutta, 1874).
4. Sir Richard Temple, *Journals kept in Hyderabad, Kashmir, Sikkim and Nepal* (W.H. Allen, London, 1887).
5. J. Claude White, *Sikkim and Bhutan* (Edward Arnold, London, 1909).
6. H.H. Risley. *The Gazetteer of Sikhim* (Bengal Secretariat Press, Calcutta, 1894).
7. *Sikkim: A Concise Chronicle* (Government Publicity Department, Gangtok).
8. William Montgomery McGovern, *To Lhasa in Disguise* (Thornton Butterworth, London, 1924).
9. Sir William Lee-Warner, *The Protected Princes of India* (Macmillan, London, 1894).
10. Mohammed Hidayatullah, 'Opinion in the matter of the Chogyal of Sikkim and the 35th Amendment of the Constitution of India' (1974, unpublished).
11. *Journal of the Asiatic Society of Bengal* (Calcutta, January 1909).
12. George Patterson, 'Conflict in the Himalayas', *The Daily Telegraph*, London, 26 October 1974.
13. Ware Edgar, *op.cit.*
14. Claude White, *op.cit.*
15. Risley, *op.cit.*
16. Percy Brown, *Tours in Sikkim and Darjeeling District* (W. Newman, Calcutta, 1917).

CHAPTER

3

SEPARATE BUT TOGETHER

'In the case of Sikkim, India in 1949 seized the opportunity of a local uprising against the ruler to send in troops, and bring the state into closer dependence as a protectorate than it had formally been under the British.'

NEVILLE MAXWELL, *India's China War.*

'It may be stated that Sikkim was not regarded as a princely state and the status of Sikkim depended on the treaty.'

MOHAMMED HIDAYATULLAH,
former vice-president of India, unpublished 'Opinion'.

Tibet was not alone in expecting independent India to atone for British sins. Before Britain had fully pulled out, Gangtok sent a ten-page memorandum to New Delhi asking for Darjeeling's return. It argued that 'on the lapse of paramountcy all sovereign powers in respect of the Darjeeling area will de jure revert to the ruler of Sikkim'.[1]

The document had been drafted by Sirdar D.K. Sen, a Bengali barrister who had been employed by the Maharaja of Kapurthala (who gave him the Sirdar title) before becoming Sir Tashi's legal adviser. His case was that the terms and conditions of Tsugphud Namgyal's cession had not been honoured by the British. The transfer of territory was solely for use as a residential sanatorium. Sovereign rights in perpetuity had not been conveyed. By paying rent, the British had acknowledged the continued ownership of successive chogyals. In any case, the land was a personal offer to the East India Company and could not be passed on to the successor government. The memorandum added that 'the deed of cession must become null and void on the lapse of paramountcy, and the rights of the ruler of Sikkim must ipso facto revert to him on the transfer of power in India'.

Since this reversion would be automatic, the durbar suggested at least a new agreement between Gangtok and New Delhi. Unless this was done, India would have no legal rights in Darjeeling and 'enormous legal and administrative difficulties will arise, as all officers and courts functioning in the territories would, after the date of transfer, be acting without any lawful authority'.

Nehru's government did not reply. It was not a happy augury. However studied the silence, new India's leaders could not have felt easy. They knew that the durbar had sent a copy of the memorandum to the International Court of Justice that had been set up in The Hague two years earlier. They must also have realised that many decisions at court were taken not by the reclusive Sir Tashi, who lived in a private dream world of the clouds and colours he so loved to capture on canvas, but by his dynamic young son who was looking forward to a period of national regeneration.

The Chogyal was then twenty-three years old, a gifted and personable young man married to a dazzling Tibetan beauty, Sangey Deki. Ordained into the priesthood when barely seven, he had been removed from St Joseph's Convent in Kalimpong and sent as a novice to the Lingbu monastery in Gyantse in Tibet. In 1933 he was installed as lama of Phodang and Rumtek monasteries; ironically enough, he replaced in the latter Lendhup Dorji who had been unfrocked and expelled by his fellow clergy. There followed seven years of instruction from the Jesuits in Darjeeling and at the Bishop Cotton School in Simla. He had planned to read science at Cambridge, but the wartime death of his elder brother, Crown Prince Paljor, who had enlisted in the Royal Indian Air Force, made him heir-apparent, again fulfilling the Namgyal tradition that elder sons did not succeed.

He was sent to the Indian Civil Service training camp in Dehra Dun instead where, by another quirk of fortune, among his colleagues were Nari Rustomji and Bipin Bihari Lal who were both to play such a vital part in Sikkim's history. Lal was known then by his caste surname Mathur. Also with them was the Chogyal's Bhutanese cousin, Jigmie Dorji. He, the Chogyal and Rustomji became friends for life; Rustomji recalling that 'young Sikkim was a shy, timorous fawn, lonely and lost in the vast Indian subcontinent'.[2]

To Buddhists throughout the Himalayas, the Chogyal was already an exalted being. They called him Gyese Rimpoche, prince reincarnate, because he was the acknowledged incarnation of both the tenth chogyal, Sidkeong Tulku, and of the Karmapa Lama. The advantage of birth was refined by office discipline. Joining the administration on a monthly salary of ₹ 300, he eventually became his father's principal adviser in judicial and administrative matters. In 1947 he became president of the state council.

The habit of work was to remain with him all his life. His office in the ADC's cottage next to the palace drawing-room resembled a research scholar's study more than a royal chamber. It was a small room stacked high with maps, books and papers, and never very tidy. An electric typewriter always stood ready for use. Every file was read and sent back with copious notes in the margins. A passion for paper work was his strength as well as his weakness. It enabled him to become familiar with problems in remote corners of the kingdom and personally attend to the smallest bureaucratic detail. But this assumption of direct responsibility also denied authority to people below him. They felt slighted and often blamed him for their own inadequacies. Nor was it humanly possible for one man to attend to everything. Some matters were bound to be delayed or overlooked. They were inevitably held up as instances of royal neglect. But the Chogyal never could delegate power.

The much older Barmiok Athing-La was in many ways his exact opposite. The patrician chief was shrewd, gracious and immensely dignified. He was rugged and hardy, yet courtly; strict on discipline, but not unaware of the advantages of compromise. The Lepcha Barfungpas had adopted the Bhutiya religion, dress, food and customs to thrive under the Namgyal monarchy. So too might Sikkim have to come to terms with renascent India. Athing-La was also better versed in statecraft. His father had accompanied Thutob Namgyal to Calcutta in 1906 for meetings with the future King George V, the Panchen Lama and Sir Ugyen Wangchuck who later became Bhutan's first king. His own labours as Sir Tashi's secretary had exposed him to Indian governance. More than his peers, Athing-La perceived the magnitude of the changes that lay ahead.

The Chogyal, Barmiok Athing-La and Roop Narayan, an Indian judge who served Sikkim for about twenty years, decided to explore the atmosphere of New Delhi. But a meeting with Sir Brojendra Lal Mitter, dewan of Baroda, was not a success. Mitter advised the Sikkimese to 'close your eyes and jump into the ocean of India', to which Athing-La retorted: 'Your freedom is not necessarily mine. If independence comes to India it should also come to Sikkim.' It was a bewildering time. The dewan of Baroda warned darkly against the Nawab of Bhopal's machinations. Pandit B. Pattabhi Sitaramayya, president of the State People's Conference, rambled irrelevantly of the cold in Delhi and how he had had to cut up a floor rug to make a jacket. Sir Benegal Narsing Rau was non-committal. C.S. Iyengar could not understand why Sikkim should not be satisfied with the status quo, and Sardar Vallabhbhai Patel merely listened in silence.

There were equally unfruitful meetings with Maulana Abul Kalam Azad and Dr Rajendra Prasad. They knew nothing of Sikkim and had no clear idea of the future.

Sir Edward Wakefield of the political department was more understanding. The delegation asked a number of pertinent questions when they called on him on 15 June 1946 and insisted on being kept informed of the exact nature of India's ties with Tibet, Nepal and Bhutan. Possibly because of this demand, the Indo-Bhutanese treaty was signed about fifteen months and the Indo-Nepalese treaty five months before relations with Sikkim were finalised. Wakefield assured the visitors that 'it should be possible for Sikkim to obtain nearly identical terms of political relationship with India as Bhutan and Nepal obtained'. Also that 'Sikkim should not be afraid of being carried away on a flood of decisions made in regard to the internal "Indian states"'. He tempted the Chogyal with hopes of substantial economic aid in return for a treaty.

More formal guidelines were set in the Constituent Assembly on 22 January 1947 when Nehru moved that 'this Assembly resolve that the committee constituted by its resolution of 21 December 1946 [to talk to a negotiating committee set up by the chamber of princes] shall in addition have power to confer with such persons as the committee thinks fit for the purpose of examining the special problems of Bhutan and Sikkim and to report to the Assembly the result of such examination'. Nehru knew that a Narendra Mahal team could not speak for the two Himalayan kingdoms. He was aware, too, that a committee formed with the express purpose of discussing terms with India's princes would have no authority to negotiate with Sikkim and Bhutan. Explaining the additional task, Nehru added that the committee would also negotiate with 'territories which are not Indian states, especially Bhutan and Sikkim...' The resolution he moved authorised the committee 'to meet representatives of Bhutan and Sikkim and discuss any special problem that may arise...'

India's first prime minister did not have to be told that Sikkim and Bhutan lay outside the jurisdiction of both his government and of princely India.

There were more conferences that year. At a crucial meeting on 16 July, the three Sikkim delegates met V.P. Menon, Sir Humphrey Trevelyan and Harishwar Dayal of the states and external affairs departments. Roop Narayan spiritedly argued that Sikkim's geopolitical location and ethnic and cultural affinities called for parity with Bhutan, but they were too diffident unambiguously to assert that the lapse of the Tumlong treaty had removed all limitations on Gangtok's options. However, Menon readily admitted that Sir Tashi's position was different from that of any Indian ruler and that Sikkim was under no obligation to join India. He also agreed that the durbar did not have to be represented on 25 July when Mountbatten would discuss their future with India's princes.

Menon did, however, express the hope that the durbar would not sever all connections with India. He suggested that even without accession, Sikkim and Bhutan could enter into agreements on defence, external affairs and communications. Finally, after assuring the visitors that India's external affairs ministry (and not the new ministry of states) would continue to handle relations with Gangtok, he asked the Chogyal to put forward concrete proposals. Jigmie Dorji, who had been appointed Bhutan's agent in India, was present at this meeting. But he did not join in the discussion beyond promising to report the proceedings to his master. His mother, Rani Chuni Wangmo (Sir Tashi Namgyal's only sister who had married Raja Sonam Tobgye Dorji, the Bhutan agent in Kalimpong, in April 1918 and had identified herself wholly with Bhutan's interests thereafter) had already taken up the question of Bhutan's status with the British. Rani Chuni had found Caroe stiff and unbending and had explained her fears to F.M. Bailey, a former PO then living in retirement in England.

The Indian government's views became a little clearer after Mountbatten's talk with the princes. A.J. Hopkinson, who had stayed on in Gangtok as PO, was instructed to write a temporizing letter to Sir Tashi on 26 July:

> I have the honour to say that the government of India have come to the conclusion that it would be in the interest of both the dominion of India and of Sikkim, Tibet and Bhutan that existing posts concerned with their political relations should continue to be maintained under the dominion government acting through the Department of External Affairs.
>
> The government of India recognises Sikkim's special positon: the presence of an officer at Gangtok simultaneously responsible for relations with Sikkim, Tibet and Bhutan, it may be observed, is the best possible guarantee of this fact. The government of India trust that in the circumstances the durbar will agree to the continuance of a post equivalent to that of Politicial Officer, the incumbent of that post having supervision over posts in Tibet.
>
> The government of India add that this proposal in no way modifies the position as understood in the recent conversations with representatives of the durbar at New Delhi.

Given the resolution with which Patel and Menon handled native rulers and brought Hyderabad, Kashmir and Junagadh to heel, it is most unlikely that they were moved by altruism to spare Sikkim. Much was written later about Nehru's feeling for the mountains. But romantic attachment to a terrain he had not even visited when his policy was formulated could not have run away with his political judgment. Patel and Menon, both single-minded men unmoved by sentiment, certainly could not have succumbed to any such emotion. More plausible is the inference that while they would have liked to merge Sikkim, they appreciated that even the successor government in New Delhi could not aspire to inherit powers that its viceregal predecessors had not enjoyed. Therefore, they sought Gangtok's consent to continued diplomatic relations. The request could have been refused. At no time did New Delhi claim suzerain authority or insist on the unilateral right to send a representative.

India and Sikkim entered into a standstill agreement seven months after Menon's clarification. New Delhi's initial draft proposed the continuation of 'all agreements, relations and administrative arrangements as to matters of common concern'. But Gangtok was suspicious of such an omnibus provision. At its suggestion, the wording was modified to cover twelve specific topics including external affairs, defence, customs, currency and coinage, and posts and telegraphs. On 1 April 1948 the durbar agreed to the proposal for the 'continuance of the post of a representative of the External Affairs Ministry at Gangtok, responsible for the conduct of relations with Sikkim and Bhutan on the same lines, and also for the conduct of relations with Tibet and having supervision over posts in Tibet'.

Two separate developments explained the pace of events that followed. The Chogyal had watched with growing anxiety as Mao mobilised his forces for the final showdown with Chiang Kai-shek's regime. He knew that a Communist China would give short shrift to Tibet's slumberous lamaist polity. Also anxious about the direction in which his father's Nepalese subjects might try to push Sikkim, he had written to Sir Basil Gould, the PO, as early as 1942 about the potential danger of immigrants taking over the country. Sir Basil replied to say that not only was he aware of the threat, but had also warned Raja Sonam Tobgye Dorji, Jigmie's father. The Bhutanese replied that since settlers were not registered as subjects they would be evicted if the need arose. But Bhutan was also worried and Jigmie Dorji responded with enthusiasm when the Chogyal mooted the idea of a Himalayan federation.

It was a hazy notion. No one had any clear idea in mind beyond a loose association of Buddhist (or semi-Buddhist like

Nepal) kingdoms that could be a buffer between India and China. They shared geographical contiguity, a cultural past and many common institutions. Tibet was not immediately included but Dzasa Surkhang Surpa, the Tibetan foreign minister, was excited by the idea when it was mentioned to him during a visit to Gangtok, seeing in the federation a possible counterpoise to China's menacing postures. The Nepalese were lukewarm at first but Tanka Prasad Acharya, the prime minister, later tried to revive the idea.

New Delhi sat up in alarm. A federation might enable the Himalayan kingdoms to slip out of its control. The concept might have even more dangerous repercussions elsewhere. Buddhist tribes on the north-east frontier might demand inclusion. Tawang monastery (Galden Namgey Lhatse, meaning 'celestial paradise in a clear night,' in Tibetan) had close links with Lhasa's Drepung monastery and accepted the Potala's ecclesiastical and administrative authority. The sixth Dalai Lama, Tsangyang Gyatso, was born there in 1683. There was some talk abroad of the scheme also offering a solution for the Naga problem. In the west, it would appeal to Ladakh whose long-dispossessed royal family still enjoyed the right to send *lapchak* (annual gifts) to the Dalai Lama. It might even tempt Kashmir whose ruler was bound to Tibet by an 1842 treaty pledging perpetual 'relations of peace, friendship and unity'.

India's bureaucracy feared that Nehru, who was easily captivated by imaginative new proposals, might be willing to consider the notion. He had already shown a distressing inclination to indulge Sir Tashi's engaging young heir. Then, as later, the administration decided to pre-empt the issue so that the idealistic prime minister had no option but to endorse a strategy that had already been enforced. The federation idea had to be scotched and its author brought under New Delhi's firm discipline. But there was no legal basis for action against the durbar. So Harishwar Dayal, who had succeeded Hopkinson as the first Indian PO, looked for other means. He found them in the mob and in Tashi Tsering who had been employed for many years as a clerk in the Residency, as the PO's establishment was then called. Loyal to the authority he had served all his life, Tsering was ready to oblige.

Political activity had been simmering in Sikkim since the end of 1945 with three main parties competing for attention. Tashi Tsering and Sonam Tshering, a rifleman who had become judicial head clerk, led the Praja Sudharak Samaj. Some Nepalese had set up the Rajya Praja Sammelan. Lendhup Dorji was the founder of a third organisation, the Praja Mandal. All three movements aimed to reduce Bhutiya-Lepcha control in general and overthrow the authority of kazis in particular, which was a bit of a paradox for Lendhup Dorji since he was both Bhutiya-Lepcha and claimed to be kazi of Chakung. All three groups also aimed at destroying the power of thikadars, as Nepalese lessee-landlords were called.

Tashi Tsering had compiled an elaborate note (presumably with the help of his Indian superiors in the Residency) on Sikkim's economic grievances. It justifiably criticised the system of land tenure, the civil and criminal magisterial powers vested in landlords and the practice of forced labour which had theoretically been abolished two decades earlier, but persisted on most estates. But these complaints had to be viewed in the light of general conditions in a kingdom of which Claude White had written 'Sikkim distinctly is, and I fear always will be, a poor country, with the problem ever before her as to how the necessary expenditure is to be met'.

The landscape presented almost insuperable problems. Much of Sikkim was mountainous. Though 97 per cent of the people were cultivators, the country produced only two-thirds of the food it consumed. High, serrated and snowcapped spurs do not make for easy cultivation, and the steep escarpments and ridges extending to the foot of Kanchenjunga remained untouched. The soil was poor and water inadequate. Hillsides had been laboriously carved into terraces banked with low bunds of rough stone, and planted with paddy, millet, buckwheat, barley, wheat, lentils and cardamom. But it was a hard grind wringing a meagre living out of the cruel terrain. Hooker noted that dense forests extended right up to 12,000 feet above sea level, 'only interrupted where village clearances have bared the slopes for the purpose of cultivation'. Some fields were too narrow even to use the plough, the soil being turned over with a hoe instead, according to L.S.S. O'Malley of the Indian Civil Service. 'Sikkim is essentially a mountainous country without a flat piece of land of any extent anywhere,' reported P.N. Bose, the noted Indian geologist.

Such wealth as the kingdom possessed was concentrated in the hands of Marwari businessmen who maintained a stranglehold on Sikkim's commerce. The firm of Jethmull Bhojraj acted as state bankers and took a cut on all transactions. The kazis may have been lords of extensive estates, but had comparatively little cash income. Even Sir Tashi was far poorer than many Indian businessmen. His lifestyle would have seemed Spartan by the standards of Bombay or Calcutta society. His daughters had been packed off to Tibet with cash dowries of only ₹ 10,000 each. The palace could have been a Victorian circuit house with wings added on. The Densapa house in Barmiok was little more than a cottage.

This simplicity did not trouble Sikkim's leaders, but those below them were acutely conscious of disparities. They were also beginning to complain of the absence of any kind of organised administration. The Lhadi Medi (with a spokesman called Kew Me who functioned rather like a parliamentary speaker) had fallen into disuse. The royal advisory council, which was entitled to discuss any matter of importance and convey its views to the king, seldom met.

Traditional democracy survived only in the bleak landscape of the Lachen and Lachung (big and little pass) valleys which were really an extension of the Chumbi terrain. They had always enjoyed a sturdy form of rustic autonomy. Claude

White observed that the valleys 'have an unusual and almost communistic government of their own'. The entire populace sat in council on every occasion. 'Nothing, however small, is done without such a meeting, even if it is only to supply me with firewood or to tell off a man to carry water. Everything is settled at these meetings, and business there may be transacted, and everything from the choosing of their own headman to the smallest detail is arranged in consultation.'[3]

Sikkim's true heart beats in these valleys of the two main streams of the Teesta that arise in a bewitching wilderness. Steep, high and dangerous Donkhya-la (the pass where even the wild yak is frozen) commands the head of Lachung valley at a height of more than 18,000 feet. The road winds shakily from the town of Lachung to Yumthang where a small hut covers a hot spring. The steaming sulphurous water is held in a stone reservoir beside which travellers boil their eternal basins of green tea. Bitter winds sweep a harsh landscape. But physical inhospitality is mitigated by the warmth of a simple people whose black yak's hair tents dot the valleys. The traveller is always invited to share a jug of frothing milk and a cake of creamy cheese laid out on a blanket on the ground.

Self-governing institutions still survived effectively here, and the *peepon* (elected headman) was a person of consequence and authority. Tibetan graziers always paid a fee in barter to the Lachen peepon for grazing in the Lhonak valley, and a formal agreement between the Lachen people and Tibet's Khamba dzongpon governed pastures and grazing. By written law the entire village migrates on the same day so that no enterprising herdsman can stake a claim to the best grazing. It is a necessary rule. In winter when pastures higher up are under heavy snow, the valley is black with thousands of yaks. Summer brings primula, rhododendron and apple blossoms. Orchids cluster on mountainsides, herds of burhel and chamois, water-driven prayer-wheels and smoke-darkened monasteries; it is a world that lives apart, preserving ancient rhythms.

Lachen and Lachung suffered no tremor while the rest of Sikkim was in tumult. But elsewhere, people were responding to extraneous appeals.

• • •

Leaders of the three political parties met in Gangtok on 5 December 1947 and called a giant rally two days later to demand abolition of lessee-landlords, an interim government with parliamentary trappings and—most significant—accession to India. The Praja Sudharak Samaj, a faction of the Rajya Praja Sammelan and Lendhup Dorji's Praja Mandal merged to form the State Congress which claimed 60,000 members in a country with only 125,000 people, including women and children. Tashi Tsering became president and demanded his party's immediate affiliation with the All-India State People's Conference which operated in Indian princely domains (Nehru had been its president) and eventual merger. The State Congress also threatened to withhold rent from landlords and taxes due to the government.

Jolted out of his dream-world, Sir Tashi summoned five State Congress leaders to the palace on 9 December and bluntly told them that union with India was out of the question. But if they cooperated, he would at once curb the power of landlords, abolish the land tenure system and look into other economic grievances. Anticipating greater administrative demands, Sir Tashi had already revived and reorganised the state council to include ten prominent citizens, lamas and retired officials. He agreed to add three politicians who would be given the rank of secretaries, the highest he could offer.

Sir Tashi was not averse to sharing authority. Details of governance were, in any case, left to courtiers. Some of them complained that the ruler consulted so many people on every issue that no one knew who was responsible for what. Servants with files under their arms were said to shuttle back and forth between the palace and the houses of leading advisers. It was an informal consultative arrangement, but not an authoritarian one. It made little difference to Sir Tashi if the system also included politicians. The Chogyal, too, advised compromise. For all the rapport between him and Nehru, the latter's government was committed to assertive republicanism. 'I must frankly confess,' Nehru had once said, 'that I am a socialist and a republican, and am no believer in kings and princes...' Under his direction, the All-India State People's Conference had not hesitated to take drastic action to twist the arms of Indian rulers who were tardy in signing deeds of accession.

The State Congress, which had raised the merger demand really only to extract reforms, readily accepted Sir Tashi's offer. Its three nominees represented Sikkim's three communities. Raghubir Prasad, a Nepalese, had been a senior clerk in the Indian public works department. Captain Dimik Singh was one of the very few Lepchas to have been promoted to an army commission. Sonam Tshering represented the Bhutiyas. With goodwill, the experiment would have defused the crisis and laid a sound basis for participative governance. But rapprochement between the ruler and his subjects did not suit the Residency. The standstill agreement of 27 February 1948 was not sufficiently binding. Sir Tashi could go back on his approval in principle of a treaty between the two countries. Interest abroad in the Chogyal's novel plan for a Himalayan federation worried New Delhi and the PO.

Public disturbances did not, therefore, end with the council's expansion. On the contrary, Tashi Tsering, as ever the Residency's creature, went back on his undertaking, and forced the three political secretaries, who were working well, to resign. They did so unwillingly and only after considerable physical harassment. Raghubir Prasad, being most vulnerable to Nepalese pressure, yielded first. The captain followed after some delay. Sonam Tshering stayed the longest at his post and was ever afterwards charged with betraying the people's cause.

Having scuttled a bold effort to break the impasse, the State Congress went on the rampage. There were strikes and satyagrahas, rowdy meetings in Gangtok's Paljor Stadium and threats of invading the palace. But the royal family vehemently denies contemporary Indian newspaper reports, based only on information released by the PO's office since there were no media correspondents in Gangtok, that Sir Tashi and his children fled to the Residency where Dayal provided them with sanctuary. The Chogyal tried to drive his jeep out of the palace, but was stopped by several hundred demonstrators who had swarmed up the drive. Clambering on the vehicle's bonnet at the bend by the little chorten, he made his first-ever speech in Nepalese and the crowd dispersed. Coo Coo La, the most beautiful and astute of his sisters, if also the most headstrong, recalls sitting on the palace steps cradling a Mauser automatic. Accustomed to the rigours of Tibet and having many times braved the hazards of bandit-infested roads between Lhasa and Gangtok, the princess was prepared to fight off attackers. None came.

Meanwhile, State Congress rallies drew impressive crowds at Namche in October 1948 and at Rangpo the following February. It was said that the demonstrations would have been peaceful if some kazis and thikadars had not sent their own men into the movement to discredit it. Violence was reported from many outlying towns. Mobs were collected in Singtam, Namche and Gyalzing, brought to Gangtok, and allowed a free run of the capital's liquor shops. Drunken brawling, street-corner orgies, and a constant repertoire of offensive songs blaring out of wayside loudspeakers marked the campaign for civil liberties.

As tension mounted, Sir Tashi sent his secretary to the Residency to complain that the PO was encouraging lawlessness. Gangtok was under curfew, six leading politicians had been jailed for breach of peace and for inciting people to defy orders to pay taxes. A warrant had been issued for Tashi

Tsering's arrest. But Dayal threatened to annex Sikkim if the warrant were executed. He also demanded that the six prisoners be released.

India's sympathies had already been proclaimed. When Tashi Tsering and a young Nepalese aide, Chandra Das Rai, travelled to New Delhi in December 1948, they were warmly received by Nehru who lavished praise on them as heroes of the revolution. Keskar carried patronage a stage further when he approvingly told the Constituent Assembly that 'one of the political parties in Sikkim, viz., the Sikkim Rajya Praja Sammelan, had sent a copy of a resolution passed in January 1949, suggesting the merger of Sikkim with India and its government as a centrally administrated area'. This was a dress rehearsal for what transpired during 1973–'75. The tactic of inciting lawlessness and then complaining that the durbar could not maintain order was later to be employed with devastating effect.

As populist demagoguery reached new heights on May Day in 1949 and the PO pressed even harder for concessions, Sir Tashi agreed to form a ministry. Tashi Tsering was sworn in as Sikkim's first (and only) prime minister on 9 May 1949. Chandra Das Rai and Dimik Singh were inducted as well. So were two durbar officials, Dorji Dahdul and Reshmi Prasad Alley, whom the State Congress selected. Two Nepalese, two Bhutiyas, and a Lepcha comprised the cabinet.

This was Sikkim's second opportunity to settle down to successful self-government under popular leaders who might in time have gained the throne's confidence. But the chance of building up a relationship of trust was again destroyed. The prime minister had no experience of administration and looked to the Residency for guidance in all matters; the ruler knew nothing of political supervision and suspected the PO's hand in every cabinet demand. Sir Tashi did not think of delineating areas of jurisdiction and Tashi Tsering did not ask for a framework of governance. Overlapping was inevitable. In the absence of a constitution, each side accused the other of encroaching, and though in office, the State Congress continued to foment agitation. Even New Delhi admitted its 'incompetence'.

When Keskar visited Gangtok at the end of May, he brought an offer. Sir Tashi was told that the cabinet would be dispensed with if he agreed to a draft treaty and temporarily placed his administration in the hands of an Indian official. The alternative could be dangerous for the throne as well as Sikkim. India's attitude had hardened because of developments in China. Though Mao's rule over a unified and centrally administered country was not formally proclaimed until five months later, Nehru was dismayed by indications of the Chinese People's Liberation Army's objectives. Keskar and Dayal held a pistol to Sir Tashi's head: he had to agree to a treaty. The dismissal of the ministry was packaged as a reward. In reality, New Delhi, too, did not want to encourage democratic populism in sensitive border areas. The Indian government did not trust either the palace or the politicians, but felt confident of being able to control the former. The decision had been taken before Keskar left Gangtok on 27 May.

It was not the king but India's representative who dealt the blow when an unsuspecting Tashi Tsering and his colleagues obeyed a summons to the Residency two days later. In the high-handed style of British pro-consuls, Dayal told the prime minister and his colleagues they had been dismissed. The ministry had lasted for just twenty-nine days. The ex-prime minister led a delegation to Delhi, but appeals were useless. Once Sir Tashi agreed to a permanent alliance, India had no further use for democracy or democrats. It was announced 'that the government of India's sole wish was to ensure a stable government in the state of Sikkim and that under no condition could India tolerate chaos and disorder. Towards achieving this goal of a stable government... the Indian government intended to cooperate more closely in bringing about the increasing association of the Sikkimese people with their government.'[4] A company of Maharatta troops was dispatched to Gangtok to underline India's resolve.

Dayal took over the administration the same day. The palace felt aggrieved over his tactics, but Sikkimese politicians were far more bitterly critical of what they condemned as duplicity. The PO's reign was consequently shortlived and John Lall of the ICS, brisk and clipped with an exaggerated British accent, became dewan on 11 August 1949. Sir Tashi allowed the new dewan the use of Mintokgang and lost the bungalow forever. It was claimed that a dewan was needed 'for the good of Sikkim, but that his administration would be for the briefest possible time'. In the event, dewans lasted for exactly twenty-three years after which there was a brief respite of only ten months before history was repeated even more drastically to justify a worse usurpation.

The Sikkim Congress was disappointed, but seemed to draw the right lessons from the denouement when it argued:

> Our demand that Sikkim should accede to India has in principle been accepted because the administration will remain in the hands of government of India's official. The responsibility to maintain peace and to see the proper administration has also remained in the hands of the government of India....[5]

Lall was acclaimed as protector. But this was after an external affairs ministry announcement on 20 March 1950 claimed:

> As regards the status of Sikkim it has been agreed that Sikkim will continue to be a protectorate of India. The government of India will continue to be responsible for its external relations, defence and communications. This is as much in the interests of the security of the state as of India and is dictated by the facts of geography. As regards internal government, the state

> will continue to enjoy autonomy subject to the ultimate responsibility of the government of India for the maintenance of good administration and law and order.

Dayal was accredited as the Indian President's plenipotentiary and had to present his credentials to the durbar when the treaty was finally signed in Gangtok on 5 December. Hidayatullah noted this conformity with international usage. He also cited nine points as the true indicia of Sikkim's sovereign status: use of the term 'treaty', India and Sikkim being named opposite each other in the preamble; the President of India's appointment of a plenipotentiary; the need for Sir Tashi to examine Dayal's credentials and accept him; cancellation of earlier treaties; use of the customary legal language; the extradition clause; sanction for an Indian representative in Gangtok; and provision for ratification.

Although Sikkim's defence, foreign relations and communications became Indian responsibilities under the treaty, none of the thirteen articles affected what the eminent Indian jurist called the kingdom's 'distinct international personality'. As Hidayatullah put it, 'in a protectorate, the protecting power only represents the same on the international plane, but the protectorate still remains a state under international law'. The comparison he drew was with the 1912 treaty of Fez which allowed France to station troops in Morocco, control the sultanate's political and financial foreign relations, and assume responsibility for internal affairs. India's view of that engagement can be deduced from the remarks of the Indian delegate during the UN debate on Morocco's claim to Mauritania: 'In determining territorial claims, no reliance can be placed on treaties concluded between expanding colonial powers such as France or Spain and declining kingdoms like Morocco.'

World history abounds with other instances of unequal treaties being nullified and of protectorates whose proper position is respected graduating to full independence. Bulgaria,

Rumania and Serbia were all under Turkish rule before World War I. Liechtenstein remains a sovereign principality in spite of surrendering much of its foreign economic relations to Switzerland. Monaco enjoys an international personality and so does Luxembourg. Even more apposite (as mentioned earlier) is the case of Tonga which placed itself under British protection in 1900. A treaty of friendship made Britain responsible for the Pacific kingdom's defence and foreign affairs while subsequent agreements extended British control to a wide range of internal matters relating to administration, police, law courts, land revenues, and legal enactments. But the Tongan monarch was still styled 'Majesty' and accorded all the honours due to a reigning sovereign. British restrictions were in time voluntarily removed to allow Tonga to emerge to full independence. Much the same process was repeated in Britain's dependencies in the Persian Gulf.

Even Puerto Rico did not foreclose its options in 1952 by voting for association with the United States of America. Unlike Sikkim, it was a total dependency to start with, Puerto Rico having been placed under US military administration when Spain ceded the colony in 1898. But far from regarding its associate status as permanent, President Dwight D. Eisenhower expressly promised 'that if at any time the legislative assembly of Puerto Rico adopts a resolution in favour of more complete or even absolute independence, he will immediately thereafter recommend to Congress that such independence he granted'.[7] This was announced at the UN on 27 November 1953.

It is a sobering thought that colonial powers such as Britain, France and the USA should display greater respect for UN principles and the rights of small nations than democratic India. Article 73 of the world body's charter calls on members to progressively remove restraints on non-self-governing territories. This was confirmed in the 1960 Lusaka declaration calling for immediate transfer of powers to the indigenous people in trust and non-self-governing territories still under foreign administration. It was repeated ten years later in the declaration of principles of international law concerning friendly relations and cooperation. Article 102 (1) of the UN Charter demands registration of all treaties, and Chapter XI expects members to regularly supply the UN with information on dependencies.

India's refusal to comply with any of these provisions—especially the registration clause—was matched by South Africa's reticence over Namibia. But only Salazar's Portugal, which displayed similar intransigence over Goa, chose, for its own reasons, to draw attention to this continued defiance. Occasional Pakistani and Chinese references were equally motivated. New Delhi's defence that the 1950 treaty was a domestic arrangement was never put to the test of domestic or international opinion. The treaty remained a skeleton in India's cupboard.

Far more damaging from Gangtok's point of view was a three-page letter the PO sent to the palace on 25 February 1951. Three of its ten clauses—promising economic and technical assistance, educational scholarships, and help in realising outstanding revenues—were promising. At the durbar's insistence, Dayal also agreed that 'the treaty shall not affect any arrangements between the Government of Sikkim and the Government(s) of Tibet, Bhutan and Nepal which were in force on the date of the treaty'. This was an important recognition by New Delhi of Gangtok's right to conduct customary diplomatic relations with neighbours without interference, and of the kingdom's traditional territorial claims in Tibet. A further clause regulating reciprocal travel excluded Indians from 'any areas in Sikkim which, on religious or other grounds, are not open to the public'. This, too, constituted acceptance of the durbar's authority and recognition of the alien status of Indian citizens in Sikkim. Clause 9 spelt out the rules relating to extradition.

Other parts of the letter were less reassuring. For instance, the durbar could not employ foreigners (including Indians) without New Delhi's approval. The first three clauses were even more ominous. First, the ruler was required to appoint as his principal adviser and executive officer a dewan nominated by the Indian Government: 'If there is a difference of opinion between the Maharaja and the Dewan on any important matter, it will be referred to the Government of India and decided in accordance with their advice.' Second, New Delhi assumed responsibility for developing self-governing institutions. Pending India's approval of a constitution, there would be an advisory council and, later, an elected council whose members would be elected by village panchayats. The dewan would supervise and implement the entire process.

It was the final provision that spelt danger. The ruler could seek New Delhi's aid in the event of law and order being threatened or of gross internal maladministration but India did not have to wait for him to ask. 'Independently of such a request the Government of India will be entitled in such a situation to give such advice as they may consider necessary and appropriate for dealing with the situation and the Maharaja shall be bound to act in accordance with such advice.' As with the treaty, all disputes arising out of Dayal's letter would also 'be referred to the Chief Justice of India whose decision thereon shall be final'.

This communication—commonly referred to as the Letter of Exchange—went far beyond the scope and contents of the treaty. It was a unilateral declaration by New Delhi that sought to create formal legal sanction for the kind of arbitrary control often exercised by British proconsuls and, in effect, brought Sikkim into far closer administrative dependence on India than had existed in viceregal times. Such a document was not enforceable in any court of law and the durbar would certainly have rejected it but for the tension created by the political upheaval of 1949 in which Dayal was suspected of having a hand. But whatever the excuse, the letter asserted the PO's watching role. It enabled him to direct the kingdom's internal affairs through the dewan. It was also taken to authorise his direct patronage of politicians who promised to oppose the durbar.

New Delhi's implicit justification for the letter was that ultimate sovereignty vested in the Indian government which had chosen to delegate some powers to Sikkim. This is not the view of jurists who maintain that, in 1950, a technically sovereign kingdom voluntarily and temporarily entrusted some of its functions to a country with which it had entered into treaty relations. No claim based on earlier usage was permissible because Article 1 of the treaty explicitly states: 'All previous treaties between the British Government and Sikkim are hereby formally cancelled.'

It is Hidayatullah's contention that: 'The relationship between India and Sikkim rested entirely on the treaty of 1950. A treaty is a compact between nations or an agreement between high contracting parties. A treaty cannot be contemplated unless each contracting party has a distinct sovereign international personality.' The treaty would obviously not have been possible if, in 1950, Sikkim were a dependency of India, as Caroe suggested. The slate had been wiped clean in 1947 when His Majesty's government repudiated the treaty of Tumlong, nothing remaining of the durbar's earlier 'subordinate alliance' with the Crown. If paramountcy lingers in spite of this categorical erasure of the past, then Britain too can ignore the Indian Independence Act of 1947 to assert continuing sovereignty over India, Pakistan and Bangladesh.

REFERENCES

1. Sirdar D.K. Sen, 'Memorandum of the Government of Sikkim: Claims in Respect of Darjeeling' (1947, unpublished).

2. N.K. Rustomji, *Enchanted Frontiers: Sikkim, Bhutan and India's North-eastern Borderlands* (Oxford Press, Bombay, 1971).
3. J. Claude White, *Sikkim and Bhutan* (Edward Arnold, London, 1909).
4. V.H. Coelho, *Sikkim and Bhutan* (Vikas, New Delhi, 1971).
5. Sikkim State Congress pamphlet (Gangtok, April 1950).
6. Sir Humphrey Waldock, QC, 'Opinion on the Effect in International Law of the 1950 Peace Treaty between India and Sikkim' (17 February 1966, unpublished).
7. Henry Cabot Lodge, United Nations General Assembly (27 November 1953).

CHAPTER

4

BURRA KOTHI

'The senior British official in Sikkim is the so-called political officer, appointed directly by the viceroy of India, and he exercises an enormous amount of power.'

WILLIAM MONTGOMERY MCGOVERN,
To Lhasa in Disguise.

'The role of the Indian dewan in Sikkim is as difficult as it is important. As prime minister and chief adviser to the maharajah, his interest must be Sikkim's. Yet he is suspect—an Indian in Sikkimese clothing—so that useful and sympathetic as he may be, Sikkim's political parties would do without him.'

PRADYUMNA P. KARAN and WILLIAM M. JENKINS, JR.,
The Himalayan Kingdoms: Bhutan, Sikkim and Nepal.

Harishwar Dayal, who was able to manipulate the 1949 disturbances to impose such unequal terms on Sikkim, was not a unique phenomenon. If the beliefs he acted upon were derived from the British, the precedents he set were avidly taken up by his Indian successors. A span of eighty-six years, from 1889 to 1975 (Claude White to Gurbachan Singh) lay between the first PO's appointment and the withdrawal of the last. All these officers had something in common: they bullied the ruler, made much of his opponents, meddled with minute details of administration, and persuaded the Indian government to look upon Sikkim and its monarch through their eyes. Official Indian policy eventually reflected the private prejudices of civil servants who were only supposed to implement the government's views. Not for nothing was the Residency locally known in Gangtok as *burra kothi,* the big house.

Chafing at restrictions, the Chogyal complained that the imperial tradition should have ended when a new relationship was forged in 1950. Article XI of the treaty said that 'the government of India shall have the right to appoint a representative to reside in Sikkim'. A representative, he argued, was the accredited envoy of a friendly nation, not a proconsul inspired by outmoded notions of paramountcy. But the most he was able to obtain was when, visiting Gangtok in May 1968, Mrs Gandhi agreed to rename the Residency India House. But there was no diminution of authority, and successive Indian POs enjoyed draping themselves in the mantle of Claude White's arrogant legacy.

Although White was only a public works department official, he cuts a resplendent figure in photographs. Walrus moustache, gold braiding on his dress tunic, a row of ribbons and medals, ceremonial sword, and white gloves epitomise imperial authority. His conduct was equally overbearing. After storming Thutob Namgyal's palace and driving out loyal retainers, White behaved abominably to the ruler and his consort. He then appropriated for himself the higher of the two elevations between which the town of Gangtok (the high hill) is now strung out. It was significant that the palace occupied the lower eminence.

The first PO does not appear to have sought Thutob Namgyal's consent in choosing his site and building a house. A thousand acres were cleared, primeval forests felled, the ground levelled, and stonemasons, carpenters, and wood carvers brought from Punjab. The furniture and furnishings were imported from London. Bhutiya and Lepcha boys were trained for domestic service. As the building neared completion, the simple Sikkimese must have realised that this grand establishment was the real seat of power.

White's Eastern version of a Swiss chalet, commanding a magnificent view of Kanchenjunga and its surrounding cluster of peaks, was also probably the world's first outpost for what eventually came to be called China-watching. Apart from controlling Sikkim, political officers maintained garrisons and post offices in Tibet, foiled the machinations of Manchu ambans in Lhasa, and struggled to influence the Dalai Lama's government. Nearer home they kept a watchful eye on wayward Bhutanese chiefs. Responsibilities in Tibet came to an end soon after 30 October 1950 when Beijing bluntly notified New Delhi that: 'Tibet is an integral part of Chinese territory and the problem of Tibet is entirely a domestic problem of China.' Nehru readily withdrew Indian military escorts from Yatung and Gyantse; surrendered the properties India owned in these towns; handed over the postal, telegraph, and telephone services operated by India; and relinquished control of twelve rest houses. Bhutan was separated from the PO's jurisdiction in 1971. Only the tiny kingdom of Sikkim eventually remained of a parish that once sprawled across the heartland of Asia.

But the past dominated life in burra kothi, whose panelled drawing-room gave pride of place to a set of massively carved sofas upholstered in yellow brocade. One chair reared like a throne, bigger and higher than the rest. The furniture had been specially made as New Delhi's gift to the Dalai Lama, but reached Gangtok too late to be sent by mule train through Nathu-la. Tibet had fallen and its pontiff was in flight. A useless gift for the exiled god-king of a disappearing society fittingly decorated the parlour of a functionary whose office was an anachronism.

Precisely because it was an anachronism, however, it clung all the more jealously to its colonial privileges. It was not just the operational theatre that had dwindled; burra kothi's grounds had shrunk to a mere 400 acres. But Indian incumbents did not allow reduced jurisdiction or any thought of the struggling, impoverished republic they represented to diminish an exalted sense of consequence. Sikkimese courtiers with a grouse against the palace were more than welcome to take their grievances to the PO. He was also widely recognised as patron of the kingdom's ever-growing Nepalese population. Disgruntled politicians relied on his sage advice. The king, too, was sometimes forced to make his way up the hill to explain himself or plead for leniency.

POs entertained splendidly. They drove around Gangtok in a pale blue limousine. From its bonnet fluttered the republic's tricolour while the number plate read merely INDIA. An army of Sikkimese servants wore pale-brown khos and tight-fitting, gold-embroidered hats. The choicest wines and liqueurs were served at his table. Silver and china gleamed on the sideboards, and the library contained rare leather-bound first editions on the Himalayas. It was a sumptuous residence, built as much for comfort as to impress. When the PO wished to journey to New Delhi, a military helicopter was always there to spare him the tedious drive to Bagdogra.

Publicly, relations with the palace oozed cordiality. The Chogyal and the PO treated each other with ostentatious bonhomie at all receptions, a bear's hug and clasped hands being the accepted form of greeting. Their letters usually ended with effusive expressions of goodwill. But private relations were always strained for the palace resented the PO's presence and his actual actions as much as the historical past he symbolised. An Indian embassy with an ambassador would have been welcome as evidence of diplomatic equality; a political officer was not only a reminder of control but his house crowning the hill constantly rubbed in the ruler's subordinate position. And so, to underline the fact that they looked on him as only an ambassador, the Sikkimese unfailingly addressed the PO as

Excellency. To make matters worse, not a single Indian bothered to learn Sikkim's language. They did not have to for they saw themselves as supreme administrators.

It must have been galling for the PO that whenever the Chogyal appeared in New Delhi, the Indian government received him with the full ceremony due to the reigning sovereign of an independent country. The army, navy and air force presented a joint guard of honour at the airport. Pilot cars and motorcycle outriders escorted his motorcade; and the Sikkimese flag flew beside India's tricolour over the President's palace while the royal visitor was in residence. Formal banquets were held in his honour, and Mrs Gandhi always made a point of calling on the ruler. To compensate for these courtesies, the PO lost no opportunity of whittling down the Chogyal's rank in Gangtok. Indian visitors were advised to treat him like an ordinary citizen.

PO after PO also managed to offend the durbar in other ways. Avtar Singh would not stand up when the Sikkimese national anthem was played in Gangtok's Denzong cinema until the Chogyal pointed out that the Indian contingent would look silly if it remained seated while all others were on their feet. Singh also set tongues wagging by quarrelling bitterly with Ivan Surita, commissioner of West Bengal's Jalpaiguri division. Not only was Surita a friend of the Chogyal's and a frequent visitor to the palace, the Sikkim government had to deal with him on a number of official matters. Trapped in the hills, Gangtok's marooned society fed on news of each fresh dispute, avidly discussing its course. Another PO kept away from Guards functions because he objected to the ruler presenting colours to his troops.

The old controversy over the Guards never quite died down. Even after Nehru agreed to the force being revived, external affairs ministry officials cautioned that an army would strengthen the durbar's position. Several generals suggested either that Sikkimese recruits should form a new battalion in the Indian army or that a force on the lines of the Jammu and Kashmir militia should be raised in Sikkim to be incorporated in India's border defence. The Chogyal's objection to both plans was that Sikkim subjects could not serve in their own country except under their king's colours. When a PO expressed the fear that a separate army might encourage the durbar to demand the recall of Indian troops, the Chogyal at once promised to place his men under India's operational command in times of emergency. But he firmly rejected the idea that only Bhutiya-Lepchas should be enrolled. Such exclusiveness would not only give the Guards a communal complexion but would also frustrate the Nepalese integration in the Sikkimese personality that was the objective of all his social and economic programmes.

One argument followed another. Most were of a minor nature, but they were irritants in the relationship. They were also intended to assert the importance of a PO who sometimes felt left out of settlements between the Chogyal and New Delhi. This happened when Subimal Dutt, the foreign secretary, agreed that all members of the royal family should have Indian diplomatic passports in which they would be styled prince or princess. Burra kothi insisted that ordinary passports were good enough, and the palace had again to appeal to New Delhi. Such petitions—and the need for them cropped up regularly—created the impression in India that the Chogyal was always quibbling over something or the other. The impression was carefully fostered by Indian diplomats who stressed what they called his obsessive concern with protocol and alleged tendency to seize upon one concession to demand another. It was the only way they could destroy the credit the Chogyal enjoyed with Nehru and counter the influence of his friends from the ICS training course.

It was a part of this campaign to contrast the Sikkimese ruler's seeming querulousness with the Druk gyalpo's supposedly benign placidity. But Bhutan was not saddled with a permanent Indian presence. The PO visited Punakha or Thimphu, the later capital, only about once a year when the Bhutanese were lavishly hospitable. After a surfeit of banquets, dances and champagne, the PO returned to Gangtok convinced that the worldly Wangchucks were far more agreeable than the nagging Namgyals. Since the road to Tibet, which was burra kothi's main concern for political as well as commercial reasons, did not lie through Bhutan but through Sikkim, successive POs took only a cursory interest in Bhutanese affairs.

Sikkim was different because of its strategic location. When, at the height of Nehru's rapport with Chou, the Chogyal asked for the restoration of his Tibetan possessions, he was charged with trying to put a spoke in the wheel of *Hindi-Chini bhai-bhai* camaraderie. When he repeated the claim after relations had worsened, he was accused of exploiting New Delhi's difficulties with Beijing. 'The government in Delhi has not always shown tact in its dealings with the young and ambitious Chogyal whose family comes from Tibet with which he also has religious ties,' wrote Dorothy Woodman.[1] It did worse. It capriciously accused him of conspiring with those who were busy destroying the only Tibetan society with which the durbar had links.

Many of India House's confidential reports against him eventually trickled back to the Chogyal. The Indian foreign secretary asked him in 1962 if it were true he had established contact with the Chinese Communists during a visit to Hong Kong. Princess Coo Coo La's shopping sprees there were viewed with greater suspicion. The PO had convinced New Delhi that the royal family's sympathies lay with China. In the early 1970s, even T.N. Kaul, with whom the Sikkimese royals were particularly friendly, accused the Chogyal of persecuting Lendhup Dorji because he was the only Sikkimese politician to lean towards India!

Relations with individual POs ranged from cold to acrimonious within this framework of suspicion and hostility.

When the Chogyal flew to London five days before the seventeenth anniversary of India's Independence, it was suggested he had timed his departure to avoid the annual flag-hoisting ceremony at India House. The Sikkimese were outraged when a PO's wife casually strolled into a formal religious ceremony in the Tsuk-la-khang with a cardigan thrown over her shoulders and her hands busy with wool and knitting needles.

N.B. Menon objected to the Chogyal meeting M.C. Chagla, the distinguished lawyer and judge, after he had quarrelled with Mrs Gandhi and resigned from her cabinet as external affairs minister (1966–'67). Chagla was especially persona non grata also because he never failed to address the Sikkimese royal couple as Majesty. Another PO, Inderjeet Bahadur Singh, felt slighted because he was not invited to the opening of the Jorethang–Naya Bazar road. He complained, too, that he might as well not be in Gangtok since the Chogyal obtained all the advice he wanted in Shillong, Moscow and Ankara. Rustomji was then serving the Assam government in Shillong, Kaul was ambassador in Moscow, and K.L. Mehta, another friend, was India's ambassador in Ankara. Jealousy among Indian officials was always an additional complication, and the Namgyals were victims of an extraordinary competitiveness in which diplomats vied with each other both to boast of the influence they wielded over the Chogyal and his relatives and to run them down. Bahadur Singh, who was a nominated member of the relatively new Indian foreign service, resented the Chogyal's friendship with several ICS officials who were above him in rank. His complaint led to a difficult interview with M.J. Desai, the foreign secretary.

Many of these personal storms revolved round the beautiful Coo Coo La whose charm, vivacity and intelligence made her numerous friends as well as enemies in India. Married by proxy at fifteen and packed off to Lhasa, she had enjoyed a high position in Tibet where her husband was the governor of Gyantse. The princess had returned to Gangtok, she always maintained, only at the insistence of the Indian government which claimed to be responsible for her safety and did not want her to fall into Chinese hands. Always addressed as Lacham Kusho, consort of the gods, she was a formidable woman who never permitted the least liberty with her rank as the wife of a Tibetan duke. Her crest flaunted the coveted five yaks' tails allowed only to a handful of Lhasa aristocrats. Durbar officials in Gangtok were under orders to formally describe her as 'Her Royal Highness the Princess Royal'. Her chillingly air-conditioned flat in Calcutta, upholstered in dark brown velvet and with a set of chairs in sold silver, contained priceless ikons and valuable porcelain silver and crystal. Coo Coo La entertained far more regally than her more restrained brother. Her guests were often more distinguished, and conversation in her drawing-room always more sparkling. Only the best French wines were poured from her heavy cut-glass decanters. But more revealing of the general sumptuousness was her style at table: her own place was set with golden coasters and cutlery to remind even the most honoured guest of the difference in rank.

But for all this glamour, Coo Coo La's fortune was her own creation, 'Money didn't make me, I made money,' was her justified boast. Nehru offered her a pension. The princess astutely asked instead for import licences and trading permits. Armed with these, she worked her way up from a single room ('a cold water flat' she called it) in a humdrum business street in Calcutta, that too lent by her cousin, Jigmie Dorji of Bhutan, to her gracious flat. She also acquired properties in Kalimpong and Sikkim. Many snide remarks could be heard of how the highest in Delhi had pampered and indulged Coo Coo La; Kaul was regarded as foremost among her admirers. His attentions were hardly surprising since European aristocrats, British politicians and American diplomats also paid court to the Chogyal's gifted sister. India House resented her prominence, her air of cool disdain and—even more—its inability to put her down. Bajpai, the second-last PO, called her 'the dragon lady'.

Relations with the durbar worsened in the 1960s when Apa Pant, the princely diplomat who was Nehru's protégé, built a temple to Hanuman on Lukshyama. It was bad enough to set up a Hindu place of worship so near the royal cremation ground on a site venerated by Buddhists; worse was what the Sikkimese saw as the temple's psychic impact. It was believed to disturb a mystic triangle among three holy shrines. The tin trident that crowned the temple shone directly into the Gyalum's Thakchi palace north of Gangtok. Another of Apa Pant's edifices, a temple to Ganesa, similarly flashed its ominous reflection into the Chogyal's palace. Pant's explanation that Lukshyama was sacred to Nepalese Hindus only added fuel to fire, convincing Bhutiya-Lepchas that India, like the British, favoured immigration and the immigrants.

That constant fear never left the Sikkimese. The Chogyal suggested a halt to future immigration during talks in New Delhi in 1965. But his official Indian hosts would not hear of it. Visiting Gangtok three years later, Kaul suggested that Indians from hilly Garhwal and Kumaon should be settled in the Lachen and Lachung valleys. Aghast, the Chogyal pointed out that these reserved areas were forbidden even to Sikkimese from nearby Chumthang. The durbar was more than ever convinced that it was Indian policy to weaken Sikkim's Tibeto-Buddhist ethic by supporting Nepalese Hindus who might be expected to form alliances with their compatriots in Darjeeling.

The Chogyal's marriage to Hope Cooke in 1963 was the catalyst that completely changed the situation. He had met her in Darjeeling two years earlier when Hope was reportedly studying Tibetology. He was forty, she only twenty-three. Hope was described as an American debutante, a graduate of the fashionable Sarah Lawrence College where Jackie Kennedy had also been educated. Her grandfather and legal guardian, Winchester Noyes, had been a shipping magnate. An uncle by marriage, Seldon Chapin, was then US ambassador in Tehran. His son later represented Washington in Addis Ababa. Her mother had died somewhat mysteriously. No one mentioned her father.

Those who had seen Hope in Darjeeling describe her as an awkward young girl in a daringly brief mini-skirt with straggling shoulder-length hair. A heavy smearing of mascara and eye shadow heightened her pale complexion. Dressed up, she could look attractive but was not a patch on the radiant Sangey Deki who had died in 1957 leaving three children, Tenzing, Wangchuk and a daughter, Yangchen. But the middle-aged widower was besotted with the young girl. Like so many Americans, Hope was probably dazzled at the prospect of becoming a queen. Later, she was the star of an American documentary titled *Yankee Queen*.

Though Nehru blessed the match and the engagement was announced on 28 November 1961, the union was by no means popular. The Lhadi Medi's consent was reluctantly given and only after a hectic day-long session behind closed doors. The lamas were sceptical of Hope's claims to erudition, and the kazis found her notions of court etiquette baffling. Athing-La and Jigdal Densapa were distinctly cool. Princess Coo Coo La was polite only because she would not be rude to her brother's consort. People were mystified by the whispering tone Hope affected. Even the omens were not propitious. A conjugation of five stars made 1962 an unlucky year and the wedding had to be postponed to 1963. Hope then surrendered her American passport to become a Sikkim subject, and the Chogyal passed a special law to allow a civil marriage. The wedding was celebrated with considerable pomp in the Tsuk-la-khang.

According to Kaul, 'the new ruler, Palden Thondup Namgyal, under the influence of his newly-wedded American wife and her friends, started giving pin-pricks to India on matters big and small'. There were silly antics like the All Fool's Day joke of sending out invitation cards to an 1 April party at India House. There were more serious charges about Hope's American friends carting off Tibetan silver and thankas to sell in a New York boutique. The allegation was unfair, for Hope and her friends paid for everything they bought, but that was no defence against gossip, and resentment mounted when Sanubhai, Gangtok's principal silversmith, stopped doing general work because he had so many American orders on hand. Indian diplomats boycotted her fashion show in the USA—adapting Sikkimese material and designs to Western modes—because cards went out in the names of 'Their Majesties the King and Queen of Sikkim'. 'Department-store diplomacy,' sniffed Coo Coo La. Taking its cue from the authorities, the Indian press levelled veiled charges of American espionage in the Himalayas.

India House was not prepared to tolerate the growing Sikkimese practice of addressing the royal couple as Majesty, though New Delhi officially recognised the ancient Sikkimese titles of Chogyal and Gyalmo in 1965. But when the *Sikkim Gazette* referred to Tenzing as 'crown prince', the PO wrote to ask whether this meant the 'maharajkumar'. New Delhi insisted on the lesser designations bestowed on Indian princes. The Chogyal was probably responsible for aiming at styles that denoted sovereign status internationally but Hope was the outsider, and so she was blamed.

Many thought the new Gyalmo a strange, unhappy woman who was unable to reciprocate her husband's doting love and was conscious of her loneliness in a court that found her faintly ridiculous. But for all the Delhi-inspired calumny, she was no Mata Hari weaving webs of espionage. The real charge against her was seldom mentioned: Hope's dreams of queening it in the Himalayas cut off the Chogyal from his throne's traditional supporters and isolated him from Sikkimese society. The circle that gathered round her consisted of men and women who were equally uncertain of their welcome. Among her closest associates were Karma Topden, the Chogyal's half-sister, Lhanzin, a bouncing, lively and warm-hearted girl whose position remained invidious, an Anglo-Sikkimese girl married for some time to an Australian teacher, young Nepalese students whom she patronised, a number of inconsequential Eurasians and Indians who were working in Sikkim, and the occasional foreign missionary. It was a rag-tag and bob-tail court, but it was the only group in which the doubt-ridden Gyalmo felt confident. They helped to move the palace farther from the thought processes of Sikkimese life, and alienated the people who could rally loyally when the need arose. As the Chogyal lost the knack of sustaining human contact with his subjects, his public appearances also became increasingly stylised.

The marriage had another effect that turned out to be unfortunate. It brought a steady stream of distinguished Westerners to Gangtok. The 1965 coronation witnessed the apogee of heady flattery when American and European newspapers fell over each other to wax lyrical about the king and queen. They talked of 'improbable magic', of 'giant butterflies and pandas and four hundred different species of wild orchid', and of 'ancient mystique' amidst 'amazing comfort'. Judy Gendel in Britain's *Daily Telegraph* adapted King Farouk's famous prophecy about five monarchical survivors to six—'Spades, Hearts, Diamonds, Club, England and Sikkim'. The *Washington Post* effused: 'Americans are well aware that Monaco is touched with Grace; now Sikkim is radiant with Hope'.

Such flights of fancy cannot have pleased the PO who felt that the Chogyal and Gyalmo were getting above themselves. Hope's advent also introduced a sense of acute social rivalry between the two establishments. The Chogyal still continued with his occasional mammoth mah-jong sessions, gambling with cronies who were seldom seen at his parties, but his wife ordered Scandinavian silver, bought crested crockery in England, imported linen from New York, and raised palace entertainment to a level of elegance where it challenged India House's established supremacy. Even if the PO was able to lay on more elegant intimate dinner parties, palace banquets were far more glittering.

There were opportunities for both as distinguished foreigners flocked to Gangtok and the palace and India House squabbled over them like ambitiously climbing hostesses. Most of these guests arrived with introductions to the Gyalmo, but the PO insisted that only the Indian government could invite them to Sikkim. He was so put out when Kenneth Keating, the American ambassador, stayed with the Chogyal that New Delhi was mischievously told that while talking to Keating, the Gyalmo had compared India's military presence in Sikkim with the US invasion of Cambodia. India House had its way with Senator Charles Percy, but the Percy children were sent to the palace. Even this was too much for the PO who so made appointments for the senator that he and his party were extremely late for an elaborate lunch hosted by the Chogyal and Gyalmo. Pique, protocol problems, and petty manoeuvres attended every major social event.

More difficulties cropped up when Hope's friends—not all of whom were as important as Keating and Percy—wanted to travel in the northern highlands. It was not easy for foreigners to get a visa for Sikkim. Permits for the north, which was under military control, were virtually impossible. The initial restriction on entering the kingdom is a relic of the Bengal Eastern Frontier Regulation of 1873. In theory, it did not affect Sikkim but in practice, it kept foreigners out of both Sikkim and Bhutan by strictly regulating access to India's border zone with the two kingdoms. The Chogyal was usually able to persuade the external affairs ministry to make an exception for palace guests. What he could not do was induce the PO to sanction visits to Lachen and Lachung.

The Sikkim government actually issued the passes but only on the basis of the PO's assurance that the army had given permission. The rules applied even to the durbar's Indian guests. Karma Topden, as chef de protocol, would telephone the first secretary in India House who, in turn, put up the application to the PO to obtain military clearance. But the procedure was never simple, complications often arising because of burra kothi's less than honest ambivalence. There were cases when all formalities were cleared, but travellers armed with valid passes were held up at Chumthang where the Assam Rifles protested they had received no information.

It was a form of harassment I was familiar with. A pole blocked the road at Chumthang where our four-wheel Jonga (lent by the Chogyal) driven by a Sikkim Guards soldier and with a palace bearer at the back was obviously expected. The sentry flagged us down. I thought he would inspect our permit, but, no, he didn't ask for it. He knew my name and had a message. The major-sahib wanted to see me. He pointed up a hill, refusing to raise the pole and let us drive on. We had to see the major. At first, the major pretended pleased surprise at my calling on him. The story changed when I told him firmly I had not called but been brought. He spoke then of landslips and landfalls ahead and of the road having been swept away three days earlier. I was most welcome to spend the night in his camp. In fact, he had been waiting for this opportunity to host me. He and his officers were enormously interested in journalism, and we would have much to talk about. He would send runners the next morning to find out if the road was safe. We had, of course, made full inquiries about the road before setting out from Gangtok, and I told him that. He then said the subsidence had taken place not three days earlier but in the last hour. Other officers dropped in. They asked innumerable questions about the Chogyal, the palace and especially, about the quality and quantity of drinks served there. Alcohol is of absorbing interest in abstemious India.

Some trivial conversational gambit or other intervened each time I stood up to leave until, finally, I just stalked out.

A couple of hours had been wasted and it would be dark when we reached Yumthang. But I still hadn't made good my escape. There was another officer waiting by the Jonga when I came down. He said nothing about the road. He even half-apologised for the major. 'Things aren't going so well for us on the border just now,' he explained. 'It would be embarrassing if it were written about.' I assured him I had no such intention and sped on my way. The same officer was waiting at the same place when we drove back two days later refreshed by the long walks, hot springs and gallons of tea and chhang. 'I hope you won't make a big thing in the newspapers of being held up at Chumthang?' he asked. I haven't written about it till now.

I discovered later that the small township of Mangan on the northern highway, a collection of cottages perched on the edge of the Teesta gorge, marks the limit of free movement. The district officer of Mangan can drive further north, but even villagers need Indian identity cards to go about their normal buying and selling. Everyone else is stopped at Chumthang and subjected to severe questioning. Curiously, though, no one asked to see the permit that the palace had issued and which India House had endorsed after obtaining the army's clearance. It allowed me, the driver and bearer to take the Jonga to Yumthang, visit Lachen and Lachung and return to Gangtok. Travel on the road to Nathu-la in the east is just as difficult.

Tourism suffered in consequence. The most attractive areas were under military occupation—ravines ablaze with rhododendron, magnolia-spangled roads, clusters of orchids, picturesque lakes, rivers teeming with trout, forests where musk deer and blue sheep could still be seen, the resting places of the Siberian water-fowl, snow slopes where the Chogyal hoped to set up skiing, the sacred mountains of Sikkim, and some of its most ancient monasteries. Japanese groups wanted to study the flora. Europeans and Americans were interested in rock-climbing. India's strict rules kept them out. The Chogyal grumbled about the revenue he was losing. Worse for him and the Gyalmo was the implicit rejection of the durbar's authority over large tracts of the country. It was an intolerable situation for them, but protests only made India House wonder why the American queen should be so anxious to take her countrymen to the Tibetan border with its Indian military installations.

The most irksome part was that the world's media trained its spotlights on the court of Gangtok. Hope's arrival changed the quality of palace life, adding a new dimension to perspectives. She aroused an awareness of the world in Sikkim, and made the world conscious of her husband's tucked away kingdom. The Chogyal had lived simply as a widower, and his staff recalls that no more than fifty cards were received each Christmas. The number leapt into several hundreds after the publicity attracted by the wedding and coronation, and Hope took on the task of shaping goodwill into support for Sikkim's aspirations. The kingdom was suddenly in the news and everything that happened there commanded international attention. Much to the PO's chagrin, India's backyard became the world's illuminated stage.

Mintokgang could not help but be drawn into these disputes. The circumstances of John Lall's appointment were not likely to endear him to the palace. His laboured Anglo-Saxon starchiness made for cultural incomprehension. The term 'dewan', recalling the nominated prime ministers of Indian princely states, was also as repugnant as 'Residency', and was eventually changed to principal administrative officer. When I.S. Chopra, a flashy cavalry officer who had served as Indian ambassador in the Middle East, was appointed to the job in 1969, he was designated 'Sidlon' which was Tibetan for prime minister. The Chogyal was edging closer to his dream of a Tibeto-Sikkimese renaissance which the PO saw as camouflage for less innocent political ambitions.

If a dewan was popular with the Chogyal (as Rustomji who held the job from 1954 to 1959 was), he, at once, incurred India House's suspicions. If he was trusted by India House, the palace was bound to be wary. Trifles were blown out of all proportion. Successive POs believed they should supervise who the dewan saw and even what he wore. Rustomji's habitual kho became a talking point. Dewans were also expected to submit confidential reports on the royal family to India House.

It was a difficult situation for these officials who were junior in rank to the PO and therefore could not act independently. They owed formal allegiance to the Sikkim government and tried to demonstrate it by following Rustomji and wearing the kho on all ceremonial occasions. But too close an identification was frowned on, and no dewan was ever allowed to forget he was New Delhi's nominee. He could be withdrawn if the PO felt he was not serving India's interests in the durbar. Other Indian officials, also seconded to the Sikkim government, were similarly caught in the tension between the palace and the PO. At one time India House's security officer, the head of the Indian intelligence bureau, and the kingdom's police commissioner (also an Indian deputationist) were all at loggerheads. They reported against each other, the PO, the dewan and the Chogyal.

It was an unhealthy incestuous world, closed in from liberating winds, circling wildly in its own ever-narrowing whirlpool of gossip and intrigue. The two leading characters, the Chogyal and the PO, were surrounded by dozens of supporting figures who spared no effort in exaggerating and spreading the least grumble or indiscreet remark. In this way the palace and India House were kept informed of each other's thoughts even if the information was always more colourful than accurate. But burra kothi had the edge, for its first, second and third secretaries were professional diplomats trained in the art of encouraging disgruntled officials, abetting politicians and letting Nepalese leaders know that New Delhi stood by them. There was also usually at least one naturalised Tibetan among them who could mingle with local society. The durbar's amateur officials were no match for those skilful operators whose task was helped by Indian intelligence networks in Kalimpong and Gangtok. Ostensibly there to look after border security, they were deeply involved in the kingdom's internal politics.

Bajpai refined and streamlined the system. Son of Sir Girja Shankar Bajpai of the ICS, he was a man of the world, educated in the US and at Oxford, knowledgeable about classical music, period furniture and Anglo-Indian art. Cooking was his relaxation; with wine and cheese imported in the diplomatic bag, he turned out recherché French dishes. Bajpai had a certain elan and could afford to be dismissive about the palace's provincialism and about what he habitually called the Chogyal's little bailiwick. It was his affectation to claim that his job in Gangtok was a bore when not an actual embarrassment. He talked longingly of experiences in more sophisticated settings. He was also adamant that Gangtok was not a foreign diplomatic posting. It was an extension of the Indian scene.

Such a man at once brought to the surface all the complexes from which the Chogyal suffered. They had got off to a bad start, for the arrangements to receive Bajpai had not been to the liking of a PO who had a highly developed sense of the deference due to India's representative. Nor did Bajpai take to Chopra whose brusque military manner, exaggeratedly rolling gait and flamboyant brocade khos never seemed very real. Shared aesthetic tastes should have brought the Chogyal and PO together, but Bajpai's blend of haughtiness and condescension unnerved the Chogyal. The PO could stalk out of the palace refusing to dine because he had been insulted. He could be smoothly dismissive. His acid letters showed up the ruler's more mundane style. He could be charming and disparaging at the same time to Hope whose royal pretensions only provoked his derision. Hurt, suspicious, irritated, and often irritating, the Chogyal's baffled resentment found expression in brooding silences or vehement outbursts. Because he felt unsure with the polished PO, he insisted on confirming every conversation in a subsequent memorandum. 'The worst thing the British could have done for him with their ICS training was to turn the Chogyal into a clerk!' was Bajpai's exasperated explosion. He made no allowances for the insecurity of a man whose sensitivity about his lack of university education would sometimes provoke him to stammer with an injured air: 'I'm only a non-graduate!'

Relations between India House and the palace had never been as bad as in Bajpai's time. Gurbachan Singh, the last incumbent, stepped into this fouled atmosphere. A grey-bearded Sikh chieftain who had joined India's foreign service when Partition robbed him of hereditary estates in Pakistan, Singh took pride in his patrician birth and claimed that Zulfiqar Ali Bhutto's palatial residence at Larkana had once belonged to his family. He had been to school in England and, but for the war, would have gone up to Oxford. Like Bajpai, Singh was polished and urbane, with diplomatic postings in London and Paris behind him. More to the point, the last PO arrived fresh from a job with the dreaded RAW though he would airily dismiss it as just a post in the prime minister's secretariat.

None of these superior (and supercilious) beings was likely to win the affections of a touchy king and his giddy young consort. When Kaul wrote that the Chogyal 'did not get along with any of India's several able dewans and representatives in Sikkim—from John Lall and Rustomji to Baleshwar Prasad and Apa Pant to Bahadur Singh respectively', he was laying the fault on the ruler's difficult nature. What he did not take into account was the manner in which Indian officials sought to dominate the Chogyal and Gyalmo. They had inherited the worst traits of Claude White and his British successors.

Lording it over little Sikkim was some compensation for all the rebuffs Indian diplomacy suffered in more equal exchanges. Many POs admitted it was embarrassing for a republic to protect a monarchy, but being able to order around a king was always a source of personal satisfaction. Conflict was inherent in the respective positions of Chogyal and PO. It would not, however, have been manifest in so many niggling details of daily life had it not been for the cultural conditioning of a foreign service that preserved the legacy of the British Raj more diligently than any other branch of India's governance.

All were bent on making their authority felt at every turn. But a few went farther. The Chogyal claimed that at least two diplomats, Jagat Mehta and Bahadur Singh, had recommended absorbing Sikkim. The Foreign Affairs Committee in New Delhi turned down the proposal only because the ground had not been prepared and outright annexation would have invited global criticism. Also, India still needed an autonomous buffer state whose monarch could be New Delhi's whipping-boy.

REFERENCE

1. Dorothy Woodman, *Himalayan Frontiers* (Barrie and Rockliff, London, 1969).

CHAPTER

5

WAR OF NERVES

'Nepal is tributary to China. Thibet is tributary to China and Sikkim and Bootan are tributary to Thibet and therefore secondarily to China.'

Hon'ble SIR ASHLEY EDEN,
envoy and special commissioner to Sikkim,
secretary to the Government of Bengal,
8 April 1861.

'I don't like seeing a friendly state on our frontier swamped by a great power, though it is the suzerain power. The consequences of a large force on our frontier must be doubtful. In a military sense, the disappearance of a buffer state, if it does disappear, will be a loss.'

LORD MINTO to JOHN MORLEY (private letter)
24 February 1910.

The psychological reasons for the PO's high-handedness were reinforced by fears of what China might be up to along the Himalayas from Leh to Tawang. India would have preferred an autonomous Tibet as the best security for its frontiers and also as guarantee of New Delhi's continued influence in the three border kingdoms: the letter Lord Minto wrote in 1910 to John Morley, secretary of state for India, expressed the permanent interest of successive Indian governments as well. But Nehru could not act on that wish. He was a prisoner of history.

Ashley Eden's report on negotiations for the 1861 treaty of Tumlong clearly set out the position. He gave the chogyal and his dewan Britain's 'most solemn assurances that we did not wish to retain possession of any portion of the Sikkim territory'. Indirectly, he also let China, Tibet, Nepal and Bhutan know that there was no 'intention of annexation' whatsoever. At the instance of Kashmiri merchants who were anxious to profit from the potentially lucrative trade between Tibet and Bengal, he did try to persuade the durbar to open a road through Sikkim, with the merchants paying 'heavy transit duties to the Sikkim government' in return for the latter's protection. But he withdrew the request when the ruler and chief minister demurred. As Eden explains: 'There is one point, however, on which my instructions were most positive, and this was that I should neither say nor do anything which should give ground for a supposition that British rule was to be permanently planted in any part of Sikkim.'[1]

The position, on the ground or in law, did not change in 1890 when a weakened China seemingly acquiesced (though Tibet did not) in the British claim of protectorship over Sikkim. The kingdom still retained its autonomy, especially in internal governance. What Eden had noted in 1861 also still remained true: 'Had any other policy been pursued, we should, I firmly believe, have been embroiled with the whole of the frontier and Indo-Chinese states, and the result would have been a long, tedious, and most expensive war.'[2]

It suited British strategy to base the entire corpus of treaties and engagements which lent legality to India's northern claims on the assumption that Tibet was subject to China. That way, the Tibetans could not threaten British actions in the Himalayas while an enfeebled China was no threat at all. History was cited to justify the tactic. The celestial emperor had ratified Maharaja Gulab Singh's 1842 treaty on Ladakh with 'the Lama Guru of Lhasa' (the Dalai Lama). Britain's 1890 convention was concluded directly with the Chinese amban without even reference to Lhasa. The British ignored Tibet's rights in the trade regulations three years later. Worse, they insulted and imprisoned the high dignitary the Dalai Lama sent to Darjeeling and allowed him no part in the negotiations. Claude White deliberately did not wait for Tibetan representatives in 1895 when he erected boundary pillars at Jelap-la in the presence of three Chinese commissioners. London felt that Younghusband's 1904 convention remained inoperative until confirmed by the Chinese two years later.

Admittedly, the British accepted Tsarong Shape as Lhasa's envoy and allowed him to sign the 1908 trade regulations in Simla. But this was only because, fearing Russian probing in Central Asia and worried about signs of Chinese restiveness, Minto thought it prudent to plug all loopholes. The pact's general effect, however, was to place Tibet still more firmly in Chinese hands. This was more explicitly spelt out in Simla in 1914 when Britain acknowledged that 'Tibet is under the suzerainty of China' and stated 'it is understood by the high contracting parties that Tibet forms part of Chinese territory'. Even so, Ivan Chen, commissioner for the Pacification of Tibet and China's special plenipotentiary at the talks, would not sign the agreement which Peking later formally repudiated.

However, the British hedged declarations of Tibet's dependent status with stringent conditions and restrictions upon Chinese movement and actions. Sir Henry McMahon's strategy was to recognise Peking's legal suzerainty over Tibet as a surety of Tibetan good behaviour, but to deny China physical access to the border marches which were to remain under Lhasa's theoretical authority. This was a typically British solution, but it was possible only because the viceroy bargained from a position of strength with a weak China and a Tibet that was only too grateful for any British recognition it could obtain. Towards the end of their long reign in India, however, the British had begun to doubt the wisdom of this ploy. The likelihood of a strong revolutionary power emerging out of the confusion of Kuomintang rule may have explained more determined efforts to endorse the campaign for Tibetan independence. Britain then tried to persuade the USA to extend diplomatic recognition to Lhasa, but the Americans refused. For them Tibet was the Dalai Lama's pontificate and no more. Not until Chiang Kai-shek had fled China and the Cold War set in, did the fear of Communism persuade the Americans to reconsider their stand on Tibet. By then it was too late for both Tibet and India.

As successor to the viceregal regime, Nehru's India could not ignore British backing for Chinese claims regarding Tibet without inviting possibly embarrassing examination of the background to the McMahon Line. One relatively new theory on this 850-mile border is that there was no agreement at all at the 1914 Simla conference, the entire supportive evidence having been conjured up by Caroe many years later, as already mentioned. This version has it that Sir Henry McMahon did indeed draw up a memorandum on the subject but it was not formally discussed and was not even endorsed by the British authorities. In evidence, it is cited that the Assam government seemed unaware of the McMahon Line right up to 1935–'36 and that the Line found no mention in official works like Aitchison's *Treaties* or generally dependable publications like the *Times Atlas.* The relevant map was published for the first time in 1960.

According to this theory, what Ivan Chen actually initialled (and later repudiated) was a map relating to Tibet's northern frontier with China, which also was drawn by McMahon. The more conventional view, however, is that though the tripartite conference in Simla failed to reach an agreement, Britain and the Tibetan delegate bilaterally endorsed the McMahon Line. Since Chen, apparently, did not object, he is presumed to have acquiesced. But this claim is flawed on two counts. First, Tibet could not at that stage enter into an international agreement without Chinese ratification, especially since Britain had made such a show of recognising China's suzerainty. Secondly, the Anglo-Russian convention of 1907 prevented Britain from entering into a bilateral engagement with Tibet. Whether or not a border agreement was signed in 1914, New Delhi was on shaky ground. Nehru had to be both cautious and placatory, which may explain the readiness with which he surrendered extra-territorial privileges in Tibet as soon as China asked, clothing the concession in anti-colonial rhetoric.

Nevertheless, India watched with dismay as the Chinese consolidated their hold on Tibet. The relatively minor worry of Lhasa's ineffectual demand for a swathe of cis-Himalayan territory yielded to the much greater danger of aggressive Chinese knocking on a door whose very existence was suddenly in question. Real fears were not aroused, however, until 1954 when official Chinese maps again showed the entire belt, including Sikkim, as Chinese. This was a reiteration of the Manchu theory that China, Nepal, Sikkim, Bhutan and Tibet were like five colours (*wuts'ai)*—yellow, red, blue, green and black—that a skilful artist could blend to produce an attractive shade, which Chang-Tin Tang, the amban, had evoked in 1906 to warn Lhasa against direct relations with British India. There were other equally vivid metaphors. Ladakh, Nepal, Sikkim, Bhutan and Tawang in what is now Arunachal Pradesh were described as the five fingers of China's Tibetan palm. Ladakh, Nepal, Sikkim and Bhutan were also the 'four teeth with which the Chinese will grind their way to the southern seas'.

India decided on an oblique gesture of defiance. At Nehru's request, the Chogyal, who was president of the Mahabodhi Society of India, travelled to Lhasa to invite the Dalai Lama to attend the Buddha's 2,500th birth anniversary celebrations. The invitation was informal enough not to suggest a head of state's ceremonial visit, but it was intended to convey disapproval of the gradual obliteration of Tibet's separate status. The Chinese authorities retaliated with expected ungraciousness. The Chogyal was kept waiting at the border while his credentials were examined. His international driving licence was not accepted in Lhasa, and he had to take a fresh motoring test. More cartographical claims followed. When the Dalai Lama finally reached Nathu-la where Sir Tashi waited to receive him, someone—presumably a Chinese agent—mischievously clipped a Chinese flag to his car fender.

Sikkim was not directly involved in this tussle but was conscious of peril, like a child caught in an adult war game. Differences over Aksai Chin (the north-eastern section of the Ladakhi plateau jutting into Tibet) and the McMahon Line were public knowledge. An entire division of Chinese soldiers was said to be deployed in the Chumbi valley. Indian troops took up position in twenty-four places in Sikkim, and a full Indian division fanned out across the kingdom, supported by a heavy arms brigade based in Siliguri in the West Bengal plains. Gangtok echoed to the rumble of military trucks on their way to the border. The road down to Bagdogra airport in West Bengal, the kingdom's only outlet, was often sealed off for convoys. Army control of the kingdom's northern and eastern districts was tightened. The Tibet trade petered out. Sikkim was turning into a gigantic cantonment. The row of shops in Gangtok's Lal Bazaar that sold smuggled imported goods not available in India were always crammed with soldiers buying lengths of nylon to be worn as sarees and cosmetics for their wives.

The durbar responded hospitably enough, giving woollen sweaters to the troops who did not initially have adequate winter wear. But the Chogyal put his foot down when the PO suggested that military families should be allowed to settle down in his country. He protested that Bhutiya-Lepchas would be totally obliterated if Lho-mon-Tsong-sum's existing ethnic imbalance was further aggravated by an influx of 100,000 Indian women and children.

Nor was the Sikkim government anxious to unnecessarily provoke the Chinese. The durbar fully supported India's defence effort. The Sikkim Guards were offered to the army, the Chogyal several times toured border installations and he spoke of India's protection with gratitude. 'India is our protecting power. So long as India is strong, we are safe,' he announced. He told a questioner on another occasion that if the Chinese attacked 'they will not find it an easy adventure. We will show them that we can defend our frontiers.' But he never really believed the Chinese would attack, though he repeatedly affirmed that the durbar had 'absolute confidence in the capacity of the Indian army to defend Sikkim against aggression'.

He also drew the line at provocative political intrigues and counter-insurgency guerrilla activity in which the PO's hand was suspected. At Nehru's request, Sikkim had accepted about 7,000 Tibetan refugees, most of them warlike Khampas from the Namgyal dynasty's own ancestral province. Many were settled in the Temi and Kewsing tea gardens; others lived in camps managed by Coo Coo La. The Chogyal expected them to become Sikkim subjects and refrain from extraneous politics. But the Tibetans refused to sign a standard form promising to abide by local laws. They ignored the government's authority, and looked for instructions to organisers in India and abroad. Many collected their rations and quietly disappeared.

Foreign secretary Subimal Dutt was told in August 1960 that at least 1,300 Khampas were missing. Durbar officials reported to the Chogyal that the KMT paid ₹ 100 per recruit to fight the Communists. The men apparently trekked through the jungles to Darjeeling where undercover Taiwanese representatives were thought to operate a clandestine recruiting centre. From Darjeeling the Tibetans descended to Siliguri to entrain for Nepal. They were probably despatched to Mustang, the nerve-centre of guerrilla operations. Gangtok suspected the

Dalai Lama's elder brother, Gyalo Thondup, who had built up important contacts in the United States and whose Chinese wife Zhu Dan was the daughter of a high KMT official, General Chu Shi-kuei. The couple lived in Darjeeling where Mrs Thondup ran a self-help institution for Tibetan refugees. Gyalo Thondup was to be accused fourteen years later of far more dangerous intervention in Bhutan. Later still, he became the Dalai Lama's main conduit for political negotiations with Peking. Even if he acted on instructions from Washington and Taiwan in this early anti-China phase, he needed at least India's tacit consent. The durbar, therefore, asked the external affairs ministry either to control Gyalo Thondup or to remove all Tibetans to camps in India.

The request was seen as pandering to Peking. It coincided with the Chinese General Chang Kua-hua's announcement in Lhasa:

> Bhutanese, Sikkimese and Ladakhis form a united family in Tibet. They have always been subject to Tibet and to the great motherland of China. They must once again be united and taught the Communist doctrine.[3]

It was one of many coincidences that suggested collusion to suspicious Indians. Nehru felt perturbed enough to justify India's military presence in the two kingdoms. He told the Rajya Sabha on 25 August 1959: 'But the fact remains that so far as Bhutan and Sikkim are concerned, they are in treaty relations with us and we are responsible for their defence. I cannot imagine any foreign country doing anything which is an infringement of their sovereignty. In any event, any such infringement would be an infringement of our undertakings with Sikkim and Bhutan....' It is noteworthy that not only did the prime minister recognise the 'sovereignty' of the two Himalayan kingdoms, he treated them at par. Three days later in the Lok Sabha, Nehru again referred to them in the same breath to clarify that 'the government of India is responsible for the protection of the borders of Sikkim and Bhutan and of the territorial integrity of these two states....' Continuing to equate them, Nehru made it clear he did not regard either as lying within India's borders.

Chou went a step further when he wrote to Nehru on 8 September:

> In your Excellency's letter, you also referred to the boundary between China and Sikkim. Like the boundary between China and Bhutan, this question does not fall within the scope of our present discussion. I would like, however, to take this opportunity to make clear once again that China is willing to live together in friendship with Sikkim and Bhutan, without committing aggression against each other, and has always respected the proper relations between them and India.

Like Nehru, Chou, too, did not differentiate between the two kingdoms. But he appeared to doubt India's claim to speak for either. In the case of Sikkim, this might have meant rejection of the Anglo-Chinese convention of 1890 or the Indo-Sikkimese treaty of 1950, or both. The ambiguity persisted during Sino-Indian talks in Delhi, Peking and Rangoon. China's refusal to be more specific may have owed something to the 1959 revolt in Tibet, revealing that the Tibetans had not been brought fully under control. Political uncertainty at home would have advised Peking to keep its options open.

Renascent China probably entertained doubts about the 1890 convention's relevance. New Delhi's case quite simply was that if the amban had recognised Britain's protectorate over Sikkim, and if Younghusband had wrung acquiescence out of the Tibetans after gunning his way into Lhasa, it did not matter how strenuously the Sikkimese and Tibetans objected to the fiat. In this version, even modern China was not at liberty to change its mind after more than half a century of cataclysmic upheavals! This was an extraordinarily static view of history. The evolving polity of the two countries had cast off the rulers who parleyed in Calcutta in 1890. Much of what had been bequeathed to India by the British, and to China by the Manchus, had been discarded without compunction. All Asia applauded lustily when such legacies were shed, seeing in the rejection (as in Bangladesh's repudiation of Pakistani rule in 1971) vigorous proof of resurgent national pride. Yet, one item in that otherwise repugnant heritage was treated as immutable. Peking's refusal to regard the protectorate claim as sacrosanct was not only deeply offensive to New Delhi but was also taken as evidence in some way of the Chogyal's disloyalty. It moved Nehru solemnly to warn China:

> We have publicly, and rightly, undertaken certain responsibilities for the defence of Sikkim and Bhutan, if they are attacked. It is very necessary for us to understand that if anything happens on their borders, then it is the same thing as an interference with the border of India.[4]

Chou En-lai visited India seven months later. As is well known, the six days he spent trying to persuade Nehru that two emerging Asian republics should be able to settle differences without relying on a discredited past achieved nothing. But another controversy developed out of the Chinese premier's press conference on 30 April 1960. Asked about claims to Bhutan, Chou told an Indian reporter: 'I am sorry to disappoint. We have no claim with regard to Bhutan, nor do we have any dispute with it. You may recall that in its letters to the Indian government, the Chinese government twice mentioned that China has no boundary dispute with Sikkim and Bhutan and that China respects India's special relations with Sikkim and Bhutan.' This is the official Indian version. According to China's official Hsinhua News Agency, Chou said 'proper relations' (as in his note of the previous

September) and not 'special' relations. Both sides claimed to have tapes to prove their versions. The distinction is interesting for 'special' is not always 'proper'. Having dismissed the McMahon Line as being 'illegally delineated through an exchange of secret notes by British imperialism with the Tibetan local authorities of China', Chou may have felt it would be only logical to denounce the 1890 convention as another fraudulent imposition.

There was no reason to expect an attack on Sikkim. But India used the Chinese threat to wage a psychological offensive against the durbar. New Delhi asserted its rights far more directly than it had done before not only vis-à-vis Peking but also in relation to Gangtok. External affairs ministry officials urged the Chogyal to stridently denounce supposed Chinese intentions. At the same time, they warned him not to expect any relaxation of Indian control until the border problem had been settled. Menacing Chinese moves near Tawang in October 1962 lent point to these warnings. The durbar proclaimed an emergency, began recruiting a home guard, and set up a people's consultative committee to advise the government. But not many Sikkimese were convinced even then of China's aggressive designs: the Chogyal somewhat imprudently told a visitor that if the Chinese really wished to invade, they would enter the Brahmaputra plains through the Chumbi valley, where the route was shorter and there wasn't a bristling wall of armour as at Nathu-la.

His complacency was not well received. Kashi Raj Pradhan, leader of the Sikkim State Congress and one of the kingdom's first elected executive councillors, claimed after a talk with Nehru that 'the prime minister said he could not give an assurance that Sikkim would not be lost to the Chinese'. Kashi Raj belonged to a prosperous thikadar family. He was one of Sikkim's first university graduates and a successful businessman. He was also a reliable witness. Nehru himself promised at the end of 1962 that 'Sikkim will be defended by us with all our strength just as any part of India', which made some Sikkimese wonder whether India did not perhaps hope for a showdown in which the durbar would be compelled to choose sides. To add to speculation, H.V. Kamath, a socialist MP whom Kazini had known well in Delhi before she married Kazi, claimed that China had set up a puppet government of Sikkim 'somewhere in Tibet'. The durbar took these alarums with a pinch of salt. It was still anxious not to awaken China's dormant claims by constantly harping on a threat.

The war of words did not erupt into action until January 1963 when Peking accused the Indian army of trespassing beyond Nathu-la and digging trenches, erecting barbed-wire fences and putting up pill-boxes in Chumbi. New Delhi dismissed the charge of 'fictitious border violations', in turn accusing Peking of making 'preposterous and baseless allegations'. As hysteria mounted and pressure on the palace increased, the Chogyal found it necessary to announce that 'Sikkim stands firmly by the side of India in prosperity and adversity and this has been amply demonstrated by the unstinted support we have given to the government of India in this hour of crisis'. Notes flew back and forth between the Indian and Chinese governments, becoming more and more acrimonious, but Gangtok was not directly involved until 31 July 1963, when the foreign office in Peking announced that 'China and Sikkim have always lived together in peace and no Chinese forces have ever crossed into Sikkim; this is a fact not to be distorted'. Two months later the Chinese complained: 'In recent years India has repeatedly made use of Sikkim territory to violate Chinese territory and deliberately created incidents along the Sino-Sikkim border in a vain attempt to undermine the friendly and good-neighbourly relations between China and Sikkim.'[5]

Peking was not trying to extend Chinese territory. But it was implying rejection of New Delhi's protective role in Sikkim (i.e., the 1890 convention) and indicating that the

Sikkimese should take their own decisions. The precise message was that while China recognised Sikkim's independence and wished to live in peace with the kingdom, relations might be impaired if Gangtok allowed Indian troops to operate from its territory. The tactic was carried a step further when Sir Tashi died on 2 December 1963. Three days later China's head of state, Liu Shao Chi, sent a condolence message direct to the Chogyal. India's attitude towards Sikkim had hardened, and Nehru's sense of outrage was reflected in the awesome language of his rebuke:

> The government of China has in contravention of normal diplomatic courtesies in its relations with the government of India, addressed a telegram from Chairman Liu Shao Chi directly to the Maharaja of Sikkim, on the 5th of December, 1963, instead of forwarding it to this government for onward transmission. The government of China is well aware that the external relations of Sikkim are entirely the responsibility of the government of India and that any communication, either formal or informal from the government of China to the government of Sikkim or its ruler, should be channelled through the Indian government. The procedure adopted by the Chinese government is, therefore, entirely unacceptable to the Indian government and they trust that in future all communications pertaining to Sikkim will be addressed to the government of India only.[6]

Gangtok felt Nehru was unnecessarily agitated, and resented such a display of asperity over a courtesy message during Sikkim's mourning. But Liu was not abashed. When the Chogyal was crowned on 4 April 1965, he again sent his message of congratulations direct to the ruler.

Relations between Delhi and Peking worsened in the time between Sir Tashi's death and the Chogyal's coronation. India claimed in January 1964 that thirty armed Chinese, two civilians, and a wireless operator had trespassed nearly three miles south of Kongra-la. Two Tibetans who had crossed Banchho-la were arrested in early August. A Chinese patrol was accused of entering through Nathu-la some weeks later. Forty Chinese soldiers were said to have intruded in November, and three transgressions (all near Nathu-la) were reported in December. The last border violation by the Chinese was on Boxing Day when 'seeing an Indian patrol, they withdrew into Tibet and, after crossing the border, fired one green eerie light into the sky'. In turn, Peking accused India of constructing twenty-seven military structures beyond Jelap-la.

There was a lull on the Sikkim frontier until India and Pakistan went to war in Kutch in August 1965. A few days later Jagat Mehta, India's charge d'affairs in Peking, was summoned to the foreign ministry and told that his government had three days, i.e., until September 20, in which to dismantle military installations on the Chinese side of Sikkim's border, to stop boundary violations, desist from harassing raids, and to return seized men and livestock. New Delhi reported that harassment, kidnapping, and confiscation were hardly feasible in a region occupied by four persons, fifty-one yaks, and 800 sheep. There was an infantile sequel when ultra-patriotic Indians drove 801 bleating sheep (not 800 because round figures are inauspicious) up to the Chinese embassy in New Delhi. Round the necks of the animals hung placards reading 'Eat us and spare the world'. The first firing across Nathu-la was reported on 21 September 1965.

More serious encounters followed when the Chinese tried to prevent the erection of a barbed-wire fence at Nathu-la. Both sides used field artillery and heavy mortar, and suffered casualties. Peking threatened to deploy its air force and a conflagration might have resulted if Lal Bahadur Shastri, who succeeded Nehru as prime minister in May 1964, had not proposed an unconditional ceasefire and a meeting between sector commanders.

China's brief spell of bellicosity has been explained in several ways. The historian John Rowland took the view that 'Peking, which sees the Himalayan states as irredentist regions to be regained as soon as possible, also assigns to them an offensive role. They can be future bases for the subversion of India.'[7] Many Indians seemed to be similarly convinced of China's malign intentions. Others suggested that pressure was mounted on the Sikkim sector to induce India to modify its claims over Aksai Chin and the McMahon Line. Another view is that China would have liked to alter the alignment at Nathu-la where Claude White's pillars stood along a 14,500-foot ridge. Indian artillery commanded the heights and the entire Chumbi valley, including military fortifications and troop movements, lay open to Indian inspection. Shastri believed that China acted in collusion with Pakistan, an argument that seemed to be borne out by the close timing between Chinese moves and hostilities in Kutch. If so, it was a diversionary tactic to unnerve India and encourage Pakistani morale. Extensions of the ceasefire to permit UN discussion of the Kutch war and the cessation of threats after India and Pakistan accepted the Soviet offer of mediation certainly suggest a nexus.

All these factors may have played some part in influencing Peking's thinking, though there is nothing to indicate that China ever seriously considered invading Sikkim, leave alone India. But Delhi's obsession with Sikkim's status played into Chinese hands and provided them with a ready instrument of irritation. The temptation to use it was strengthened by the repugnance that Communist leaders instinctively felt for treaties that had been forced on China during its vulnerable decades. They found the 1890 convention morally almost as objectionable as the Simla agreement.

Sikkim was only incidental to this problem, but the Indian government did not see it that way and made Delhi's relations with the kingdom dependent on India's ties with China.

Talking to reporters in Gangtok in 1967, the Chogyal complained: 'There has been flippant talk that we may lean toward our neighbours in the north, to spite our other friends.' But the talk was not flippant and the Chogyal's choice of words— 'neighbours' and '*other* friends'—only fed suspicion. Such freedom as the durbar had earlier enjoyed seemed inadvisable after India began to feel threatened, and the Gyalmo's international social contacts only deepened the sense of a foreign net closing in. When Morarji Desai visited Gangtok in March 1968 as deputy prime minister, he inadvertently confessed to his government's paranoia. He recognised Sikkim as an independent country, he said, but India could not say so in black and white because the Chinese would at once want to set up an embassy in Gangtok.

That fear impelled the PO to take an even closer interest in the palace and its activities. Nervousness manifested itself both in tightening restrictions and in a curious kind of sanctimoniousness. When Kaul went up to Nathu-la in September of the same year, for instance, being able to speak Chinese, he asked a photographer on the other side of the fence whether the man was a friend of India's. The photographer did not reply whereupon the question was repeated several times until the Chinese, his patience worn down, angrily bawled out 'No!' This was the cue Kaul was waiting for. He at once trumped the photographer's ungraciousness with a long and pious homily in Mandarin on the close bonds between Asia's two great nations and how and why all Indians were inspired only by undying friendship for the Chinese.

REFERENCES

1. Parliamentary papers, India Office, London, Vol. 20, 1862.
2. Ibid.
3. *The Times of India* (8 August 1959).

4. Lok Sabha (10 September 1959).
5. Note from the Chinese Ministry of Foreign Affairs to the Government of India (19 September 1963).
6. Lok Sabha (28 December 1963).
7. John Rowland, *A History of Sino-Indian Relations: Hostile Co-existence* (D. Van Nostrand, New York, 1967).

CHAPTER

6

EIGHTFOLD WAY

'We shall not remain content until we have banished from Sikkim whatever traces may remain of poverty, ignorance and disease; we shall not cease in the struggle until the light of knowledge, health and happiness shines bright in every home of our lovely land.'

CHOGYAL PALDEN THONDUP NAMGYAL,
Coronation speech, 4 April 1965.

'The main problem is that the present electoral system and government were evolved with the government of India's blessings. In order to change all this, all parties and the government of India have to be involved.'

CROWN PRINCE TENZING,
The Statesman, 14 April 1973.

While India and China bickered over the border, the newly-enthroned Chogyal was busy recasting Sikkimese society in a modern frame. It was a period of economic reconstruction and political emancipation, at the end of which the kingdom boasted a per capita income of ₹ 750, while India's stagnated at around ₹ 320. Politically, each Sikkimese enjoyed not one but five votes. The judiciary was revised to leaven the Indian Penal Code with the traditional features of Buddhist justice. The civil service was reorganised as a formal hierarchy. Panchayats were formed and entrusted with rural administration, and development plans launched for both agriculture and industry. New roads opened up the interior, and there were suddenly all the signs of bustling life stretching out eager hands to the future.

Though Indian aid made all this possible, the awakening was not entirely to Delhi's liking. For, in its forward march, the durbar looked to the past for inspiration, reviving forms and institutions (like the titles of chogyal, gyalmo, gyalum and sidlon) that had fallen into disuse. One such institution was the modest Sikkimese army that put up such a gallant resistance when Indian troops attacked the palace in 1975. The origins of the Sikkim Guards are lost in the mists of the thirteenth century when it was the practice for every village to send an able-bodied youth to court in return for a reduction in house tax. The men were fed, clothed and armed by the durbar, and used to repulse invaders and put down rebellion. But they had not fought since Rinchingpong. Numbers and importance steadily declined as menial tasks replaced martial duties and the court moved restlessly from Chumbi to Rabdentse and Tumlong to Gangtok. The guardsmen often had to chop wood, draw water, pitch tents and tend horses for the royal entourage.

But the force was never disbanded. Hooker recorded in 1849 that he was 'met by a large party of armed Lepchas dressed in blue and white striped kirtles, broad loose scarlet jackets, and the little bamboo wattle hat lined with talc, and surmounted by a peacock's feather'[1] that remained the formal dress uniform until recent years. He also noted that scarlet-coated Bhutiyas bearing bows and arrows flanked the monarch's throne. Guardsmen armed with matchlocks conducted the British botanist when he was returning to India. Colman Macaulay reported in 1894 that 'the Sikkim army was drawn up to receive us in the courtyard' when he called at the Tumlong palace with its burnished copper gilt spire. Even in the 1920s, a JCO commanded ninety-six men equipped with rusty muzzle-loaders that had been a gift from Queen Victoria. There was also the military band—woodwind, gongs, and drums—which accompanied chogyals wherever they went. They received Lord Wavell with a musical cacophony when he paid a farewell visit to Sir Tashi.

The Chogyal had to marshal all this evidence when he revived the force in the 1950s. He dredged up old photographs of resplendently attired guardsmen posing outside the old dzong where the royal family lived until the building collapsed, to prove he was reorganising an extant force, not reviving an extinct one. His argument, based on the treaty of Tumlong, was that Indian protection did not deprive the Sikkimese of the right to self-defence. Nehru agreed, but external affairs ministry officials were less understanding, and a formal agreement was not reached until early 1961. Indian MPs were told then that Indian army officers would command the Sikkim Guards and that India would pay about ₹ 2.6 million for one company, Sikkim being responsible for the second.

This revival was part of a campaign to rediscover the country's roots. The Chogyal had warned in his coronation speech that '... we have to ensure also that, with the material progress towards which we are striving, we do not lose sight of the spiritual values that are our precious heritage, that the right legacy of our past and the lovely things of Sikkim are not engulfed in the ocean of change'. Nari Rustomji, his ICS colleague, who succeeded Lall as dewan, was his ardent supporter. 'Dress, language, architecture, religion, social customs, music, painting—in these were centred the heart of Sikkim's culture,' he wrote. According to Rustomji, 'the hour had struck for Sikkim's cultural renaissance, with the young prince as its shining inspiration'.[2] It was a heady era as cottage industries were encouraged to combine traditional motifs with modern functionalism and a new architectural style blended Tibetan monastery and dzong with contemporary utility. The secretariat in Gangtok was renamed Tashiling. The palace was redecorated, with the High Court and Council House following suit.

The mission was sustained by the Chogyal's Buddhist convictions. He led a delegation to the world Buddhist council in 1954, represented Sikkim at Japan's Buddha Jayanti celebrations five years later, and was alternate leader of the Indian team at the World Fellowship of Buddhists Conference in Cambodia in 1961. Later, he went on pilgrimage to the sacred places of Ulan Ude in Soviet Mongolia. These travels brought home to him the scholastic background to religion, resulting in the unique collection of monastic implements, bronzes, coins, thankas, xylographs, palm-leaf manuscripts and books housed in the Namgyal Institute of Tibetology set up by royal charter in 1958. The library acquired many priceless Tibetan translations of ancient Hindu works whose originals had been lost in India. It also defied the orthodox prejudice against texts of different sects being housed under the same roof to extend the collection even beyond Mahayana scriptures.

Not only did the Institute, rearing like a small castle from nineteen acres of woods, gardens, and flowering orchids, serve students of the chhos, but it provided material for scholars with an interest in the culture of the great landmass stretching from the southern Himalayan slopes to the northern sweep of the Altai Karakoram. The Gyalum led a delegation of scholars to inspect monasteries near Baikal in eastern Siberia in 1967, a return visit being paid by a team of Soviet Buriats under an incarnate monk whose predecessor had been adviser to the thirteenth Dalai Lama.

In trying to reawaken a consciousness of Sikkim's art and culture, the durbar also exposed its own inherent weakness: it represented the minority ethic in a Hindu Nepalese-majority country. Nepalese leaders were warned that the Chogyal's emphasis on Sikkim's past was designed to exclude them from the political and administrative mainstream. India House also feared that grand plans to encourage tourism—a luxury hotel in Gangtok, traditional guest houses in Lachen and Lachung, and a ropeway from Yumthang to the contemplated skiing slopes above—would bring in hordes of dreaded foreigners. Schemes to extract the pharmaceutical properties of medicinal herbs, grow mushrooms, start a piggery and export gladioli and orchids invited disapproval. The Chogyal was accused of squandering money on fancy projects to impress his friends abroad.

The point is that in spite of the promises of aid and technical assistance written into the 1950 treaty, New Delhi was not at all anxious, at first, to allow Sikkim to emerge from medieval somnolence. What changed this attitude was not the Chogyal's ambition for his country, but Nehru's concern for Sikkimese loyalty once deteriorating relations with China underlined the attractions of a rival system. Paying his first visit to the kingdom in April 1952, the Indian prime minister told listeners: 'You must build up your united strength for the permanent safety of your country.' Returning to Delhi, he sent a team of planners to tour Sikkim and draw up its first economic plan for coordinated growth.

This seven-year plan cost ₹ 32.4 million. India spent ₹ 125 million on Sikkim's development in the two decades after 1947 in addition to loans of around ₹ 5.6 million and the Darjeeling subvention, a word India preferred to 'rent'. Nehru raised the amount from the final British figure of ₹ 12,000 to ₹ 300,000 when the 1950 treaty was signed—a noble sum by contemporary Sikkimese standards but paltry compensation for not pressing claims to one of India's richest tea-growing and tourist districts. Four economic plans absorbed ₹ 360 million by 1976, the entire cost being met from India's exchequer. The third plan period (1966–'71) was reduced to five years to synchronise with India's own fourth plan.

The change in the countryside was spectacular. There was a sense of personal achievement in outposts like the 200-acre Geba experimental farm near Gyalzing (royal meadow) whose

Lepcha manager, E.T. Tasho, a Balaclava helmet pulled over his ears to keep out chilly winds, proudly displayed giant red and white Japanese radish. It had been a satisfying day in Gyalzing where an excited crowd watched as the district officer called bids for an orangery. The sale had earlier been announced by beat of drum, and 1,500 trees (an estimated 45,000 fruits) were knocked down for ₹ 3,205 in the weekly market. The deal over, the successful buyer retired to an eating house to order bowls of steaming thukpa for all his friends with the contented air of a man who can afford to stand a round.

Oranges covered about 1,800 acres and would have been even more lucrative but for poor communications with the main market in the plains.

Cardamom, occupying some 14,000 acres, became the most paying crop under the Chogyal's management. Incentives were shrewdly offered to plant the low bushes that march with roads ribboning their way through the hills. Cultivation spread rapidly, and a jaunty young farmer, cap perched rakishly on his gleaming locks, red velvet jacket thrown across square shoulders, presented himself before the Gyalzing magistrate, seeking permission to convert his grandfather's fields to the new cash crop. The market price was high, and he expected a harvest of at least six maunds. He would be taxed at ₹ 18 a maund, but would be exempt from land revenue. Grinning, the farmer admitted that profits would be much higher than the levy. By 1971, cardamom was the single-most important item in the ₹ 400,000 that Sikkim earned from exports.

Directly as a result of such measures, the kingdom's revenue rose from ₹ 600,000 in 1950 to ₹ 4.1 million only four years later. By 1967, when much bigger Bhutan could mobilise only ₹ 9 million annually, Sikkim raised ₹ 12 million. The kingdom's income was said to be ₹ 35 million in 1973. New Delhi's economic pundits even complimented Sikkim on using investment funds more constructively than India.

As plan succeeded plan, the literacy rate rose from 12.3 per cent to 15.9 per cent. Malaria, once rampant, was eradicated. Three new hospitals and twelve dispensaries laid the foundations for comprehensive health care. The establishment of two high schools, a junior school, and ninety-one primary, upper primary, and middle institutions enabled the Chogyal to claim in his coronation speech that no child lived more than two miles from educational facilities. The Thondup College for night students confirmed he had set his sights on a university but that needed New Delhi's clearance. A thermal plant in Gangtok and the Rongnichy hydroelectricity project were other early achievements.

Seed multiplication centres improved the quality of paddy, wheat and maize. The Hilley-Ribdi farm developed wart-resistant potatoes. Lachen and Lachung were brought under scientific apple cultivation. Tea gardens were laid out, forests planted, Jersey bulls and Landrace pigs distributed to farmers, and an extensive cattle inoculation scheme started. Jorethang was the site of a bacon-curing centre, while sheep stations were opened at Zemu and Dentam. Far-flung irrigation and drinking water projects, a State Trading Corporation, the Lagyap hydroelectricity project, and a highly successful distillery and fruit preservation factory at Rangpo continued the advance. When the state-owned transport service was launched, the Chogyal himself took the wheel of the first SNT or Sikkim Nationalised Transport bus from Gangtok to Siliguri. Copper, limestone, and graphite deposits were surveyed; a paper and pulp factory planned; more roads and bridges were completed; and India's permission obtained for a jewel-bearing factory that the Chogyal hoped would lead to watch-making. The Palden Thondup Cottage Industries Institute trained more than 300 boys and girls.

'Our progress and achievements have been in large measure due to the friendship and goodwill of India, who has not only assisted generously with funds, materials and expertise for our various projects but has also been the source of much of the inspiration behind our efforts,' announced the Chogyal. But the external affairs ministry accused him of ingratitude while the PO complained the official publication *Sikkim through Figures* did not adequately acknowledge India's aid.

Differences had cropped up towards the end of the first plan. The Chogyal was keen on sophisticated small-scale industries. Nehru, who at home attached greater importance to heavy industry than to cultivation, was more interested in improving Sikkim's agriculture. A compromise was reached, but when the Sikkimese went to Delhi with a draft fourth plan that would cost ₹ 260 million, India demanded that the kingdom should substantially increase its share of the outlay. Then, India insisted that Gangtok should pay more for Indian experts. Eventually, the Chogyal had to be content with a ₹ 185-million outlay. But Kaiser Bahadur Thapa, militant editor of the fortnightly *Sikkim* with the grandiloquent motto *Dulce et decorum est pro patria mori* (It is sweet and honourable to die for one's country) wasn't satisfied.

Thapa was an intrepid man who had braved British displeasure during World War II to accompany escaped German prisoners to Lhasa. He wrote angrily about the bargaining: 'We must remember that Sikkim was here when the plans were not, and will continue to be here if we decide to discontinue the development plans.' Thapa complained of pressure and accused India of not allowing Sikkim to generate its own resources. He advised the durbar to refuse all aid 'if our larger interests are to be jeopardised', and suggested New Delhi's tactic was to force the Chogyal to impose heavy taxation in the hope that unpopular measures might trigger off a revolt against the throne.

Politics had lain just below the surface ever since 1947. The palace and the political parties had not wholly recovered from the psychological effects of the confrontation they were forced into only two years later. That memory lay between them like a drawn sword. And like the monkey in the fable, the PO advised both and nibbled away at the disputed cake.

The balance changed somewhat when, apprehensive of being swallowed up, and worried about the hordes of Nepalese rallying to the State Congress banner, Sonam Tshering broke away to form the National Party. The new group's conservatism was reflected in a flag that closely resembled the national standard. The only difference was that instead of the eight-spoked wheel in the centre of the red-bordered white field, it displayed a large yellow star, representing the monarchy, presiding over three lesser satellites which stood for the Bhutiya, Lepcha and Tsong communities. Again by implication, the majority Nepalese had no place in Lho-mon-Tsong-sum. The party symbol was the equally orthodox device of a swastika.

The National Party announced on 30 April 1948 that it was 'resolved that Sikkim shall not, under any circumstances, accede to the dominion of India' for:

> Historically, socially, culturally and linguistically, Sikkim has closer affinities with Bhutan and Nepal.
>
> From the geographical and ethnic point of view, Sikkim is not a part of India. She has only political relations with the latter, which were more or less imposed on her.
>
> From the religious point of view, being lamaist, she is quite distinct from India.

Draftsmanship was never the National Party's strongest point. But its purpose comes through clearly enough from the resolution that 'the policy of the party is to maintain intact by all means the indigenous character of Sikkim and to preserve her integrity. The party would make all-out efforts to establish a separate entity and to remain outside the Indian Union.' It felt that the land tenure system could not be abolished overnight and that Sikkim would only gradually evolve towards representative governance.

India House at once dubbed it the 'palace party'. But Sonam Tshering had opposed Sir Tashi for far too long to become a pliable tool. Believing that the durbar did not sufficiently safeguard the country's Tibeto-Buddhist traditions, the National Party refused to take part in the panchayat elections in December 1950. Its philosophy appealed to Bhutiya-Lepchas who had formerly rallied to the State Congress. Though the leaders were assertively non-aristocratic, the party's programme was also tacitly endorsed by kazis, officials and courtiers who were not anxious to take an overt part in politics. All of them agreed that relations with India could only be 'on the basis of equality'. The manifesto went on to elucidate:

> From India's point of view, a happy Sikkim as a buffer state would be of greater advantage than an unhappy Sikkim in India on one of her future international boundaries of great importance which would be a disadvantage, indeed a danger, to India.[3]

Worried about this emergence, the Indian government summoned the Chogyal as well as State Congress and National Party leaders to New Delhi. The Rajya Praja Sammelan was also invited partly because it had once opted for union with India and partly because some of its members had objected to merging with the State Congress in 1947. But the only outcome of the conference held in March 1950 was an advisory council to work with the dewan. Two State Congress representatives and two from the National Party were appointed to it; the Rajya Praja Sammelan was not included and soon disappeared. But John Lall did not define the council's jurisdiction or entrust members with any responsibilities. It was, in fact, a truncated and ineffective version of Sir Tashi's earlier council which could at least directly address the ruler. The new council was supposed to advise the dewan who would then convey its advice to Sir Tashi.

The conference the Chogyal called in May 1951 to draw up a constitution was more productive. Like his father in 1947, he, too, was convinced that the Sikkimese would have to close ranks. He realised the need for a formal basis of governance, and also understood the importance of enlisting Nepalese support. The State Congress was represented by Captain Dimik Singh and Kashi Raj Pradhan. Sonam Tshering spoke for the National Party. Representing Sikkim's three communities, the delegates agreed that since Bhutiyas and Lepchas were virtually indistinguishable and also too weak to stand individually, they would be bracketed together for political and administrative purposes. It was also decided that the Nepalese would enjoy legislative parity with Bhutiya-Lepchas. Each group would elect six councillors through adult suffrage, the durbar nominating another five.

Tashi Tsering tried to repudiate the agreement but was ousted in a coup that made Kazi Lendhup Dorji president of the State Congress. The former twenty-nine-day prime minister still didn't understand that India House called the shots: the PO wrote to Sir Tashi on 25 October 1951 approving the constitutional framework that Tashi Tsering had tried to kill. But New Delhi expressly forbade a written constitution that carried the imprimatur of all the political parties. Instead, the durbar was ordered to issue a proclamation. This was a clever move, exposing the palace to the charge of ruling through royal fiats. A proclamation also distracted attention from the fact that the country's two political parties had helped to draw up a blueprint that enjoyed New Delhi's sanction.

With minor revisions, the State Council and Executive Council Proclamation of 1953 remained in force until 1974. It set up a bicameral dyarchy with eighteen elected members, seven each from the Nepalese and Bhutiya-Lepcha communities, one each for the Tsongs and Nepalese Hindu scheduled castes, a representative of the kingdom's fifty-four Buddhist monasteries, and one from a general seat elected by the entire populace on a simple majority. In addition, the durbar nominated six councillors.

The council could 'enact laws for peace, order and good government of Sikkim' and had specific charge of education, health, excise, transport, bazaars, forests, public works and press and publicity. Some of its members were appointed to an executive council and entrusted with portfolios with limited financial authority. But councillors could not discuss foreign affairs, relations with India, the appointment and emoluments of the dewan and other Indian deputationists and law officers. The judiciary, sub-judice matters, secret and discretionary expenditure, the civil list, and the royal family were also out of bounds. Budgetary proposals were subject to the ruler's approval. In addition, the durbar retained control of ecclesiastical affairs, state enterprises, home, finance, police, land revenue, rationing, the administrative establishment and foreign relations.

If this seemed heavily weighted against the council, it should be remembered that the palace had little say in many of the matters excluded from legislative purview. In practice, reserved subjects came under the jurisdiction of the PO or dewan. But the Proclamation envisaged expansion of the council's powers. The token inclusion of foreign affairs gave notice that the transfer to New Delhi was not necessarily permanent.

Political leaders were disappointed, however, not so much because they demanded a greater share of authority as because they hankered after sonorous designations. The calibre of Sikkimese politicians was not high. Tashi Tsering, Raghubir Prasad and Sonam Tshering had all held clerical jobs. Netuk Tsering, who later became National Party president, was another unfrocked lama like Kazi. His predecessor, Martam Topden, was a simple man who proudly claimed to be of the land. Among younger entrants, Krishna Chandra Pradhan, though the son of a rich Rai Sahib, had drifted in and out of jobs in Sikkim, Bhutan, Nepal and India. Nahakul Pradhan was a former havildar.

Men with natural ability developed by education were not drawn to politics because of the much more attractive opportunities available in the durbar's rapidly expanding administration. At least 90 per cent of the 3,000 educated Sikkimese had comfortable bureaucratic jobs. Some 200 gazetted officers formed an influential and exclusive club within this meritocracy. Though some councillors sought enhanced spending powers, most would have been happy enough if the council had been glorified as Parliament, the executive council described as the cabinet, and the rank of prime minister bestowed on the majority party leader.

India would not tolerate the sovereign implications of such terminology. Just as the Chogyal could not be called king or addressed as 'Majesty', his government, too, had to be content with the subordinate status that the British allowed in the princely states. Privately, Indian officials also agreed that it was unthinkable to invest the people's representatives with full powers since they could not be controlled as easily as a monarch. But the palace was publicly criticised for curtailing democracy. The Chogyal did not dare to disclose the extent to which all decisions were taken in New Delhi.

• • •

The National Party captured all seven Bhutiya-Lepcha seats in the first elections held in 1953. The State Congress did the same in Nepalese constituencies. Under inspiring guidance, a hesitant experiment in power-sharing might eventually have matured into a responsible administration. But like many ICS officials, John Lall, who, as dewan, presided over the council, could do things for people and nothing with them. He introduced welcome measures like the abolition of house tax and forced labour, but did not bother to encourage councillors to ask pertinent questions, examine official decisions, and initiate legislation. Most members merely read out speeches that had been written for them. The few enterprising councillors were immediately slapped down, and the right to frame laws they enjoyed under Clause 13 of the Proclamation was never invoked. The council served only a decorative purpose in its ornate little bungalow, grey stone ornamented with scarlet lattice-work and gold appointments. The dewan ruled Sikkim in the Chogyal's name.

But even this token democracy provoked fierce animosities. There was much anguish in 1953 when only Sonam Tshering and Kashi Raj Pradhan were appointed executive councillors. Hectic intrigues also tore into party unity. After the second election in 1958, when the State Congress accounted for eight of the fourteen elected councillors, but still did not think of demanding the majority party's right to form an executive council, Kazi left to form the Swatantra Dal. His partner in the enterprise was an inconsequential man called Namgyal Tsering whose only qualification was that his father had been a senior officer in the Residency, and whom we will meet again in very different circumstances. It was an incomprehensible move except for the fact that Kazi's ambitions were beginning to surface and he felt overshadowed by Kashi Raj Pradhan.

The latter did not survive for long. An election tribunal removed him and his nephew, Nahakul, both appointed to the executive council in 1958, from office. The younger Pradhan was easily re-elected, but his uncle was roundly defeated by Chandra Das Rai who had returned to politics after leaving it when Tashi Tsering was sacked. Rai had studied at Varanasi and become a magistrate. But in spite of his handsome victory over the party president, Rai was not made an executive councillor; he had thrown up a good job for nothing.

The National Party also faced difficulties. Corruption charges were levelled against Sonam Tshering, and India's Central Bureau of Investigation asked to look into them. The allegations were not proved, but Martam Topden, by then a rich contractor and landowner, replaced him as party president.

Sonam Tshering complained of victimisation. Chandra Das Rai felt aggrieved. Kazi's Swatantra Dal had not made any impact. The three disgruntled politicians convened a meeting at Melli in September 1959, and a more ambitious rally in Singtam the following May. The Sikkim National Congress was born there with Kazi as president and Sonam Tshering as vice-president. The new party, which included some remnants of the Rajya Praja Sammelan, demanded responsible government, a written constitution, universal adult suffrage on a joint electorate and guaranteed fundamental rights. With Kazini in the background, it was far superior to the National Party when it came to language and rhetoric. 'Sikkim run by proclamation cannot be called a democratic country,' thundered Kazi. 'Never before in the history of India and China has Sikkim come within the orbit of both India and China. In such a critical period, therefore, the aspirations of the people of Sikkim must find expression in the formation of responsible government based on a written constitution. Nothing short of this will satisfy the people of Sikkim....' It was Kazi's voice but whose were the words, people wondered, for the new champion of democracy had little education and no experience of anything beyond running taxis and a petrol pump.

The main complaint was against an electoral system that was said to violate the 'one-man-one-vote' principle, but which, as the Chogyal argued, gave every Sikkimese five votes. A Bhutiya-Lepcha voted for representatives of his own community and for those of the Nepalese, Tsong and scheduled caste groups, as well as for the all-Sikkim seat. The rules stipulated that 'the candidate securing the highest number of votes of the community which he represents will ordinarily be required to have secured also at least 15 per cent of the total votes of the rest of the electors to entitle him to be returned'. It was the durbar's prescription to facilitate communication across communal barriers, prevent the creation of ethnic ghettos, and ensure the evolution one day of an integrated society. Though the SNC complained that the system was far too complicated to be functional, the turn-out for the elections held under the 1953 Proclamation rose from 30 per cent to 35 per cent between 1953 and 1958.

Then, as later, the SNC talked at, rather than to, the durbar. It directly addressed the Indian government, and a memorandum incorporating the Singtam demands and threatening the palace with satyagraha was sent to Nehru. The Chogyal was then in Moscow, leading the Indian delegation to a conference of Orientalists. Without waiting for his return, the Indian prime minister invited Kazi, Sonam Tshering, Rai and four other SNC delegates to Delhi where these opposition politicians were received with almost official honours on 10 August 1960. Baleswar Prasad, the dewan, shepherded them on the trip.

Nehru met the politicians on 26 August, read their memorandum, expressed sympathy for their aims and advised them to discuss details with the external affairs ministry. With such assurances of support, the satyagraha became unnecessary. But Kazi found other reasons for repeatedly petitioning New Delhi. He objected to separate representation for Tsongs, complained that the Sikkim Guards would be used to suppress dissent, and, always with an eye to placating the majority community, denounced the 1961 Sikkim Subjects Regulation as a device to disenfranchise the Nepalese. Again, the Chogyal did not divulge that none of these steps had been taken without India's explicit clearance, or that subjecthood rules had been discussed with New Delhi for more than five years. Instead, he promised to amend them if the council unanimously voted for amendments, but the offer was ignored.

• • •

Rightly or wrongly, the durbar blamed the PO for encouraging SNC assertiveness. This carping attitude owed something to the frustrations experienced by Sikkim in economic affairs. The revolution of rising expectations held the seeds of conflict. There were interminable wrangles with India over the amount of aid, identifying projects and the appointment of technical advisers. At home, the emerging new class of contractors, tradesmen and officials demanded a lion's share of the money that was earned locally or received from New Delhi. Gangtok was convinced that, but for a restrictive treaty, Switzerland would finance watch-making in Sikkim, Japan would set up an electronics plant and the Netherlands invest in dairy farming. The durbar criticised tied aid, demanded the right to collaborate with industrialised countries and sought to relax India's stranglehold.

'Your children go to foreign universities but ours have to study in India,' grumbled the Sikkimese, referring to the 400 annual scholarships provided by New Delhi. 'You import technicians from abroad but we are allowed only Indians!' Even those were not readily available. The fifth clause of Dayal's letter elaborating the treaty stipulated that 'the government of Sikkim will not in future employ any person other than a subject of Sikkim without the consent of the government of India, but may obtain professional advice from Indian nationals without such consent'. In practice, New Delhi never approved of any foreigner, and the PO made scathing comments about the qualifications of a Swiss architect who gave shape to some of the Chogyal's visions of a distinctive building style. New Delhi even tended to frown upon the durbar's direct offers of employment to Indian specialists of renown. Only the Indian government's nominees were allowed. 'Indians don't have enough experience of the hills, all their problems are geared to problems of hunger in the plains,' remarked Madan Mohan Rasaily, then secretary for trade, commerce and industry. 'We want to associate with small but developed countries that share our difficulties.'

The Sikkimese had claimed to detect a direct nexus between aid and politics ever since Nehru financed the first plan in the wake of Chinese rumblings. Subsequent gestures were similarly related to events on the border. If New Delhi had nothing to fear from Beijing, it did not bother to respond to Gangtok's pleas.

There were inordinate delays in sanctioning proposals. Indeed, most, if not all, the projects that suddenly sprang to life after the kingdom was annexed, and which were then paraded as tangible evidence of the benefits of merger, had been mooted by the durbar and either rejected or deferred by India. Some were subjected to extraordinary deviousness. After persistent requests, New Delhi agreed to a ropeway. But when completed, it was found that the installation was of no use to the Sikkimese. Constructed in a region under exclusive military control, it was used only to carry rations, stores, petrol and equipment for Indian troops. The durbar was informed that the ropeway would revert to Sikkim when conditions permitted the army to be withdrawn; meanwhile, its cost would be set off against India's aid to the kingdom. The Chogyal's dream of a watch-making factory fared as badly. India's nationalised machine tools industry said it would set up a jewel-bearing factory only when Sikkim produced evidence of Swiss interest, but the project report Gangtok prepared and submitted to Delhi before forwarding it to the Swiss was implemented in Kashmir instead. The political challenge there demanded immediate generosity.

The money given to Sikkim was shown as aid to a third country to enable India to obtain more Colombo Plan funds.

But for all practical purposes, the kingdom was treated as an integral part of India, as was again emphasised when the durbar's request for a foreign exchange account with the Reserve Bank of India was turned down. 'We could earn nearly ₹ 30 million if we could sell direct to third countries,' Rasaily calculated, explaining the economics of cardamom exports. Sikkim's annual output of about 50,000 maunds (a maund equals 37.32 kg) was bought locally by Marwari traders for ₹ 460 a maund. They then exported it to the Middle East where the ruling price was in the region of ₹ 2,000 per maund. Sikkim's request to export direct was refused. At the same time, New Delhi rejected an application to import machinery on the grounds that Sikkim could not expect to spend foreign exchange without earning any.

Trading rights were manipulated. Sikkim charged no duty on India's trade with Tibet which was booming until relations with China worsened. Until then, KMT dollars alone, melted down and sold as silver bars, yielded an annual profit of ₹ 3 million. Nor did Indian merchants, many of whom became millionaires, have to pay any taxes or costs towards using the kingdom's roads and halting stages. This was in accordance with Article V of the treaty which provided for reciprocal exemption. But India violated it to levy excise duty on every scrap and morsel that went into Sikkim. The National Party's Ashoke Tsering complained that New Delhi 'heaped tax upon tax for the benefit of the Indian public and to the detriment of Sikkimese consumers'. A watch, which cost only ₹ 300 in Calcutta, sold for ₹ 1,300 in Gangtok. Such imposts drained the kingdom of about ₹ 10 million every year. On the other hand, Sikkim's own wines and liqueurs could not be sold in adjoining West Bengal; even durbar officials taking the occasional bottle of locally brewed alcohol down as a present were stopped at Dum Dum airport, searched and made to pay duty as well as a fine.

Gangtok was not impressed by the plea that it was administratively impossible to separate those commodities that would be consumed in Sikkim from those that were intended for India or Tibet. A lump sum was offered instead as reimbursement, that too, not until Morarji Desai's 1968 visit. Though the deputy prime minister admitted that India owed Sikkim about ₹ 140 million in arrears, nothing was done until, after repeated representations, Mrs Gandhi increased the annual ad hoc refund from ₹ 7.5 million to ₹ 12 million.

With Gangtok obsessed by scores of such grievances, Chogyal Palden Thondup would periodically get away from it all and retire to remote reaches of his kingdom where life was still untouched by argument. He needed those respites to draw confidence from the simple trust of his subjects and renew his own ties with people who often seemed more real than Kazi Lendhup Dorji or Netuk Tsering. They provided a refuge from the Gyalmo's nagging, from political wiles and the thinly veiled insolence of successive POs.

Northern Sikkim was his favourite retreat. There was trout fishing there, as also the warm hospitality of Thangu's peasants, and always a steaming thumba of chhang. Gyalzing too, where the past lived on in stone and wood, was a favourite. The road wound past Tashiding (the elevated central glory) monastery crowning a wooded mountain, foaming torrents washing its feet. A *mending*, or prayer wall, inscribed with the mystic chant *Om Mane Padma Hum* commanded the approach to the town. Above it stood Pemayangtse monastery, Sikkim's biggest and oldest, built for celibate youths from good families of Tibet. Captain Yongda of the Sikkim Guards had been initiated there. Some 6,920 feet below that sanctuary shimmered the white chorten where the three Tibetan monks had consecrated Phuntsog Namgyal as the first chogyal. Burning lamps had to be set adrift in the lake for the kingdom's welfare.

An old dak bungalow near Pemayangtse sufficed for the Chogyal's needs. A log fire crackled in the living-room hearth and hot water was sloshed into a massive zinc bath that was dragged in. The wailing notes of a flute threaded the night. It was Tasho's young Nepalese assistant at the Geba farm, playing to the empty hills and to the fireflies glowing above the valley. The inevitable chhang was served, and a young chicken, bought in the bazaar, quickly killed, dressed and fried in a smothering of blazing chilli.

Such vignettes of contentment could not be simulated. 'Sikkim distinctly is, and I fear always will be, a poor country, with the problem ever before her as to how the necessary expenditure is to be met,' was Claude White's gloomy prediction. But the only jarring note was at the gates of the garish stucco profusion of Rumtek's new Dharma Chakra Centre. There beggars sought alms, the only place in Sikkim where the traveller was troubled. But then, the exiled Karmapa Lama, who lived there, drew legions of the faithful from India, Europe and the United States. Smart converts brought with them habits that were alien to Denzong. They paid handsomely for the privilege of watching His Holiness don his fabled hat, and generously scattered largesse to buy a slice of nirvana, corrupting the poor who strayed across their path.

The ragged old men who warmed rheumatic joints in Gangtok's watery sun, or the ancient crones muffled in tattered wool, would never dream of asking for charity. Nor in Kewsing, cradled in a bowl of dust in the western hills, where an Indian shopkeeper looked around him to murmur: 'They might be poor, but not in spirit.'

REFERENCES

1. Joseph Dalton Hooker, *Himalayan Journals* (Ward, Lock, Bowden, London, 1891).
2. N.K. Rustomji, *Enchanted Frontiers: Sikkim, Bhutan and India's Northeast Borderlands* (Indian Council for Cultural Relations, New Delhi).
3. National Party resolution (Gangtok, 30 April 1948).

CHAPTER

7

SPIDER'S WEB

'Madame X was most assuredly a femme fatale. At least I had been assured that she had been twenty years before, and the years having dealt with her very kindly she was still a femme considerably fatale.'

GEORGE N. PATTERSON,
Up and Down Asia.

'The woman behind Kazi Lendhup Dorji's ascendance in the politics of the tiny Himalayan kingdom was Mrs. Langford-Rae, a French-speaking Belgian, who was well-known in social and political circles in the fifties and sixties. She took off for Sikkim for pastures new and married Kazi, a feudal lord, and acquired the traditional title of Kazini of Chakung. She and Hope Cooke, Chogyal's American wife, fought like Kilkenny cats, paving the way for the merger of Sikkim into the Indian union.'

BLITZ,
27 October 1979.

A stately woman with honey-blonde hair drawn into a tight bun swept into the room, long skirts rustling about her ankles. 'I am the Kazini of Chakung,' she announced. Her face was a thick smooth white, resembling the chalk masks of Japanese kabuki dancers. On it arched a pair of thin blue-black eyebrows and the scarlet gash of a painted mouth. Her long lashes were stiff with mascara. Only the eyes were real, glittering like live coals.

Kalimpong was wilting with ennui in 1961. The kindly Macdonald sisters who ran the Himalayan Hotel had suggested that a visit to Kazi Lendhup Dorji's European wife was obligatory. She was one of the few human enigmas left in a town that had known tingling excitement and was now stranded by history's receding tide. David Macdonald, their father, a small wrinkled man beaming under his knitted cap, belonged to that legendary past. The son of a Scots tea-planter and his Sikkimese Lepcha wife, he had been a British trade agent in Gyantse in Tibet and married a Nepalese woman. Their three elderly daughters, Annie Perry, Vicky Williams and Vera Macdonald, wryly described themselves as a Himalayan cocktail.

Nehru had called Kalimpong a nest of spies. Chinese Communists saw it as the command centre of British imperialism. Clinging to the foothills at about 4,000 feet, Kalimpong was once the world's pot-pourri. Its inhabitants could not always explain why they had elected to live in this particular corner of India. Each followed the discreet strand of his interests in a tangled skein of many hues and textures.

The thirteenth Dalai Lama had found asylum there. So had relatives of the deposed King Theebaw of Burma. Elderly Afghan princesses who had fled Kabul with King Amanullah could still be seen in the weekly market. Prince Peter of Greece and Denmark and his wife, Princess Irene, were said to be studying Himalayan flora until their residence permits were abruptly cancelled. Sir Tashi's sister, Rani Chuni, had retired to Bhutan House. A Tartar prince evoked memories of the court of St Petersburg. A neglected villa was pointed out as having once been Rabindranath Tagore's home. In another house had lived the Russian painter Svetoslav Roerich and his Bengali actress wife, Devika Rani. Some residents had known Denis

Conan Doyle, son of the creator of Sherlock Holmes. Buddhists, Christian missionaries, writers and retired military officers from Europe and America graced the social circle.

There was also an older Kalimpong recalled by the name: meeting place of kalons or ministers. Emissaries from Sikkim, Bhutan and Tibet used to gather there long before Kalimpong became British territory in 1865. It belonged to Sikkim until the Bhutanese seized it in 1706, the ruins of the Damsang and Dalimkote dzongs testifying to 159 years of Druk rule. But the town acquired importance only in 1900 when the trade route to Tibet was opened. Then, Kalimpong became a vital link in Lord Curzon's chain of imperial communications. Lhasa lay 350 miles to the north; the road winding for seven days through Pedong, Rishi, Rhenock, Phadamcheng and Zutuk in Sikkim to the Jelap pass. Then for another three weeks it followed the Younghusband trail across the Tibetan plateau to the forbidden city.

Kalimpong's glory lasted for about half a century until Indian and Chinese inflexibility closed the gates. From being a throbbing caravanserai on one of Asia's busiest highways, the town declined into a forlorn outpost at the end of a blind alley. Nature conspired in that decay. A ferocious cyclone swept away the toy train that chugged from Siliguri to Gyalkhola. Steam-engines were hurled down the Teesta gorge, and strips of railway line dangled from the trees.

But there was a spurt of wanton excitement just before the end. Trade had never been so prosperous. Money poured in. With the daily turnover in the busy winter months estimated at ₹ 400 million, the State Bank of India opened a branch to rake in the profits. More than 10,000 men were employed in sorting out mounds of dirty white, grey, or black wool from Tibet into neat bales for onward journey to Britain and the US. Thousands more provided fodder and maize for mules, and exotic entertainment for their masters who were determined to enjoy themselves during a ten-day respite from the privations of a bleak and dangerous road. Apart from wool and KMT silver, the caravans brought yaks' tails, musk, borax, curios and Chinese rice. They took back cement, kerosene, all the manufactures of Indian factories, and even a car for the Dalai Lama that was dismantled and carted up piece by piece. Officials turned a blind eye when rations and equipment for Mao's men and army, including jeeps from Calcutta, were similarly exported.

All this found an echo in Kalimpong's frantic pleasures. Muleteers drank and diced at the notorious Tenth Mile; eating houses remained open day and night. It was a town of lavish hospitality, intense rivalries and sudden death. A man might be bursting with arrogant exuberance one night and lying with a broken neck at the bottom of a ravine by dawn. A prominent Lhasa nobleman, known as the Rockefeller of Tibet, had given his house to the Chinese government and become Beijing's deputy trade agent. Thousand-year-old eggs were served at his parties and the guests included many exalted personages as well as outlandish seekers after strange truths in the border marches. Hordes of men employed by New Delhi's far-flung intelligence network, not only RAW but also the Subsidiary Intelligence Service which had a formal local presence, kept a close watch over this shifting cavalcade.

Vigilance was thought necessary not only because the Chinese were feeling their way into Tibet, and the Himalayan wall was no longer the 'barrier of unparalleled strength' that Sir Charles Bell had called it, but also because this shift in the balance of power threatened to have extended repercussions all along the frontier. In Bhutan House, Rani Chuni's children, Jigmie Dorji and his sister Tashi, were quietly determined to lead the Druk kingdom to full independence. In Gangtok, the Chogyal was probing the limits of India's patience. It was a time of fear and exhilaration, both sharpened by an awareness of impending change. As the shadows closed in, Kalimpong's death-rattle could be heard in the nervous gaiety of its inhabitants. If the town pondered on Tibet's fate, it was more directly involved in the tussle in and over Sikkim: between Delhi and Gangtok over the Chogyal's dreams of independence, between the palace and politicians over the trappings of power.

Lha Tsering was one of India's many agents in the game, a Tibetan by birth and, therefore, especially valuable to the intelligence service since he could mingle with the locals without exciting comment. He was accompanied in 1950 by a strange and striking European woman whom he abandoned in Kalimpong. She took a room at the Himalayan Hotel, gave lessons in English and French and lived quietly with her books. She called herself Elisa-Maria Langford-Rae, but Vicky Williams, who had peeped into the register of foreigners at the police-station, let it be known that the glamorous if no longer young blonde had been christened plain Ethel Maud. Her first appearance in Sikkim was apparently with Taya Zinkin, the journalist wife of Maurice Zinkin who retired from the ICS for a business career when India became independent. Taya was for many years the *Manchester Guardian's* India correspondent.

All that was known for certain about the mystery woman came from the not always reliable recollections of people whose paths had crossed hers. An elderly Englishman said he had met her when she was the wife of an English tea-planter in Jorhat. Delhi journalists described her as a fixture in H.V. Kamath's bachelor establishment. They had also known her as married to a director of India's health services, carrying on a vendetta against Rajkumari Amrit Kaur, her husband's minister. Mrs Langford-Rae had taught boys at St Columba's school in Delhi as well as civil service cadets. She had worked as an interpreter for the external affairs ministry. Pasupati Shumshere Jang Bahadur Rana, the royalist politician in Kathmandu, remembered her as his governess when he was a child in Delhi and his father the Nepalese ambassador. A missionary woman from Gangtok had actually run to earth Mrs Langford-Rae's sister, a doctor's widow, in the middle-class respectability of an

Edinburgh flat. 'A tiny woman pushing a shopping trolley,' the missionary reported. That was the closest that anyone ever got to her origins.

Her own stories were far more colourful. But the different versions she trotted out seldom agreed, dates never. She was Scots by birth and had been brought up in a Belgian convent. No, she was Belgian but had studied medicine in Edinburgh. The sepia photograph of a woman in veil and bustle, taken three-quarters from behind in the style of fifty years ago, was her mother, 'a dear little German baroness'. Her mother had been a French countess settled in Geneva. She had a flat in Brussels crammed with period furniture, cut-glass and antique silver. Her treasures were stored with Harrods in London, and she had ordered the store to send flowers to Sir Tashi after an operation at the London Clinic.

Her son was in the British Foreign Office. He was in the Bank of England. He had been in the colonial police. He was really her stepson. Her own son, Rory (Roderick), had been in tea and was killed in a motoring accident in north Bengal. The Macdonalds remembered him as a pleasant young man who had visited Kalimpong but, to their surprise, stayed at their Himalayan Hotel instead of with his mother. She talked of Kemal Ataturk and Chou En-lai, of Mussolini, Sarvepalli Radhakrishnan and Pasupati's grandfather, Maharajah Mohan Shumshere Jang Bahadur Rana. She claimed an uncle had taken her for safety across Siberia to China when war broke out, but no one was sure whether it was World War I or II or some minor Balkan conflict. She said she had lived in Burma and Hongkong, and recounted precise incidents about anonymous people of many nationalities in vague places. Her husbands seemed to have been legion.

Late one evening, after the chhang flagons had been filled many times, she peremptorily ordered 'the photograph' to be brought. It turned out to be the silver-framed portrait of a splendidly moustachioed officer covered in ribbons and medals. 'My father!' she announced with a superb flourish; then as the gathering waited expectantly, 'Marshal Carl Gustaf Mannerheim of Finland.' Could that, I wondered, explain an ambiguous accent that was never quite pukka and the sudden mispronunciations that had always intrigued me.

By 1961 she had been married to Kazi for several years, her account of how it happened predictably embellished into an improbable fairytale. 'I was just going to bed in Delhi when Maya Devi Chhetri (Kalimpong's MP, Nepalese naturally) phoned to say she was bringing some people to see me. I was so tired and didn't want to be bothered, but what could I do? Dear Maya Devi was so insistent!' So Mrs Langford-Rae struggled back into a dress and quickly laid out some snacks. 'And then they arrived and Maya Devi, who really is a sweetie, had this rather strange creature with her who didn't say a word and I said to myself, "Oh dear, another of those dumb hillbillys" and put him out of my mind.'

The visitors stayed on and their reluctant hostess, though weary and nearly dropping off to sleep, was too polite to say so. 'I was bored and exhausted when suddenly Maya Devi suggested we should all go out to dinner. I grabbed at the chance to get some rest and at once said "You go on, do!"' But her guests would not hear of it. 'A sandwich and a cup of tea with a book was all I wanted but they were ever so persistent. The argument went on and on and I didn't want to go out at all, I only wanted to get rid of them, when our mountain friend, who hadn't opened his mouth all evening, suddenly said, "You come too!" and I said to myself, "Good heavens, it speaks! Well at least that's something". You know, I really had begun to think it was a vegetable or something.' So she changed again and then, just as all of them were setting out, Kazi grabbed her hand and mumbled 'You marry me, yes?'

'It was so weird I didn't know what to say, whether to laugh or cry. I mean, he couldn't possibly have been serious, could he?' There was a peal of thunder just then. As the rain poured down in buckets, Kazi clapped his hands and let out a guffaw of pleased boyish laughter. 'It really was delightful to hear, so simple and unaffected. They told me that rain and thunder are auspicious omens in Sikkim.'

So they were married by a magistrate and the marriage lines were safely locked away with a firm of solicitors in Calcutta.

They could not have been a more ill-matched pair. The bride claimed to be fluent in several European languages. Kazi spoke only Sikkimese and broken Hindustani. The language of the kitchen, in which memsahibs give household instructions to bearers, was her only means of communicating with her husband, an appropriate one as it happened. She was an accomplished woman of the world, wrapped in an air of rococo intrigue. Kazi had never ventured beyond the subcontinent. Both had enigmatic pasts but Kazi's was slightly less inaccessible. Many doubted his claim to the Chakung title. Even more questions were asked about the source of his wealth. Kazi was nearly sixty at the time and already married to a woman of property. His family was implacably opposed to this unsuitable second alliance. Rumour had it that his nephew offered Mrs Langford-Rae a blank cheque as her price to quietly go away. There were tantrums, too, in Chakung where the women folk barricaded themselves inside the family house and pelted the foreign intruder with pots and pans. The family never did accept her; years later Kalimpong watched in amusement while Kazini and her husband's great-nephew shrieked abuse at each other in the market-place.

There were stormy scenes with her husband, too, and shrieking tantrums that any passer-by could hear. A friend whom Kazi summoned once to calm her down found Kazini 'prostrate on the drawing-room carpet, as though she had been biting it in her rage'.[1] Nevertheless, the marriage was the turning-point in Kazi's life. He had someone to write his petitions and proclamations. His first wife conveniently dying, her fortune was used to renovate the Kalimpong bungalow and furnish it for comfort as well as Sikkimese elegance. It was named Chakung House. At the same time, Lendhup Dorji, who had always signed himself L.D. Kazi, adopted the Western-style territorial dignity of Kazi Sahib of Chakung. On occasion his wife even prefixed it with 'Excellency'. The metamorphosis was reflected in the well-cut tweeds and khos of soft Tibetan wool or glowing Chinese brocade that Kazi began to wear. He and his wife took to sending out Christmas cards decorated with a Sikkimese symbol cunningly stylised to resemble a European heraldic crest. But more significantly for Sikkim, Kazi became the symbol and spearhead of a relentless campaign against the durbar.

The cause of this enmity was never revealed. The Chogyal confessed bewilderment. Kazini herself talked righteously of democracy and human rights. Sonam Tshering thought she had expected a senior position in Sikkim's education department. Others felt she had married Kazi in hopes of dazzling the simple Sikkimese with her worldly elan and was bitterly disappointed to discover that not only did her husband not have a grand position at court but that her own talents seemed tawdry in comparison with the cosmopolitan refinement of the Chogyal's stylish sisters. A few sniggered that the Chogyal, with always an eye for a pretty face, had given offence by completely ignoring Kazini's overripe charms.

One of her earliest clashes with the durbar was over a photograph caption in *Onlooker* (a glossy society magazine in those days) in which she had imaginatively described herself as consort of a liberal ruler who had introduced many reforms in his 'state'. When Sir Tashi's secretary protested, Kazini explained she had meant 'estate'. On another occasion she told reporters that Kazi was president of Sikkim. After another royal reprimand, she corrected the description to president of the Sikkim National Congress.

Kazini's posturing reflected her thwarted longings. She had a generous word only for people who could be of use or whom she could patronise. Lhanzin-La, never quite in the durbar's charmed circle, was therefore the only connection of the Chogyal's she spoke of with kindness. Athing-La's birth and title, both superior to Kazi's, aroused all her fury. When Karma Topden married into English county society, the great-granddaughter of a Scottish earl, the unwitting bride provoked sharp ridicule. The fashionable Coo Coo La was particularly resented. Kazini never referred to the proud princess as anything but 'Mrs Pheunkhyang'. She was initially ambivalent towards the Chogyal, perhaps still nursing dreams of eventual royal favours, until Hope's advent killed all hope.

Rory had just died and since she did not attend many palace ceremonies in any case, the Chogyal rather hoped that mourning for her son would keep her away from the wedding. But he had reckoned without the feminine curiosity and strategic sense of an adversary who would not for anything in the world miss this opportunity to take stock of Sikkim's Western first lady and impress her own presence on the important foreign visitors who were expected. Other guests say Kazini strolled among the festive throng, tears of mascara streaming down her heavily powdered face, hysterically pouring out her inconsolable grief to anyone she managed to buttonhole. They woke up next morning to find on their bedside tables a typed verse making fun of 'Hope with her Bowery accent'. No one in Sikkim had heard of the New York district, Bowery. But Kazini wiped her tears, slapped on fresh mascara, and returned chuckling to Kalimpong. The show of grief had been an act anyway for she told someone 'she had no maternal feelings and was quite indifferent to her son... His death had not affected her in the slightest.' During his visit to Kalimpong, 'Kazini took no more notice of him than if he had been the most casual of casual visitors.'[2]

Such games added piquancy to the town's rather dull social life. Kazini also turned out to be a racy raconteuse, full of scandalous accounts about the royal family. Most of her stories were libellous. All were in bad taste. But they could be funny. They depicted the Chogyal and Hope as empty, vain and tyrannical. The tales spread, and people who knew nothing else about Sikkim came to hear maliciously witty descriptions of the royal family's idiosyncrasies. As the years passed, Kazini's blonde hair thinned, whitened and was stained with henna, the face behind the mask crumpled into a fissured field of wrinkles. The upright figure bulged in its stiff encasing brocade. But the campaign continued, poisoning Indian and foreign opinion. As Satyendra R. Shukla put it in *Sikkim: The Story of Integration*, 'Their house at Kalimpong became the frequent rendezvous of the journalists and politicians looking for facts—or fiction—which she doled out with ease and poise with every peg of whisky.'[3]

Diplomats, civil servants, politicians and newspapermen were the special targets of her attention. They were regaled with grave allegations of corruption in the durbar, of political machinations and administrative chaos enlivened with spicy anecdotes of the Chogyal's liaisons and the Gyalmo's affectations. Whether entirely fabricated or grotesquely exaggerated, the stories found a mark, not least in Gangtok where the Chogyal seethed with impotent anger. Eventually, he persuaded the West Bengal authorities to withdraw her special permit to live in Kalimpong. It was a short-lived victory, for Kazini soon bounced back venomously, vowing revenge. 'I was burning with fever,' she exclaimed dramatically. 'They just seized me and flung me into the aeroplane wrapped in only an old blanket in which I was shivering.' In a burst of histrionics, she flung herself across the room to lie huddled on a divan, simulating fever-racked agony. 'I went to see Mrs Gandhi, whom I had known, you know, when we were in the same sanatorium in Switzerland,' and her voice became soft and pleading as her hands folded in supplication to describe the appeal. "'Induji," I said, "what have I done wrong that this tyrant should have me driven out of my home? And why should the West Bengal government abet his nefarious schemes?"' Whatever Mrs Gandhi, who was not then prime minister, may have replied, Kazini claimed to have access to a higher court. 'Sir Alec Douglas-Home himself wrote to demand "Why has this woman been separated from her husband?"' This was delivered in tones of rousing indignation. At this point in the narrative, Kazini brought out an envelope emblazoned with the House of Commons portcullis and waved it in the air. '"One seeing is worth a thousand hearings," as Chou En-lai always used to tell me.' But no one ever saw the name on the envelope or, for that matter, if it had any inscription at all.

But it was not all fun and frolic. Around Kazini gathered a number of educated young Nepalese men who were intoxicated by her eloquence and convinced that destiny had singled them out to re-enact the French Revolution. Lal Bahadur Basnet, who had been an education corps NCO and spoke French passably well, was an early protégé. Krishna Chandra Pradhan came later and so did N.K. Subeidi. But the most favoured was Nar Bahadur Khatiawara, a peasant lad from near Gyalzing whom Kazini adopted and put through school and college in Kalimpong. Khatiawara was by far the most promising of the lot. He brought in several other youths and talked with gusto of the village organisation he was building up: 'Our Nepalese members are called "garam dal" while the Bhutiya-Lepchas are the "naram dal". One is for fighting, the other for agitational propaganda.' The distinction between 'garam' and 'naram', militant and moderate in political terms, also revealed Sikkim's great divide of ethnicity and temperament.

There was no doubt as to where young Khatiawara stood. 'I will drink this Chogyal's blood!' he would scream, raising clenched fists to the ceiling. But Kazini was his adored 'mama'; publicly he would say of Kazi and Kazini: 'They are our *rashtriya pita* and *rashtriya mata*, national father and national mother.' Kazini preened with satisfaction. One day she added: 'Actually, you know, they call Kazi sahib the Mahatma Gandhi of Sikkim!' The hint was at once taken, and for a few weeks Kazi basked in the new honorific.

Basnet, who became the SNC's joint secretary, recalled in *Sikkim: A Short Political History* that Kazini took over the party's publicity, produced a steady stream of political propaganda and built up her husband's public image. 'If the activities of the party lacked colour, it was amply supplied by the fertile imagination of the Kazini; and where the party leaders failed to exhibit courage and determination, the Kazini's vigorous language lent all the fire needed.' But as Basnet admits, propaganda outstripped reality, and 'newspaper cuttings, the end product of the Kazini's toil' boasted of winning many more battles than were ever even attempted. 'The Sikkim National Congress was kept alive and kicking, its image shining, almost wholly by the efforts of the indefatigable Kazini.'[4]

If newspaper claims were hollow, they nevertheless irritated the Chogyal who set a high price on press coverage. He was constantly upset by the personal and political invectives published in the *Himalayan Observer,* a Kalimpong periodical, and occasionally complained to the PO, who merely shrugged to say that India believed in free expression and an uncontrolled press. He should have anticipated the snub, but prescience was never one of the Chogyal's strongest qualities. He bungled even more badly over a series of three articles on Sikkim's political and land rights that Basnet wrote for a leftist Calcutta weekly, *Now*. Since the magazine had a limited circulation, the provocation could have been ignored. Instead, the durbar arrested Basnet and charged him with sedition. The charges were not pressed, but the case seemed to confirm misgivings about Sikkim's ruler.

The action taken against one of Kazini's very few female protégés was equally ham-handed. Ruth Karthak Halim was a

Lepcha woman married to an Indian businessman. Possibly prodded by Kazini, she claimed descent from Thekong-tek and suggested that the throne was hers by right. She then formed an Independent Front to contest the polls which she could not do, having forfeited her status in Sikkim on her marriage. In any case, Mrs Halim was totally without influence. But instead of just debarring her, the durbar kept her in jail for about four months.

All this was grist to Kazini's mill. She complained that the state of emergency proclaimed in Sikkim in 1962, during India's war with China, was only another bid to suppress popular rights. She denounced the new thirty-one-member people's consultative committee as an instrument of the durbar. She told everyone she would hold on to her British passport until such time as she could be a citizen—not subject—of Sikkim. Political machinations absorbed much of her energy in the middle and late 1960s. A piqued Basnet had walked out of her circle to form the Janata Party. She hoped the National Party would succumb to quarrels among Martam Topden, Netuk Tsering and Phurba Maila who was elected president in 1969. Her husband was locked in a tussle for leadership with Bhim Bahadur Gurung, the SNC general secretary. In a farcical denouement, Kazi and Gurung expelled each other from the party. But Gurung, Netuk Tsering and Nahakul Pradhan were made executive councillors even though Kazi won the general seat in the 1967 elections by a substantial margin, and his party returned eight members. The National Party had five and the State Congress only two.

Kazini was bitterly disappointed, and the SNC stridently returned to the demands of domestic revolution and closer ties with India. The State Congress had lost its radical fervour. Kashi Raj Pradhan had been removed from the leadership, and his nephew, Nahakul, was a circumspect man. If the Chogyal would not make her husband executive councillor, Kazini would not recognise the durbar's status. 'I don't know what Sardar Patel was thinking of,' she would say. 'Why on earth he left out these three Himalayan states when the princes were merged, I just cannot imagine!'

No one was quite sure at this time of Kazi Lendhup Dorji's own views. He had very little to say for himself, and nothing when his wife was around. But in reflective moments, he would muse aloud on how the Namgyals had been unjust to the Khangsarpas, recall an ancestor who had apparently saved a ruler from the Tibetans, talk of the services of Phodang Lama and complain of being deprived of the well-endowed abbotship of Rumtek. He was proud, too, of his labours as executive councillor in charge of agriculture. If his wife were not present, Kazi would pull out a report he had compiled on the Geba farm and draw the visitor's attention to the Chogyal's note of approval at the bottom. His platform rhetoric notwithstanding, Kazi thought only in terms of personal equations. No sense of mission inspired his conversation; he certainly did not appear to be an ardent republican. The impression he conveyed was of an amiable old man who barely understood the things that were said and done in his name.

His wife was far more complex. The title she affected, the emblems she flaunted, the names of the great she so casually dropped and her punctilious insistence on social niceties suggested the tarnished glitter of European salons and boudoirs before World War II. She might have been Mrs James, the humble subaltern's wife from Dinapore, who became Lola Montez the Spanish dancer, was courted by Tsar Nicholas at St Petersburg, and captivated Ludwig of Bavaria who created her Baronne de Rosenthal and Countess von Lansfeld. She was delighted when I sent her a postcard of Lola Montez's portrait among the court beauties in Munich's royal palace with the inscription 'Thinking of you!' I am told she showed it round at her dinner parties.

She was obsessed by rank. Her campaign for Mrs Halim's mythical pretensions was a feature of this fixation. She sometimes said that Taring Raja, then living quietly in the exiled Dalai Lama's entourage, was Sikkim's real king. Carried away by her dreams, Kazini even once or twice hinted that her husband had a better claim to the throne than the Chogyal. She would sometimes suggest, with Kazi vigorously nodding away, that he had been adopted by Sidkeong Tulku, the tenth ruler. But vain, ambitious and scheming though she was, Kazini also knew that royal fantasies would not help to promote her husband's position or earn the Indian government's backing. On the contrary, his appeal in Sikkim as well as for Indians lay in his continuing opposition to the durbar. Asked if she wanted to be the next Gyalmo, Kazini drew herself up to her full height to announce: 'No, but I shall be the first lady of the first president of Sikkim!'

The mystery was that after the one abortive attempt at deportation, the Chogyal always treated Kazini with more than the consideration shown to the wives of other prominent Sikkimese. There were greeting cards at Christmas, warm replies to Kazini's occasional letters, and gracious courtesy when they happened to meet. That was always his way, grumbled palace officials, who were sometimes obliged to take measures against the Sikkim National Congress. They were convinced their master would not have been half as affable if Kazini had not been European. Kind and sensitive though he was, with a deep pride in his country and its traditions, he yet seemed sometimes to trust suave Indians more than the most devoted Sikkimese, and any Westerner in preference to the most suave Indian. It was a typically Asian weakness. The Sikkimese talked of the hospitality he lavished on Indian army officers, the demands of European guests who were not particularly exalted or useful, and about the Chogyal's graciousness to Karma Topden's English wife. The durbar was baffled and never quite sure of how he really felt towards Kazini.

REFERENCES

1. Sangharakshita, *Precious Teacher: Indian Memoirs of an English Buddhist*, (Windhorse, Birmingham, 2007).
2. Ibid.
3. Satyendra R. Shukla, *Sikkim: The Story of Integration* (S. Chand, New Delhi, 1976).
4. Lal Bahadur Basnet, *Sikkim: A Short Political History* (S. Chand, New Delhi, 1974).

CHAPTER

8

POISED IN TIME

'The old year was expelled and the new year ushered in with a pantomimic display; and a form of dance also played a part in the ritual concerned with the exorcizing of maligned spirits and the destruction of human enemies.'

THE EARL OF RONALDSHAY,
Lord of the Thunderbolts: Sikkim, Chumbie and Bhutan.

'The contemporary polity of Sikkim is passing through a process of integration of tribalism, the lamaist traditionalism and liberal democracy.'

AWADESH COOMAR SINGH,
Politics of Sikkim.

The Iron Dog year drew to an end with slow ceremony, the dances dragging out in a watery Himalayan sunshine. The light caught the Tsuk-la-khang's golden pinnacle. It glowed on the velvet and brocade of Bhutiya-Lapcha dignitaries, their kazinis dripping with turquoise and corals, and on the jewelled sarees of Indian wives. Nepalese officials wore jaunty embroidered caps, dark jackets and white jodhpurs.

It had started early in the morning, the Kagyet ritual unreeling like a slow-motion film. The performers were all monks and acolytes from Pemayangtse. Their first number was the *a-tas-ras,* a frolic of nimbly leaping clowns, followed by one ponderous presentation after another. Cavorting stags and rattling skeletons, swooping birds, pounding yaks and rolling waves of blood reflected Denzong's vivid imagery. Most dancers were of fearsome aspect. The black-hat warriors, massive in ornate masks and cascading robes, the *thromo-tsoglen* female deities symbolising wrath accepting divine prasad, cymbal dancers, the *tro-thromo* spirits also depicting anger in male and female masks. An intense, exacting and, to the uninitiated, somewhat monotonous drama. It paused only for *sungkhor*, portraying the death of the demon when the lamas chanted prayers and rejoiced at the victory of good over evil.

The Gyalmo, shimmering in silver and blue, stepped hastily back on her sandalled feet to escape any contamination from paper effigies of the dying year's sins as they were ritualistically burned. 'It's terribly unlucky for the ashes to touch you,' she whispered. 'The Sikkimese were probably the first to invent the fall-out!' Hope had reason to flee. For superstition was reinforced in 1957 when Sangey Deki, the Chogyal's first wife, died six months after a scrap of charred paper from the *hom* fire fluttered to the edge of her kho.

It would be another couple of days before the Losoong festival ushered in the year of the Hog. Based on the Kali Chakra, which Tibet imported from India, the Sikkimese calendar runs into a cycle of twelve years, each named after an animal: rat, bull, tiger, hare, dragon, snake, horse, sheep, monkey, bird, dog and hog. There is a shorter governing cycle called after the five elements (earth, water, fire, tree and iron) and each of these lasts for two years, though the animal year changes roughly every twelve months. The year of the Iron Dog was, therefore, followed by the year of the Iron Hog, to be succeeded in time by the Earth Rat year and then the Earth Bull year. But the lunar chart, which determines the Kali chakra, does not always exactly synchronise with Western calendar dates, and there was an interregnum of a few days between the end of the Dog year and the beginning of that of the Hog. It was symbolic of the suspense in which Sikkim was poised. The Denzong kingdom hovered between a discarded past and an unrevealed future.

T.N. Kaul blamed the Gyalmo for this uncertainty. He believed that the Chogyal's 'American marriage, perhaps, made him believe that through extraneous influence he could ensure American and Canadian support for his claims to independence'.[1] Her advent certainly added a new dimension to perspectives. Hope aroused awareness of the world in Sikkim and made the world conscious of her husband's tucked-away kingdom. The first entry in the palace guest-house visitors' book reading 'Hope Cooke, Seale Harbor, Maine, USA' always made me wonder if there were no visitors before her advent or no book to record them. But though guests and guest-house, even perhaps a register to record arrivals and departures, may have always existed, Hope replaced casual usage with method and a sense of purpose. She tried to choreograph Sikkim's cultural heritage for presentation on an international stage and commissioned Satyajit Ray to make a film about the kingdom. She was disappointed with the product. To her chagrin, it hardly dwelt on vivacious national pageants like the Kagyet dances or traditional arts as displayed in monasteries.

What Rustomji attempted in architecture, the Gyalmo accomplished in interior décor, dress design and school curricula. The palace's heavy Victorian furniture was sent into storage and replaced with low cushioned divans, carved and gilded chokseys, and wondrously woven carpets. A series of textbooks was planned to inspire national pride. Promising young men and women were helped to study abroad, especially in the US, where Hope's contacts enabled them to gain college admission. The Palden Thondup Cottage Industries Institute embarked on more imaginative new production lines. Even her own personality altered. Gone was the casual young girl in a scanty dress who had romped gaily in Darjeeling. There blossomed instead a willowy woman with a string of pearls twisted in her high coiffure and eyes shadowed to darken her fairness. Hope wore khos on ceremonial occasions, but otherwise favoured the Nepalese saree drawn tightly under her arms, or a length of fabric wrapped about her in Lepcha style. Her movements became slower, her smile more distant, and her voice dropped till it was hardly audible. She wisped along barely seeming to touch the ground, an ethereal being who, critics murmured, overlooked Sikkim's flesh and blood to go into ecstasies over the country's spirit.

In their different ways, the Gyalmo, Kazini, and Princess Coo Coo La were spurred by similar ambitions. Each wanted recognition for a more important Sikkim. But each wanted it for herself. There were operational differences too. Hope may have believed that her connections abroad would exert themselves on her behalf. Coo Coo La had powerful friends in New Delhi and expected them to yield to her persuasion. Kazini hoped that her political and newspaper contacts would benefit her husband, though it was never certain whether the public personalities she mentioned so glibly really were close friends. The Chogyal could not have found it easy coping with three domineering females. Happily, he was spared Kazini's proximity and, therefore, had no direct experience of her tantrums. But he, too, believed resolutely in Sikkim's destiny.

Politicians and civil servants shared the king's faith and approvingly read Kaiser Bahadur Thapa's fulminations in *Sikkim*. 'If you keep a servant you have to pay his wages,' was Netuk Tsering's curt dismissal of Indian aid. Four senior officers—Jigdal Densapa, Rasaily, Kunzang Sherab and Dorji Dahdul—had formed an external affairs committee to advise on relations with India and future ties with other countries. The initiative gave oblique warning of Gangtok's intention one day to manage its own foreign policy. Two of its members always accompanied the Chogyal to New Delhi, and everyone knew the committee was unlikely to take any step without royal clearance.

Gangtok's study forum was another such initiative. Its 150 members were also drawn from the upper reaches of the civil service. Densapa and Rasaily were again the leading figures, but the group included Chandra Das Rai, who had returned to administration after his unrewarding political flirtation, and Keshab Chandra Pradhan, the chief conservator of forests. About thirty or forty of these rather staid bureaucrats met at irregular intervals over tea or drinks to discuss administrative reform and future strategy in a somewhat casual fashion. No resolutions were ever adopted. Politics was strictly avoided, and the Chogyal did not consult the forum. None of the members of either group was in the first flush of youth; many were of noble birth, all were men of substance. All held responsible jobs. Yet, ludicrously, they were viewed in India as dangerous revolutionaries. B.K. Daschowdhury, a Lok Sabha member, warned the Indian Parliament that there existed in Gangtok a 'young study group on the very lines of the Red Guards in China with the help and aid of Chinese funds and that this organisation has started very strong anti-Indian propaganda in Sikkim and neighbouring border areas creating great trouble throughout north Bengal and thereby threatening the security of India'.

The charge was as laughable as the language. But it is true that, taking their cue from the ruler, some articulate young Sikkimese let it be known that they felt they had to live under stifling restrictions. They did not actually mention independence, but said they were anxious to express themselves and to project their country's identity. The demand for a radio station, which had dragged on since 1957, was a case in point.

Nehru had agreed to grant Sikkim a transmitter, and his consent was reported in Indian newspapers. But the PO convinced the external affairs ministry that Bhutan, Nepal,

Tibet and China would see broadcasts from Gangtok as proof of Sikkim's sovereignty. It was impossible to officially retract the prime minister's public commitment. But even if foreign service mandarins could not cancel a prime ministerial decision, they could obstruct execution. Unaware of these machinations or, perhaps, to keep up the charade, Keskar, who had moved to the information and broadcasting ministry, told Parliament on 20 April 1960 that preliminary investigations had been completed and installation would depend on the conclusion of All-India Radio's technical discussions with the durbar. The minister added that the station would entail an initial investment of ₹ 184,000 and a recurring annual charge of ₹ 250,000. Though India would provide most of the money, Sikkim would also make a small contribution.

Four months later, Subimal Dutt advised the Chogyal not to press the demand, hinting that accommodation would be suitably rewarded. A consolation prize was offered in December when the Chogyal was promised an 'important' position on the advisory committee for AIR's Darjeeling station. It was about to start broadcasting to Tibet's restive Khampas, and the Chogyal's participation would lend credibility to propaganda. But when the Chogyal called on Nehru the very next day (9 December), the prime minister again assured him that a small transmitter for internal radio programmes had already been sanctioned. Nehru also said the necessary departmental instructions had already been issued.

The bureaucracy then countered by provoking a controversy over the name. The durbar wanted 'Radio Sikkim'. The external affairs ministry insisted on 'All-India Radio, Gangtok'. Deeming half a loaf better than nothing, the Chogyal reluctantly agreed, but officials at once pointed out that since all available frequencies were booked, it would be impossible to find a free slot for the kingdom. First, they suggested that Sikkim should be content with allotted time on the Indian intelligence network transmitter, which would beam short Sikkimese programmes every day; then they proposed the alternative of a daily half-hour feature from AIR's Kurseong station.

A team of experts was sent to Gangtok when neither alternative was accepted. It reported that the only building suitable for studios, laboratories, recording rooms and offices was the White Hall, just below the Ridge, then used as a club. The durbar offered to build a house to specifications, but the team was not agreeable. It had to be the White Hall or nothing. When the Chogyal agreed even to this, J.C. Mathur, AIR's director-general, raised an even more insuperable objection. Aware that the White Hall had barely any grounds, he demanded at least seventy acres for a 50-kilowatt station and its transmission aerials. The durbar suggested nearly a thousand acres of vacant land around Namphong hill, but Mathur said the shadows there would interfere with sound-waves.

One obstacle after another was raised. New Delhi also became increasingly dilatory in its correspondence, not replying to letters from Gangtok until several months had elapsed and then only after repeated reminders. Eventually, communications were altogether ignored and the matter petered out. The file was presumably closed and put away in some dusty cupboard in South Block. Nehru's consent was never withdrawn but the calculated procrastination in which India's civil servants excel won the day. 'You know what the prime minister was like,' a senior Indian diplomat confessed to me many years later. 'He made these extravagant promises and left us to wriggle out of them.'

South Block officials could not similarly prevent the construction of Sikkim House, the most exquisite example of the new building style, in New Delhi's Chanakyapuri diplomatic enclave. But the external affairs ministry flatly refused to sanction the appointment of a Sikkimese representative. Even Indian state governments had their own men in the capital, but the durbar was told that it could not communicate with the Indian government except through the PO in Gangtok.

There had been other setbacks. Faced with criticism in the Indian press which accused Gangtok of insufficiently applauding India's military efforts to save Sikkim from China's aggression, the durbar had issued a terse statement on 16 February 1961. It explained that the Sikkim government was perfectly satisfied with defence arrangements and did not wish to alter Sikkim's protected status. But in the course of talks in New Delhi in September 1962 the Chogyal suggested that India sponsor his country's admission to the Colombo Plan. The study forum later endorsed the plea. So did Sikkim's legislative council. The request was extended to include membership of the Universal Postal Union, World Health Organisation, International Labour Organisation and a number of other UN agencies.

Though Kaul and other friends encouraged these hopes, the external affairs ministry retorted that a protected kingdom could not join international organisations. However, the Chogyal had done his homework. Marriage and increased travel had widened his outlook. Leading jurists abroad were ready to advise him. He had profited from the enterprise of his Bhutanese cousins. New Delhi discovered that it was no longer dealing with a backwoods potentate, but a lively prince conversant with international law and usage. Irritated by this surprise, Kaul and others, who feared the erosion of their own influence in Gangtok, blamed the Gyalmo. They warned her husband that his foreign friends were trying to destabilise India and create a beachhead for Chinese expansion.

The Chogyal's conduct could not be faulted. When Chester Bowles, Washington's extremely popular ambassador in New Delhi, offered economic help, the ruler at once advised him to route it through India. At the same time, he reminded South Block that the Colombo Plan had already admitted dependencies such as Borneo and Sarawak. San Marino and the Vatican were both members of the UPU. San Marino and Liechtenstein were parties to the statute of the International Court of Justice under Article 93(2) of its charter. Monaco was in the UNESCO and WHO. Kuwait and Mauritania had belonged to several UN agencies before they joined the UN. Though North Vietnam was denied UN membership, it had been welcomed into the ILO, WHO and UNESCO. His case was that these technical and cultural organisations did not insist on full sovereignty. Bhutan provided the obvious precedent: India had led it into the Colombo Plan in 1962 and into the UPU seven years later.

Some Sikkimese affected a mild contempt for the more successful Druk kingdom. 'They were still rolling up their land records and storing them in the rafters when we had a proper system of registration,' exclaimed Jigdal Densapa. Bhutan had no economic plans until Athing-La went there in 1961 as secretary-general of development. Bhutan was the bigger and more populous country but it was not unified under a single government until the end of 1907, when Sir Ugyen Wangchuck, the Tongsa Penlop, was installed as the first hereditary king. The Namgyals had reigned for six centuries. Their ancestors had ruled in Tibet and India since the beginning of time. Sikkim boasted elected councils and an organised administration when bloodthirsty chieftains held Bhutan from its towering dzongs.

Many of the Sikkimese kazis had opposed Rani Chuni's wedding in 1918 to Sonam Tobgye Dorji. They felt that Thutob Namgyal's daughter should aim higher than a Bhutanese chief who was not of equally grand lineage. But disapproval turned to chagrin when they discovered that, though only recently ennobled by the British, the Dorjis were a rich and splendid clan with vast estates in Ha and magnificent properties in Kalimpong and elsewhere. Sonam Tobgye Dorji's father was in effect prime minister of Bhutan. He was as trusted by his royal master as by the British viceroy, and exercised a decisive influence in shaping Indian policy along the border. The Dorji position was later to be further consolidated when Raja Sonam's and Rani Chuni's beautiful younger daughter, Ashi Kesang, married King Jigme Dorji Wangchuk, the third Druk Gyalpo. Her brother Jigmie, the Chogyal's friend and cousin, became Bhutan's prime minister.

The British styled the Bhutanese ruler Maharaja and granted him a fifteen-gun salute. When the treaty of Punakha was executed in 1910, Sir Charles Bell, then PO, informed London: 'By one o'clock the signing and sealing of the treaty was over and Bhutan was incorporated in the British empire.' Sir Edward Grey, then British foreign secretary, confirmed three weeks later: 'That treaty puts Bhutan, as far as the conduct of its foreign relations is concerned, on the same footing with Sikkim, whose status is recognised by the *wai-wu pu* (as the Chinese foreign office was called after its reconstitution in 1900)'.[2] Right up to 1940, the *Memorandum on Indian States* listed Bhutan with such minor principalities as Alwar, Dewas and Jaisalmer. Ten years later, Sir Benegal Narsing Rau admitted in *India's Constitution in the Making* that 'the precise status of the territory may be said to be left undetermined'. We know that Nehru always bracketed together the two Himalayan kingdoms. But his successors recognised His Highness the Maharaja of Bhutan as 'His Majesty the King' and posted a special officer in Thimpu in 1968.

The Chogyal knew that Bhutan's path had not been easy. New Delhi had not been amused when the kingdom's national assembly, the Tsongdu, met in May 1960 to express reservations about Article 2 of the 1940 treaty which stipulated that 'the government of Bhutan agrees to be guided by the advice of the government of India in regard to its external relations'. The Dorjis had obtained assurances from several countries that they would recognise Bhutanese passports and stamps before India would yield to the fait accompli. Jigmie Dorji's murder in 1964 was never fully explained. His younger brother, Lendhup, and sister, the indomitable Ashi Tashi, were forced to flee to Nepal; and Queen Kesang was all but supplanted by the king's Tibetan mistress whom the Indian authorities treated to royal honours.

New Delhi's tepid support for the 1965 international convention on the transit trade of landlocked countries was explained by fears of the benefits that the three Himalayan kingdoms might demand. Considerable pressure was exerted three years later to exclude Bhutan from the Vienna conference on the law on treaties. Among the topics on the agenda was the Vienna convention's provisions for the denunciation, suspension and termination of unequal agreements. If knowledge of this right had carefully to be kept from the Bhutanese, it had to be concealed no less scrupulously from the Sikkimese.

The durbar learnt during the Kagyet dances that India and Bhutan were about to exchange accredited envoys, and that the PO, already deprived of Tibet, would now lose jurisdiction in Bhutan. It had heard only two weeks earlier of Thimpu's application to the UN secretary-general. The effect was electric. Jigdal Densapa had studied international law at Exeter University in Britain. An Australian diplomat once described him as the only modern man in Gangtok. Meticulous in speech, punctilious, even cautious to a fault, the Chogyal's bachelor secretary was entirely dedicated to his master's cause. With a thorough grasp of diplomatic etiquette, he understood the implications of the India-Bhutan agreement on envoys. The Sikkimese could not but contrast this concession to Bhutan's status with the ungraciousness with which their own king had been treated a few months earlier when King Birendra of Nepal was married. The Chogyal refused to go because, acting on New Delhi's advice, Kathmandu decided to seat him with heads of government and not of state. Three Sikkimese councillors were given ministerial rank and sent instead, but as an India House official caustically pointed out, the elevation could not mean anything since Sikkim did not have a ministry.

• • •

Attention drifted away from the slowly spiralling figures outside the Tsuk-la-khang. 'Truly, truly,' lisped the Gyalmo as gyrating lamas laboured into a second session, 'we could be of great help to India at the United Nations'. Densapa had all the figures at his fingertips. There were smaller countries in the world body. Some members were less populous. Many could not claim the streamlined administration, independent judiciary and thrusting planning system that were Sikkim's pride. The group around the royal family watched the Chogyal brooding in his canary-yellow satin kho frosted with gold embroidery, the colour of kings according to the antique prescription of China's Chi'ng dynasty. The *wu-sha norbui tok shen,* Sikkim's fur-trimmed crown, a short jacket, the sleeveless vestment called *nazah,* and appliqué felt boots completed his striking ensemble. The two senior princes, Tenzing and Wangchuk, slim athletic youths, also glowed yellow and gold like their father.

A woman's voice rose hissing into the silence. 'Look at Genghis Khan pottering about his tin-pot state!' It must have been audible to everyone, though not a head turned. Kazini had announced her presence.

Husband and wife had taken time off from intrigue to make one of their rare appearances at court. They had driven up the dustily winding road from Kalimpong in Kazi's ramshackle jeep and set up camp in a borrowed basement room below Deolali bustee. It was a humble abode for a woman who claimed such grand antecedents and had set her sights so high. Her rancour was raspingly evident as palace bearers, stocky little Lepcha lads in scarlet-trimmed white khos, swept past with trays of beer and champagne and mounds of Tibetan delicacies. 'Bouncing British brigadiers with bone between their ears...,' she sang out as the Sidlon, I.S. Chopra, strolled up with his rolling cavalry officer's gait. Taken aback, Chopra smiled weakly and edged away. Just then the Chogyal's two youngest children, Palden and Hope Leezum, streaked past and Kazini exclaimed, 'Aren't they delightful little Anglo-Indians!'

Kazi stood away from his wife. Shy and gentle, he seemed awkwardly aware of his ambivalent position at court. He had not yet summoned up enough courage publicly to challenge the durbar. Nevertheless, Kazi was not sure of his welcome. He had taken a momentous political step and was anxious to test the atmosphere. In all his blazing finery, Kazi seemed ill at ease, as always nervously wringing his hands, eager for any opportunity to talk.

His discomfiture arose out of the 1970 elections, significant because, for the first time, Sikkimese politicians demanded the right to form a government. Initially, 114 candidates entered the lists for eighteen seats; though most of them dropped out, interest was high and more than 50,000 people cast their votes. For the first time, too, political ferment reflected the durbar's anxieties. Nahakul Pradhan's campaign speeches demanded that Sikkim should enjoy the same privileges as Bhutan. Janata Party leaders promised to end Indian protection. The National Party was most vociferous, threatening countrywide disturbances if Gangtok were not allowed to manage its own foreign relations. 'We are like slaves under the treaty,' said Ashoke Tsering. Even Bhim Bahadur Gurung's branch of the SNC promised to curtail India's supremacy. Kazi alone resisted the fever that swept the country, not deviating from his 1966 pronouncement (obviously drafted by someone else) that: 'The issue of the revision of the Indo-Sikkim treaty of 1950 is ill-timed. It is neither essential, nor is it of immediate or vital importance to the people of Sikkim. The people here do not stand to get any benefit from a revision of the treaty.'[3]

Some Indians suspected that the SNC chief was only driving a hard bargain with the durbar. The National Party, State Congress, Janata Party and Gurung's SNC were campaigning for international change in the expectation of subsequent political concessions at home. Kazi was thought to be pressing for constitutional reforms as the price of support for the independence movement.

This rather cynical interpretation seemed to be borne out when the results were announced. The two National Party groups (led by Martam Topden and Netuk Tsering) won eight places, Kazi's SNC five, and the State Congress four. The Gurung faction made no impression. 'There were only stones and *biri* ends in Bhim Bahadur's ballot box!' Kazini croaked.

To everyone's surprise then, Kazi made a move that was without precedent in the kingdom's politics. In taking this step, he spurned the State Congress to which he had once belonged and whose democratic programme made it the SNC's natural ally. In a parallel and equally curious move, Netuk Tsering seemed strangely disinclined to close National Party ranks and join forces with Martam Topden. Instead, the two unfrocked lamas, one Lepcha, the other Bhutiya, decided to petition the durbar. They were implacable public enemies. Kazi accused Netuk Tsering of being the Chogyal's creature. Tsering saw Kazi as India's agent. Yet they joined forces to plead that though no party had secured an absolute majority, the SNC and the National Party could together muster thirteen members in a council of eighteen, and were 'now in a position to form the government, if Your Highness so pleases'. Then followed three supplementary demands. The petitioners wanted the executive council to be called by some other 'appropriate nomenclature (either in the Sikkimese language or English) befitting the status of Sikkim and the aspirations of its ruler and his people'. They asked to be included in the development and planning committees and for these committees' reports to be discussed by the full council before acceptance. Finally, they suggested that food, commerce and industries should be placed under an executive councillor.

Many heads must have been put together to produce this quaint document. The obsequious language was the work of Kazi's legal adviser. The hankering for a grand designation points to Kazini's vanity. Kazi's shrewd financial acumen was probably responsible for the demand for some say in planning, which accounted for the bulk of government spending and could, therefore, be expected to offer easy pickings. The basic plea for a ministry is credited to Netuk Tsering's desire for power. The rubicund ex-lama did not share any of Martam Topden's humility. He was ready to support the durbar's campaign against India for the restoration of foreign affairs, defence and communications, provided the Chogyal allowed him political control at home.

The petition also confirmed that the SNC's real expectations were somewhat more modest than its propaganda aims. Even its inaugural platform in 1960 had not shown much desire to cast aside the fundamentals of the durbar's framework. All that Kazi seemed to want then was to expand the council to twenty-two and juggle with its numbers so that he was sure of a permanent majority. He was keeping his options open even now.

The most remarkable feature of the exercise was Kazi's willingness to make common cause with his opponent. This exposed an inherent flaw in Sikkim's embryonic politics. Party differences usually dissolved once the results were announced. Individual and group commitments were easily forgotten in the scramble for places in the executive council. Those who were nominated to it at once became the government, irrespective of the platforms on which they had been elected. Those who were left out also readily suppressed their avowed beliefs and functioned together as the opposition.

The Chogyal should have seen the wisdom of conceding at least some points of the petition. Kazi's amour-propre would have been assuaged. His wife would have felt less neglected. Netuk Tsering's loyalty would have been confirmed. There was an even more important gain to be reaped. Once the SNC was seen to be cooperating with the National Party in a government that was obviously loyal to the throne, it would lose many of its extremist Nepalese supporters. That would have compelled Kazi to tone down his radical demagoguery and take a more realistic stance.

The induction of a full-fledged ministry might even have cleared misunderstanding between palace and politicians. By strengthening the government, it would also have improved the Chogyal's bargaining position in New Delhi. Tactics apart, Sikkim's amateur politicians needed training in administration. Kazi told me at the time he was prepared to serve under his lifelong rival.

This was to reckon without India House. The PO did not want a reconciliation or a unified government that supported the durbar. It was easily able to play upon the palace's permanent and unreasoning aversion to ambitious politicians. It was even easier to whip up politicians' fears of royal autocracy. The Chogyal continued to pick and choose executive councillors. 'We seem to manage quite well with coalition governments,' was his laconic explanation for not responding to the overture.

But they were neither coalitions nor governments. They were self-seeking individuals bound only by temporary interest and kept under the firm discipline of the dewan and PO. Those two really constituted the government.

Rebuffed, Kazi hit back when the entire council voted for the deletion of Clause 15(ii) of the 1953 Proclamation which forbade discussion of 'the external relations of the state, including relations with the government of India and any commitments entered into by the Maharaja with the government of India'. Martam Topden moved the motion and the four executive councilors—Nahakul Pradhan and Kaloo Rai of the State Congress, and Ashoke Tsering and Harka Bahadur Basnet of the National Party—endorsed it. Kazi alone refused. He argued that it was not in the public interest to enhance the throne's authority and that ordinary Sikkimese would be crushed out of existence if India's protection were diluted. Independence, he said, would benefit only the palace. In private, Kazi explained that he was opposed only to piecemeal amendment. He would support the deletion of Clause 15(ii) if the Chogyal agreed to revise other passages relating to the distribution of powers.

But the PO was delighted. Kazi's objection allowed him to claim that the people did not want independence; the council had only obeyed the durbar's bidding. Clause 15(ii) was India's safety valve. It protected New Delhi's colonial authority, concealed the extent of actual control from public view, and prevented elected representatives from expressing any opinion on a vital aspect of their country's affairs. The PO also told reporters that the Chogyal was drumming up a public campaign without ever having made a formal approach to New Delhi.

This was quite untrue. He had never ceased to harp on the need to revise the treaty. A new relationship was hinted at in March 1965 when the Chogyal paid his first visit to New Delhi after ascending the throne. The occasion was marred by a minor faux pas. The Chogyal and Gyalmo were state guests and protocol demanded that the Sikkimese flag should fly beside the President's standard from the Rashtrapati Bhavan dome. But the presidential ADC would not accept the flag from the Chogyal's aide, saying he had received no orders. Indian officials later apologised for the incident and made adequate amends.

The talks with Lal Bahadur Shastri were cordial enough. The prime minister made no promise, though he listened patiently and did not accuse Gangtok of flirting with Beijing, as others did, whenever adjustments were mooted. Emboldened, the

Chogyal let it be known he had discussed 'minor administrative problems' with India's leaders. No details were disclosed, but three weeks later, the Chogyal told a journalist he had asked Shastri to consider Sikkim's views on 'administrative arrangements'.

Other feelers followed. 'We have mentioned this matter to the external affairs ministry in Delhi verbally,' the Chogyal admitted on 4 February 1966 when asked if he intended to seek revision of the 1950 treaty. 'We fully appreciate India's vital interests in Sikkim.' He seemed also to suggest that 'some changes', not necessarily complete sovereignty, had to come about, adding that the durbar would continue to employ Indian dewans 'until a properly qualified person from Sikkim was available for the job'.

In June Hope published an article on the Sikkimese theory of landholdings and the Darjeeling grant in the Namgyal Institute of Tibetology's bulletin. It created a furore, for the author disputed the legality of India's possession. She argued that no Sikkimese monarch was empowered to alienate territory. Tsugphud Namgyal's gift to the Company was 'in the traditional context of a grant for usufructage only; ultimate jurisdiction, authority and the right to resume the land being implicity retained'. All owners, she maintained, were only tenants in a system of centralised indivisible landholding which did not permit transfer in perpetuity. Echoing Sirdar D.K. Sen's memorandum, the Gyalmo claimed that Darjeeling's cession was the 'gift of a certain tract for a certain purpose and does not imply the transfer of sovereign rights'.

Shastri was dead by then, and Mrs Gandhi, who had succeeded him, assured Parliament that 'there has been no demand from any responsible quarter in Sikkim laying claim over the Darjeeling district'. But India's private reaction was so strong that the Chogyal had to dismiss his wife's scholarship as a 'purely academic exercise', adding: 'My government is quite competent to handle any matter concerning the rights and well-being of my country and my people... without resorting to the assistance of an academic body like the Namgyal Institute or its bulletin.'

If the article irritated Indians, it raised Sikkimese hopes, suggested other areas of dispute, and stirred uncomfortable memories of the duplicity that had been practised on the seventh chogyal to obtain Darjeeling. New Delhi remembered, too, that Sir Tashi's 1947 memorandum had never formally been withdrawn. There were other reasons for unease. The study forum had called for rejection of Indian aid if not given 'with grace', arguing that Gangtok's willing cooperation was essential for the effective defence of the Himalayas. Kaiser Bahadur Thapa's *Sikkim* continued to expound its views with customary bluntness. He was a tubby Nepalese, bubbling with cheerfulness, who had seen military service in the ranks and evaded British and Tibetan vigilance on the eve of World War II to escort a banned team of German explorers to Lhasa. 'Revision of the 1950 treaty there must be,' proclaimed his journal, 'and in keeping with the present-day trend, not only should our treaty be revised but it should also be registered with the United Nations Organisation. If our rights are not given to us gracefully, we are prepared to get it anyhow. But in doing so let us hope that we will not be driven to the extreme so that we are compelled to repeat the underground Naga story.'[4]

Strong words indeed, for the Naga rebellion was then in full spate. As always, however, the clinching factor seems to have been provided by Beijing. The Indian government later admitted that the Chinese had started a propaganda offensive through loudspeakers installed on the border from 3 July 1966. Kaul was sent to Gangtok in December to soothe the Chogyal with informal assurances. In February of the following year, New Delhi agreed to depict the Rangpo frontier as the official international boundary between India and Sikkim.

These negotiations were a closely guarded secret until May 1967 when the Chogyal addressed a press conference at the palace to announce that his country's goal was political freedom and that 'he awaited the convenience of the government of India. They have got more important things on their hands than we have.' Sikkim's case was advanced in conciliatory tones. Stressing the 'identity of purpose and interests' that bound the two countries, he expressed his firm conviction that the matter would be resolved to the satisfaction of both. The Chogyal stressed the importance of 'mutual discussions', ruled out any suggestion of anything like an ultimatum from Gangtok, and promised that 'everything will be in mutual interest'.

'Your interests are my interest,' he told Indian journalists. 'We have chosen to throw our lot in with the south. We share the ideology that you follow. But that does not mean merger with India.'

Details of the kind of arrangement he had in mind were first spelt out on 6 June when the Chogyal said: 'We want India to look after our defence and leave the rest to us.' Then came one of those grieving monologues that often embarrassed friends and were exploited by enemies. 'We have been pushed around too much by not only Indian officials, but also by others who see even in our simple statements a deep and sinister meaning.' The charge had sufficient basis, but it was just the kind of remark that the PO and the press would describe as anti-Indian. It was but a short step from that conclusion to accusing the Chogyal of being soft on China.

India's opportunity to make the allegation arose on 15 June when three executive councillors, Netuk Tsering, Nahakul Pradhan and Bhim Bahadur Gurung, issued a statement:

> Since Sikkim signed the treaty with India, it was within her sovereign rights to demand its revision as one of the

> signatories... Every country has the inherent right to exist and maintain its separate identity and to review its treaty obligations in the wake of the changing circumstances.

New Delhi was furious. Hope's article could have been dismissed as an academic exercise, the Chogyal's private pleas dealt with explanations and promises, but a public demand by politicians in office was quite another thing. There were stormy showdowns with the PO until, fearing the consequences of displeasure, the durbar announced that Sikkim's relations with India lay 'outside the purview of the powers and functions of the executive councillors'. It was not a satisfactory exercise in mending fences. While India remained suspicious, the three party leaders felt their king had abandoned them.

But the threatened crisis produced an invitation to the Chogyal and Gyalmo to visit India for fifteen days as guests of the government. There were no hitches to start with as the red carpet was unrolled when the Chogyal, Gyalmo and Prince Wangchuck reached New Delhi in September. Mrs Gandhi was waiting at Palam airport with cabinet colleagues, senior officials and the mayor of Delhi. The three services presented a guard of honour. Nine motorcycle outriders, three each from the army, navy and air force, preceded the ceremonial cavalcade to Rashtrapati Bhavan. Sikkim's red, white and yellow flag fluttered along with the Indian tricolour above the palace. Dr Zakir Hussain, the President, entertained the royal visitors to a formal lunch. Mrs Gandhi was hostess at a more elaborate banquet. The President's aeroplane took the Chogyal and his family on a tour of south India.

Hope, however, complained that the car in which Wangchuk travelled did not have the royal complement of flag and escort, such distinctions being reserved only for her husband. The Chogyal noted, too, that the military band at Palam had struck up the general salute instead of Sikkim's national anthem. There was an awkward moment in the Meenakshi temple in Madurai when the royal tourists were shown a frieze carved with a mantram: anyone who recited it, explained the priest, could charm listeners into agreement. The Chogyal loudly observed that he would like to test its efficacy on the Indian government.

Kaul was back in Gangtok the following year, still lavishly promising the moon, but also to complete arrangements for more important visitors. Morarji Desai arrived soon afterwards. Then, in May 1968, Mrs Gandhi paid her fourth visit to Sikkim. Though some courtiers noted her reserve, the prime minister graciously announced that a presidential state visit would take place in April 1970. Kaul, who accompanied her, seemed optimistic about the future, and the Chogyal made many flattering references to the Indian connection. 'We have made a modest, but significant, stride in the development of our country with a view to achieving a self-reliant economy,' he said in his welcoming address. 'This advance has been possible largely through the generous assistance and sympathy received from India.'

External affairs ministry officials say this was the high point in Indo-Sikkimese cordiality. Chinese bellicosity as well as stirrings within the kingdom had underlined the need to ensure that the Sikkimese were not too dissatisfied. Mrs Gandhi was inclined to be indulgent to the Chogyal. Indian officials claimed that though Hope did not evoke anything like the same warmth, her husband could have had anything he asked for. But they really meant personal privileges by way of money or facilities. The Chogyal did not want such favours. He wanted only recognition of Sikkim's rights, and that the prime minister was not prepared to concede. Afterwards, the Sikkimese complained she arrived in Gangtok empty-handed and went away laden with gifts.

• • •

The memory of these arguments, the uncertain outcome of continuing negotiations, and disappointment over India's unresponsive attitude on all matters of substance clouded the air as the Chogyal walked through the pavilions at the Kagyet dances, acknowledging the greetings of his guests. Elderly kazis doffed their brocade hats to measure the ground with their richly robed bodies, years of practice ensuring that ankles, knees, waist, arms and head moved in a single flowing sweep of unbroken grace. More restrained in their obeisance, Nepalese officials bent double, hands folded in a respectful namaskar. India House wives, anxiously clutching ceremonial scarves, received a smile and a kindly word. For his own blood, the Chogyal reserved a special courtesy. As nephews, nieces and cousins dropped in prostration, they were gently helped up and heads gravely knocked in token of kinship.

There were special visitors too. Bajpai lolled on a sofa. Beaming genially next to him sat K.C. Pant, India's minister of state for home affairs, who had travelled from New Delhi with his wife as Mrs Gandhi's special emissaries. A Brazilian count, convinced he had been a Himalayan Buddhist in another incarnation, had journeyed all the way from Rio de Janeiro in search of his spiritual ancestry and to lay his curly ginger head on 'His Majesty's sacred lotus feet', ignoring the Chogyal's gentle discouragement. George Griffin, political officer in the American consulate in Calcutta and suspected by Indians of being in the intelligence, had also invited himself with his wife Chrissie: the two made a consciously handsome pair. 'Present them to me,' Kazini ordered one of the ADCs, 'and don't forget that I am Her Excellency the Kazini Saheba of Chakung'. She acknowledged the introduction with a cool nod and shot off across the lawn to proclaim, 'Watch out, the CIA's here!'

Most of the time, however, her mascara-ed stare was fixed hungrily on Bajpai and Pant in the special enclosure where even she did not dare venture. They carefully avoided her gaze, not wishing to provoke comment with public confabulations. But

Kazini was not to be deterred. Her moment came in the buffet tent where protocol barriers were lowered and guests pushed and jostled each other to pile their plates high with rice, noodles, pork, beef, prawns, mushrooms and bamboo shoot. Pouncing on Pant while the embarrassed minister grappled with knife and fork, she dragged him into a far corner with whispered urgency. 'Shhh! They're listening,' she cried. 'The secret police are watching us!' The penetrating warning drew all eyes to the huddled pair. Gangtok was convinced Mrs Gandhi had sent a politician not in honour of the Kagyet dances, but to plan tactics with the durbar's avowed enemy.

A resplendent symbol of Kanchenjunga—*kanchen dzonga* or fortress of gold—watched the manoeuvre from a special throne in an enclosure facing the Tsuk-la-khang. Fabled home of the abominable snowman, the brooding mountain is worshipped in Sikkim. It is the house of the five treasures (mineral, salt, Buddhism's sacred books, foodgrain and wealth), an all-powerful monarch glistening under a sparkling mantle of snow lacquered by the rising and setting sun. The sublimity of the world's second highest peak towers over the kingdom even as its representation guards the festival.

Sir Tashi was not at all happy in 1955 when a British expedition asked to climb the mountain. He eventually gave permission, but only on condition that the appropriate propitiatory ceremonies were first performed. The team was provided with sacred banners to plant on the heights and was strictly forbidden to set foot on the sanctuary of the ultimate peak. 'He's even claiming Kanchenjunga now!' exclaimed an irate Indian diplomat. When the Chogyal heard this, he retorted: 'We don't claim it. Kanchenjunga has always been ours!'

• • •

The worship of the snowy range, Phanglabsol, is a separate festival in early September. The rites were laid down 270 years ago by the third chogyal, Chador Namgyal, who also invented the Sikkimese script, basing it on Tibetan, which, in turn, was an adaptation of Devanagri. The dance is a stirring spectacle of martial resonance with the mountain god in flaming brocade robes, wearing a red mask mounted with replicas of human skulls, and flanked by snarling snow lions, ministers and armed retainers. It is a spirited performance with caparisoned horses, boots and breeches, swords, daggers and shields, masks and helmets, all ferociously tumbling together until Mahakala, the guardian, calls on Kanchenjunga to drive out evil with good, to protect the faith, and to bring peace and prosperity to the people.

There is a smart march past by the Sikkim Guards; the Chogyal takes the salute; special prayers are offered in the Tsuk-la-khang; and offices and other establishments remain closed. Phanglabsol is also marked by deep carousing and all-night mah-jong sessions for high stakes.

At year's end, however, Kanchenjunga is content with a passive role on the sidelines. Other deities dominate the Kagyet ceremonies while Sikkim's protector watches over a monarchy and a way of life that are unaware that time is running out. The beat of drums muffles acerbic comments. Generous hospitality covers up the clash of personalities. Even Shankar Bajpai looks as benevolent as the Laughing Buddha as champagne glasses are raised to the hope of the new year, and lumps of dough called *tormas* are carried in colourful procession to be burned near the Tsuk-la-khang's main entrance. It is another symbolic destruction of past evil. The warriors, witnesses of the triumph of good over evil, worshippers of the snowy range and of Mahakala, circle the chapel three times to signal the end of the festivities. A gong booms across the lawn to be followed by the thunderous clash of cymbals. Then utter silence. The Iron Dog year is over.

The royal family walks slowly back across the gravel and up the shallow flight of steps to the palace verandah. As they turn round to wave farewell, Sikkim's nobles again fall flat on their faces in a swift, fluid movement of homage. But Kazini stands upright, mouth set in acid disapproval, feet firmly planted, hands tucked deep into the wide sleeves of her silken kho, almost as if fearing that some zealous courtier might drag them out and force her down to the ground like the rest. Kazi looks uncertain, eyes darting round the recumbent forms, ashamed to be different, yet not daring to follow his peers. His wife has resolution enough for two. 'My husband does the *dhok* only to Buddha Bhagwan.' Her announcement is really an order.

• • •

The Chogyal stood a little longer than usual on the edge of the verandah after his wife and four children had gone in, a strangely lonely figure in his golden satin. He had never looked more regal or more lost, not fully comprehending the tide of political fortune in which he was caught. Events carried him along, a simple man sustained by his understanding of duty but increasingly estranged from the people he sought to serve, seemingly far removed from the lyrical warbling about daffodils and silver mists with which Hope wove the enchantment of her fantasy court. There was no hint as yet of the gathering storm that was to darken the palace as Sikkim waited for the year of the Hog.

REFERENCES

1. T.N. Kaul, *Diplomacy in Peace and War: Recollections and Reflections* (Vikas, New Delhi, 1979).
2. Sir Edward Grey to Sir John Jordan, Minister in Peking (23 December 1910).
3. *Hindustan Times* (15 February 1966).
4. *Sikkim* (Gangtok, 6 August 1968).

CHAPTER

9

SHORTER LEASH

'If we give way in respect to Sikkim, we must be prepared to do so, at some future date, not only with regard to Bhutan and Nepal, but with regard to Kashmir and her feudatories, such as Hunza and Nagar, and with regard to any of the smaller Himalayan states which may have committed themselves.'

SIR MORTIMER DURAND,
Foreign Proceedings, Secret E, May 1889.

'In the case of Sikkim it was inconceivable that she would continue as a "protectorate" of India for long or that India would like such a millstone round her neck.'

T.N. KAUL,
Diplomacy in Peace and War.

There was consternation in India House. It was 15 August 1968, the twenty-first anniversary of Indian Independence, an occasion for somewhat stilted rejoicing. The royal family and all important Sikkimese, as well as leading members of the Indian community in Gangtok, were expected to attend. But word reached the PO that a small crocodile of boys and girls carrying placards was wending its way towards the hill. An official sent down to investigate came back with startling news. The banners were uniformly hostile. 'Indians get out of

Sikkim', 'We are a buffer but not a duffer' and 'We want independence' were some of their slogans. Never before had the public thus raised its voice.

The flag-hoisting ceremony was not interrupted. Indian diplomats had carefully studied the unflappability of their British predecessors. Their attitude to the locals had been modelled on the phlegmatic superiority of empire-builders like Hermaan Kisch of the ICS who received the Sikkim Campaign's medal and clasp for organising the army's field postal service in 1888. 'The inhabitants of Sikkim are quite uncivilised,' Kisch had written, 'though the Maharajah himself is an intelligent man with some education. The letters that the Bhutan and Sikkim Rajahs write to British officials are sometimes extremely amusing.'[1]

Condescension and a stiff upper lip saved the day. The PO and his staff pretended not to hear the high-pitched bursts of sound that rose above the resonance of *Jana Gana Mana,* India's national anthem. Nevertheless, the PO was uneasy. Although used to demonstration as a daily routine in New Delhi and Calcutta, he had not expected one in Gangtok.

Nervous echoes reached the Lok Sabha some months later when twenty-five MPs demanded an explanation from Mrs Gandhi for what they called a 'Quit Sikkim movement'. The prime minister was soothing. She told indignant parliamentarians that only 'local schoolboys' had staged a 'minor demonstration outside the residence of the government of India's political officer'. The situation was well under control. There was nothing to worry about. New Delhi had 'taken up the matter strongly with the Chogyal of Sikkim'.

So 'strongly' indeed did the PO threaten reprisal that the durbar was bullied into issuing a statement on 9 September deploring and condemning the incident. 'Sikkim is a Buddhist country and hence pledged to peace and non-violence,' it announced. Two school teachers who had organised the protest were severely reprimanded. R.N. Haldipur, the dewan, was summoned to New Delhi and given a dressing-down for permitting such an outrage. The Indian authorities, who turned a blind eye to regular and far more violent disturbances against the US, British and Chinese missions, treated this feeble display almost as a *casus belli.* Kaul again appeared in Gangtok, for only two days, and this time full of sombre warnings to the Chogyal to mend his ways. Much to the latter's surprise, he also said that New Delhi had been on the point of transferring control of posts and telegraphs to the Sikkimese, but would not now do so because the durbar could not be trusted—it had not suppressed the outburst of public opinion with a heavy enough hand.

Kaul added that Delhi would never now agree to an overall review of the treaty. Nor could Sikkim, as a protected kingdom, apply for membership of such UN agencies as the WHO or even the Tuberculosis Association. It would have to be content with indirect links through India. The Chogyal regarded this as a stab in the back from the man whom he had always looked upon as a close friend and who had in the past promised so much. As always however, the ruler was generous enough to make allowance for the political orders that Kaul had presumably been given.

Talks with Raja Dinesh Singh, who visited Gangtok the following May, seemed to justify his indulgence. The new external affairs minister, a titled landowner from Uttar Pradesh, seemed far less rigid. He compared Sikkim with Monaco and appeared to accept the Chogyal's correction that Luxembourg offered a more accurate comparison. Dinesh Singh also suggested that Sikkim might soon be able to issue her own postage stamps. Perhaps the raja was expressing a personal view. Perhaps he had been sent to soften up the Chogyal. No one in Gangtok examined the minister's motives or the extent of his authority. They were too buoyed up with hope not to accept his assurances entirely at face value.

It was a period of tremendous exuberance. Krishna Chandra Pradhan, who was always in and out of political parties, and Namgyal Tsering, Kazi's partner in the moribund Swatantra Dal, mustered about 300 activists under the banner of a United Front. They plastered walls with posters, distributed pamphlets, addressed street-corner meetings, and missed no occasion to denounce the treaty which, they alleged, had been signed 'under duress and deception'. 'Independence is the people's demand and not the king's,' Pradhan said. 'The Chogyal can't go against the nation's wishes.'

Physically, Namgyal Tsering was the more imposing personality: tall, ramrod straight, with a face the colour and texture of a dry walnut and a few wisps of grey hair doing valiant service as a beard. An ancient trench coat, ragged but debonair, draped his spare frame. In another age, the man might have passed for a cavalier or a soldier of fortune. He repeated Sikkim's economic grievances, warned that there would be communal violence unless the electoral system were revised, and complained that Sikkimese applicants for passports had to cool their heels for at least two years. (Sikkimese subjects travelled on Indian passports which described them, at the Chogyal's insistence, as 'India-protected', a term that many Sikkimese resented deeply).

The UF demanded instant and complete withdrawal of Indian troops. But, as always with Sikkim's poorly educated politicians, its charter was both confused and contradictory. 'We have no hostility with China and no historical background of animosity' Namgyal Tsering declared, going on to throw an unconvincing sop to New Delhi: 'We are safer with the Indian army.' Then returning to his original thesis: 'China won't invade Sikkim.' His case was that India and Sikkim could draw closer emotionally if there were no institutional compulsions. 'India is our nearest neighbour and eldest brother... We want to strengthen relations on an equal basis.'

Kaiser Bahadur Thapa also returned to the attack with an editorial which, after pointing out that conditions had changed since 1950, announced that 'as is the present-day trend today, we shall not be satisfied with anything less than the revision of the present treaty and a complete independent status to be tied up in eternal bonds of friendship through mutual agreements and defence treaty'.[2] The editor of *Sikkim* was punished by being kept waiting for his 'India-protected' passport when he was invited to a journalists' conference in Hong Kong.

Many other such irritants and petty harassments did much to further offend and alienate Sikkimese opinion. Ashoke Tsering was not allowed to go to a world Buddhist Council meeting in Bangkok, and Sanu Sakya, Gangtok's most skilled silversmith, could not attend the opening of the World Crafts Council in Lima. India was paranoiac about the most inoffensive Sikkimese presence abroad. The Indian embassy in Washington took such umbrage when the highly regarded Asia Society in New York planned to create a Sikkim council in line with its units for other countries, that the state department persuaded the society to abandon the idea. New Delhi's policy became more and more obstructive. Permits for foreign visitors to Sikkim involved interminable complications, and even some of India's legitimate obligations were avoided. For instance, although India had agreed to equip the Sikkim police with weapons and wireless equipment, delivery was repeatedly delayed until the Chogyal took the matter up with Morarji Desai. A meagre consignment of ten rifles and sixty helmets (far short of the promised equipment) was then belatedly sent to Gangtok.

• • •

If the Independence Day agitation created difficulties for Sikkim, it also obliged India to ponder in embarrassment on the colonial anachronism of its supremacy. It had always been a contradiction for a socialist republic to control a monarchy. Nehru, sensitive in his idealism but with a shrewd grasp of political reality, had long ago admitted the incongruity. New Delhi had also begun to realise that it had been a mistake to borrow the language of the 1890 convention when drawing up the 1950 treaty. According to Article II, 'Sikkim shall continue to be a protectorate of India and subject to the provisions of this treaty, shall enjoy autonomy in regard to its internal affairs.' No one had asked uncomfortable questions while the British ruled the subcontinent, but a protectorate had since acquired a definite connotation in international law. World opinion was veering round to accept protected status as a passing phase in the life of a nation, and all protecting powers were thought to be under an obligation to help their protectorates attain independence. A number of international charters, manifestos, declarations and resolutions stressed this point.

The Western powers had too many skeletons in their own cupboards to raise the matter, but the Chinese compared India's position in Sikkim with the Soviet Union's in Czechoslovakia. They said that New Delhi had 'inherited the colonial policy pursued by Britain in the nineteenth century by taking Sikkim as a protectorate and carrying out colonial rule over it'.

The charge was too near the bone, not only in Sikkim but all along the border, to be ignored. The wind was blowing against inherited privileges and unequal treaties. But the catch was that India's only valid defence—the claim that far from being ruler and ruled, India and Sikkim were in willing partnership—would have opened up even more unwelcome possibilities. Vincent Coelho, a former PO, made precisely this (from India's point of view) tactical mistake in his book, *Sikkim and Bhutan,* by arguing that New Delhi exercised direct control of external affairs, defence and communications only because 'Sikkim of her own free accord passed on these special responsibilities to India'. The book further pleaded: 'This word "protectorate" would therefore imply, and correctly so, a voluntary association between Sikkim and India where the former has literally placed herself under India's protection.'

A voluntary alliance logically implies the right to withdraw. However, the least attempt by the Sikkimese to even hint at that right was treated as political treachery. Like the British viceroys in India, Mrs Gandhi's government too had convinced itself that nationalism was the aberration of a small minority of troublemakers who had only to be quelled for the populace to quietly settle down to alien rule.

Inducements were first tried under the impression that if the Chogyal were sufficiently rewarded, all murmurs would die down. Nehru's gift of trading licences to the ruler's first wife and sisters had already made their fortunes; Mrs Gandhi matched it with generous foreign exchange permits for the expensive English education of his two elder sons who were both at Harrow. The Chogyal was able to buy two flats in London's fashionable Mayfair. There were no problems about importing luxurious furniture and fittings for Sikkim House in Delhi. Nor were questions asked about the royal family's increasingly frequent tours abroad. Renaming the Residency India House and recognition of customary Sikkimese titles (chogyal, gyalmo, gyalum and sidlon) were also features of her conciliatory diplomacy. But the strategy was based on a superficial reading of the Chogyal's character. Just as Sidkeong Tulku had disappointed the British, his reincarnation failed to live up to Indian expectations.

The Chogyal was never a man to spurn comforts, but he would not accept them as the price of conscience. When he persisted in his demands for Sikkim, Mrs Gandhi, Morarji Desai and T.N. Kaul all hurried to Gangtok. Looking for a way out of the legal and moral obligations of protectorship, and for a form of words that sounded less offensive to twentieth-century radicalism than a recognisably colonial term, they proposed to alter Article II of the treaty to read: 'Sikkim shall be in permanent association with India and, subject to the provisions of this treaty, shall continue to enjoy autonomy in regard to its internal affairs.'

A qualitative change in Indian politics explained the purpose of this ingenuity. New Delhi's political responses had lost their consistency once thinking was no longer guided by Nehru's philosophical beliefs. Reverses in the conflict with China, the 1965 war with Pakistan, and Mrs Gandhi's tenuous hold on Parliament after the 1967 elections had made for some flexibility, explaining the token gestures of placation made to the Chogyal. It was even suggested then that he should bide his time until the prime minister was stronger, when she would meet all his expectations. But the heady triumph of the Bangladesh war, India's emergence as the most important power in South Asia, China's UN membership (which was expected to reduce the pressure on border defence) and Mrs Gandhi's crushing majority in the 1972 elections changed all that. There was no longer any question of accommodation.

When New Delhi finally made up its mind to be firm, it cited the example of the US and Panama in respect of the canal zone. History could hardly have provided a more unfortunate parallel. Kaul, otherwise a polished and astute diplomat, tried to persuade the Chogyal to agree to a form of association that is probably the modern world's most blatant instance of might and chicanery triumphing over justice. When the ruler hesitated, he was accused of prevarication.

Whoever in the external affairs ministry dredged up this analogy and briefed Kaul could not have been informed of world reactions to the canal zone agreement. For the 1903 treaty between John Hay, the US secretary of state, and Philipe Bunau-Varilla, a French commercial adventurer who had bought up a number of Colombian delegates representing the Panama secessionist movement, has long been recognised as a cruel hoax perpetrated on nationalists through fraud, political subversion and military aggression.

In a world of their own—the Chogyal and Gyalmo

The Sikkim Guards in dress uniform outside their headquarters

Jawaharlal Nehru and Indira Gandhi (in Sikkimese dress) with Sir Tashi Namgyal and his family

Bayonet to bayonet —India and China face each other at Nathu-la

Jawaharlal Nehru regarded the Chogyal with almost paternal affection

Burra Kothi, originally the Residency, then India House and now Raj Bhawan

Kazi Lendhup Dorji and his mysterious European wife who may have been the daughter of a sergeant in the British army

Sandwiched between Kewal Singh and Shanker Bajpai, the Chogyal receives the 8 May agreement from Karma Topden

A demonstration below the Palace secretariat

Kewal Singh and B.S. Das look on as Kazi presents a khada to the Chogyal in an unusual gesture of respect

The Chogyal receiving the author at the wedding of his daughter, Princess Yangchen, to Simon Abraham, a New York-based British businessman

The author's wife, Sumita, the Chogyal's ICS friend, Nari Rustomji, and Sem Lhanzin-La, the Chogyal's half-sister

A bamboo bridge in North Sikkim

The author with the Gyalmo at the Kagyet dances ending the Iron Dog year on the lawn between the Palace and the Tsuk-la-khang royal chapel

The Palace gates where Indian troops shot dead the sentry, nineteen-year-old Basant Kumar Chhetri of the Sikkim Guards

The Chogyal at the coronation of King Jigme Singye Wangchuk of Bhutan. His secretary, Kazi Jigdal Densapa of Barmok, sits behind him flanked by the two loyal Sikkim Guards captains, Roland Christopher Chhetri and Sonam Yongda

Sikkim's first Indian governor, B.B. Lal, swearing in Kazi Lendhup Dorji as the first chief minister

An all-party meet at Burra Kothi

The author with (left to right) an India House official, Kazi Tse Ten Tashi of Rhenock, formerly secretary to both Sir Tashi Namgyal and the Chogyal, his daughter-in-law, Sem Lhanzin-La, and Trateng Sherab Gyalsten, chief secretary

Kazi and his Assembly colleagues with B.B. Lal at Burra Kothi

Queen Kesang Wangchuk of Bhutan and Dasho Landhup Dorji, first cousins of the Chogyal, outside the Tsuk-la-khang royal chapel at the funeral

The end of the road for the Chogyal. Princess Yangchen can be seen in front as the bier makes its way to the royal cremation ground on Lukshyama hill

'The succession is automatic'—Tenzing Topgyal Wangchuk Sisum Namgyal, thirteenth consecrated Chogyal of Sikkim, at his father's funeral

(Pictures: Courtesy Government of Sikkim Information and Public Relations Department, Namgyal Institute of Tibetology, Estate of the late Princess Pema Tsedeun Yapshi Pheunkhang, Sem Lhanzin-La Tashi, Keshav Chandra Pradhan and others.)

The promise of US support for their secessionist goal persuaded the Colombian rebels to allow the Frenchman to negotiate on their behalf. The treaty Bunau-Varilla achieved granted the US 'in perpetuity the use, occupation and control of a zone of land' and further allowed it 'all the rights, power and authority within the same... which the United States would have if it were sovereign of the territory... to the exclusion of the exercise by the republic of Panama of any such sovereign rights, power or authority'. Under these terms, Panama was excluded from exercising any sovereignty over a portion of its own territory. The US position was that Panama retained titular jurisdiction, but nothing more. Almost all that the Latin republic was able to secure after more than seventy years of striving was that its flag would fly with the Stars and Stripes.

It would be interesting to know what General Omar Torrijos Herrera, who ruled Panama for many years, might have had to say if he ever learnt that Mrs Gandhi had tried to force a similar iniquitious arrangement on a small neighbour. At the 1976 Non-aligned Nations Summit Conference in Colombo, the general spoke with moving deference of Mahatma Gandhi's liberal spirit to which India was heir. Mrs Gandhi was foremost among the Afro-Asian leaders in encouraging Herrera's determination to recover lost territory, roundly denouncing American imperialism. The Third World shared Latin America's justified resentment of the deceit that had been practised on Panama. Leading Americans were equally critical. Dean Rusk compared the canal zone agreement to the unequal treaties imposed on the Manchu and Ottoman empires. He was convinced that the Hague court would strike it down. Even Henry Kissinger admitted it was not 'an equitable and freely negotiated agreement'.

Panama took its grievance to the UN Security Council in 1973. Among the fourteen countries to support its contention were such staunch friends of the United States as Australia, Austria, France and Kenya. An embarrassed Britain, still saddled with vestiges of its own colonial empire, thought it more prudent to abstain. The move to liberate the canal zone was frustrated only by the US veto. Eventually, however, world pressure, the demands of liberal opinion at home, and the need to refurbish the American dream after the long nightmare of Vietnam, persuaded the Carter administration to initiate steps to restore what had been so unfairly acquired.

This was the model of power and arrogance, devoid of morality, on which Kaul sought to rebuild India's relationship with Sikkim. 'One of my efforts as foreign secretary', he recalls, 'was in September 1972 to have a democratic autonomous Sikkim as long as defence, communications and security remained with us, and remove the incongruous and ugly appellation of "protectorate" from the treaty.'[3]

A more astute tactician than the Chogyal proved to be might, at this point, have thought of explaining his dilemma and the implications of India's demand to his politicians. But there is little evidence that even the study group or the external affairs committee were taken fully into confidence. Instead, the Chogyal sought Bajpai's permission to consult an eminent British constitutional lawyer, Sir Humphrey Waldock, who was at All Soul's College, Oxford, and later became president of the International Court of Justice. He was asked to comment exhaustively on the Indian proposal's legal and constitutional implications. Nani A. Palkhivala, the Indian jurist, was asked to temper some of Waldock's views in the light of political reality. The Chogyal then suggested to Kaul that the amended clause should read:

> There shall be perpetual peace and friendship between the government of India and the government of Sikkim and between the people of India and Sikkim. Sikkim in full sovereign rights enters into a permanent association with the government of India and entrusts to them the rights and responsibilities stipulated in this treaty hereunder.

When Kaul questioned the phrase 'in full sovereign rights', the Chogyal drew his attention to the 1817 treaty of Titalya which recognised the Namgyal dynasty's rule over Sikkim 'in full sovereignty'. He could also have said that the 1950 treaty could not have been signed except between sovereign powers and that even if sovereignty were still restricted, Sikkim was entitled to hope—as India did before 1947—to graduate to full independence. But the question was an idle one. Delhi had no intention of giving away anything. Kaul tried to convince the Chogyal that the durbar could at once operate its own posts and telegraphs if he unconditionally accepted the amendment. Sikkim would join the Colombo Plan six months later, and the WHO and the ILO after a further interval. The only reason for this staggered advance was to avoid upsetting Hindu extremists in the Jana Sangh and the militant Rashtriya Swayamsewak Sangh, who regarded the entire subcontinent as *Akhand Bharat,* undivided India. Or so Kaul pleaded.

When the Chogyal went to Delhi on 4 May 1972, Kaul stepped up the demand to include the abrogation of the sixth paragraph of Harishwar Dayal's letter which excluded from India's purview 'any arrangements between the government of Sikkim and the governments of Tibet, Bhutan and Nepal which were in force on the date of the treaty'. The reason given was that the provision had lost its meaning since Tibet was no longer an independent state. But the Chogyal countered that Nepal and Bhutan were daily becoming more so. Moreover, whatever the practical application of the clause, its true value lay in demonstrating Indian recognition of Sikkim's capacity to enter into relations with other countries.

Swaran Singh, who had taken over from Raja Dinesh Singh, told the Chogyal the next day that permanent association ranked higher than protection. But the new external affairs minister, who was a lawyer by training, would not countenance any reference to the UN. Mrs Gandhi, who had not till then been directly involved in the negotiations, confirmed her dislike of the word protectorate on 8 May; permanent association 'sounded better' to her.

Kaul's version is that the Chogyal was quite happy with the proposed revision until mischief-makers abroad put him up to be difficult. 'A draft agreement was drawn up and approved. Thondup said he would send it back duly signed from Gangtok within a week. He never did, because some foreign advisers misled him into believing that he had a cast-iron case for independence. I sent word to him, week after week, that the opportunity would not recur, but he showed no response.'[4]

What Waldock and Palkhivala actually told him was not that Sikkim had a cast-iron case for independence, but that if he agreed to permanent association, India would have a cast-iron case for annexation. The 'opportunity', on which Kaul harped so magnanimously, was in fact a trap. For though there was no general rule indicating the relative positions of protectorates and associate states, or governing either, the law accepted that a protectorate possessed an international personality distinct from that of its protecting power. The UN's 1970 resolution had specifically laid down that 'the territory of a colony or other non-self-governing territory has, under the charter of the United Nations, a status separate and distinct from the state administering it...'Protected countries also enjoyed the right of ultimate self-determination.

But permanent association was a vague term without precise juridical meaning. West Bengal could be said to be in permanent association with the Indian Union. The bond could be given any meaning that the stronger partner chose. Once the Chogyal accepted this connection, India could claim that Gangtok had definitively exercised the right of self-determination that the UN held so dear and had closed its options for all time. India could also argue that by accepting the New Delhi government as the supreme central authority, the kingdom had merged its international identity with India's. Sikkim would then lose its juridical identity and be reduced to the level of the princely states under British paramountcy. It would also be deprived of its international personality and be regarded by world law as being under India's jurisdiction.

The 'distinct sovereign international personality', as Hidayatullah called it, without which Sikkim would not have been able to sign the treaty, would disappear. The kingdom would have no access to the Hague court. It would not be able to approach the United Nations; nor would the UN feel sanguine about taking an interest in the affairs of a country that had voluntarily surrendered its rights. Sikkim would only be left with internal autonomy which was already circumscribed by the treaty, Dayal's letter, economic and geopolitical factors, and above all, by India's treatment of the kingdom. The Chogyal would not be left with any grounds for objecting if at any time India unilaterally decided to take the short step from permanent association to merger.

These dangers had to be anticipated because the UN had very little experience of associated states. There was Puerto Rico's connection with the United States. The UN General Assembly had also approved of the association between New Zealand and the Cook Islands. But the American and New Zealand constitutions expressly allowed the associated territory freedom to change its mind. India's did not. Britain's association with Antigua and some other West Indian islands was also based on the understanding that they could ask for revision whenever they chose. But Mrs Gandhi's India did not contemplate any such freedom. It sought to bind the kingdom in a permanent subordinate relationship.

Little wonder the Chogyal baulked. He tried persistently to talk things over with Mrs Gandhi who was never in a hurry to respond to his requests for appointments. Though she continued punctiliously to call on him whenever he was in Delhi—not usually allowing him to visit her—she confined the conversation to social generalities. With Bajpai he could not communicate at all, while he had begun to mistrust Kaul with whom he had been friendly since the 1950s when the Kashmiri was posted in the Indian high commission in London. In spite of this absence of any real dialogue, the Chogyal suggested another alternative. Let the new Article II read, he said, that 'though separate, Sikkim and India shall continue to be in close association with each other'. But close was not permanent, and it was turned down. So was the rider 'though retaining her separate identity...' In fact, India was not prepared to consider any modification at all. The negotiations that dragged on for four or five years—there was never any question of a settlement 'within a week' as Kaul claimed—did not really amount to an exchange of views. Not once did New Delhi budge from the stand it had taken.

Unable to resist pressure and fearing veiled threats of more drastic action if he did not knuckle under, the Chogyal agreed towards the end of 1972 to accept Kaul's draft. But he would do so, he said, only if Mrs Gandhi's government unconditionally endorsed a letter from the durbar which would spell out:

> It is the understanding of the government of Sikkim that Article II, as so amended, means that, though separate, Sikkim and India shall continue to be in close association with each other and conduct their relations in a spirit of mutual friendship and cooperation. In this spirit, the two governments shall, as appropriate, consult together on matters of mutual concern, and in particular on those referred to in the treaty of 1950.
>
> It is also the understanding of the government of Sikkim that Sikkim and India shall continue the association between their two countries within the framework of the purposes and principles of the charter of the United Nations; and that the government of India shall assist Sikkim in promoting its economic and social progress and in developing its participation in international cooperation.

It was a brave attempt to snatch victory from the jaws of defeat. If India agreed, Sikkim's constitutional position would fall within the UN's purview, and the Chogyal could insist on the documents being registered with the world body. But India's backyard would then be open to public inspection. Mrs Gandhi is believed to have exploded angrily that 'any international association would bring in outside interference and pressures in Sikkim'. Swaran Singh again firmly told the Chogyal that no reference to the UN would ever be permitted. Kaul tried to reason more artfully that such involvement was redundant since, as a founder member of the UN, India would naturally always uphold its highest principles. If so, countered the Chogyal, India had no reason to shrink from an explicit undertaking to abide by ideals it had helped to frame and claimed to adhere to.

He was adamant that his country would not willingly commit judicial suicide. All manner of rewards were again held out to obtain acceptance of permanent association. The Chogyal was told he could follow Bhutan into a number of UN agencies. It was conveyed to him that Kazi would not be patronised any longer. The Namgyal dynasty's perpetual reign was guaranteed. He was again offered limitless funds, especially in foreign exchange. 'Name your figure and we'll sign the cheque,' they said, with no particular attempt at finesse.

But with his back to the wall, battling for Sikkim's survival, the ruler refused as determinedly as Mrs Gandhi pursued her goal. New Delhi abandoned the correspondence in the stalemate that followed, but not its intentions. Somehow or other, Sikkim would have to be brought into a tighter orbit. The exercise still needed a democratic gloss. It would also have to claim some semblance of legality. Both imperatives suggested a local accomplice who could be built up as the people's representative and thrust into the limelight as an alternative to the durbar. Indian intelligence had not wasted its time. Thanks to Kao's RAW, New Delhi had all the information it needed. The obvious candidate was waiting in the wings in Kalimpong.

It was from about this time that official Indian displeasure began to be reflected in public whispers of what the Chogyal and Gyalmo were accused of being up to. Specific charges were never laid, but there were innuendoes enough to suggest that both, especially Hope, were acting in concert with America and China to destabilise India and set up a centre for covert activity in the Sikkim Himalayas. Some of the suspicion was directed at Princess Coo Coo La, too. The international border at Rangpo all but disappeared in practice. India quietly returned to Coelho's assertion in his book that 'one can assume that India's frontier with China is the Chumbi valley and the crest of the Himalayas along Sikkim's northern border with Tibet'.

This insistence on complete control flew in the face of geopolitical reality. The durbar fully recognised that the sovereignty it hoped for would always be subject to certain practical limitations. 'We can never be independent in the true sense,' admitted Karma Topden, explaining that Sikkim would stand in relation to New Delhi almost like some of the autonomous republics of the Soviet Union vis-à-vis Moscow. The Chogyal, too, tried several times to convince Kaul that by liberalising economic and political ties, India would also gain an additional vote at the United Nations. The explanation was put down to the belief that Hope was acting at the CIA's behest. She was believed to have set her heart on being a full-fledged queen. Her besotted husband would do and say anything to keep her happy. There were also always Kazi and Kazini to claim it was the palace and not the people that demanded independence.

Relations became so bad that New Delhi cancelled the state visit by the Indian President that had been planned for 1970. Kaul went to Gangtok instead and blamed 'bad weather' for the cancellation, but it was common knowledge the PO had warned that the President might have to face hostile demonstrations. Nevertheless, Kaul spiritedly denied any tension, insisted that relations were 'based on mutual understanding, trust, confidence and cooperation and [were] bound to increase in future despite some press reports to the contrary'.

These fine words were not matched by any spirit of understanding or private assurances. Netuk Tsering met Mrs Gandhi in 1972 when Sikkimese executive councillors were invited to tour India. He complimented her on the liberation of Bangladesh and her election victory, then pointedly asked: 'When will you also make us free?' The prime minister's reply was that since the treaty had been negotiated with the king and not the people of Sikkim, she could discuss changes only with the Chogyal.

She did no such thing though they met at least twice later the same year. On 5 May in Parliament House, the prime minister talked only of Rashtrapati Bhavan catering. A subsequent encounter was equally brief and fruitless. Mrs Gandhi confined her conversation to such topics of absorbing interest as an injury to her toe, the Chogyal's rheumatic back, and the attractions of holidays in the hills. She was adept at using small talk to hide her intentions.

REFERENCES

1. Hermaan Kisch, *A Young Victorian in India: Letters of H.M. Kisch* (Jonathan Cape, London, 1957).
2. *Sikkim* (Gangtok, 27 March 1972).
3. T.N. Kaul, *Diplomacy in Peace and War,* (Vikas, New Delhi 1979).
4. Ibid.

CHAPTER

10

VOTE FOR FREEDOM

'We agree that the idea of 'protectorate' definitely belongs to the bad old days of colonialism and is entirely outmoded, if not actually offensive to Sikkimese ears.'

KAZI LENDHUP DORJI and SONAM TSHERING,
letter to the editor, *The Statesman,* 16 February 1966.

'The Sikkim National Congress under the leadership of Kazi Lendhup Dorji had been the government of India's greatest ally, for the Kazi, while professedly practising nationalism, was so blatantly pro-Indian that in Sikkim political circles he was known as the agent of the government of India.'

LAL BAHADUR BASNET,
Sikkim: A Short Political History.

Scarcely a prayer-wheel paused in its eternal rotation as Sikkim prepared for its fifth general elections. The outlook had changed completely since the fourth polls in April 1970, when Kazi and Netuk Tsering had briefly come together. A sort of truce seemed to have been established between Gangtok and New Delhi, and few of the kingdom's 107,062 voters expected the results to make much difference to the contented rhythm of their existence. Touring Sikkim on voting day I found a relaxed holiday mood. Chhang shops were closed, but simply lazing in the sun seemed pleasanter than queuing at polling booths.

The calm was deceptive, for all three parties had undergone some change. Martam Topden, old and ill, had retired from the leadership of the National Party, leaving the sixty-six-year-old Netuk Tsering in undisputed command. He was a tough old practitioner whose appearance—a blotchy round face under close-cropped white hair—recalled the Teling monastery, a day's march from Gyantse, where he had spent his early childhood. Though he had long ago abandoned the monkhood, people still called him Netuk Lama. But there was little trace of monastic austerity in the incongruous opulence of a crowded sitting room whose piece de resistance was a large English doll with flaxen hair and staring blue eyes. It was an ugly intrusion in the profusion of Chinese porcelain, delicately chased Sikkimese silver and rich Tibetan carpets.

Netuk Tsering was of humble birth. He did not belong to the durbar's inner circle. The kazis viewed him with considerable misgiving for his loyalty to the throne did not mellow a naturally aggressive temperament. India House was even more suspicious of his uncompromising nationalism. 'Is the map of Sikkim separate or is it shown just like one of your states?' he would ask belligerently. Netuk Tsering also claimed that V.V. Giri, India's President, had agreed with him that Sikkim should be independent. He had been politically baptised in 1948 when it seemed likely that the State Congress might press for merger. 'We would have been a small drop of water in the vast Indian Ocean,' he once remarked, recalling those hectic times. His prescription for the future was simple: 'We must remain Sikkimese. There can be no merger with India, Tibet, Bhutan or Nepal.' But though Netuk Tsering wanted Sikkim to issue its own passports, trade abroad, and receive direct aid from third countries, he was politician enough to know that India would not willingly make concessions. The Sikkimese would have to coax them out of India.

As part of this more persuasive approach, his National Party was making a conscious effort to dilute its ethnic exclusivity. It had a Nepalese councillor from the north and two other Nepalese office-bearers, the general secretary, Man Bahadur Basnet, and a vice-president, Harka Bahadur Basnet. The party's 1973 election manifesto, a mere two pages, promised to serve 'the country, the king and the welfare of the Sikkimese masses.' It announced that 'the main objective of the party is to work for and to lead the country and her people towards prosperity and advancement commensurating *(sic)* the progress of the world under the able guidance of the Chogyal Chempo'. It talked of drainage, cardamom cultivation, roads, canals and drinking water, schools and markets—modest parish pump issues that would appeal to ordinary folk.

In contrast, the SNC's thirteen points continued to stress lofty political principles. Calling for 'abolition of the prevailing communal election system', it demanded a written constitution, fundamental rights and an independent judiciary, and argued that 'it has been very clear from the last four general elections that no substantial political and administrative reforms can be brought about in Sikkim unless a single party majority (i.e. at least ten out of eighteen elected seats) in the Sikkim council can be gained by any political party'. The charter's last clause appealed for 'strengthening of friendly relations between Sikkim and India'.

Many Sikkimese wondered why Kazi at all contested under a system of which he disapproved so thoroughly. He had earlier said that 'it is common knowledge that the Sikkim council is a puppet council and enjoys neither powers, prestige, nor the confidence or respect of the people of Sikkim'. But in spite of this derision, the SNC president strove desperately for a voice in the council. His volte-face in what became notorious as the *Bulletin Number 2* controversy showed just how anxious he was to become a member. In fact, Kazi almost did not make it in 1973 because of a head-on collision with the durbar over the party bulletin which appeared on 26 January 1972. An article titled 'Sikkim at the Crossroads' accused the Chogyal of absolutism, warned that 'there can be no king without a people' and hectoringly demanded reforms. It also quoted ominously from the Bible's *Book of Joshua*: 'And the princes said unto them—let them live, but let them be hewers of wood and drawers of water'—to denounce the durbar's treatment of its subjects. The article rumbled on to recall 'the stormy coup of 1949 before the palace in Gangtok', concluding in ringing tones: 'And to those who persist in seeking their own petty, personal benefits, who will neither listen to the voice of wisdom nor decency, who will not read the writing on the wall, for those whose pastime is a desultory indulgence in barley-water diplomacy. Kerensky's words to the Duma in 1917 are pregnant with meaning: "If you will not listen to the voice of warning, you will find yourself face to face with facts not warnings".'

Everyone knew who had written that! Joshua and Kerensky meant as little as Bowery accents to native-born Sikkimese. But action could only be taken against Sikkim subjects and SNC officer-bearers. Summoned by the Chogyal, Kazi presented himself at the palace, profusely apologising for the article which, he said, had been published against his advice. But the written apology that he promised to submit was never produced; Kazi slipped out of Gangtok that afternoon and went to ground in Kalimpong where he was assured of Indian protection.

The council met in early April with Sonam Tshering in the chair. All fifteen members present, including four executive councillors, voted for a National Party resolution condemning the bulletin and demanding action against the SNC. Another unanimous motion expressed the council's lack of confidence in Kazi. His party colleagues stayed away, but some of them let it be known they were not averse to some kind of punishment that might curb Kazini's bossiness.

Armed with the two resolutions, the government filed cases against Kazi, Khatiawara, by then SNC general secretary, and against the party's publicity officer, D.B. Gurung, whose signature appeared on the bulletin. Kazi was also dismissed from the executive council at the end of May. Fearing further reprisals or even extradition proceedings, the SNC chief and his wife set out for Europe, while Khatiawara and Gurung remained in Chakung House in Kalimpong. Gurung was only an innocent victim of Kazi–Kazini stratagems. No sooner had husband and wife departed than he made his way back to Gangtok, sought out a magistrate with the customary tribute of a basket of eggs, and pleaded he could not read or write English and was not responsible for the bulletin. The charges against him were dropped when Gurung signed a confession describing the publication as the handiwork of Kazi, Kazini and Khatiawara. Warrants were then issued to arrest Kazi and Khatiawara. The British Kazini living in India was, of course, beyond the reach of Sikkimese law.

Husband and wife were in a quandary when they returned from Europe in August 1972. The fifth elections were due the following January. Kazi could not participate with an indictment hanging over his head. The SNC was in danger of disintegration, and his own career seemed to be in peril. He could not even return to Sikkim without courting arrest.

Two men came to his rescue at this critical juncture. Athing-la persuaded the Chogyal that though troublesome, Kazi—to whom he was related by marriage—was a safer bet than any demagogic Nepalese politician representing the all-Sikkim seat would be. No other Bhutiya-Lepcha leader could command Nepalese loyalty, and Kazi was really a safety-valve for populist passion. Bajpai proved a no less persuasive champion. He told the Chogyal that *Bulletin Number 2* was mild by the standards of Indian political invective, and that New Delhi would not approve of harsh punishment. 'I had to tell these chaps not to use a sledgehammer to crush a fly,' he explained.

In the end, the Chogyal agreed to accept an apology. Kazi wrote on 21 October 1972:

> May it please the Miwang Chogyal Chempo.
>
> The Chogyal and the government of Sikkim have expressed displeasure at the publication of the *Bulletin no. 2/1972*, dated Gangtok, the 26th January, 1972, entitled 'Sikkim Today', and captioned 'Sikkim at the Crossroads', published by the publicity secretary of the Sikkim National Congress, Shri D.B. Gurung.
>
> And, thereafter, criminal proceedings were instituted by the government.
>
> As an expression of my deep sorrow over these most unfortunate developments, and in token of loyalty to the Miwang Chogyal Chempo, and to my country, I do hereby tender my unqualified apologies.
>
> I do this with the honesty and sincerity of one who has always cherished these virtues above all else.
>
> I would, therefore, pray for the withdrawal of the cases against me in the court.
>
> And for which act of graciousness I shall ever remain the Miwang Chogyal Chempo's most obedient subject.

Khatiawara wrote a similar abject apology and the two politicians duly received royal pardons. The charges against them were withdrawn. But in private, both men admitted that the apology was only a tactical move. 'It was the only way,' said Kazi. 'I wouldn't have been able to contest the elections otherwise.' Khatiawara gleefully told everyone how he had hoodwinked the durbar. They had cause for jubilation. For the Chogyal agreed under pressure to delay the deadline for enrolment of candidates so that Kazi could stand. He also agreed not to damage Kazi's public image by publicising the apology.

But Kazi's political standing was less secure than it had been. Many former supporters like Lal Bahadur Basnet had already left, piqued by the intrigues and jealousies of his wife's court. Kazini's ceaseless promotion of Khatiawara, and the latter's unrestrained language and disturbing drift to hooliganism, worried sober politicians. They feared that he might try to convert Sikkim into a militant Nepalese state. Nor did his association with Kalimpong Marxists endear Khatiawara to the Sikkimese. SNC members who went to Kalimpong complained that Kazini ordered them about like servants. D.B. Gurung had left the party because of the shabby way he had been used in the bulletin affair. Incipient communalism had driven away Sonam Tshering, the party's veteran vice-president. Other Bhutiya-Lepchas followed. Though the SNC initially filed nominations from fourteen constituencies, two Bhutiya-Lepcha candidates in the north and east stepped down. Even some of the more mature Nepalese were perturbed at the party's increasingly strident communal tone. Kazi, though president, was like the painted wooden figure on a ship's prow: the SNC was becoming an organisation of rowdy young Nepalese.

Not everyone was dismayed by this disarray. Nahakul Pradhan calculated that with Kazi under a legal cloud and the SNC in chaos, he had a good chance of capturing the all-Sikkim seat and emerging as Sikkim's elder statesman. Krishna Chandra Pradhan, who had seized the Janata Party presidentship, promised to help, and the two called on the Chogyal to propose a bargain. As Nepalese, they would win the majority community's vote they said, but they were also loyal Sikkimese and would naturally campaign for an independent kingdom. In return they asked for an end to legislative parity, for a common register of voters, and, somewhat curiously for defenders of democracy, that the palace should advance money for their election costs.

Instead of readily agreeing as they had expected, the Chogyal read the Janata Party leader a stern avuncular lecture on his disorderly lifestyle and the grief he had caused his father and elder brother, as well as on his running feud with the Densapas. The Chogyal touched a raw nerve. Krishna Chandra was tired of living in the shadow of an eminent father and a successful brother and of being regarded as the family ne'er-do-well. Desperately anxious to be taken seriously, he had expected the overture to be received with gratitude. Nahakul Pradhan's presence, while he was scolded like an errant schoolboy, made things worse. He stalked out of the palace swearing vengeance.

The two Pradhans agreed on 15 August 1972 to merge their parties and called a *maha samiti* at Melli on 26 October to ratify the decision. Older members of the State Congress who tried to prevent the liquidation of a respected organisation say that hoodlums were posted in and around the Melli hall. Delegates who opposed the move were threatened with violence. The closed-door meeting agreed to form the Janata Congress with Krishna Chandra Pradhan as president. Bhim Bahadur Gurung joined them and also a few men who claimed to represent the forgotten Rajya Praja Sammelan. 'And thus on the ashes of the Sikkim State Congress they raised the edifice of the Janata Congress!' commented the SNC. 'We are sure that the hearts of the Sikkimese people must be breaking over such a sudden and sorrowful demise of the Sikkim State Congress, and that, too, without even having any mourners and pall-bearers thereof.'

'We have the old flag, the old symbol and the old programme,' retorted Nahakul Pradhan in Rangpo where he had been propitiating the gods before the contest; a wisp of rose petal in his hair and a smear of sandalwood paste on his forehead betokened his devotions. Kazi's apology and rehabilitation had upset the apple-cart, and Nahakul Pradhan must have realised he had burned one boat without acquiring another. He was worried too because one of the seventeen candidates, a Bhutiya-Lepcha, had cried off, frightened by Krishna Chandra's outright racism. He therefore tried to insist that the old identity remained intact. The two parties, he argued in a display of semantic acrobatics, had 'amalgamated' and not 'merged'.

The Janata Congress manifesto ingeniously tried to explain that the State Congress had to change its name since Sikkim was not an Indian state but a separate country where the Janata was supreme. The document promised to guarantee Bhutiya-Lepcha rights and professed loyalty to the throne while undertaking to revise the 1953 Proclamation to introduce the one-man-one-vote concept. 'The main aim and objectives of the Sikkim Janata Congress are equal rights for the people and a democratic form of government under the Chogyal Chempo as its constitutional head.'

This moderate charter was far removed from Krishna Chandra's vituperative demagoguery. He accused senior civil servants by name of corruption, gerrymandering and ethnic discrimination. Complaining that the Nepalese were being persecuted, he passionately declaimed that like Uganda's Idi Amin, the kazis were out to liquidate immigrants. Equipped with chalk and blackboard, Krishna Chandra regaled audiences with a diagram to prove Bhutiya-Lepcha domination in all fields. 'Our national language is a version of Tibetan. The state religion is Tibetan Buddhism. There is no such thing as Sikkimese!' He also questioned the royal family's rights. 'If we have parity then let it be taken to its logical conclusion. Sikkim should also have a Nepalese Hindu king.' Some durbar officials wanted to lock him up and disqualify the Janata Congress for inciting racist friction. But since the Chogyal would not hear of such extreme steps, Krishna Chandra continued to infuse communal poison into politics.

As always, personal animosity spiced political rivalry in the run-up to the vote. Kazi could not forgive Nahakul Pradhan for trying to steal his Nepalese constituency. Kazini was terrified that Krishna Chandra might outshine her beloved Khatiawara. She had not forgotten her old vendetta against

Bhim Bahadur Gurung either. She and Kazi had also mustered ammunition against the Janata Congresss general secretary, Santosh Kumar Rai, who had been accused the previous year of complicity in a ₹ 687,000 fraud over supplies of cement and bitumen. The main allegation was against his brother Kaloo Rai who had been dismissed from the post of executive councillor in charge of public works. Standing on a bridge on the road to Pakyong, Santosh Kumar Rai hit back by proclaiming that the SNC's campaign costs were paid by India.

The government, too, had changed its character. I.S. Chopra retired in July 1972, forced to leave a comfortable job as much because his contacts in New Delhi had failed to further Sikkim's cause as because of Shanker Bajpai's dislike. The sidlon's post was vacant. The Chogyal did not want an Indian officer recommended by the external affairs ministry, and the PO did not trust anyone the Chogyal chose. Nor was there an obvious Sikkimese successor. Athing-La would have been able to handle the job, but the Chogyal had outgrown his old mentor. Jigdal Densapa could not be spared from the palace secretariat. Moreover, Sikkimese civil servants were beginning to grumble that Indian administrators were paid much more than they were so that a substantial portion of India's aid was repatriated in salaries.

So the king became his own prime minister. Files were sent to him and all departmental chiefs reported direct to the palace. It was a temporary arrangement, but Kazi and Krishna Chandra Pradhan accused the Chogyal of setting the clock back again to the age of absolute monarchy.

Sikkim's 69,254 Nepalese voters, 22,658 Bhutiya-Lepcha, 8,060 Tsongs, 5,710 scheduled caste electors and 1,370 lamas voted against this background. But no one expected any major turmoil. Even India House seemed complacent. Bajpai contrasted the relatively peaceful campaign with the anti-Indian tirades heard during the 1967 and 1970 elections to explain a little smugly that the public had at last realised that

Sikkim's national polls were like local self-government elections elsewhere. 'They're interested in roads, drinking water and irrigation—the topics that would normally concern a small tehsil in India.' He was convinced that the honours would go to whichever party promised to solve day-to-day problems, voters not being interested in constitutional abstractions. 'The treaty and relations with India are not an issue this time,' added Bajpai. Even the National Party had said nothing about independence.

• • •

The results were not really surprising. The rout of the Janata Congress had been predicted for it was identified in the public mind not with the hallowed State Congress, but with Krishna Chandra Pradhan's intemperate outbursts. The State Congress had four seats in the 1970 council; three years later, the Janata Congress won only two. After serving in the council for twenty years and as an executive councillor for thirteen, Nahakul Pradhan was pushed into the wilderness. Bhim Bahadur Gurung and Kaloo Rai were also defeated. It was a sad fall for the party that had aroused political consciousness twenty-six years earlier. The SNC retained its five seats: three Nepalese, a Tsong and Kazi's general constituency. Victory belonged to the National Party which emerged with eleven councillors. Seven Bhutiya-Lepchas and two Nepalese were returned on the party ticket. They were supported by Pechying Lama who had been elected uncontested from the monasteries, and by the scheduled caste representative Purna Bahadur Khati.

Watching the trend as votes were counted, Netuk Tsering issued a statement on 9 February, six days before the result became public. He pointed out that the two Janata Congress seats were both the subject of petitions to the Election Commission. He criticised politicians, meaning Kazi, who impeded Sikkim's constitutional advance, accused them of working for the country's 'disintegration' and promised to serve 'in a spirit of dedication'. Then came the rub:

> As the president of this party, I also take this opportunity to convey our thanks to the government of India for the generous assistance in our development activities and for the economic aid for various projects. We look forward to this continued assistance and feel confident that the government of India will not lag behind in fulfilling the ambitions of our people in enabling us to enjoy the status like that of Nepal and Bhutan.

If India House was taken aback, there was a surprise in store for the palace too. It was not only in foreign affairs that Netuk Tsering was preparing to assert himself. The majority party leader was just as determined to stand on his rights at home. He objected strenuously when, instead of calling on him to form a government, the durbar appointed the usual coalition with six members. Netuk Tsering was made senior executive councillor with three men (Nima Tenzing, Kunzang Dorji and Harka Bahadur Basnet) from his own party. But Bhuwani Prasad Dahal of the Janata Congress and either Chhatra Bahadur Chhetri or Durga Prasad Razalim—the final choice had not yet been made—from the SNC were also nominated.

There were other murmurs. The first complaint was over an incident at Bikmat, a two-hour pony trek from Namche, where the presiding officer mistakenly gave five instead of six ballot papers (one for each candidate) to about 150 voters. Kazi's agent at once accused him of saving an extra slip for the National Party; the charge was not withdrawn even when the SNC won the seat. Secondly, it was discovered during counting in the White Hall that some ballot papers from Rawang had not been separated along the perforation. Since these were in the National Party candidate's box, SNC and Janata Congress leaders again accused the government of rigging. A headstrong young Bhutiya kazi from Kewsing, Rinchen Wangdi, later to marry Princess Coo Coo La's daughter Sodeun-La, angrily rejected the charge and the altercation led to fisticuffs. The Janata Congress and SNC men present walked out of the White Hall saying the polls were not valid.

These minor episodes did not seem to cause any serious unrest since all eighteen elected and six nominated councillors took the oath of allegiance. Obviously, the SNC and Janata Congress had no intention at this stage of impugning the elections. The first real hint of trouble appeared only when the lamas proposed 20 March as an auspicious day for swearing in the new executive council. There would be the usual ceremony in the council house followed by lunch at the palace. The durbar was told that the two SNC men were being difficult. Razalim was in Namche and reluctant to journey to Gangtok. Chhetri had left Gyalzing for his sister's home in Kalimpong. When Karma Topden dispatched a messenger to bring him back, Chhetri seemed flattered by the executive councillorship and was getting ready to leave Kalimpong when Khatiawara intervened with a gang of young SNC toughs. The durbar's messenger was driven off and Chhetri taken to Chakung House.

He disappeared from view for seven days. The *Himalayan Observer* of Kalimpong reported under the heading 'E.C. at gunpoint' that Chhatra Bahadur Chhetri claimed to have been 'hounded and pounded by the Sikkim intelligence men at Namche, Gyalzing, Jorethang and also at Kalimpong from March 18–20 to take him to Gangtok for E.C. at gunpoint'. Chhetri also reportedly told the West Bengal police that the Chogyal's men were 'harassing' him and his sister. 'To escape from all these depredations on my personal safety, I came of my own free will and accord to seek shelter at Chakung House, the home of my president Kazi Lendhup Dorji Khangsarpa.' But the story he told me in Gangtok two weeks later recalled D.B. Gurung's helplessness. Kazi had sent for him, said Chhetri, to discuss the SNC's strategy in the council. When he reached Chakung House, they locked him up in the servants' quarters with Khatiawara's gang keeping watch at the door. He had been forced to sign a document that Kazini had typed out, but did not know what it said since he could not read English.

Meanwhile, Chhetri's father went to the Gangtok police and laid a charge against Kazi for kidnapping his son and holding him prisoner. The old man also trudged up to the palace to thank the Chogyal for honouring Chhatra Bahadur who had apparently smuggled out a message saying he accepted the executive councillorship and would take up the post as soon as he was free.

The Janata Congress representative was also missing when the executive councillors assembled. Bhuwani Prasad Dahal had been eager to serve. Nahakul Pradhan, wishing to make his peace with the durbar, had told Topden that Dahal would garland the Chogyal before the ceremony. But when the day dawned, a letter arrived instead of the Janata Congress representative. Signed by several members, it announced that the party reserved the right to choose its own nominee and that it would not be able to do so before 29 April.

Apparently, Krishna Chandra Pradhan, still smarting from his humiliation and his party's subsequent rout, had summoned all his colleagues to a conference the night before in Santosh Kumar Rai's flat near Gangtok's Denzong cinema. Overriding Nahakul Pradhan's protests, the Janata Congress decided to sit on the sidelines until the SNC's course of action was clear.

It was the National Party that proved most unpredictable. Netuk Tsering was offered the public works department and Kunzang Dorji given charge of forests. The Chogyal explained that it had not yet been decided what duties would be delegated to Nima Tsering and Harka Bahadur Basnet. But though all four took the oath of office, Tsering and Dorji declined their portfolios. It was for the party president, they said, to allocate responsibilities. Netuk Tsering also let it be known that he preferred to be called prime minister and not chief executive councillor. Even if the higher designation was not possible, he would insist on increased financial powers for himself and his colleagues and on collective responsibility in the council.

Kazi agreed. The National Party had eleven members, and the SNC president was ready to support its right to form a government provided he was recognised as leader of the opposition.

Among the compromises suggested was a plan to restrict the executive councillors to National Party members so that, in practice, a two-party system was introduced. Another suggestion was that Netuk Tsering should preside over legislative sessions as the sidlon had done. But the Chogyal was not at liberty to make innovations. Many durbar officials feared and disliked Netuk Tsering. They pointed out that once the two-party principle were conceded, there would be nothing to stop Kazi from one day heading the government. Taken to its logical conclusion, politicians' rule would mean majority rule, and that would be the end of Sikkim's indigenous language, religion and culture.

Civil servants were even more disapproving. They comprised the most powerful group in the country and provided the six nominated councillors who exercised the greatest influence after the king. One of them had presided over council meetings since Chopra's retirement. These men knew that political power could only be extended at the expense of bureaucratic authority. Having been answerable only to the palace, they were not willing to report to elected councillors.

The strongest pressure was applied by India House which found little that was reassuring in Netuk Tsering's record. It was even more apprehensive of the future. Politicians who derived their strength from the ballot box, and were willingly confirmed in power by the durbar, would not need the PO's patronage. Even Kazi might dispense with guidance under these circumstances. Indian diplomats were also as averse to a Nepalese majority as the most crusty Bhutiya-Lepcha nobleman. The Nepalese in adjoining Darjeeling district had for years claimed special recognition, and the demand for a separate Uttarkhand (later Gorkhaland) state to include a large slice of the Terai was gathering momentum. It suited New Delhi to retain an amenable monarch in Gangtok. If the process made the Chogyal seem intractable to his subjects, so much the better for a strategy that demanded several weak elements that were inherently incapable of cohesion. The PO therefore reminded the durbar that it could not introduce any revision of the constitutional proclamation of 1953 without New Delhi's approval. When people thought the Chogyal was unyielding, it was really the paramount power that feared democratic change.

Though India House was able to stall political progress, New Delhi was beginning to realise the limits of its divide-and-rule policy. The actions proposed by the National Party, SNC and Janata Congress had already indicated that in spite of deep personal and other differences, their political thinking was moving towards ultimate coalescence. They were capable of agreeing on the general terms of policy towards the durbar. If they held out long enough and advanced their views with sufficient vigour, the Chogyal might have no option but to yield. He might even welcome a common front with all his politicians. The vacillations of Chhatra Bahadur Chhetri and Bhuwani Prasad Dahal had also revealed that India could not rely on the permanent loyalty of any party or politician so long as the throne offered them alternative choice. Even the faithful Kazi was prepared to cooperate with Netuk Tsering. If that cooperation fructified, the eleven National Party men, six nominated councillors and five SNC representatives could convert the innocuous council into a potent forum of national revival.

It was too late to cast off a political system that had stood the test of five elections. It was too late to alter results that had already been proclaimed. It was impossible to wean away councillors who had taken the oath of allegiance. There was no constitutional way, in fact, of preventing the National Party, with its commitment to independence, from assuming control. But the new council could be strangled before it began working.

CHAPTER

11

THE BIRTHDAY PARTY

'RAW agents were despatched to Gangtok, Mangan, Namche and Gyalzing, the four district headquarters in Sikkim. They slowly gathered operational data required for planning the operations in case India was forced to take action.'

ASOKA RAINA,
Inside RAW: The Story of India's Secret Service.

'Under Kao's overall guidance, the RAW team helped the pro-democracy leaders build up their organisation and make their weight felt in the politics of Sikkim. This process had started several months before the storm broke in April 1973.'

P.N. DHAR,
Indira Gandhi, the 'Emergency' and Indian Democracy.

Tension crackled in the air as Gangtok observed the Chogyal's fiftieth official birthday on 4 April, just two weeks after the fiasco of the swearing-in ceremony. Though a little wan, the Chogyal sat serenely erect behind the palace drawing-room's high choksey. He could have been a deity in gold brocade above a carved and gilded altar, receiving homage, greetings and gifts. Relatives knocked heads, officials presented khadas. Bajpai brought a rare piece of south Indian statuary. Indian army officers saluted and shook hands with cheerful bonhomie. Visitors came in from the verandah, through the rather dark hall with its slippery polished wooden floor, with the stairs going up to the first floor, and into the drawing-room. They went out by a small door to the lawn by the ADC's cottage where tea and sandwiches had been laid out under the magnolia tree.

The Chogyal had sat down punctually at nine o'clock that morning for the audience which did not last more than half an hour. But it was a time of strain and speculation, for everybody was aware that something was happening in the world beyond the palace. No one mentioned it in his presence, but discipline snapped once guests had left the drawing-room. The rising hubbub of conversation in the lawn echoed the tremulous fears that gripped the kingdom. The durbar's intelligence had totally failed to anticipate the situation. It didn't even know RAW had been busily beavering away in the villages.

The next function was at 10 am when the Chogyal held a levee in the pavilion (Yabring) facing the Tsuk-la-khang. He put on his fur hat and formal vestments for the occasion and, followed by Hope and the children, crossed to the flagpole to take the Guards' salute. Sikkim's soldiers had never looked smarter in their starched khaki and gleaming brass. Then to the Yabring where a high chair stood in the centre of the dais. The royal family and important Sikkimese sat on the Chogyal's right, the PO, army generals and prominent Indians on his left.

It was an uneasy two hours, a low hum of whispering providing the background as three red-robed monks chanted the benediction. The chief secretary read out the year's administration record, and the Chogyal pinned gold and silver medals, awarded in the birthday honours, to brocaded chests. The decorations had been ordered from Spinks of London and a case of gold medals was lost in transit. But there was little time for disappointment. Jigdal Densapa, Karma Topden and Rasaily slipped out every so often and returned looking even more harassed. The PO alone seemed to be without a care as he crossed one plump leg over the other, rocked his chair back and forth, beaming and waving at acquaintances. The Sikkimese were scandalised at Bajpai's insensitivity.

The news that Densapa and Rasaily brought back at noon must have been worse than anything heard before, for the rest of the celebrations were abruptly cancelled. Bajpai heaved himself out of his chair, ambled across to the Chogyal to shake hands and was driven away in scattering rain. Reaching India House, he telephoned the palace to say that Avtar Singh, secretary in the external affairs ministry, would reach Gangtok that afternoon.

The year of the Bull had started badly when a flagpole collapsed during the Kagyet dances. Then a crack appeared in one of Tashiding's massive stupas. In Thakse palace, the Gyalum was haunted by a repetition of the visions that had come to her on the eve of the 1949 disturbances and which troubled her whenever the royal family was in danger. The high incarnate monk that the Dalai Lama sent to offer oblations for Denzong's welfare was killed on the road to Gangtok. This succession of sombre portents recalled ancient prophecies of doom. Coo Coo La recounted the writings of a medieval female seer called Mache Labdeun who had anticipated trouble. Lepchas talked gloomily of the curse of the Buddhist Namgyals because they had not kept Khye-Bumsa's promise to Thekong-tek to honour the indigenous faith. That was also said to explain why eldest sons never succeeded and why so many rulers had a physical disability like the Chogyal's stammer and his father's near-blindness. Twan Yuan, a writer and painter of Chinese extraction, long resident in Gangtok, claimed it had always been known that the twelfth Chogyal would be the last.

The crisis had been building up since the SNC and Janata Congress had organised a rally in Gangtok and petitioned the Chogyal to set aside the February elections. Kazi and Khatiawara made inflammatory speeches at Melli on 24 March.

Santosh Kumar Rai delivered similar orations in Singtam's Bhagwati temple the next day. Late the following evening, the government belatedly invoked the Security Act against Krishna Chandra Pradhan for fomenting communal unrest. He was tracked down and arrested in the home of Chatur Singh Roy, an elderly Nepalese who had settled down in Sikkim in 1965 after retiring from the Indian excise service. He was one of the SNC's joint secretaries. Trouble on a much bigger scale started almost at once as demonstrators poured into Gangtok.

They were a mixed crowd of Sikkimese and Indians. The Indians were politically motivated but Sikkimese reasons for congregating in the capital were mixed. Simple villagers had been told that the royal birthday was being celebrated on a grand scale and there would be food, chhang, and presents for all comers. Many came to discuss their future: they had been led to believe the Chogyal was about to ban the Nepalese language and outlaw Hindu worship. Many more came out of fear because households in the south and west had been threatened with reprisals if they did not each send at least one male. A small group did indeed take part to press for political reforms. They had been rounded up by Khatiawara's youth organisation which was determined to force a show-down with the durbar. They saw Kazi as the only Bhutiya-Lepcha leader to defend majority rights.

Politically articulate Indian Nepalese from Darjeeling and Kalimpong who were foreigners in Sikkim provided the stiffening. Deo Prakash Rai, secretary of the All-India Gorkha League, called a meeting in Darjeeling's Chowkbazaar to pledge solidarity with the SNC and demand New Delhi's instant intervention. So did Tarak Kumar Karki, a minor local functionary of India's Samyukta Socialist Party, who claimed that 5,000 people had attended his rally. 'Many people have come from Darjeeling, Kurseong and Kalimpong,' he boasted in Gangtok. Roop Narain Dahal, secretary of a Gorkha League faction in Kalimpong and Kazi's legal adviser, was equally busy.

So were Khatiawara's Marxist friends from West Bengal. They were illegal infiltrators, but they increased numbers and lent political purpose to an exercise that took the Sikkim government by surprise.

The mood was peaceful on 27 March when 700 or so spectators waited outside the council house for the Chogyal's arrival. Kazi and other SNC and Janata Congress councillors, seven in all, were inside. They took the oath with the eleven National Party men, and heard the Chogyal promise gradual reforms. The house was adjourned sine die; but Kazi thrust a sheet of paper at the Chogyal, as he was leaving. It turned out to be a memorandum listing three demands: Krishna Chandra's release, one-man one-vote, and a democratic administration. Councillors and spectators then followed the royal car to the palace.

Once there, Kazi, Nahakul Pradhan, Bhim Bahadur Gurung and Kaloo Rai asked for an audience and were received as soon as lunch had been cleared away. They warned the Chogyal that the crowd, which had by then reached the Tsuk-la-Khang, was becoming impatient, and suggested that he promise to release Krishna Chandra, inquire into allegations of rigging, and consider alterations in the electoral system. Since the politicians claimed to speak in the people's name, the Chogyal said he would himself address the crowd and, much to the pleased surprise of the gathering around the Tsuk-la-khang, he made a short but pertinent speech in Nepalese. He told them that Krishna Chandra Pradhan had been arrested for a cognisable offence and the law would have to take its course. It would be improper for the throne to tamper with the course of justice. The Chogyal promised that the election commissioner would listen to all polling complaints but appeals would lie to the throne.

Finally, he reminded listeners that the constitution was not his private invention or imposition. It had been approved in 1951 by Sonam Tshering, Dimik Singh and Kashi Raj Pradhan representing all the country's communities and political parties. If the people's new leaders felt the constitution had outlived its usefulness, they should again discuss alternative proposals and send him a list of recommendations which he would consider. But he could not unilaterally foist a new system on the country.

What the Chogyal might have added was that he could not change the constitution, however obnoxious, without India's consent. Harishwar Dayal's Memorandum of Government of India's Views on Constitutional Scheme of Sikkim (25 October 1951) explicitly forbade almost all the reforms the politicians demanded. It still tied the durbar's hands. It forced the Chogyal to appear far more illiberal then he was or wanted to be.

The crowd burst into applause. The gathering broke up, and people streamed down the hill and out through the palace's back gates. But two young students who had not been noticed before and who did not appear to belong to any organisation suddenly announced they would not leave until all three demands had been met. Upstaged, Kazi and the others went away, leaving the limelight to Ram Chandra Poudyal, Khara Nanda Uprety, and two or three hundred other young men who said they, too, would stay back.

It did not seem to be a premeditated decision. In fact, it was the first of many impetuous gestures that made Poudyal such an uncertain political quantity. He was a quiet studious youth, known to be a favourite of Hope's. Nobody had guessed until then his predilection for the dramatic. Uprety merely followed Poudyal on a road that neither then expected to lead to highly dramatised martyrdom. For though nothing had been said about a hunger strike, the absence of food lent their vigil the aura of self-sacrifice. Their companions trickled away over the next day and night, but it was not until 1 April that Poudyal and Uprety, both weak and grubby, were forcibly removed to the Thutob Namgyal Hospital in a blaze of glory.

• • •

It was a time of frantic developments on many fronts. As the ten-member Joint Action Committee that the SNC and Janata Congress set up wrote to Mrs Gandhi, 'The black flag demonstration by more than fifteen to twenty thousand people at Gangtok on the day of the Chogyal's birthday, and total boycotting of such celebrations throughout with black flag demonstrations, go to show growing unpopularity of the Chogyal amongst his people.' Khatiawara urged villagers to seize police-stations, raid government armouries and prepare for guerrilla warfare. Nanda Kumar Subeidi was also mobilising men while Kaloo Rai busily collected funds. Always with an eye on India House, Marwari traders in Singtam, Namche, Jorethang and elsewhere gave the demonstrators money. The JAC also boasted it had the blessings of the Karmapa Lama at Rumtek. The durbar heard on 1 April that a mob armed with kukris and lathis was marching on Gangtok. Bigger crowds were reported the next morning.

Sikkim's Bengali police commissioner, S. Dutta Chowdhury, an Indian officer on secondment, was at his wits' end. His professional duty was to Sikkim and its king. However, like the Sikkim Guards' Indian commander two years later, he was expected to obey a higher allegiance. But the policeman's chemistry was different. With his professional pride and sense of loyalty, he pleaded with the Chogyal's secretary to invoke Section 144 of the Criminal Procedure Code which forbade the assembly of more than five persons. This is the routine way of controlling mobs in all Indian cities. 'How the hell do you expect me to carry on without Section 144?' Dutta Chowdhury raged when the durbar demurred. 'I can't act without the government's authority. I'll resign rather than make a mess of things!'

He had cause for anxiety. His little force of 350 constables and forty-five officers had only 110 .303 rifles of World War II vintage. India was supposed to provide additional equipment in an emergency but the PO turned down the durbar's request for 200 self-loading rifles and 20,000 rounds of ammunition. Dutta Chowdhury's anguished messages to his opposite number, the police superintendent of Darjeeling, asking for weapons, ammunition, gas masks, shields, batons and tear-gas were also ignored. When his demands became more and more insistent and the Darjeeling SP couldn't prevaricate any longer, he sent a paltry consignment of thirty-eight tear-gas shells, three gas-masks and three rifles. The commissioner poured out his woes at the unofficial meetings that civil servants held every day to discuss the crisis. Sherab Gyaltsen, the chief secretary, was always present. So were Densapa, Rasaily, Chandra Das Rai and Kunzang Sherab. The gatherings were usually in the finance secretary's room in the Tashiling. A sudden clap of thunder during one of these conferences and the blackout that followed convinced the superstitious they were battling against fate.

Interminable arguments produced crippling paralysis. Rasaily, Chandra Das Rai and Tulsi Sharma, the most senior among the Nepalese officials, regularly held parallel conferences. Sonam Tshering, chairman of the birthday celebration committee and still able to communicate with Kazi, had to be kept in the picture. So had Athing-La. Ananda Bhattacharyya, a West Bengal-based Bengali lawyer who was Sikkim's legal adviser, had come up from Siliguri and was installed in one of the dak bungalows. It was Karma Topden's duty to liaise between all of them and also keep the Chogyal informed. No one was in overall command. Several centres of authority had sprouted overnight. Everybody was bursting with self-importance. Everybody had a solution.

Rasaily and Kunzang Sherab wanted to call out the Sikkim Guards; Densapa feared retaliatory violence against the Chogyal. Topden was for waiting for more precise information. Dutta Chowdhury continued to plead that Khatiawara, Kaloo Rai and Subeidi should be arrested and Section 144 imposed in Gangtok and other towns. But, still afraid of offending New

Delhi, the durbar's cautious officials proposed on 1 April that the Indian army should be asked to restore peace. They instructed Topden to obtain the palace's approval. The Chogyal, who was lying on his bed reading a book on European military history, looked up just long enough to tell his deputy secretary that though he would personally prefer a reconciliation with the politicians, it was up to his officers to take a decision.

Eventually, they agreed to partially accede to the police commissioner's requests with a restricted application of Section 144, Karma Topden again being sent to the palace. The Chogyal was sitting in the bay window of the drawing-room when his deputy secretary appeared shortly after breakfast on 2 April. He talked at length and with obvious sorrow of the 1949 riots, suggested that it might still not be too late to try for a compromise with the JAC, and brooded on past, present and future. The ruler was especially troubled by what he saw as his own failure with his people. But Topden's mission succeeded. Late that night, the district magistrate of East Gangtok issued prohibitory orders under Section 144 valid for three days and operative from 3 April. The ban was subsequently extended for a week. The effect was to forbid more than five persons to collect in a small area of Gangtok between the Paljor stadium, police lines and bazaar. The 2,000 or so demonstrators holed up in the grounds of Kazi's petrol-pump could not emerge, except in ones and twos but never more than five, without falling foul of Section 144.

There was a cocktail party at India House that evening. The Tashiling officers sent Karma Topden as their representative to find out how the wind blew. But Bajpai pre-empted the move by showing him at once into a small study where a formidable galaxy of dignitaries was waiting. Topden knew General Kowcher, the Seventeenth Mountain Division's Sikh GOC, quite well. The others were introduced as Brigadier Hoon, Gangtok area commander, and General Roy, the corps commander from Siliguri. India House's two political secretaries, Gurdip Singh Bedi and Sudhir Devare, were also present. The PO plunged into an interrogation.

'What do you want the army to do? The government of India and I are ready to be of assistance.'

'I am happy sir, that you should...' began Topden, but was curtly interrupted.

'You can leave out all that! Tell us exactly what you want.'

'That's unfair, sir,' began Topden a second time. 'I have no official authority...' but he was again cut short.

'In that case why were you sent? You're wasting our time!'

Fumbling for words, the flustered deputy secretary stammered out an apology on behalf of his seniors who were still closeted in Tashiling, and explained that he had come to give the PO his assessment of the situation and to learn India House's views. To General Roy's specific question as to what the army could achieve, Topden replied they were expecting a crowd of about 5,000 and that the Guards would take over only if the police failed to control the mob. Asked again about the army's specific role, Topden suggested that Indian troops could watch the power-house, telephone exchange and other vital installations. Bajpai murmured something about seeing that the water supply was not poisoned, but General Roy did not think they needed to worry about such sophisticated tactics. Did the PO and the army generals know then of RAW's role? Or was it still a closely kept departmental secret?

The telephone rang, just then—Kazini was calling from Kalimpong. 'Tell her I'm not at home,' snapped Bajpai. 'I'm tired of that woman bothering me all the time!' Turning to Topden, the PO then said he was worried by reports of Crown Prince Tenzing strolling about the bazaar without an escort. He had also heard the Chogyal was thinking of going down to the petrol pump with a white flag. He cautioned against rash gestures, blamed the crisis on Rinchen Wangdi's fracas at the White Hall, and repeatedly stressed the army was at the

Chogyal's service. Clearly, he wanted a lead role for the Indian army, but only at Sikkim's request. The meeting broke up. Nothing had been decided. Karma Topden did not know India House's intentions, and the PO had failed to manoeuvre him into declaring the Indian army alone could save Sikkim.

While the Chogyal's deputy secretary was parrying the PO's questions, Densapa, Sherab Gyaltsen, Kunzang Sherab, Chandra Das Rai, Tulsi Sharma and Rasaily—three Bhutiya-Lepchas and three Nepalese—were engaged in even more momentous talks in Tashiling. It was a meeting of all the talents, official and political, Bhutiya-Lepcha and Nepalese. Kazi, Nahakul Pradhan, Bhim Bahadur Gurang, Bhuwani Prasad Dahal, Kaloo Rai, Chatur Singh Roy and Adhik Lal Pradhan represented the JAC. The National Party had sent Netuk Tsering, Martam Topden, Ashoke Tsering, Kunzang Dorji, Nima Tenzing, and Man Bahadur Basnet. Sonam Tshering in the chair held the balance. The meeting dragged on for hours but agreed at last on the one-man-one-vote principle. The civil servants, JAC and the National Party decided that individual proposals for other changes would be considered at a second session, and would then be submitted to the Chogyal as the conference's unanimous recommendations. On behalf of his master, Jigdal Densapa promised in advance that the palace would accept all suggestions. The durbar was at last reconciled to surrendering power.

Some of those who were present realised that such a constitution, expressing the views of all the groups that mattered in Sikkim, would in the long run strengthen the kingdom's position. The external affairs ministry, which was ostentatiously urging the Chogyal to democratise his administration, could not oppose the consensus view. In short, it was a shrewd attempt to seize the initiative and transfer decision-making authority from New Delhi to Gangtok. Differences resolved, civil servants and politicians, Nepalese and Bhutiya-Lepchas, were congratulating themselves on success when Kazi suddenly announced he would first have to consult his party.

It made no sense. All Sikkim knew that Kazi was the SNC. Chatur Singh Roy, the party's general secretary, had also taken part in the discussions and endorsed the decision, so that there was no question of the president being isolated. Nahakul Pradhan and Bhim Bahadur Gurung protested that the SNC had ceased to function as a separate entity when it joined the JAC. The Kazi's followers were now bound by the latter's collective undertakings. Kazi had already given his word, they pointed out. But if he still had reservations, he and Roy could talk things over in private for a few minutes. Kazi was not to be persuaded. He demanded a telephone and refused to allow Chatur Singh Roy to accompany him to the room where there was an instrument. The call did not last long. Kazi came back almost at once to say that the agreement had fallen through.

They were thunderstruck. The SNC president had not been away long enough to book a trunk-call to Kazini in Kalimpong. Nor would he have left Roy behind if he was only going to talk to his wife. There were no colleagues in Gangtok whom he would dream of consulting. In fact, there was no one in the SNC who would not unquestioningly follow the president's lead. Everyone was convinced that Kazi had telephoned India House. The PO must have told him to call off the deal.

Stunned, the civil servants tried to reaffirm the agreement with more independent leaders. But their attitude had stiffened after the unexplained mystery of Kazi's telephone call. Nahakul Pradhan, Bhim Bahadur Gurung and Chatur Singh Roy were now unwilling to take risks. Instead, they suggested that the JAC's young militants should be involved in a settlement. Rasaily, too, agreed that Krishna Chandra Pradhan might be more receptive. He was released on parole and taken to the Tashiling where he seemed amenable, but said it would be wise also to obtain Khatiawara's consent. So the negotiators piled into a jeep and drove to Nahakul Pradhan's bungalow where the JAC had shifted its headquarters from Kazi's petrol pump. Responsibility for this undertaking rested with Rasaily who expected to be able to thrash out the problem on a man-to-man, Nepalese-to-Nepalese basis. He probably hoped that an ethnic front would not only wrest political power from the durbar but would also frustrate Indian ambitions.

Reaching Nahakul Pradhan's house, Rasaily and his colleagues explained that the Chogyal was so afraid of the country being annexed that he would do anything to arrive at a Sikkimese solution. This was their chance of asserting majority rights, throwing off Bhutiya-Lepcha domination, and also strengthening Sikkim's independence. The new dispensation would reduce the Chogyal to a figurehead. While Khatiawara vehemently rejected all mediation, Krishna Chandra suddenly made a dash for it and disappeared. Their last card had gone.

Events moved fast after that. Defying Section 144 early in the morning of the Chogyal's birthday, the crowd began to pour out of Kazi's petrol pump. The offensive had been carefully planned. Women and children surged forward first. Behind them, led by Khatiawara and Kaloo Rai, came a solid phalanx of men menacingly brandishing kukris and lathis. They ignored warnings to disperse broadcast through loudspeakers. Tear gas was ineffective as the mob marched with the wind which carried the gas back to the police who had no protective masks. Some of the shells were intact and the demonstrators hurled them back. As bricks and stones rained down and Dutta Chowdhury was hit on the head, the police broke ranks and fled, with the crowd in pursuit. A column climbed the hill to the old bazaar. The rest almost forced down the barrier that had been erected across the road. The police commissioner was afraid they would seize the armoury and wireless station.

'It was at that stage that firing had to be opened as a last resort to disperse the mob,' he reported. 'Only seven shots—five from revolvers and two from rifles—were fired. No one was killed, and only two in the mob suffered gun-shot injuries.'[1] But the JAC screamed blue murder about the 'indiscriminate use of tear gas and shooting with live bullets on the peaceful procession of the people... as a result, several persons were injured and the condition of three persons is reported to be serious'. The 'curfew' and 'ruthless firing' clearly indicated, they told the PO and Mrs Gandhi, 'that law and order in this tiny Himalayan kingdom of Sikkim have collapsed'. Briefed by the external affairs ministry, India's press and radio magnified a minor fracas of a kind that passes unnoticed in the streets of Indian cities almost every day into a major and murderous confrontation.

The JAC also wrote to Mrs Gandhi that 'the arming with lethal weapons and free use of Tibetan refugees and parading them within the areas under curfew to suppress the people's peaceful movement is indeed a matter of gravest concern to the safety and security of the Sikkimese masses'. Rumour, fuelled by India House diplomats, swept through Gangtok that Dutta Chowdhury had armed hundreds of muscular Tibetans who would fall upon the Nepalese and slaughter them. As with many fantasies, there was a grain of truth in the allegation. The commissioner admitted that 'in Gangtok where a handful of police officers and men were engaged in containing thousands of lawless elements for days without rest or relief, thirty able-bodied and respectable citizens were enlisted as special police officers under Section 18 of the Sikkim Police Act to help the regular police maintaining law and order.'[2] These recruits were, however, Doptha-pas and, therefore, Sikkim subjects. They looked like but were not Tibetans.

The Chogyal was still sleeping when Karma Topden burst into his bedroom with an eye-witness account of what had happened at the petrol-pump. He listened aghast, then burst into tears. 'It's the first time in Sikkim that we have had to fire on my people. I shall never forgive myself for shedding Sikkimese blood.' The Chogyal bitterly blamed himself for not pursuing his original idea of a compromise with the JAC. He carried the pain of his self-reproach to that morning's drawing-room audience, grieving through the rituals while Kazi and his advisers prepared for another attack. It was launched in the afternoon of 4 April, not long after the Yabring celebrations were cancelled, when the mob again tried to rush the police barriers. The crowd had swollen by then to about 8,000, but a firm stand by the police seemed to have a salutary effect. Many demonstrators were reported to be trickling back to Singtam and Raniphul.

• • •

The rising might have fizzled out then but for a piece of foolishness by Crown Prince Tenzing who decided to venture out in his Jonga, Mrs Gandhi's gift in happier times, to see what was happening. His companions, Captain Roland Chhetri, Rinchen Wangdi and Dorjee Dahdul, a youth in the Sikkim intelligence, were all in their early twenties. None of them was noted for prudence. They were four high-spirited young men out for adventure.

The drive to Singtam, just an hour away, was uneventful. Knots of people stood about along the road, but they seemed to bear no ill-will to the handsome young prince. Most stared, some folded their hands in greeting, a few even smiled and waved. Singtam was peacefully deserted. But the mood had changed when Tenzing, still at the Jonga's wheel, and his companions were returning. A barricade had been flung across the road at Raniphul, eight miles south of Gangtok, and Tenzing, who was driving, had to pull up as smooth-faced young Nepalese boys wearing scarlet armbands and waving the JAC tricolor, swarmed into the road. Not only was the crowd bigger but it was surly, and some volunteers began pounding the Jonga's sides. Captain Chhetri lost his nerve and fired into the air. He feared for the prince's safety and hoped to frighten the mob into scattering. Simultaneously, Tenzing pressed hard on the accelerator, crashed the barrier and the Jonga was soon lost in a speeding cloud of dust.

'You can't go around taking pot-shot from the windows of a Jonga!' Kazini screamed over the Kalimpong–Calcutta line when I telephoned her. 'Times have changed, you know, and their blood is up. The boys have said, "*Bus!* This time it's *khatam.*"'

Bajpai dolefully shook his head to mourn that while he was doing everything possible to save the royal family, it was determined to ruin itself through its own follies. 'Yes sir, you couldn't possibly do more to help them,' Bedi, his ever-faithful factotum, echoed sycophantically. From pulpit and forum, Kazi denounced the Chogyal's son's murderous activities which had resulted in three deaths, he thundered. The JAC even identified one of the 'victims' as Miss Kamal Tsong of Assam Lingsey village in east Sikkim. But far from having been gunned down in Raniphul on 4 April, an outraged Miss Tsong issued a proclamation on 18 May: 'I am very much alive and request you to consider this grave defamation that they have tried to bring on me.'[3] Ram Chandra Poudyal, by then encamped in the Paljor stadium, also denied Kazi's charge that the crown prince had made an attempt on his life.

There were other canards. Ganja Bahadur Gurung sent frantic messages to the palace, army and India House on 5 April to complain of terrible atrocities by Tibetans in Sichey bustee, where he lived. He was a shopkeeper in the bazaar and had unsuccessfully fought the elections as an independent candidate when he warned voters the political parties 'will throw you in the ditch alive.' He had thrown his lot in with the JAC since then. When he complained of houses being looted and set on fire, women raped, and children butchered, the Chogyal at once sent Rasaily, Keshab Chandra Pradhan, Chandra Das Rai and Karma Topden to Sichey bustee to inquire. Dutta Chowdhury and a police escort accompanied them. The place was quiet and a little apprehensive because many people wondered whether Gurung's mischievous story might not be an advance warning. But there had been no untoward happenings. The police commissioner telephoned India House to explain that the JAC was spreading panic. 'This particular incident would show how the organisers of the current agitation had deliberately tried to whip up communal frenzy with a view to hamper restoration of normalcy and create maximum possible mischief,' he pointed out. A copy was sent to India House which took no notice.

The Sikkim Guards meanwhile had cleared Raniphul of demonstrators and were marching towards Singtam. In spite of Tenzing's frivolity, there seemed every reason for supposing that the insurrection—if such it could be called—was running out of steam.

That possibility must also have occurred to Kazi and his sponsors. At about 10 o'clock on 5 April he and four other JAC leaders climbed the hill to see the PO. They needed advice on fresh tactics to mobilise villagers, maintain pressure on the palace and continue to dominate lurid headlines in India's only too obliging newspapers. But it was the durbar that came to their aid. For Dutta Chowdhury raided the petrol pump while they were away; and though he collected a mass of incriminating documents to show that the JAC had planned the upsurge only to invite New Delhi to take over Sikkim, the conspiracy was forgotten in the blaze of publicity attracted by the drama of the five leaders' appeal for political asylum. They sensationally petitioned Mrs Gandhi 'to intervene quickly and fully before we are massacred'. India House sent the message which was at once relayed to the press and radio. It was a masterstroke dreamt up by RAW, Bajpai and his officials who at once extended full hospitality to the five JAC men.

Conditions deteriorated rapidly throughout Sikkim. Police stations, often only a hut with a constable in charge, were burned down in the Nepalese-inhabited south and west. Loyal officials were beaten up. The country's few armouries were looted and wireless equipment and stocks of petrol seized. Anyone who tried to resist this reign of terror was locked up by the mob. Singtam's Bhagwati temple was converted into a jail for lamas and civil servants who were made to chop wood and draw water for the people's leaders. An excise official was put to work in a poultry farm, and the Densapa family home in Barmiok razed to the ground. Rare thankas, ikons, Tibetan brass and bronze and ancient Buddhist manuscripts—a priceless collection matched only by the Namgyal Institute's treasures—went up in flames. Eventually, the relics were brought to Athing-La; a pitifully battered little tin trunk in which rattled a few blackened and twisted pieces of metal saved by a faithful servant who had hidden in the jungle and travelled furtively by night to Gangtok. The fear that gripped loyal Sikkimese was not lessened when Phurpa Maila, a former president of the National Party, was murdered in cold blood.

Enraged by such vandalism, the National Party threatened to bring down its own men from the Bhutiya-Lepcha strongholds of the north. But the army, which had stood by when JAC cadres and infiltrators from India terrorised the countryside, quickly threw a barrier across the North Sikkim Highway. Even the Chogyal would not allow the National Party to put up a fight. 'You must tell their leaders that the last thing I want is a communal holocaust,' he instructed an aide when told that 6,000 sturdy men of Lachen and Lachung awaited his orders at Mangan. 'If they don't listen, I will go there myself and ask them to return home.' His circumspection was not to everybody's liking. 'The minority has been made to feel like a defenceless minority in its own homeland,' was Karma Topden's bitter complaint.

• • •

The purpose behind the disturbances was also becoming clear. When a friend telephoned Tenzing from Cambridge, the prince told him that the PO was pressing his father to surrender the government to—and the Indian Telephones line went dead just as Tenzing was about to reveal who the nominee was to be. Bajpai's charter of demands, which the Chogyal was ordered to sign as if it were his own letter, supplied the censored passage. The first draft ordered him to write: 'As agreed by you, I hereby appoint the GOC 17 Mountain Division as the administrator of Sikkim,' There were angry exchanges when the Chogyal refused. He was hysterically accusing, Bajpai cuttingly derisive. India House presented six drafts one after the other. The palace turned all of them down. They bound the Chogyal to abide by Indian advice, seek New Delhi's protection for himself and his family, and commit the durbar to carrying out extensive political changes. The Chogyal would also have to promise to withdraw all charges against the demonstrators, including Krishna Chandra Pradhan. He was expected to condone violations of the law, allow an Indian judge to investigate election complaints, and order fresh polls within twelve months instead of allowing the new council to serve its full term of three years.

Though Bajpai threatened and bullied, storming out of the palace when he failed, the Chogyal might have persisted in his refusal if violence did not again seem imminent. Khatiawara, who had fled Gangtok when the first shot was fired at the petrol pump, had collected another mob in Kalimpong and borne down on Singtam. The Guards were sent to defend the town; but stricken to the core by the petrol-pump firing, the Chogyal would not allow them to use force. The police were given similar instructions. Hamstrung by their orders, the Guards fell back on Sankhola. Then, as the mob advanced, they retreated to Raniphul. The Chogyal yielded to pressure rather than fight. Police action of the kind that is almost a daily occurrence in Calcutta would have quelled the riot. The Chogyal would not hear of retaliatory official violence.

Bajpai and Avtar Singh were both at hand on 6 April when he agreed to ask India to man the Rangpo, Rhenock and Melli police stations. Next day the PO presented another document under which responsibility for law and order throughout the kingdom was transferred to India. This, too, was granted. Finally, on 8 April the Chogyal signed the last of Bajpai's drafts handing over his government to the PO.

• • •

This was the climax of a process that had been conceived in 1971, as soon as RAW had completed its work in what was still East Pakistan. According to Asoka Raina, author of *Inside Raw: The Story of India's Secret Service*, intelligence operatives were given two years to finalise strategy with not even the government in New Delhi being aware of what was afoot. This version suggests that even Mrs Gandhi was not told of RAW's plans until eighteen months later, when the stage was set for action. 'The Prime Minister is reported to have asked when RAW would be in a position to go ahead and is said to have been surprised when told that the operation would commence within twenty-four hours.'

The Sikkimese didn't know details but were not surprised by the overall thrust of these disclosures. All Kalimpong knew of Kazini's friendly relations with the Subsidiary Intelligence Bureau there. Only a special dispensation allowed her to live permanently in the border town at a time when Indian officialdom was paranoiacally suspicious of all foreigners, especially Westerners. It had been noted she had access to classified documents like Harishwar Dayal's dos-and-don'ts letter. More than once Densapa had complained to India House that Indian undercover agents had been identified in remote places in the north where they had no ostensible duties. Employees of India's extensive military intelligence network seemed to spend more time fraternising with the Sikkimese than on the border with China that they were supposed to guard. Doubts had been voiced, too, about the true functions of India House's ethnic Tibetan employees. In fact, the Chogyal had taken advantage of an informal meeting with Mrs Gandhi at the Mountaineering Institute in Darjeeling to say he had received reports that some kind of a 'Naxalite-type' rebellion was being fomented in Sikkim.

Coo Coo La was less mealy-mouthed. She had warned for years that a SIB agent called Tejpal Singh, locally known as 'Go-kar' (whitehead) on account of his thatch of grey hair, was distributing money to the durbar's opponents. She was shopping in Hong Kong, buying vast quantities of mushrooms, seaweed, ferns, mao-tai and other Chinese delicacies for her second daughter's wedding, when the April disturbances began. The princess at once called a press conference and repeated all her old fears, though she also tactfully suggested that an over-zealous intelligence agency might have exceeded its brief. Even so, Mrs Gandhi was not amused. Kazini was mocking. 'I was amused at Coo Coo La calling a press conference in Hong Kong,' she wrote from Kalimpong. 'I wonder if George Patterson, who always accused her of "dabbling", was present. It did not appear to cut much ice.' Soon afterwards, the *Himalayan Observer* (5 May 1973) printed a particularly vicious article on Sikkim's 'dangerous dabblers'.

Raina's book confirmed that Indian intelligence had encouraged and promoted, if not actually initiated, a rising that Mrs Gandhi's government tried so hard to project as a spontaneous national movement to which it was forced to respond.

> It was not difficult for RAW to reinforce the idea, which was already widely prevalent, to get rid of the Chogyal. Select individuals, who were popular amongst their respective communities, were asked to further propagate the idea. Funds were made available for this purpose; a few were assured 'danger money.'[4]

The sequel is worth noting:

> Four years later RAW was still mopping up loose ends. There were still a few people who had to be paid off for services rendered. Their involvement had hastened the process for the formation of the 22nd Indian state. Payments had been delayed, for the Congress government had fallen and the Janata Party had taken over. Fresh authority for funds to be released had to be sanctioned. These never came through.[5]

This default may help to explain why Nar Bahadur Khatiawara, pampered darling of Kazi and Kazini, trusted protégé of Indian officials in Gangtok and Kalimpong, wooed by Indian politicians twice his age, became the most pungent critic of the revolution of which he was the acknowledged hero. None of the manoeuvres in 1973 and subsequent years would have succeeded if Khatiawara had not produced a mob to back every Indian decision with a semblance of popular Sikkimese support. Yet, in the historic memorandum that he presented to Morarji Desai on 1 August 1977, a bitterly disillusioned Khatiawara described the deceit that was practised on the Sikkimese in 1973 to conclude:

> The sum total of the whole sordid episode has been that we are today branded as leaders who have sold away our country—a not very palatable compliment for any political leader anywhere in the world.[6]

Asoka Raina blames Desai's straitlaced morality for India failing to honour her debt to the Sikkimese collaborators who did her bidding.

• • •

It was a harrowing time in the palace. Hope's nerves were unequal to the strain; her poise was completely shattered. Nine year-old Prince Palden woke with a start one night, the rhythmic chanting of demonstrators still ringing in his ears, to ask his mother if people ever killed their king. The Chogyal spent his long evenings in black dejection. 'India already has everything, what more can they want?' he would ask over and over again. It was true, for New Delhi controlled communications in the landlocked country. Indian soldiers had almost turned Sikkim into a vast cantonment. The PO gave all the orders. The Sikkimese would have starved if Indian aid were cut off. Marwari traders dominated commerce. The Chogyal's throne was a flimsy rocking-chair in the hollow of Mrs Gandhi's hand.

There was no scope for increasing India's effective power. All that New Delhi lacked—was seemingly most envious of—was the technical sovereignty that still vested in the Denzong monarchy. It did not seem an important enough gain to justify the operation; but that the operation was succeeding was evident from the ambivalence of some of the Chogyal's most trusted officials. None of the civil servants who daily reported at the palace was anxious to fall foul of India House.

Their calculations became evident when the Chogyal sought the advice of the kingdom's twenty most senior officials before submitting to the PO's demands. He warned them of the consequences. 'We are going back to dewan's rule. It means that twenty-five years of working towards an independent Sikkim will go down the drain.' He told them he was prepared to hold out if they would support him. There was more in this vein, pleading, remorseful and sentimental, but also appealing to their patriotic instinct. 'Canny to the end, the old man wasn't going to take a step without passing the buck to his officers' was Bajpai's acid comment when one of the officers invited to the palace meeting lost no time in reporting the conversation to him.

Buck or no buck, Sikkimese civil servants were not going to stick out their necks and advise against yielding. They were ready to welcome the rising sun. An aide produced a sheet of paper on which someone wrote: 'In the best interest of the country, under circumstances prevailing at the present moment in Sikkim, arising out of the recent and destructive politics, we accept the attached draft between Sikkim and India.' The reference was to the third and most drastic of Bajpai's propositions; it was endorsed by all the twenty men present, including the Chogyal's trusted secretary, Jigdal Densapa.

Even then, many Sikkimese believed the transfer of authority under the agreement signed on 8 May 1973 was only temporary. Bajpai told reporters he had hoped for agreement between palace and politicians. 'We regret it did not prove possible.' He added: 'We intend to assist the durbar also for a long-term solution of other problems, including political ones, in consonance with the spirit of the age.' The Chogyal and others noted that the PO implied resumption of Gangtok's authority. Avtar Singh was more categorical at Dum Dum airport when he explained that the Chogyal remained head of state and that India would hand back the government 'soon after restoration of law and order'.

However, the PO's actions seemed designed to destroy rather than restore the peace. His first move as supremo was to revoke Section 144, which had another six days to go, without even the required magistrate's sanction. The result, which Bajpai must have foreseen, was to bring a massive body of potentially turbulent men, then waiting eight miles away, right into the heart of Gangtok where they had the run of the town without any restraint at all. Questioned about his motives in inviting the invasion, the PO blandly ignored precedents at home to tell an India House press conference that 'peaceful demonstrators pursuing a legitimate form of protest could not be stopped by force'. He preferred to use 'persuasion'. But the only form of persuasion visible was the hospitality of Indian troops who set up camp for the demonstrators in Gangtok's Paljor Stadium and provided them there with food and water.

It was a secure base, protected by the Indian army, from where the JAC could lead daily sorties against the palace and every so often go on the rampage in town.

Two further decisions made it clear that Sikkim was being thrown to the mob. Bajpai ordered the Sikkim Guards into the palace grounds from where they watched helplessly as the country sank into planned anarchy. Then, the Sikkim police was stripped of its uniforms and the men confined to barracks, which the crowd in the stadium above systematically bombarded with stones. Their food godowns were looted. Dutta Chowdhury, to whom the restrictions did not apply since he was Indian, voluntarily laid aside his khaki to share the humiliation that had been forced on his men. Though the Guards and police were gone, the PO did not depute soldiers or the Central Reserve Police to maintain the peace. JAC cadres manned checkposts and barricades when I drove up from Rangpo on 10 April. Indeed, taxis and private cars were off the road. I would never have reached Gangtok if the PO had not with quixotic graciousness allowed me to travel with the diplomatic pouch in an India House jeep. The JAC cheered our jeep with its India plates all along the way, but turned back consignments of grains and vegetables.

This encouragement of anarchy synchronised with mounting psychological pressure on the palace. Bands of demonstrators were allowed up to the gates several times every day to scream abuse at the Chogyal and Gyalmo, burn their portraits, and tramp round the grounds to deafening roars. But when the National Party led a counter-demonstration, it was peremptorily stopped at the pavilion on the Ridge where a young Indian army lieutenant nervously fingered his revolver lest the Chogyal's friends try to advance closer. They had to halt there so that the royal family couldn't see or hear this brave show of loyalty. 'K.C. Pradhan, go to hell, L.D. Kazi, you as well,' read one of their placards. Man Kumar Basnet strode up and down like a champion wrestler surveying his fans, and a gnarled old Nepalese labourer, complaining of hunger, demanded to be fed like the JAC men in the stadium.

It was a spontaneous rally, laughter mingling with tears, without the steely resolve of Khatiawara's crowd, but reflecting in microcosm the variety of Sikkimese society—comfortable women in khos who knitted, and chewed paan, village elders who invoked heaven's wrath on those who had insulted their king, civil servants who still believed in India's good faith, sprigs of Bhutiya-Lepcha nobility, and a sprinkling of bright young Nepalese students. The PO's aides assured Indian reporters fresh from Delhi and with no knowledge of local conditions that the palace had hired all these men and women.

Kewal Singh, India's foreign secretary, who had arrived that morning, had to make his way through this crowd. Every inch the superior ICS man, he looked on in thin-lipped distaste as a weeping Bhutiya patriarch unwound his long braided plait and swept Singh's feet with it in token of ultimate submission. He was suing for clemency for his king and country, but the foreign secretary brushed the man aside to stride to his car.

India House propaganda constantly stressed that the true representatives of Sikkimese opinion were down in the stadium and that, but for Indian vigilance, they would long ago have murdered the Chogyal and his family. 'We've had information that one or two small groups of Nepalese might try to slip into the place and bump off the old man... we are not taking any chances with his life,' confided Bajpai. He had become the kingdom's absolute ruler, citing assassination conspiracies to justify his decision to place the palace under siege. Poor Manuel found it difficult to do his shopping. The Indian military cordon allowed hostile groups to march right up to the palace gates. It kept only friends and neutral visitors away.

Driving to the palace to see the Chogyal by appointment, I was halted by an Indian army officer and told no one was allowed in. Those were the GOC's orders. So I drove to India House where the PO emerged from a meeting to shake a doleful head and again murmur they couldn't be too careful with security since the palace might be stormed any moment and the royal family massacred. No demonstrator had stopped me, I explained, only the Indian army, but I doubt if he listened. However, courteous as ever, he provided me with a military escort to go through the army cordon. That is what gave his first secretary the chance to tell other newspapermen that the army had to protect me from being torn apart by the angry public. I had appealed for protection in this version and he had given me an escort!

The claim that 20,000 people, or a tenth of the entire population, had assembled in the stadium—repeated in the Indian media—was another grotesque exaggeration. Not more than 2,000 could have been camped there. Even they began to lose interest in the whole business after a few days. Some men tried to slip away but militants stabbed two of them. Into this restive throng stormed Lhanzin-La Tashi, a rotund little whirlwind in a patched blue anorak over her dark kho, determined to defend her half-brother. They listened to her in surprisingly respectful silence. But up in Nahakul Pradhan's bungalow, Roop Narain Dahal typed out another resolution condemning 'the Chogyal's sister's provocative and unpatriotic action'.

There was chaos in the bungalow. No one knew how the men had got into the stadium, who was in command, what the next step would be and where it would all end. In a room hung with portraits of Sir Tashi Namgyal, as well as the king and queen of Nepal, the host told reporters he had merely asked for political and administrative adjustments under a constitutional monarch. A Delhi journalist, with only the external affairs ministry's briefing to guide him, thought the revolt had been triggered off because the durbar was forcing Nepalese to wear the Bhutiya kho. Misunderstanding the question, Nahakul Pradhan, a simple man with limited English, rummaged in a drawer to fish out a coloured snapshot of himself in ankle-length brocade taken outside the ADC's cottage. 'Of course, I wear kho for palace ceremonies,' he exclaimed indignantly. 'I never refused!' 'Then what's it all about?' asked the visitor, but Nahakul Pradhan did not know.

Krishna Chandra thought he did. Self-importantly strutting up and down the verandah, he explained that the Chogyal's abdication was 'the central point' of the agitation. The 1950 treaty was no longer valid because it had not been negotiated by the sovereign people; Sikkim and India would have to agree on a new alliance. 'Its terms will be decided when we sit down and talk over things... but our country will not be sold again for money or privileges.' Kazi was on tenterhooks lest his wife, left in Kalimpong with strict instructions not to stir out of Chakung House, materialise at any moment, upset everybody, and shove her husband out of the limelight. *'Kazini uder acchha hai... hiya ane-se kiya bol dega aur sub gol-mal ho jai-ga...'* (Kazini's better off there... if she comes here she might say something and upset everything...) he whispered anxiously, every so often glancing down the road as if her jeep might sweep up without warming. His attitude seemed to strengthen the view that for all her vitriol, Kazini had ceased to wield much power. Kazi looked elsewhere for orders.

But there was no trace of hesitation or indecision as Bajpai briefed the press on the JAC's ultimatum. 'Their demands have increased considerably,' he said with seeming regret. Each visit to India House by the JAC leaders had, in fact, added to the list. The three points Kazi had presented to the Chogyal on 27 March had been inflated to fourteen. They included new citizenship rules, an elected advisory council to assist the Indian administrator, eviction of all Tibetans, agrarian reforms, an inquiry into the distribution of Indian aid, investigation of police conduct during the disturbances and exoneration of all demonstrators. The new list also demanded Dutta Chowdhury's 'summary dismissal' and examination of the Ranipul incident involving Tenzing. The last clause said that 'unlawful activities resorted to by some anti-social elements' who had exploited their movement should be punished. JAC leaders explained that Kaloo Rai and his cronies had extorted protection money and ransacked private and business houses that refused to oblige.

No one talked of a merger with India. But the expanded charter wanted the 1950 treaty to 'be scrapped and a new treaty of perpetual friendship between the peoples of India and Sikkim to be signed to strengthen the existing bonds of friendship between the peoples of the two countries, making it more secure and lasting'.

Kewal Singh received the charter on 11 April with every appearance of graciousness. He was the saviour sent by Mrs Gandhi. In that incarnation, he lectured the Chogyal, scolded the crown prince, conferred with JAC leaders, expressed his strong disapproval of the National Party's counter-demonstration, and promised everybody a new constitution for Sikkim. Obligation discharged, the foreign secretary returned to India, taking Tenzing with him. The PO was left to pursue New Delhi's objectives.

As the false claim about the military protecting me from demonstrators showed, manipulation of information was revealed as an essential feature of the strategy. Though foreign correspondents in New Delhi were clamouring for permission to go to Sikkim, not a single one of them was given the inner line permit that still controlled entry. They had to rely for news on the semi-official Press Trust of India whose reporter was Gurdip Singh Bedi's house guest in Gangtok. PTI's version was frequently quoted in the Indian Parliament and prominently printed in all Indian newspapers. In the absence of any more independent news, it was also often picked up by agencies abroad.

The external affairs ministry also emerged as a major source of stories that it asked newspapers to publish as if written by their own reporters in Gangtok. When the *Statesman* in Calcutta objected that readers knew it didn't have a correspondent in Sikkim, the ministry ingeniously suggested the opening: 'Reports reaching us from Gangtok indicate...' The paper's Delhi edition eventually published a bizarre piece of fiction datelined New Delhi and supposedly by one of its special representatives there. The supposed author claimed that 'according to reports reaching Calcutta from Gangtok...' This piece of fiction had obviously sped through Calcutta without a whisper penetrating the *Statesman*'s head office in the city. Being near the seat of power, journalists in Delhi were more easily influenced.

The Chogyal's complaints about biased coverage predictably had no effect. He cabled Mrs Gandhi on 9 April to say that All-India Radio was giving the world 'the impression that democratic forces have been suppressed and peaceful demonstrators fired upon' and also that it was entirely incorrect for AIR to claim that the Indian army was feeding Gangtok when in fact the army was 'feeding the demonstrators only'. Gullible as ever, the Chogyal also pleaded for Mrs Gandhi's 'personal intervention in the interest of abiding friendship and closest relations between India and Sikkim'. He still clutched at the hope that New Delhi meant no harm to his country and that the Sikkimese would be allowed to resolve their differences. 'We have had misunderstandings before but they always come back to me in the end,' he told a press conference in the palace. 'It is not a question of being optimistic... we have to reach an agreement.'

The JAC announced on 9 April that the agitation was being called off. On 13 April the Chogyal promised to convene an all-party conference in May to discuss constitutional changes. Five days later Kazi and Krishna Chandra merged the SNC and Janata Congress to form the Sikkim Congress.

• • •

An unnoticed consequence of the turbulent birthday party was the political debut of a good-looking young Nepalese schoolmaster whose presence and talents did not then arouse interest. At thirty-three, Nar Bahadur Bhandari could not have been more different from Khatiawara or Krishna Chandra Pradhan. A slender man of medium height with pleasant ways and a winning smile, he said little in private and that too was quietly restrained. But Bhandari was a rousing speaker on a public platform. He was eloquent and impassioned in Nepalese.

He had been born in Malwasi bustee near Soreong in the west on 5 October 1940, studied locally up to class eight, then gone to high school in Namche, and eventually taken an arts degree from Darjeeling's Government College. Unlike Krishna Chandra, Bhandari was the son of poor peasants who could not afford to pay for his education. Unlike Khatiawara, he did not have a rich patron. 'As a student I didn't get a Sikkim government stipend or an Indian scholarship.' He had to work his way to pay fees and buy books, collecting firewood for his schoolmaster. He held this against the Chogyal. It was evidence, he said, of the durbar's indifference to Nepalese without money or influence.

The injustice rankled all through the young teacher's early career in modest schools in Soreong, Chakung, Rangeli and Namche. He was working in Gangtok's West Point School when trouble broke out, and was at once drawn to the JAC's objectives as publicly announced. Being without political grooming or axes to grind, Bhandari did not initially suspect outside direction or more sinister motives in the JAC's limited democratic agenda. But though convinced that the administration had to be reformed, he was worried by the rank communalism of men like Khatiawara and Krishna Chandra. He threw in his lot with Kazi because he felt the SNC president needed and wanted the support of moderate Nepalese.

Bhandari's illusions lasted a bare four weeks. On 5 May he advised a sizable crowd in Namche to take a long hard look at the JAC's composition, methods and real aims. The warning was publicly repeated at another meeting in Peling. Nepalese and Bhutiya-Lepchas were brothers, said Bhandari, and should not quarrel among themselves; if they did, outsiders would exploit the dispute and that would be the end of Sikkim. Even Nar Bahadur Bhandari could not have guessed then how prophetic his words would turn out to be.

REFERENCES

1. Report by Commissioner, Sikkim Police (Gangtok, 11 April 1973, unpublished).
2. Ibid.
3. From the 'Tsong Union to All Tsongs of Sikkim: Appeal' (pamphlet, 18 May 1973).
4. Asoka Raina, *Inside RAW: The Story of India's Secret Services* (Vikas, New Delhi, 1981).
5. Ibid.
6. Nar Bahadur Khatiawara and nine others, 'Sikkim's Merger—A Brief Resume' (Gangtok, 31 July 1977, unpublished).

CHAPTER

12

FOOT IN THE DOOR

'The real power in the kingdom (or is it chiefdom now?) is exercised by the Indian Chief Executive who wears many hats.'

V. GOPAKUMAR,
Far Eastern Economic Review, 20 September 1974.

'These people are intolerable apathetic, and prefer being tyrannized over to the trouble of shaking off the yoke.'

SIR JOSEPH HOOKER,
Himalayan Journals.

B. S. Das was an odd fish in bureaucratic waters. Technically, he was still a member of the Uttar Pradesh police force and held the rank of deputy inspector-general; but unusual assignments had taken him into very different and diverse waters. He was political counsellor in India's missions in London and Moscow, flown to Hanoi 'to investigate a serious breach of security' in India's consulate there and asked in London to inquire into the charge that Salman Haidar, then second secretary but later India's foreign secretary, was 'feeding information to his counterpart in the Pakistan high commission'. He had also for four years represented New Delhi at the court of Thimpu. In fact, Das was sent there as the first envoy when India and Bhutan agreed in 1971 to exchange diplomatic representatives and had, by all accounts, walked a trickily narrow path with skill and dexterity.

The job was of something more than just an ambassador. Das was the only one in Bhutan, representing a powerful neighbour that was not yet quite reconciled to shedding its quasi-imperial responsibilities and determined, therefore, to extract the most advantageous terms for itself. His presence symbolised both the Druk kingdom's emergence to sovereignty and the restraints within which that sovereignty was still obliged to function. Over the years he acquired intimate knowledge of the royal family and its secrets. But King Jigme Dorji Wangchuk, K3, had astutely made a friend of him, seeking Das's advice even in delicate matters affecting his family. If Queen Kesang's Dorji relatives were less enthusiastic about New Delhi's man, they had to admit he was never unfair. Moreover, they liked his shyly pleasant wife Nirmala, the daughter of an historian of some note, and herself the author of the slim volume on Bhutan cited earlier.

This was the man Kewal Singh sent to Gangtok on 10 April to relieve the PO of the additional duty of administering Sikkim. Das's instructions were to extend full support to the mob and compel the Chogyal to yield to New Delhi's demands, threatening, if necessary, to depose him and annex the kingdom. His memoirs make it clear both he and Bajpai recognised this as the real purpose of the appointment. They had to devise the means to make annexation look plausible. A percipient West Bengal civil servant says Mrs Gandhi's dismissive attitude to the Chogyal when he called on her at Darjeeling's Raj Bhavan made it abundantly clear that whatever she and her ministers and officials might find it expedient to say in public, she had decided 'to get rid of the king and grab Sikkim'.

Das was a prim, dapper little person with slicked-back hair and a fine-drawn moustache, stiff and even a little pompous in comparison with Chopra's flamboyance and Bajpai's aplomb, but probably more genuine than either and pleasant company once he had been persuaded to thaw. In 1973, Das was commissioner of Delhi Municipal Corporation; later he became chairman of the International Airports Authority and of Air-India. Gossip had it that only an intelligence (RAW?) background could equip a man for such varied assignments. Das always laughed off the suggestion but the Chogyal's old friend, Nari Rustomji of the ICS, spoke of Das and Bajpai's successor, Gurbachan Singh, being weaned 'in the sinister machinations of RAW'.

The new administrator's initial reception at the palace was not warm. The Chogyal was still smarting from the previous week's turbulence. But the Bhutanese had spoken well of Das, and his deferential manner was a relief after Bajpai's hectoring. The JAC might have preferred someone who declaimed belligerently on the medievalism of monarchy and the righteousness of people's movements, but it, too, found little to complain of in the administrator's unobtrusive style. 'I will meet everybody who wants to meet me,' Das announced, following up the promise by restoring the Sikkim police to their normal tasks and rescinding Bajpai's licence for anarchy by reimposing Section 144 in Gangtok. He then drove down to Singtam to convince the mob still lingering there that the party was over. He also brought in 1,500 men of India's Central Reserve Police Force to make it still clearer that law and order could no longer be disregarded. At the same time, Das wooed the Sikkimese with generous promises of development funds.

Three young Indian civil servants were inducted to serve as officers on special duty and assist the new administrator. K.M. Lal was placed in charge of Gangtok, Davy Manavalam in Namche became responsible for the south, and Jayanta Sanyal ruled the west from Gyalzing. Only the northern district, with headquarters at Mangan, was spared an Indian administrator. It continued under a Sikkimese district officer.

In spite of Das's obvious qualities, an anomalous situation continued to encourage uncertainty. There was the Chogyal in the palace, a brand new administrator in Mintokgang where dewans and sidlons once lived, and the PO literally looking down on both from the heights of India House. In the days following the storm, no one was quite sure who the real ruler was. Nor did anyone know where he, she or, indeed, the kingdom, stood. Each viewed the future in terms of the immediate past, calculating how the upheaval could be turned to private gain. The revolution was losing momentum. Das ordered the arrest of Kaloo Rai and Shebchung Bhutia, another JAC leader who had once been the Densapas' driver, both accused of making money out of the riots. Several of the Singtam revolutionaries were also jailed. The JAC itself seemed threatened. An attempt to break it and revive the State Congress petered out only when Nahakul Pradhan, who had never ceased to wonder at the rag-tag company he found himself in, suddenly died.

There were other indications too that Khatiawara was no longer the rising star. There were no villagers now to hustle, no marchers to lead to glory. Instead, the much sharper ethnic Nepalese in Darjeeling and Kalimpong were casting covetous eyes on Sikkim's virgin land and business opportunities. The fear of being swamped prompted each community to sit up in alarm, overnight destroying the Chogyal's painstaking efforts to integrate society under a common Sikkimese label. So strong was racial antagonism that each leader saw salvation in carving out his communal constituency. While Kazini pestered *The Statesman* with letters stressing her husband's 'pure Lepcha' ancestry, Kazi resurrected a Lepcha Association that had been moribund for years. That prompted the National Party's Rinzing Tongden Lepcha to set up a rival Denzong Rong Sezum. There were parallel demonstrations and fears of violence. Tsongs (also called Limbus) were worried about being lumped with the Nepalese, and the scheduled castes were demanding more explicit constitutional favours as in India.

Even the Nepalese did not any longer present a united front. Badri Nath Pradhan, who had taken a law degree in Calcutta and been prominent in the JAC, admitted that the 1950 treaty would have to be revised to permit 'full-fledged democracy'. Krishna Chandra talked even more quizzically of the need for national reconciliation. He had forgotten his grievance against the palace and his vituperation against the kazis; he now described Bhutiyas, Lepchas and Nepalese as three brothers born by some curious biological process of a common father embodied in the person of that descendant of Khampa forbears, the Chogyal. The JAC was not only divided on ethnic lines but also between old and young, moderate and extremist. The blade of revolutionary unity had splintered into a number of smaller instruments, some sharply gleaming, others ineffectually dull, each guided by a different hand. Even Kazi seemed less rigid as he brooded on how often he had advised the Chogyal to avoid a clash.

This irresolute introspection was not to Khatiawara's liking. He set up a guidance committee in Singtam to hold the JAC to its commitments and make sure it did not agree to any compromise. Kazi was heckled at Melli and asked brusquely to explain his future programme instead of gloating over past triumphs. He had promised to parcel out the royal estates, they said; if that was not immediately possible, he should make a beginning by redistributing the extensive holdings of Bhutiya-Lepcha nobles, which would have meant divesting himself of property. Hundreds of young Nepalese were brought together in Singtam on 26 April to take a solemn oath in the Bhagwati temple and vow on the Gita to continue their campaign until its ends had been achieved. Khatiawara was showing signs of impatience with Kazi's bumbling and Kazini's imperiousness. At his urging, the Sikkim Congress adopted a series of resolutions asking for a written constitution, democratic rights and strong ties with India, requesting Mrs Gandhi to take 'steps to give effect to our mandate'. Many Sikkimese saw the

'Foreign Hand' behind these rumblings. They believed that, worried lest the politicians should tire of demonstrations and seek a rapprochement with the palace, India (RAW again?) was using Khatiawara to push Kazi into a position of militancy from which he would not be able to retreat. At the same time, the Sikkim Congress prudently demanded a ban on the entry of Indian Nepalese.

Kazi's life was said to be in danger, and Chakung House bristled with CRP soldiers. Their presence and the tents in the garden added tremendously to Kazini's sense of consequence after all the years of neglect. She hung a thanka in the verandah and told everyone that a poor busteewallah had trekked for miles to bring it to her with Buddha Bhagwan's blessings for Kazi's safety. 'Heaven knows he needs it!' she added meaningfully, kohl-ringed eyes swivelling round the circle to make sure her message was understood. I already knew her meaning for she had written to me with her usual flourish: 'Kazi presented me with the bullet that nearly sent him to another world and asked me, with a twinkle in his eye, "Will you have it encased in gold or platinum?" Poor darling, they have made three attempts on his precious life... and we know all about who instigates and who carries out, etc... etc.' More later of that particular drama.

There was a reaction too. A young Gangtok kazi, Kunga Topden, no relation of Karma's, had grouped together a number of Bhutiya, Lepcha, and Nepalese boys and girls under the banner of the Youth Pioneer movement. Though Das refused to register them as a formal organisation, the Youth Pioneers were determined to fight for the Sikkimese way of life.

India House shot down the administrator's first attempt to reconcile all these strands. Conditioned by Bhutan where he had successfully installed a royal advisory council before the cabinet system was introduced, Das tried to repeat the experiment in Sikkim and at once ran into objections. The National Party, which was given five out of fifteen seats, grumbled that its electoral majority had been cancelled by executive order. The JAC complained that separate allocations (five seats each) for the Janata Congress and SNC indicated the administrator did not recognise their merger. Though Khatiawara welcomed the innovation as 'the first step and a practical device in the existing circumstances of Sikkim's politics', others objected that the council did not enjoy executive or legislative powers. Some felt the Nepalese (eight against seven Bhutiya-Lepcha) should enjoy greater weightage. More conclusively, the PO pointed out that a royal advisory council was inappropriate since the word 'royal' denoted sovereignty.

The council died a natural death even before New Delhi struck the next blow at a late-night ceremony in the palace drawing-room. Photographs show Kewal Singh and Bajpai flanking the Chogyal under the massive thankas, Karma Topden in immaculate black kho in attendance, 'the tyrant sitting amidst members of the Joint Action Committee, the elected representatives of the people, the Political Officer, Gangtok, and the foreign secretary to the government of India' according to the *Himalayan Observer* (12 May 1973). Its story was titled 'Sikkimese Magna Carta—Kazi, Father of Democracy in Sikkim'. The event so hailed was the endorsement on 8 May 1973 of a tripartite agreement. There were eighteen signatories: the Chogyal, Kewal Singh, Bajpai, and five representatives each of the National Party, SNC and Janata Congress. Nar Bahadur Khatiawara was not among them.

The agreement reiterated Sikkim's dependent status, and Indian responsibility for defence, territorial integrity, and foreign relations. It also extended New Delhi's supervision to communal harmony, good government, and economic and social development. The parties to the arrangement agreed to instal a fully responsible government with a more democratic constitution, guarantee fundamental rights, establish the rule of law and an independent judiciary, give greater legislative and executive powers to the elected representatives of the people, introduce a system of elections based on adult suffrage giving equitable representation to all sections of the people on the basis of the principle of one-man one-vote, and strengthen Indo-Sikkim cooperation and inter-relationship. The new assembly would have jurisdiction over home and establishment, finance and land revenue in addition to all the subjects enumerated in the 1953 Proclamation. Some of its members would be nominated to an executive council.

The tripartite pact was a considerable gain from India's point of view. The disputable claims of Harishwar Dayal's informal letter were publicly stated and accepted, thus confirming New Delhi's right to take a direct interest in the kingdom's internal affairs. The monarchy ceased to be even formally treated as the fount of all authority and as the final arbiter. Though the Chogyal's authority over the palace and Sikkim Guards was recognised and it was stated that he would perform his functions in accordance with the constitution, his role was nowhere spelt out.

In contrast, the chief executive—Das's new designation—was exalted far above the original understanding of a temporary incumbent to help tide over a difficult period. He became head of the administration, speaker and chief minister, presiding over both the assembly and executive council. He selected the latter's members, distributed portfolios and supervised even the management of departments entrusted to individual councillors. The chief executive also enjoyed special responsibility for introducing constitutional and administrative reforms, upholding fundamental rights, and for economic planning. Though he was expected to 'submit all important matters to the Chogyal for his information and for his approval of the action proposed to be taken,' he could also take unilateral action in the Chogyal's name. In the event of differences between them, disputes would be referred to the PO 'who shall obtain the advice of the Government of India, which shall be binding'.

Since the chief executive was highly unlikely ever to take decisions without consulting India House (or for that matter any action that had not already been decided on by the external affairs ministry and PO to further New Delhi's interests), the net result of this clause was to deny the durbar the right of appeal to an objective or even disinterested party. In fact, the chief executive became an all-powerful nineteenth-century British proconsul governing a dependency through its decorative monarch and dummy legislature. The assembly was forbidden to discuss the royal family, sub-judice matters, the judiciary, the chief executive and India's responsibilities. Its newly acquired right 'to propose laws and adopt resolutions' was far less comprehensive than the 1953 power 'to enact laws for the peace, order and good government of Sikkim'. It was not clear either whether the 1953 Proclamation was still valid or had been abrogated. The final absurdity was that an internal arrangement appeared to supersede an international treaty. No one knew where the 1950 India–Sikkim treaty stood since the 8 May agreement overlapped it in many matters.

The more perspicacious members of the JAC pointed out that though all three parties had demanded responsible government, the 8 May document said nothing about a party system or the majority group's legislative rights. Even the National Party's modest claim to be able to choose its own executive councillors was turned down. Nor was the promise 'to ensure that no single section of the population acquires a dominating position due mainly to its ethnic origin' compatible with the assurance of 'equitable representation to all sections of the people on the basis of the principle of one-man-one vote', which would mean a permanent Nepalese majority. 'I would have added a dissenting note to say that the communal parity granted was illusory', commented the veteran Sonam Tshering.

Others, who would normally have welcomed reduction of the throne's powers, knew that the authority of which the palace had been stripped had all been transferred to Mintokgang and not to the people. The Sikkimese had not profited from their rising. They had expected the agreement to be a lucid, exhaustive and binding exposition of the kingdom's governance and relations with India. It should have defined roles, allocated functions, and created a framework within which the Chogyal and his subjects could harmonise their separate but not mutally exclusive aspirations. Instead, the document bristled with omissions, ambiguities and contradictions. No one knew, for instance, whether New Delhi could intervene in all disputes between the Chogyal and the chief executive or only in those relating to communal harmony, democracy and administrative efficiency. It wasn't clear whether the executive council was to be the upper house of a bicameral legislature or a cabinet of ministers. The more charitable complained that the document bore the marks of haste, inept draftsmanship and a desire to please everybody. Others were convinced it was deliberately woolly to permit further encroachments. Part treaty and part constitution, it was held together only by the linchpin of an Indian civil servant who owed his job to Mrs Gandhi and was not answerable to anyone. In Sikkim, the 8 May exercise replaced a feudatory monarchy with the contradiction of a feudatory democracy.

The Chogyal alone seemed to be content in those weeks after the signing ceremony. The palace had recovered some of its spirits. Hope was more like ordinary flesh and blood, still a little fey, perhaps, but a concerned mistress of the household determined to keep up spirits in a crisis. She drew visitors into playing scrabble on the library floor, and organised rehearsals for Jean Giradoux's play, *The Enchanted.* Maurice Valency's English version of the play was staged first in New York's Lyceum Theatre in 1950, which Hope may have seen. All her friends—Karma Topden, Lhanzin-La, and the handful of Europeans, Americans, and Eurasians in Gangtok—had parts. Even the Chogyal was drawn in, cast in the somewhat unfortunate role of executioner. Between his loud hamming, Lhanzin's giggles and the broad Scots of Ishbel Ritchie, a missionary schoolteacher in Gangtok, the palace drawing-room, where the rehearsals took place, became quite a boisterous place. The Gyalmo also talked of going down to Calcutta to find someone who could repair her grandmother's bentwood chair. Holding forth on Sikkim's schools, she promised that Palden and Hope Leezum, her children, would be educated there and not in England like the Chogyal's two elder sons by his Tibetan first wife. It seemed a time of peace in the palace, of fences being mended and loyalties pledged anew.

The euphoria was unreal: the mystery was cleared after lunch one afternoon. 'You haven't seen the agreement,' the Chogyal suddenly boomed. 'I mean the real one!' He waved to an ADC who produced a green leather folder impressively embossed in gold with India's lion capital. 'This is very, very, confidential,' he said, possessively caressing the leather. 'No one must know of it.' Promise of silence extracted, he at last let me have the folder and sat back to watch, beaming with satisfaction as, mystified by all this secrecy, I turned the cover.

In it was a four-part typed document titled 'Agreement between the Chogyal and the Government of India' signed in Gangtok on 23 April. It was at once clear why Kewal Singh had paid what the newspapers called an 'unannounced' visit to Gangtok on 21 April and stayed two days. It also explained the rumours that were rife in Kalimpong, and Kazini's searching questions revealing her fear that New Delhi might restore the durbar to power and sell the JAC down the Teesta. But the document itself was not substantially different from the tripartite agreement reached fifteen days later except for one crucial point: its opening clause promised that 'The honour, position and personal privileges of the Chogyal and his dynasty reflect the identity of Sikkim and must, therefore, be preserved.' The concluding sentence—'The Chogyal will perform the functions of his high office in accordance with the constitution of Sikkim'—was almost as comforting. A further reference to the monarchy stipulated that the country's future constitution would have to guarantee 'the constitutional position of the Chogyal of Sikkim'. The rest anticipated what was agreed upon on 8 May.

But the durbar was relieved because it rightly believed that Sikkim could not be absorbed while its throne survived. Kewal Singh also promised the Chogyal verbally that the administrator would be another dewan, and would be withdrawn as soon as the political situation had stabilised. If all this was reassuring, the durbar was baffled and worried by the foreign secretary's insistence on complete secrecy. It would have liked the tripartite agreement either to confirm the earlier one or to repeat that the monarchy and Sikkim's status as a protectorate remained unimpaired. But Kewal Singh assured the Chogyal that the 8 May document was only for public consumption, a sop to Kazi and his colleagues, and that the 23 April agreement was the operative one. Moreover, he continued, any reference to the monarchy or to relations with India might have suggested to the fifteen signatories that both matters were within their jurisdiction. Replying to one of the Chogyal's frequent letters, Kewal Singh wrote early in 1974.

> Your Highness had also raised the question of the treaty of 1950 and the exchange of letters in 1951. I would like to confirm that the relations between India and Sikkim established by the treaty of 1950 and the letters exchanged in 1951 have been further strengthened by the agreements of April and May 1973: the latter being additional to the 1950 treaty and the 1951 letters which remain in force... the Government of India will also safeguard the honour, dignity and position of the Chogyal of Sikkim and his heirs, and trust that he will continue to guide the people within the framework of the agreement to which he is a party.

But the foreign secretary adamantly refused to match this solemn private pledge with any kind of public admission. He warned the durbar that if politicians in India or Sikkim so much as heard of the April pact, New Delhi would at once repudiate its commitments. Obviously, India never did intend to honour an agreement that was only a device to placate the Chogyal after the trauma he had undergone and to obtain his consent to the tripartite agreement. When I asked Bajpai about the April document he shrugged his dismissal: 'Oh, that was superseded long ago!' But the Chogyal continued to repose his faith in the sanctity of India's pledges.

There were other worrying signs too. Das's stewardship was not continuing as well as it had started. L.B. Chhetri, a divisional engineer well disposed to the durbar, was kidnapped from the Jali power-house and taken to Singtam where he was forced to pay homage to the JAC. When Kazi accused the Chogyal of pocketing Indian development aid, the PO made no attempt to explain that India House received monthly accounts of how the money had been spent, or that Sikkim's financial adviser—always Indian—presented a progress report every six months to the Planning Commission in New Delhi. Kazi's further complaint of the royal family squandering investment funds on its foreign tours was just as silly, for Sikkim had forged ahead economically under the Chogyal and all the state-owned enterprises were prospering. The fruit factory in Singtam supplied juice to Air-India and British Airways, and Sikkim Distilleries in Rangpo had increased its capital from ₹ 400,000 to ₹ 26 million. All these undertakings paid handsome dividends. There was no question, either, of exploiting loopholes in Indian excise laws to make clandestine fortunes: the later tobacco licence scandal would have been unthinkable under the Chogyal's strictly moral regime.

No one in Gangtok paid any attention to Kazi's allegations. Nor did they believe him when he accused Princess Coo Coo La of smuggling out antique bronzes and thankas from monasteries and selling them abroad. But India's press and radio dutifully played up the charges so that opinion hardened against the palace. This psychological offensive did not lack partisan support. The *Himalayan Observer* nicknamed the Chogyal's deputy secretary 'Tikka Topden' after the notorious General Tikka Khan, butcher of Bangladesh[1], and the American magazine, *Newsweek*, peering at the durbar through long-range binoculars from Kalimpong, where its reporter obviously talked to Kazini, described Hope as 'a Himalayan Marie Antoinette'[2]. It was the last straw for a young woman whose forays into statecraft provoked far more hostility than they deserved. All this was most gratifying to Khatiawara who, fortified by his faith in 'private understandings' and 'gentlemen's agreements' with New Delhi, regretted that his men had not invaded and occupied the palace, driving the Chogyal and his family back to Tibet.

Even Das appeared to be abandoning initial attempts at objectivity: he seemed powerless to control the three Indian OSDs who had become deeply involved with the JAC. K.M. Lal, in particular, was Kazi's alter ego; if the official grapevine was to be believed, he suggested what steps the Sikkim Congress leader should take, drafted his letters and statements, and egged him on to further confrontations with the durbar. Kazini was languishing irritably in Kalimpong; but in Gangtok, her husband suddenly acquired a commanding voice and a fluent pen, proclaiming novel points of view with a legal conciseness that surprised everyone who had known him before and were well aware he had hardly any English. All three officers were supposed to serve the durbar under the chief executive's orders, but they were obviously closer to India House and did not bother at all with the Chogyal or his officials. They had become Sikkim's de facto rulers, working in close cooperation with Khatiawara, Subeidi, and other young Nepalese activists.

They were partly responsible for the disgraceful displays that RAW organized when the Chogyal toured the south and west.

His earlier visit to north Sikkim had proved a triumphal success; but the northern district, which turned out to greet its ruler with flags, bunting, khadas, gaily caparisoned yaks, chhang, and cheering crowds, was still governed by a Sikkimese civil servant posted at Mangan. There were very few Nepalese settlers in a region that was integral to the kingdom's Bhutiya-Lepcha ethic and Buddhist monarchy. The west and south were demographically and administratively different. Bhutiya-Lepchas had been driven away many decades earlier, and Manavalam and Sanyal turned a blind eye to preparations for one of the country's most inglorious exhibitions. Rows of demonstrators screamed abuse at the royal entourage, arches were strung with old shoes and tattered petticoats, even dogs were garlanded with derisive placards. 'Chogyal sex crazy bastard', 'Chogyal the murderer', and 'Drunken bastard go home' were some of the slogans said to have been painted by schoolchildren in their classrooms. The CRP helped to put them up.

Giggling wantonly, Kazini wallowed in intimately embarrassing descriptions of some of the more vulgar physical displays along the royal route. She also presented callers with a broadsheet titled 'Chogyal's Bid Foiled', which compared him to England's beheaded Charles I and Edward VIII who abdicated. She denounced as 'opportunists, deceivers, illiterate and crude' both 'the despised and loathed Karma Topden and Captain Roland Chhetri' who had organised the tour.[3] The Chogyal bore the ordeal in dignified silence, taking no notice of the insults and humiliations suffered in Namche and Gyalzing. Even the chief executive was impressed by his restraint.

But Das had his orders, which became clear when he wrote to Tarachand Hariomal, judge of the Central Court and head of Sikkim's judicial department, to ask why the judiciary should not report to the chief executive. Hariomal did not know that the 23 April agreement had expressly laid down that the judiciary would remain independent, but he had grown old in the service of justice and would not be budged from his understanding of propriety. Hariomal had qualified as an advocate in 1935 and had practised in Karachi until Partition when he migrated to India to join Uttar Pradesh's higher judicial service, retiring as a sessions judge in 1968. R.N. Haldipur, then Sikkim's principal administrative officer, offered him the post of chief magistrate, equivalent to district and sessions judge in charge of the kingdom's four districts. The appointment was originally recommended by New Delhi's law ministry which had studied Hariomal's service record and been impressed by his honesty, integrity and wide experience. The Chogyal merely approved it, but when the kingdom's judiciary was reorganised, Hariomal became in effect the chief justice of Sikkim.

He was not prepared to yield to bureaucratic pressure. The judge politely explained to the chief executive that an independent judiciary was answerable only to the head of state even in a constitutional monarchy, and that the prized principle of separation of powers would be violated if he took orders from the administration. He declined to send his files and explain his decisions to Das and also maintained that the chief executive could not act as head of state in the Chogyal's absence. There the matter rested for the time being.

The 1974 elections, arbitrary because they were not due, were held against this background of muted tension. Hope had packed her bags and returned to New York with Palden and Hope Leelzum, apparently on a visit, but actually never to return. Tenzing was back in Cambridge studying land management. India's chief election commissioner had visited Sikkim and divided the country into thirty constituencies, fifteen for each community, representatives to be chosen on the basis of the magic one-man-one-vote formula. But since more than 80 per cent of the voters in some of the southern seats earmarked for Bhutiya-Lepchas were Nepalese, it was clear that these legislators would not represent the interests of their own people. So it was suggested that each candidate would have to be proposed and seconded by forty voters, which only ensured a wider base of Nepalese support.

Convinced that the Bhutiya-Lepcha heritage was doomed, the National Party said, why bother? It fielded only six men which induced many disappointed members like Rinzing Tongden Lepcha to cross over to the Sikkim Congress. Tsong fears were realised when they were deprived of separate representation and lumped with the Nepalese. Some Lepchas threatened protests because they were still bracketed with Bhutiyas. The Scheduled Castes League announced a boycott when it was refused seven seats. Nar Bahadur Bhandari, who had formed the Prajatantra Party after severing links with Kazi, was not allowed to register it as a political organisation. Recognition was similarly withheld from Sonam Gyatso's nationalist group of United Independents. The two might effectively have challenged Kazi, but Das was not taking any chances. Undeterred, the Prajatantra Party and United Independents sponsored fifty-one candidates.

The Sikkim Congress put up sixty-four candidates from the thirty constituencies, this curious duplication being explained by Kazi's inability to offend Khatiawara and his radical peasants' organisation which disapproved of many of the party's official nominees. Khatiawara himself had formally been selected to contest both Soreong and Gyalzing when Kazi agreed that he, as well as Indra Bahadur Gurung, should also stand from Dentam. But Dentam already had an official Sikkim Congress candidate in the person of Chhatra Bahadur Chhetri who had not been trusted, however, ever since his ambivalence over the executive councillorship the previous year. Unable to throw him out, Kazi and Khatiawara hit on another strategy: with three Congress rivals in Dentam, the Indian election officer, a service colleague of the three OSDs, decided they would all have to be independents. The party machinery then supported only Khatiawara who won with 758 votes against Gurung's 102 and Chhetri's thirteen.

The manner of his victory brought enemies in its wake: 'Roop Narain Dahal, Nar Bahadur Khatiawara get out of Sikkim Congress' was painted on the culvert six miles out of Gangtok when I drove up. Krishna Chandra Pradhan, who had secured nearly 96 per cent of the votes cast in Jorethang, the highest by far, felt emboldened to argue that Khatiawara, being an independent, need not be taken into account. 'The party consists of Kazi and me,' he boasted. Krishna Chandra had also emerged as the latest favourite in Kazini's court of youthful males. She had fallen out with Khatiawara, and Gangtok lapped up spicy details of the lurid tales they told about each other. Another anonymous pamphlet, 'An Evil Star on the Political Horizon of Sikkim', the surest indication of the venom streaking out of Chakung House in Kalimpong, accused Khatiawara of bigamously marrying Hemlata Chhetri, the representative for Gyalzing, and of falsifying his age.

In spite of internal quarrels, the Sikkim Congress captured thirty-one out of thirty-two seats (sixteen Nepalese, nine Bhutiyas and six Lepchas) including the monasteries' constituency. Nar Bahadur Bhandari was defeated from Soreong by Chatur Singh Roy's 1,400 votes to his 300. Kazi, Bhim Bahadur Gurung, Bhuwani Prasad Kharel, Subeidi, Badri Nath Pradhan, Ram Chandra Poudyal and Shebchung Bhutia were all elected either unopposed or by handsome margins. Only Kabi voted for the National Party's Kalzang Gyatso Bhutia, and the Sikkimese were convinced that this had been 'given' to them out of deference to the ancient pact between Khye-Bumsa and Thekong-tek. In fact, the scale of the victory confounded everyone. They claimed that intelligence reports had initially given the Prajatantra Party a decisive lead. But the margin narrowed, wavered and disappeared; the massive crowds that always turned up to applaud Bhandari seemingly unable to make any impact. There was much talk of door-to-door intimidation, of Bhutiya-Lepcha houses being singled out for arson and violence, and of the CRP's dubious role. It was noted, too, that by allowing the Sikkim Congress to use the red and white national flag as its campaign banner, Das and the election officer had misled illiterate voters into believing they were supporting the durbar.

Sitting in the drawing-room at Mintokgang five years later, by when he had become chief minister with a landslide victory, Nar Bahadur Bhandari told me an amusing sequel. Apparently, the 1974 poll results were so unbelievable that outraged Sikkimese smashed at least sixty radio sets when AIR broadcast the news. But only one radio was destroyed after the 1979 elections when Bhandari's Janata Parishad emerged victorious and Kazi and his men did not get even a single seat. 'It was in this very room and it was kicked to pieces by Kazini herself!' said the man who had worsted her husband. As chief minister, Bhandari also saw to it that the 1974 elections were officially impugned. The Chogyal's old civil service colleague, Bipin Bihari Lal, who succeeded Das as chief executive and was promoted to be governor after the annexation, was forced to eat humble pie in his first inaugural address to the legislative assembly. In a speech written by the chief minister, as is the custom, the governor had to proclaim that the 1979 legislature was 'constituted after a free and fair election held in Sikkim for the first time under the auspices of the election commissioner in accordance with the provisions of the constitution'.[4]

It took five years and Mrs Gandhi's defeat for anyone to admit publicly what everyone in Sikkim was certain of in 1974.

But, however sceptical people may have been of the result, they did not expect Kazi to erase Sikkim from the world map. In view of his later actions, it is necessary to understand exactly what his party's election manifesto promised:

> The Sikkim Congress will seek to strengthen the bonds that already exist with the government and the people of India and to draw them even closer. The Sikkim Congress is aware that the democratic development of Sikkim has benefited from the

> interest shown by the government and people of India. Although for historical reasons our progress towards democracy has been slower, we also aspire to achieve the same democratic rights and institutions that the people of India have enjoyed for a quarter of a century.

At no time did it seek a mandate to abolish the throne and incorporate Sikkim in India.

There was no hint of betraying Sikkim either when, protesting that the Chogyal had not felicitated him on his electoral success, Kazi refused to attend a palace lunch in honour of the new legislators and sulkily stomped off to Kalimpong. The Chogyal's explanation that a constitutional head of state could not take pleasure in the victory of one party over others, and that he would congratulate Kazi when he formed a government, did not soothe the latter's inflated ego. Devout Buddhist though he professed to be, Kazi also announced that neither he nor any other Sikkim Congress member would take the oath of allegiance in the Tsuk-la-khang. In the event, the Chogyal swore in Das as assembly president. The 1973 council, which was still in legal existence, was summarily dissolved.

• • •

Buddhist lamas, a Brahmin priest and a Christian pastor invoked heaven's blessings on the new assembly when it was convened on 10 May. The thirty-one Congress members who had refused to go to the Tsuk-la-khang took the oath and signed the register after which B.S. Das, unfamiliar in a kho presented by the Chogyal, called the house to order, welcomed members, and received a khada from Kazi. He reminded the house that 'the fundamentals and the legality of the system have been clearly defined' by the 8 May agreement and that it would be expected to function within the 'parameters' laid down. It was an ironic warning, considering what was to follow. The Chogyal arrived a little after noon to deliver a short inaugural speech. He complimented members on their election and warned that though 'constructive criticism is an essential ingredient of a healthy democratic system, it is far easier to criticise than to shoulder responsibility'. Reminding everyone that Sikkim's earnings had increased from only a million rupees to ₹ 40 million in twenty years, he thanked India, briefly outlined the tasks ahead and advised legislators to bury past rancour and settle down to cooperative endeavour. It was an unexceptional address and the Chogyal was heard in respectful silence, even by Kazi.

The bomb burst the next day when Kazi rose to propose thanks 'for the inaugural speech of the constitutional head', as he put it with studied insolence. The fumbling old man from Chakung, nagged and bullied by his wife, trailing a whiff of Rumtek's lost tranquillity, disappeared in a welter of acidic, yet astute, political pronouncements that bore the hallmark of India's legal experts. The sophistication of Kazi's language and the far-reaching implications of his constitutional observations indicated that he had had access to far better brains than his own during the previous evening. If marriage marked one turning point in Kazi's career, this was another. His conversion into a ventriloquist's dummy was apparent to all on 11 May as Kazi read in Sikkimese from a prepared text. English and Nepalese translations had already been given to Chatur Singh Roy and Poudyal.

Kazi gave notice that the 8 May agreement could not limit aspirations. 'Yet, society is a growing thing and the evolution of democracy being a continuous process, those who fail to adjust themselves to the changes of time and circumstances will have perforce to face stark reality in all its consequences, and that too, with a modicum of grace.' Where had Kazi Dorji learnt such words? Did he even understand their meaning? Sikkim wondered, but Sikkim also realised that though speaking in the assembly, he was addressing the Chogyal. 'In democracy, in the ultimate analysis, the people constitute the prime and vital factor that matters. Without the people there can be no government, no state, no ruler. The voice of the people, therefore, is to be heard, honoured and respected.' Kazi was also sending Mrs Gandhi the message that RAW must already have advised her to expect. India's media lapped up every word of this playacting.

The actual motion of thanks was in three parts with three clauses in the first and six each in the other two. The third paragraph of the first part provided the initial surprise.

> The role and functions of the Chogyal cannot be more than those of the constitutional head of the government of Sikkim. In consideration for the discharge of these titular functions, the government of India are requested to afford him such honour, privileges and emoluments as are considered appropriate.

The presiding officer should at once have ruled out of order this flagrant violation of the stipulated 'parameters'. The assembly had no business discussing the Chogyal. Nor could it express any views on what India should or should not do. But here was Kazi not only speaking as if the ruler's functions and emoluments were to be determined by the assembly, but also as if Sikkim were an Indian colony and its king New Delhi's pensioner. Das's acquiescence was tangible evidence of his equivocation, if not worse.

The motion's second part asked for Sikkim to be included in the Indian Planning Commission's ambit and for Sikkimese students to be given educational and employment opportunities 'at par with the nationals of India'. The fifth and sixth clauses of the third part took this suicidal process much farther. Kazi asked for an Indian constitutional adviser; demanded that the positions of the Chogyal, chief executive, assembly, and executive council should be defined; and twice called for immediate steps for Sikkim's 'participation in the political and economic institutions of India'.

The cat was out of the bag. A separate country, however limited the exercise of its sovereignty, does not seek to take part in another nation's political and economic activities. But Das saw no incongruity in Kazi's requests. On the contrary, he rejected the Chogyal's protest about a motion that was so irregular and ominous as to bear no resemblance to the conventional vote of thanks. Kazi himself seemed unaware of the flood-gates he had opened. 'But India already controls everything!' he exclaimed, echoing the Chogyal when I asked if he knew what he was up to. 'All I asked for was that they should pay more for our plans, give something to the Chogyal, send our children to good schools and find them jobs.' His ingenuousness remained intact even when G.R. Rajagopaul, a retired secretary in the Indian law ministry, arrived soon afterwards, ostensibly in response to Kazi's invitation, to flesh out the constitution.

Kazini was beginning to be suspicious of events that had passed out of her control. She was jealous of K.M. Lal's influence over her husband and she resented the fact that Khatiawara, the village boy she had mothered and groomed, had also outgrown her tutelage. Reading the writing on the wall, she began to fear that the monarchy's abolition and Sikkim's merger with India would mean the end of all her own grand dreams. The British army sergeant's daughter had hoped the durbar would be the stage on which she would play out the most dazzling role of her life. Dismayed by the turn of events, she watched preparations to dismantle the props. No such craving inhibited her former protégé. Khatiawara told me he had been assured the 8 May agreement was only an arrangement for just one election; it was necessary to create a two-thirds majority in the assembly which would then vote to depose the Chogyal. Reminded that the agreement promised no such thing: on the contrary, it restricted the assembly's powers, Khatiawara snorted his contempt. 'I was not a party to the agreement and I am not bound by it. I don't like a system that equates 80 per cent of the people with 20 per cent. As an elected representative of the people, I can interpret the agreement as I think fit.'

Not everyone agreed. 'Khatiawara can do what he likes,' retorted Krishna Chandra Pradhan. 'He's only an independent member.' Krishna Chandra too was embarking on a new path. 'We will keep the chief executive as an adviser,' he explained, 'but his only function will be to provide a link between the Chogyal and the people.' For him the tripartite pact was an opening to a more assertive future.

Each actor was trapped in the part created by his dreams. Perhaps the most optimistic, then, was Chatur Singh Roy, at sixty-five one of the best educated and most articulate men in Kazi's party, with an intelligent awareness of events outside Sikkim. The new member for Soreong had been Gangtok's councillor from 1967 to 1969 and held executive charge of health and education. Roy told me there were typographical errors in Kazi's resolution. 'We didn't ask for participation in the political and economic institutions of India, it should have read *as in* India.' Bhim Bahadur Gurung, who had once asked for India's complete withdrawal from Sikkim, nodded in agreement. Perhaps they really believed in the mistake.

REFERENCES

1. 'Chogyal's Bid Foiled', off-print from *Himalayan Observer* (Kalimpong, 22–29 December 1973).
2. Lauren Jenkin, 'Queen of the Mountain,' *Newsweek* (2 July 1973).
3. 'Chogyal's Bid Foiled', off-print from *Himalayan Observer* (Kalimpong 22–29 December 1973).
4. *Inaugural Address by the Governor of Sikkim to the Sikkim Legislative Assembly* (25 October 1979, Sikkim Government Press, Gangtok).

CHAPTER

13

DEATH WARRANT

'Perhaps our leaders have fooled us. Perhaps they themselves have been fooled.'

KHARA NANDA UPRETY,
The Statesman, 5 September 1974.

'We had certainly not asked for a merger with India which was imposed on us as a political trickery and debauchery, for no one, however meek or small, has ever in the entire history of the world, signed away his country as has been made to appear to have been done by the Sikkimese leaders.'

NAR BAHADUR KHATIAWARA,
'Sikkim's Merger—A Brief Resume',
a memorandum to Morarji Desai,
1 August 1977.

Not a single taxi at Bagdogra was prepared to undertake the journey to Gangtok on 20 June 1974. They all pleaded that the army had closed the road, and Sikkim was cut off for all traffic. Eventually, the Siliguri manager of Sikkim Nationalised Transport, a friend from my many earlier visits, lent me his jeep and driver and we set out on an uneventful, if lonely, journey until Singtam. Gangtok was less than eighteen miles away, and fears seemed to have been groundless.

We were abruptly halted at Topkhani, just beyond Singtam, where the road drives through a dark tunnel cut into the rock. A heavy military truck, pulled up diagonally under the arching masonry, blocked the way. The vehicle had broken down, explained an Indian officer in khaki, and could not be moved until spares had been brought from an army depot or military headquarters. It was a foreign vehicle and some parts might even have to be imported. A breakdown van to haul it away would not be available until next morning at the earliest. Having set out these insuperable obstacles, the officer somewhat enigmatically suggested that I obtain permission to drive on from his superiors in Gangtok. He was far more helpful to Coo Coo La's son-in-law, a Gangtok doctor, who was also waiting to go on; the doctor was promised clearance within a short time.

Instead of sticking to the doctor, I made the mistake of driving back to telephone Gangtok from the Singtam police station. A furious young chain-smoking Bhutiya police officer flooded me with all the angry questions that were troubling him. Was the road closed or open? Was it an accidental breakdown or a deliberate blockage? Was he to stop traffic? Did the durbar still rule in Gangtok? Was he in charge of Singtam or had the Indian army taken over the country? It seemed impossible to obtain clarification. Telephone calls yielded little. Das was not at Mintokgang. Bajpai had left India House. From the palace, Captain Chhetri said that both were closeted with the Chogyal. But he took in a message while I waited and returned with the chief executive's assurance that the road was open and I could continue on my way.

I drove back to Topkhani to discover that the tunnel had indeed been cleared during my absence to let the doctor through. But the truck was again firmly back in position. The officer I had spoken to earlier had gone but a knot of soldiers on the roadside did not any longer bother with pretence. The truck would be moved, they said, only on explicit instructions to allow me to travel. Not before.

Back to Singtam to make several more futile calls under the glowering eye of the young Bhutiya policeman who continued to smoke cigarette after cigarette and fumed as if I and not the Indian army had usurped his charge. Das and the PO were still not available. But Bedi answered from India House this time, oozing unctuous concern. He rambled on at length about the hazards of landslides, infuriatingly apologised for not being able personally to shovel away rock and boulder, and regretted that the political office did not operate vehicle-removal squads. The chief executive sounded just as solicitous when I finally spoke to him on an extension in Captain Chhetri's office, facetiously inquiring why I was dallying in Singtam. When my predicament was explained all over again, Das assured me with utter conviction that the road had been cleared. Just in case it hadn't, I was to tell the soldiers from him to remove the truck.

A third trip to Topkhani revealed that everything was exactly as before. Shadows were closing in over the hills, and the way was still barred. The soldiers reasonably pointed out they had no means of verifying my account of the chief executive's instructions. In any case, they could take orders only from the GOC.

The next forty minutes were spent trying to enlist help from anyone I could think of in Gangtok. Chhetri said Das had stalked out of the palace in a huff, not replying to the ADC's question about me. From Mingtokgang I learnt he had been in for a minute but had gone out again. Bajpai was still not available. There seemed no alternative to calling the Chogyal, but the police telephone decided to fade out just as I was about to be connected to the palace.

Govind Ram, head constable of A Company, 5 CRPF, who was attached to the police station, had all this time watched me struggling with the telephone and witnessed my frustrating journeys to and from Topkhani. He now suggested I make the call from the home of a well-to-do

Marwari businessman who patronised the Sikkim Congress and was popular with Indian officials. Thither we both went, and when I got through to Mintokgang, Das was at last in and affable as ever. He had heard of my difficulties, apologised for not having been able to attend to me before and assured me that the road was open. He said he was looking forward to seeing me in Gangtok to discuss exciting new developments.

Remembering what the soldiers at Topkhani had said about orders, I thought it would be a good idea if Das spoke direct to Govind Ram, who was waiting at my elbow. The head constable took the receiver, standing stiffly at attention, murmured, '*Ji sahib*... yes, sir,' three or four times into the instrument and put it down. The way seemed clear at last but as we were strolling down to my jeep, I asked, more out of curiosity than anything else, precisely what message Das had given him. 'The chief executive sahib said that if the road happened to be open you could go,' replied Govind Ram, 'but sahib, the road is not open and he said nothing about opening it!' My irrational anger with the man gave way to concern for his safety when an NCO caught up with us to give Govind Ram a severe dressing-down. He had acted without orders. He had helped people who were not to be helped, and he had abandoned his post at the police station. He could be court-martialled for dereliction of duty. It was a shaming exhibition.

I went back to the Marwari businessman's house to make more telephone calls. Das had again gone out; the palace line was engaged; and Bedi at India House was as synthetic and supercilious as ever. But of course, the PO had long ago issued instructions for me to pass, the chief executive too. There really was no need to trouble the Chogyal who, hearing of my predicament from his ADC, had quite unnecessarily telephoned Bajpai several times. Bedi said he could not understand why I was hanging about Singtam. However, a fourth expedition to Topkhani disclosed the tunnel was still blocked.

There seemed to be no alternative to spending the night in the police station with its single table, two or three upright chairs, dingy barred cell and still grumbling, but hospitable, officer. We sat there gloomily until, suddenly, the telephone shrilled back into life. It was the Chogyal himself. 'Are you having a party there?' he joked, irrepressible as ever. He had spoken to Bajpai and Das and both had guaranteed that no further obstacles would be placed in my way.

I went back to Topkhani. The tunnel had been cleared. No trace remained of the truck or of the soldiers on the verge. The road ran empty and we sped through the night, trying to make up for the four hours lost in Singtam. It was well past 10 pm when the lights of Gangtok twinkled into view and we drove through slumbering Deolali, past a ring of men in khaki round Kazi's petrol pump, and up the hill to the chill sweep of the Ridge. We passed clusters of soldiers carrying long staves and enormous wire shields trudging back. The roads and pavements were littered with debris.

• • •

A momentous step in the history of two countries had been taken while I was in effect a prisoner in Singtam. It is clear in retrospect that the blockade had been staged to keep the media—me—out. India had prepared the ground to extend its territory through legerdemain. The kingdom of Sikkim had moved a stage nearer annihilation. Both moves arose out of Rajagopaul's Government of Sikkim Bill. Das had summoned the assembly, tabled the document, and invited members 'to consider the draft, discuss it and give their views'. Instead, they had adopted eight important amendments without any attempt at debate. The most significant change was in section 30(c) which already enabled legislators to 'seek participation and representation for the people of Sikkim in political institutions of India'. Exceeding even Rajagopaul's expectations, the assembly had enlarged the scope of the clause by adding 'and parliamentary system of India'. The frame for merger was ready. The session also recommended seven other changes, and it was agreed that the fifteen proposals would be incorporated in a final document that would then have to be moved and adopted.

What the assembly most emphatically did not do on 20 June was to enact legislation. Writing to the Chogyal that morning, the PO correctly admitted that 'it was the position of the government of India that at this stage the assembly could only consider any document or proposal and express its views on it in the form of a resolution. The decision of the assembly must then be submitted to you for your decision.' If the Chogyal approved, the document would go back to the assembly as a formal bill which would have to be proposed, seconded, read and adopted, becoming law only on the Chogyal's assent. If he disagreed, he was to inform New Delhi and the assembly of the changes and alterations he wished for 'and the matter would then be reconsidered by the government of India after consultations with you and the members of the assembly'.

The impression created was that there was nothing left to discuss. All details had already been thrashed out, and the 'Government of Sikkim Bill', which had been passed by the legislature, was held up only because of the king's unconstitutional last-minute refusal to give his assent. Sikkimese nationalists, who angrily paraded the streets of Gangtok, were under the misapprehension that a final measure was about to be enacted. Six assembly members—Ram Chandra Poudyal, Nanda Kumar Subeidi, Kusu Das, Tasa Tengay Lepcha, Bhuwani Prasad Kharel, and the sole opposition legislator, Kalzang Gyatso Bhutia—went into hiding to avoid being a party to their country's liquidation. Even Khatiawara, later regretting his role, believed that the measure had become law. As he wrote in a memorandum submitted to Morarji Desai's Janata Party government:

> Being MLAs of the present Sikkim assembly and having worked as close associates of Kazi, the conditions under which the Government of Sikkim Act 1974 came into existence can be stated here without hesitation. All our questions with regard to the bill were harshly brushed aside by the chief executive Shri B.S. Das inside the assembly, and by the political officer Shri K.S. Bajpai and his senior staff members outside the house. We were threatened to support the bill or else face the consequences.

He went on:

> On 20 June 1974, when the bill was to have been passed by the assembly at ten'clock in the morning, it could not be done because there was a spontaneous demonstration by about ten thousand people of Gangtok, including government employees, objecting against passage of the bill. The members of the assembly and the leaders along with Kazi were virtually confined to the famous petrol pump the whole day. None dared to come out and were kept hidden by the CRP throughout the day. The demonstrators had collected below the assembly house and were there throughout the day. Tear-gas was fired at the demonstrators and lathi-charges made by the CRP on men, women and children trying to prevent them from encircling the assembly house.

The memorandum finally observed:

> It was only after the demonstrators left that around 9.30 pm, under heavily armed Indian army personnel and the CRP under overall command of Brigadier A. Hoon, that all

> the MLAs were taken in covered army jongas to the assembly house.

The armed escort was as much to protect the MLAs from public fury as to prevent them from escaping. According to Khatiawara, the assembly proceedings were over in less than sixteen minutes, 'which gives an indication as to the indecent haste with which the assembly was forced to pass the Government of Sikkim Act in a midnight session of the assembly'. He continues:

> The Act was in English and over twenty members were not at all conversant with the language. Even the ten or twelve of us who had a little knowledge of the English language were not in a position in that brief spell of time to go through, leave alone understand, the bill. The chief minister Shri Lendhup Dorji Kazi was not conversant with the language at all.

Confusion was understandable since agreed procedures were changed from minute to minute. The original understanding was that the Chogyal and assembly members would informally discuss Rajagopaul's draft and submit their joint recommendations to the PO so that a constitution could be drawn up on the basis of proposals by all three parties. Instead, India had quietly abridged the process to present the durbar with a fait accompli. The manoeuvre created the impression that the Chogyal was thwarting the people's wishes as expressed through valid legislation. The Topkhani blockage seems to have been staged only to prevent me from witnessing this shabby operation. And, indeed, it was quite a drama I missed.

• • •

A new constitution had been in the air ever since 8 May 1973. The Chogyal told Bajpai and Sardar Swaran Singh, India's external affairs minister, that he had only three conditions. Any new constitution must ensure maximum Sikkimese participation in the government, recognise the kingdom's separate juridical identity, and protect India's legitimate security and other interests. He sought no guarantees for himself or his dynasty. But the actions of the chief executive and the three OSDs did not, he said, seem to respect basic factors. He was also worried about Sikkim Congress pronouncements, such as Kazi's vote of thanks, that seemed to ignore the kingdom's constitutional position. The Indians assured him that the bill on which Rajagopaul was working would take into account the 1950 treaty as well as the 23 April agreement.

At this stage, the PO invited him again to go to New Delhi to continue discussions with Mrs Gandhi. Das, who was included in the party, told reporters at Dum Dum on 12 June that the Chogyal would remain head of state and the treaty would continue to determine relations, no matter what constitution was adopted. The Sikkim delegation was courteously received at Palam airport the next day and conducted to a suite at the Ashok Hotel where N.B. Menon, a former PO and then joint secretary in the external affairs ministry, gave the Chogyal a memorandum dated 10 June with a fourteen-page document titled 'Recommendations of the Constitutional Adviser'. Much to the Chogyal's surprise, it was in the form of a bill. Before he could even read it, however, Menon told him that his acceptance of the bill would be announced at a banquet the following evening. The document would then be presented to Sikkimese legislators on 15 June as the joint recommendations of the Chogyal and the Indian government. The Sikkim assembly would ratify it the same day. Clearly, the elected legislators had as little say in the matter as their king.

A blindfolded monarch and subservient politicians were being hustled into signing their country's death warrant. For even a cursory glance at the draft told the Chogyal that not a single one of India's commitments had been honoured. The chief executive was to become the permanent ruler of a colony. In fact, the old aim of permanent association was to be achieved through the back door. Meetings with Swaran Singh, Kewal Singh and Menon, and finally with Mrs Gandhi herself on 14 June, yielded little comfort. They told him that Rajagopaul's draft was immutable, though the prime minister talked disarmingly of her high regard for the Namgyal dynasty, her affection for the Chogyal whom she wished to see in a more secure position to guide his people and help Indian defence, and of her respect for Sikkim's history and culture. Mrs Gandhi tried to persuade him that the bill would maintain continuity in Sikkim and reinforce ties with India so that the throne was strengthened and the Sikkimese could make better use of Indian assistance.

The Chogyal was not to be flattered, wined, and dined into surrendering. When New Delhi realised after five days of fruitless haggling that the bill could not be presented to the assembly as a gift from the ruler, it decided to force it on him as the assembly's handiwork. India House distributed copies to legislators on 15 June with instructions as to what was expected of them. Das returned to Gangtok the following day to make sure of obedience. Predictably, the Sikkim Congress responded with enthusiasm. The bill might have been its own invention! Kazi and his men promised a 'mass movement' to push it through.

The Chogyal stayed back in Delhi to continue his pleadings. Reminding Mrs Gandhi of the three points he had insisted on from the very beginning, he wrote on 15 June: 'Nothing in our constitution should contain or omit anything that detracts in any way from these objectives.' He also asked for ten days' grace to study the bill but was forced to return to Gangtok when Das issued notices on 18 June to convene the assembly two days later. The Chogyal decided then to warn members of the implications of the bill in the customary speech from the throne. 'I trust that due courtesy and decorum of the house are maintained when I am making the short address,' he wrote to the chief executive.

This was before Gangtok exploded in anger. As the bill's contents leaked out, people realised that extraneous pressure and Kazi's festering feud against the palace were driving the Sikkim Congress into a trap. Poudyal and Subeidi announced their opposition to the bill. The United Independents held protest meetings. The Prajatantra Party also organised rallies at which Bhandari and Khara Nanda Uprety boomed defiance at India's stratagems though Das's administration refused them permission to use microphones. They threatened to gherao the assembly to prevent it from meeting. Two new organisations, the All-Sikkim People's Committee for Joint Action and the Constitution Bill Protest Committee, were formed to resist the measure.

The administration was paralysed. Led by a militant clerk, Mrs Kalavati Subba, about 2,700 junior civil servants struck work. They were followed by the country's seniormost officials. Jigdal Densapa, Rasaily and others returned to their offices after a week's protest strike, but sporting black armbands. Some tried to explain to Kazi the consequences of what he was about to do; others led delegations to Bajpai and Das. Seventy-eight officers pointed out in a six-point memorandum that the bill contained 'many provisions which need more elucidation, clarification and amendments'. Arguing that several clauses 'violate and run counter to the very essence of the Sikkim–India treaty of 1950 as far as Sikkim's status as a protectorate and a separate state is concerned', the signatories said the bill 'should have confined itself to the rights and responsibilities of the people of Sikkim without inclusion of any extraneous provisions'. The only Sikkimese official to continue functioning normally was the chief secretary, Sherab Gyaltsen, who explained he had to keep open a line of communication with the Indian authorities.

Das coaxed and scolded, reminding officials they were transgressing bureaucratic codes. He assured the United Independents that since no part of India could claim a separate constitution, the question of Sikkim's merger did not arise. He also told the Chogyal that the assembly would only informally discuss Rajagopaul's draft and suggest changes to be incorporated in a final document, which would also take note of the ruler's proposals. In any case, he repeated, fears of a request for closer ties with India were groundless since no request could be made under section 30 of the bill until the bill itself had received royal assent and been entered in the statute book. If a request were then made, that too, would need the Chogyal's endorsement. But as protests continued, Das threatened to call out the CRP.

'The chief executive, Mr B.S. Das, has attempted to defuse the dangerous potential of such demonstrations by ordering the government staff back to work,' commented the *Hindustan Times*. 'Unfortunately, such anxiety to prevent demonstrations has not been apparent in the case of the "mass movement" organised by the Sikkim Congress.'[1]

Bajpai was more openly partisan than Das. 'Unless this nonsense stops, the government of India will take note,' he thundered at the Chogyal. Protesting schoolboys who went in a body to India House were told that Sikkim had always been a princely state and part of India. He was more circumspect with knowledgeable complainants. Uprety, who led a Youth Congress team to the PO, reported that Bajpai had explained 'that it (political participation) only meant that we Sikkimese could watch the functioning of Indian democracy as "observers" and that there was no question of Sikkimese members in the Lok Sabha and Rajya Sabha.'

Gangtok was tense on 19 June. The kingdom's red and white flag fluttered defiantly from every rooftop. Shops and offices remained shut. In spite of his 'mass movement' warning, Kazi and his men were nowhere to be seen though Mintokgang claimed they had sent word to say the Sikkim Congress would walk out if the Chogyal so much as set foot in the assembly. There were again fears of a Bhutiya-Lepcha swoop from the northern highlands to rally round the king, but as during the previous year's riots, the army quickly intervened to seal the highway. The Chogyal wrote again to Mrs Gandhi asking for a postponement of the assembly session. She had not replied to his 15 June letter and ignored this one too. Neither would Das accede to the head of state's request. Instead, he posted CRP men and regular soldiers on both sides of the road leading to the assembly and all round the building.

Against this background of unrest and intimidation, the Chogyal wrote to him late at night on 19 June expressing his inability to address the next morning's session. He had no wish to take part in the deliberations of a legislature that had to meet under the protection of foreign bayonets. Neither would he legitimise with his presence the disloyalty of politicians who were so clearly bent on defying public opinion at another government's behest.

• • •

The anti-bill processions began at eight o'clock in the morning of 20 June. The assembly gates were rushed an hour later. At one time the CRP cordon seemed likely to break under the onslaught, but the soldiers had orders to stand firm. Manavalam, watching the mêlée from a rise, is accused of casting the first stone. Whoever was responsible, heavy pelting followed, and women and children, including Sodeun-La, the eldest of Princess Coo Coo La's daughters, were hurt. Even Das admitted that excessive violence had been used as the CRP laid about them with lathis. Dr Lekhi Dahdul at the Thutob Namgyal Hosptial gave first-aid to eight soldiers and eighty-five Sikkimese, while seventeen civilians (including eight women) had to be admitted with injuries.

Though the army did not intervene, its presence on the sidelines—kneeling with rifles at the ready, prepared to fire if the CRP seemed likely to be overpowered—added to the atmosphere of menace. But unarmed reinforcements still kept flooding in from the valleys and villages, and it was not until six in the evening that the last battered defender of Sikkim's rights limped home. The morning session had fallen through. It was then that, worried by the tide of hostility, Bajpai wrote in placatory terms to the Chogyal explaining that the Sikkimese were unnecessarily exercised since the assembly could not at this stage enact legislation. Legislators were summoned again late at night. How that second gathering fared we already know from Khatiawara's graphic description.

He was not the only legislator to misunderstand what exactly was accomplished at that hasty and surreptitious nocturnal session. Chatur Singh Roy still believed in his typographical error. 'We have no confidence in the Chogyal but we want to keep our own identity under Indian protection,' he told me. He was also under the impression that a simple majority in the assembly could overhaul or repeal the constitution bill whenever it chose. Revision was inevitable, he explained, because of a major discrepancy between Rajagopaul's draft and the 8 May agreement. The latter had granted fourteen subjects to the legislature, but the bill had kept back two of these (home and establishment, and finance) for the nominated Indian chief executive. Roy was sceptical about Bajpai's explanation that since home and establishment included law and order, the police, and the CRP, politicians would be better protected against the Sikkim Guards if security powers were exercised by an Indian administrator. He seemed to think, too, that Kazi would eventually become prime minister with full authority, Das functioning in only an advisory capacity. This kind of optimistic interpretation may have owed something to ambivalent morality. 'Don't quote me on any of this,' Roy pleaded. 'They have promised to make me deputy speaker.' Similar promises were made to others too.

The demonstrations that followed increasingly took on a despairing quality. Sober men, who had all their lives staked existence itself on propriety, cast off their sustaining creed to mouth slogans outside Mintokgang—Jigdal Densapa, always so correct and courtly, flailing a loose fist in drizzling rain, Chandra Das Rai, back with gusto in the political maelstrom from which he had escaped years earlier. They were all there: Pradhans, Sharmas, Tserings, Thapas, Tamangs, Lamas, Dahduls, Tashis, Gurungs, and Chhetris, names that mirrored the multi-ethnic quilt of Sikkim's demographic variety, transcending the narrower definition of Lho-mon-Tsong-sum in their pathetic determination not to be extinguished; thousands of men and women loyally rallying to the defence, aware of being doomed. Only the 'notorious Tikka Topden' was absent. Das had astutely assessed the deputy secretary's capacity for organisation, as well as his taste for metropolitan pleasures, and had flattered him into working for the State Trading Corporation of Sikkim in Calcutta. A well-appointed office, a spacious flat, cars with distinctive yellow number plates, and a quasi-diplomatic status were expected to keep him happy. But politics was Karma Topden's life's breath. In addition to buying and selling for the Sikkim government, he also busied himself in circulating the durbar's statements, organising protest letters to Indian newspapers, and preaching unity to expatriate Sikkimese students.

Whenever the Chogyal passed through Dum Dum, the STC representative was there with a band of loyal followers to receive and see him off with ceremony. A reporter once remarked on the fine silk of his khada. 'It's Indian,' Karma retorted. 'Everything comes to us readymade from India these days, even constitutions.'

New Delhi's methods and suspected objective drove some Sikkimese to extreme demands. The Prajatantra Party called for untrammelled democracy, special protection for Bhutiya-Lepchas, a sovereign monarchy, and the right to conclude treaties with other countries. The People's Committee demanded the recall of Das and the CRP, expunction from the records of the 11 May and 20 June resolutions, and the assembly's dissolution. It accused members of 'conniving with the dictator's administration and the PO against the wishes of the people and of passing resolutions which were against the interests of the Sikkimese people and their very existence'. Poudyal and Subeidi went a step further to begin a protest fast against the bill. Nine men—three Bhutiyas, four Nepalese, and two Lepchas—began the vigil under a canvas awning just outside the assembly gates; eventually, only Poudyal remained. 'We are fighting for democracy. We want justice. Keeping the most important departments in Indian hands does not make for responsible government,' he told me when I visited his place of vigil. It was unfair for Sikkim's constitution to be rushed through in five days, he argued with impeccable logic, when India's had taken nearly three years. Poudyal wanted a committee of Indian and Sikkimese constitutional lawyers to spend at least two years on the draft. Nor would he be fobbed off with a puppet parliament. 'The chief minister will be just like the leader of any Indian state under this bill. We were promised a prime minister and told Sikkim would be linked to India only by the treaty. We are a separate country and our identity must be respected.'

But the Press Trust of India reported that Poudyal and Subeidi were fasting because they objected to the Chogyal being given 'any role in the constitution'. India's premier news agency had earlier dismissed crippling strikes and countrywide demonstrations as minor disturbances by only a few 'pro-palace elements'. Its bias was so resoundingly echoed in most Indian newspapers that Patrice de Beer, a senior correspondent of the prestigious French daily, *Le Monde*, cooling his heels in Calcutta after being refused permission to visit Gangtok, reported that all the news about Sikkim bore New Delhi's imprimatur. 'With its extensive control of communications with Sikkim, New Delhi has been able to monopolise the flow of news and views from here,' wrote Cheng Huan in the *Far Eastern Economic Review* in Hongkong. 'Sikkim's lips are, in effect, Indian-sealed.'[2] Mrs Gandhi was not so far out when she later claimed that Indians had to look to the foreign media for the truth. Her contempt for domestic purveyors of news was amply justified. Jigdal Densapa wryly acknowledged this subservience when he concluded a New Delhi press statement by quoting: '"Take your pen, Matucouvic," said Talleyrand to the Russian Pole who wrote all his despatches. "You know all the neutral words."' But the press was far from neutral. Dancing to the Indian government's tune, it was belligerently hostile to Sikkimese nationalism.

The world was beginning to wonder what was happening. So, to turn up the heat and lend credence to New Delhi's professions, the RAW operatives masterminding the operation persuaded Kazi to creep out of hiding once the numbing shock of the anti-bill agitation had worn off a little. Ever ready to oblige, he told a Gangtok rally on 26 June that 'the Chogyal is not a fit and proper person to remain even as a constitutional head' and assured listeners that the Sikkim Congress had made eight important changes in Rajagopaul's draft. 'We now find that this was not so,' Uprety complained when he discovered that the 20 June resolutions had no legal force. He also expressed dismay and surprise at the new forms of association with India that had been foisted on gullible legislators: 'The assembly members were never given a chance to discuss the resolution— drafted by an Indian officer—whose legal terminology is not easily understood in Sikkim. It was read out once in English, which 80 per cent of the members do not understand, and then passed by a show of hands. Protesting against this haste, the method of ensuring passage and the contents of the draft, six assembly members refused to sign the resolution.'[3]

For being so outspoken Uprety was deprived of his Sikkim government scholarship to study in a Calcutta college.

• • •

The Chogyal received copies of the 20 June proceedings on 22 June with Das's assurance that the assembly had not made a valid request to be represented in India's Parliament and could not do so until the bill had become law and the Chogyal had agreed to the application. But this attempt at setting out the correct legal position was contradicted the very next day when the PO wrote:

> As you are aware, the members of the Sikkim assembly have taken the strongest exception to the efforts made by certain elements, including some officials, to prevent the session to which they had been summoned on 20 June. They have emphatically reiterated their decision that the proposed constitutional framework endorsed by the assembly and its accompanying resolution should be given effect to forthwith. They have sought the government of India's intervention to this end.

Gone was the reasonableness of Bajpai's letter after the abortive morning session only three days earlier. In four sharp paragraphs, the PO conveyed New Delhi's surprise, regret, and concern over developments for which the palace alone was held responsible. Warning that legislators would 'assert their rights with the support of the public', he ominously added that there were 'widespread demands for a demonstration' against the ruler; 'either the Chogyal must give his assent or they must seek other peaceful means of ensuring that the people's aspirations are fulfilled'.

This was a blunt enough threat of violence: India House would help Kazi's abortive 'mass movement' to fructify. By peremptorily demanding ratification in India's name, the PO also abandoned the pretence that the bill was a Sikkimese matter: 'We believe this framework is in the best interests of the Chogyal and all the people of Sikkim. The assembly has given its endorsement and it has now become urgently necessary for you to give your assent. The assembly members have requested that it be given within two days. We hope and trust that you will heed their urgings.' It was not the first time that the Chogyal learnt from the PO what the assembly members were supposed to want!

The PO's ultimatum reached the palace at about half-past three in the afternoon of 24 June. Earlier in the day the Chogyal had written to Das advising against another meeting of the assembly until the tension had eased a little, explaining that he had compiled notes on the bill's far-reaching implications and wished to discuss them with the Indian government. 'You are aware that I am leaving for Delhi, and I hope the situation here will remain calm and peaceful so that our talks can be successfully concluded.'

The journey had been planned for 26 June, but the Tsuk-la-khang monks, without whose advice the Chogyal did not stir, decreed that he should start the journey before daybreak. So the royal motorcade left the palace shortly after midnight on 25 June, the Sikkim Congress promptly accusing the Chogyal of escaping under cover of darkness. No sooner had he gone, than Kazi's men poured into Gangtok, tore down the national flag, and burned portraits of the ruler. The 'mass movement' had begun under Indian protection. Das's administration did not try to prevent vandalism. Nor did the police or CRP intervene when Man Bahadur Basnet, National Party president, was dragged out of his house and manhandled in the bazaar.

• • •

The Chogyal's mission to New Delhi was doomed from the start. The external affairs ministry let it be known that he had not been invited and was not particularly welcome. Menon complained about the civil servants' demonstrations. Kewal Singh said the 23 April agreement was no longer operational. On the point of setting out for Bulgaria, Swaran Singh, himself a lawyer, cautioned the Chogyal against seeking legal advice or taking a stand on constitutional points. Kazi telegraphed the Chogyal ordering him to return at once to be a 'father figure', sent another message to the Sardar urging him to ignore a ruler who had fled 'in fear of his own people', and a third telegram to Mrs Gandhi asking her unilaterally to promulgate the bill. It is very likely that the befuddled Kazi still did not fully comprehend the implications of his actions. He had said in Gangtok on 26 June: 'The very fact that India had helped us to have our own constitution does prove that Sikkim is not a part of India but is still a protectorate.' But the Sikkim Congress leader was floundering out of his depth. The Chogyal was given fresh evidence of this on 28 June when the ministry forwarded to him a telex message in which Das reported that the assembly, which he had convened in his master's absence and against the latter's express wishes, had unanimously voted for the bill and had given the Chogyal forty-eight hours to give his assent to it. The chief executive added that he awaited the Chogyal's 'orders'.

Mrs Gandhi was no more straightforward. She pleaded with the Chogyal during a long conversation on 29 June to 'give the bill a try'. They met again the following evening when she beguilingly repeated how necessary the monarchy was to preserve Sikkim's heritage and how the Chogyal alone could guide his people through a difficult transitional period into political emancipation and economic prosperity in dynamic partnership with India. There was no question of eroding Sikkim's identity, but the people wanted a closer connection with India (no more talk of democracy), and their wishes had to be respected. She did not refer at all to the nine-point letter the Chogyal had sent her from his hotel suite and in which he had again pleaded for a joint committee to examine a bill whose effect, he said, was 'that Sikkim, its people and all official authorities from the Chogyal downwards are reduced to a status even less than that enjoyed by the governors and states of the Indian union'.

It was never Mrs Gandhi's style to face unpleasant truths or attempt an honest answer. The son of Khampa warlords was no match for her drawing-room duplicity. While she continued to be smoothly coaxing, and the Chogyal was driven near to hysterics by her composure, it was left to external affairs ministry officials to let newspapermen know that India could ratify the bill if the Chogyal would not.

Before leaving New Delhi, he sent her another anguished appeal begging for 'a final and frank talk... without any reservation.'

> A time has now come to decide whether I really have any useful role to fulfil in the service of my people and also in the larger sphere of Indo-Sikkimese relations.
>
> The more I think of the events in the last 14 months, it seems there is no role for upright, frank and honest dealings. The unscrupulous and treacherous seem to succeed in forcing forward the short-term gain in preference to the long-term principles and considerations.
>
> I may sound bitter and depressed but I am still writing to you in all frankness as a friend and from one human being to another.

Again, the prime minister did not reply. Foreigners in New Delhi who saw the Chogyal at the end of his tether speculated that he might abdicate in favour of Tenzing who was still in England. But Das knew better. 'He's a born fighter, he'll never give up.'

Nor was there much sign of yielding as he faced a battery of reporters at Dum Dum. That day's newspapers carried front-page stories about the rebuff he had suffered and how high Kazi stood in New Delhi's favours. Most gloated over his discomfiture. But the Chogyal was still battling. 'I am prepared to talk to any person any time anywhere,' he promised when asked if negotiations with Kazi were on the cards. He gently rebuked journalists who tried to draw him into accusing Mrs Gandhi of annexation by saying, 'I have always been assured that the preservation of a separate identity for Sikkim is foremost in the mind of the government of India.' To another mischievous question about appealing to world opinion, the Chogyal retorted: 'It is the Indian government that controls the external affairs of Sikkim.' But he would not compromise on constitutional issues. 'The bill has first to go back to the assembly for final reading. I will give my comments on the bill only after it has been discussed clause by clause by the legislators.'

It was a dismal homecoming made worse by nature's hazards. Because of bad weather, the Chogyal could not use the military helicopter waiting at Bagdogra. A landslide between Sevoke and Teesta had closed the road. The royal party had to take a circuitous route by way of Darjeeling and Jorethang; it was nearly midnight of 1 July when he reached the palace and sat down to a pile of reports on all that had happened in Gangtok during his infructuous odyssey to the court of Indira Gandhi.

• • •

Das had called the 28 June session ostensibly in deference to Kazi's demand, citing 'the urgency of this problem in view of the critical situation prevailing in Sikkim'. Two members, Kalzang Gyatso Bhutia and Tasa Tengay Lepcha, were missing when the house assembled, reports indicating that they were trying to mobilise villagers against the bill. The chief executive ran through the 20 June minutes, recapitulated the Chogyal's reservations and asked for views. This was the pre-arranged cue. 'This assembly and the entire people of Sikkim are shocked at the tactics adopted by the Chogyal and his ill-advised advisers to delay the adoption of the bill,' rumbled Kazi from a long, belligerently argued text that someone had clearly written for him. 'Now that the Chogyal has run to Delhi and has had yet more talks with the government of India, we would have liked, as we have already appealed, that the government of India should exercise its responsibility under the 8 May agreement and tell the Chogyal that this bill must become law forthwith.'

It was obvious that Kazi merely parroted what his Indian 'advisers' wrote out for him without grasping the purport of his words. The sophisticated language allowed no other conclusion. Central to his verbal pyrotechnics was the supposition that the bill had been drafted in consultation with the palace and that New Delhi could enact it if it chose. 'It is our view that the bill still leaves too much of the feudal system and preserves too much of the powers and privileges of an out-of-date hierarchy.'

Assuming that Kazi's fulminations were genuine, Das may have overlooked them as political hyperbole. But he had a duty as presiding officer to disabuse Kazi of the notion that India had any unilateral rights in respect of legislation. Clause 8(iv) of the 8 May agreement permitted the chief executive to report to the PO differences of opinion between him and the Chogyal; the PO would then seek New Delhi's verdict, which would be binding. But this power of arbitration did not extend to differences between the Chogyal and legislators. Nor could India invoke the treaty because that provided for only disputes between the Chogyal and the PO which had to be submitted to the chief justice of India for adjudication. In spite of this clear delineation of powers, Das saw no incongruity in Kazi's request that he report the Chogyal's dilatoriness to the PO so that 'the bill comes into force immediately whether the

Chogyal likes it or not'. The chief executive made no pretence of objectivity. He did not demur when, supporting the party president, Khatiawara spoke of writings on walls and adjusting to altered circumstances, warning that 'this is the last chance for the Chogyal; after this there will be no role to play except to abdicate'.

Neither these oratorical flourishes nor the speed with which Das rushed through individual clauses as the bill was introduced, moved and seconded, could remove the unease experienced by those few members who had a smattering of English and some awareness of the direction in which events were heading. Rinzing queried the chief executive's enormous powers while Khatiawara and Subeidi demanded that the home and establishment and finance departments should be placed in Sikkimese hands. Again protesting they had been promised a prime minister, Poudyal suggested inclusion of an amending procedure as well as scrutiny of the document by a Sikkimese constitution committee assisted by Indian experts. Several members also questioned the bill's definition of minorities. They noted, too, that the measure did not include the 20 June amendments which Bhim Bahadur Gurung reiterated. Poudyal, more persistent than the rest, said he 'would like to ask again about the amendments proposed by the members last time'. Sikkim's simple legislators were dumbfounded by the casuistry of Das's reply:

> These amendments were read out. The amendments you would like are in your resolution; copies of this are with you. These amendments do not yet amend the bill, but your views and wishes are incorporated in a resolution which will form part of the records.

In other words, though the 20 June proceedings had been used to bludgeon the Chogyal, they were not allowed to make any impression on Rajagopaul's draft. Indulged like children, assembly members could only play at law-making. Das snubbed Rinzing, Poudyal, Gurung, Khatiawara and Subeidi into silence. As gazetted on 6 July, the bill bore no trace of what the Sikkimese had unanimously recommended. The Chogyal was not the only victim of duplicity. The assembly too was taken for a ride. Khatiawara later succinctly described the fraud that Das had practised on him and his colleagues:

> During the debate of the Sikkim assembly on the Government of Sikkim Bill 1974 some of the members of the assembly had raised questions with regard to the various sections of the bill, particularly with regard to the necessity of inserting a chapter on fundamental rights as embodied in the constitution of India. The chief executive Shri B.S. Das, who was also the speaker, and not even an elected representative of the people, informed the house that the amendments would not form part of the bill. They would, however, be kept in view as an expression of the people's wishes.
>
> As persons who were comparatively young in age and inexperienced in constitutional processes, we had fully reposed our trust and confidence in the hands of the government of India.
>
> [But] with the hasty step taken to introduce the Government of Sikkim Act 1974, it led to the total subversion of the people's aspiration for democracy.[4]

It should have been perfectly clear why the chief executive so strictly controlled, channellised and distorted the proceedings. A full-fledged assembly would sooner or later have cast off the foreign yoke; members had to be severely discouraged from democratic expression while being urged to intensify pressure on the durbar. For it was through the legislature that New Delhi was planning to strike at the Chogyal and at Sikkim's sovereignty. Therefore, though Das dismissed substantive motions, he treated as sacrosanct Kazi's ultimatum to the

Chogyal and demand that India 'should take necessary steps under the provisions of the 8 May agreement that the bill is enacted immediately'. This was the motion that the external affairs ministry forwarded to the Chogyal in Delhi.

To mark its achievement, Das's administration declared 28 June 'Janata Raj Day'. Sikkim Nationalised Transport trucks ferried revellers from the districts to Gangtok. There were fireworks and illuminations, and the Sikkim Congress tricolour, so closely resembling India's flag, was hoisted on public buildings.

In spite of the pressure and the pontification, India could not legally validate the bill. Mrs Gandhi was also anxious to ensure some semblance of constitutional propriety. The Chogyal was, therefore, told she would brook no further obstruction: he would have to sign or face the consequences for him, his family, and his country. Willy-nilly, he had to be a party to his country's liquidation. Unable to halt the bulldozer, he tried to delay it, writing to Bajpai on 1 July that he would not withhold consent 'if after making my views, recommendations and apprehensions known to the house, the assembly still decide to pass the bill' at the emergency session that Das had called for the next day. This was a risk the PO was not prepared to take. The strings were noticeably tightened, and Kazi jerked convulsively around like a puppet at the end of a string for twenty-four hours. He turned down an invitation to talk things over at the palace, threatened to depose the Chogyal, and again telegraphed Mrs Gandhi to demand New Delhi's intervention. A round-robin letter, signed by twenty-eight legislators, also flatly refused to allow the Chogyal to address the assembly. 'If the Chogyal does not assent to the bill tonight, then we depend on the government of India to give effect to it tomorrow.'

The 2 July session, too, fell through. It was to be convened the next day, and Bajpai had thirty Sikkim Congressmen taken to India House for a final briefing on tactics. They were advised to stand firm in their opposition to the Chogyal's presence in the assembly but not to boycott the meeting. Instead, they were to refuse even to hear what he had to say. The bill was to be adopted as if the Chogyal had not spoken. The PO then considerately informed the Chogyal that his appearance in the chamber would provoke a walk-out and that India could not permit such an insult to the throne. It would, therefore, save embarrassment all round if he were to let Das who, after all, represented him, read out his comments on the draft.

Kalzang Gyatso and Tasa Tengay were still missing when the chief executive initiated the proceedings by reading out the Chogyal's 542-word statement on 'the sacred task of framing a constitution for the country which will have far-reaching effects on Sikkim, her people and her very close relationship with India, our protecting power'. There was no indication of grief or betrayal in the statement, nor any recrimination. After candidly admitting differences 'which is inevitable in a democratic process' the Chogyal stressed: 'Our duty is to ensure that these differences do not ultimately bring unhappiness and suffering to the people at large.' It was a dignified exposition of his reasons for interceding with Mrs Gandhi on a measure that endangered the kingdom's 'separate identity' and suffered from 'important lacuna and anomalies'. The Chogyal repeated the three points to which he remained 'irrevocably committed'. He sought no reservation for himself; nor was he inclined to interfere with the assembly. 'My viewpoints have been laid before the hon'ble house for considering the bill in the larger interests of Sikkim, her people and Indo-Sikkim relations.'

They were spelt out in fuller, if cumbersome, detail in a twenty-eight-page annexure titled 'Detailed Comments on the Draft Government of Sikkim Bill 1974'. Though something of a heavy lawyer's note, it was a clause-by-clause demolition of a document that violated the treaty and the relationship of protector and protectorate to vest all executive and legislative power in an Indian civil servant who was 'a head of state, governor and chief minister rolled into one'. It explained that elected leaders gained nothing from the anomalous position in which the kingdom was being placed, or from its throne's demotion. New Delhi would permanently rule the kingdom through an authoritarian functionary. 'The council of ministers is reduced to the position of merely echoing his decisions and direction.'

To take one example, the note said, ministers could advise the throne only through the chief executive. But he was at liberty to refuse to forward their views or to 'require the council of ministers to modify the advice' to suit his own ideas. The assembly could not thwart him. If it adopted any measure affecting the chief executive, the Chogyal would have to submit it for New Delhi's consideration. The Sikkim assembly was, in fact, a permanently hamstrung body, institutionally subordinate to the Indian government, allowed only to voice those views and take those actions that had already been dictated by New Delhi's interests. Its charter allowed no scope for independent initiative. If the chief executive chose to merge Sikkim with India, the assembly would have no option but to ratify the decision.

'This is tantamount to reducing the council [of ministers] to less than that of an advisory body,' wrote V. Gopakumar in the *Far Eastern Economic Review*. 'This would also mean that the advice tendered by the chief executive could be his own, rather than that of the council. Therefore, the chief executive is in a position to persuade the council members to take decisions acceptable to him and the Indian government. Indeed, his sweeping powers make a mockery of democratic traditions.'[5] Gopakumar also remarked on the irony of Das taking over ecclesiastical affairs which formed part of the establishment portfolio: 'It is paradoxical that a police official-turned-administrator, whose primary task is to ensure law and order in the kingdom, now has to preside over the arcane Mahayana Buddhist order.'[6]

But true to the orders he had been given, Kazi rose to say there was no need to bother with the Chogyal's note, and that the bill should at once be adopted. Some Sikkim Congressmen may have been carried away by their vendetta against the durbar. Many more had little comprehension of what was happening and could not make head or tail of the note's legal language. Others had been promised ministerial or public-sector appointments. They looked forward to handsome salaries, official bungalows and cars, police escorts, flags, ceremonial receptions, and rich pickings from lavish Indian aid. During the first six months of his tenure, Das spent ₹ 2.5 million more than the whole year's total sanctioned expenditure. Though the money was meant for development projects, much of it lined private pockets, as in India. Everyone knew there was plenty more where it came from: a windfall was in store for anyone among the 200,000 Sikkimese who displayed a modicum of ingenuity.

So Chatur Singh Roy, dreaming of his deputy speakership, rose to give the Chogyal 'another three hours either to assent to the said bill... or he has to quit the Sikkimese political scene for good'. Amidst giggles, Roy repeated Kazini's ancient joke about royal divinity: 'In the ultimate analysis it is the people of Sikkim that count and not the Chogyal who claims to be half-divine.' He also repeated the canard that the half-divine monarch had 'slipped out of Gangtok in the dead of night rather than face his people'.

The assembly voted for Sikkim's constitution amidst this puerile jeering. Having discharged that duty, members trooped up to India House for a pat on the back from the beaming PO. Bajpai boasted to reporters he had succeeded in averting a major crisis.

The last scene was enacted in the palace shortly after one o'clock in the afternoon of 4 July. Kewal Singh had arrived from New Delhi to sit with Bajpai, Das, and the thirty-two legislators as the Chogyal signed the bill and announced: 'I hereby approve the Government of Sikkim Bill 1974 for promulgation with my formal assent and under my seal and signature.' Congratulatory speeches followed, and Kewal Singh entertained the company to a victory celebration at India House. It was an appropriate setting, for the Sikkim Congress and Chogyal had both lost out. The latter's fears were expressed in yet another letter to Mrs Gandhi:

> The events of the recent weeks have been disastrous to all of us.
>
> After much agony the Government of Sikkim Bill 1974 has received my assent since your excellency had advised me to give it a try, after my constitutional right of firmly placing my views before the assembly had been completed.
>
> I still have fears over clause 30 of the act which I pray, under your protection, will never be invoked to destroy our separate identity which has been given us under the treaty and has been reassured to us.

It was a vain prayer. The ink was not dry on the Chogyal's signature before New Delhi began creating the psychological atmosphere for the next offensive. Presumably to discredit the resistance of loyal Sikkim government officials, the external affairs ministry told reporters that pro-Chinese elements had in the last two years infiltrated the middle ranks of the Sikkimese civil service and that the durbar was under the thumb of Tibetan refugees, presumably meaning Princess Coo Coo La. There was a conspiracy afoot, it was said, to weaken India's position, build up the royal family, and bind an independent Sikkim to China. 'But the dramatic developments since May last year to now go to prove that India has the upper hand,' was the smug verdict of Calcutta's *Hindustan Standard*. More presciently, the Indian press reported that major constitutional changes were being discussed, and that India would gladly consider amendments 'if the wishes of the Sikkim assembly are to be met, say, for political association with India and extending the jurisdiction of the Supreme Court to the

Himalayan kingdom, not to speak of Sikkimese citizens seeking equal privileges with Indians'.[7] Clearly, New Delhi had primed the media to prepare the ground for the application of clause 30 that the Chogyal had warned against. He was not consulted in any 'discussions'.

Instead, India's campaign continued with flattering overtures to build up Kazi and company. Mrs Gandhi sent an air force jet to Bagdogra to reward them with New Delhi's hospitality, and Kewal Singh waited at Palam to escort the Sikkimese to the Ashok Hotel where the Chogyal was usually put up. It was almost a state visit. Kazi in his kho, Rinzing wearing a fur hat and striped Lepcha draperies, Khatiawara in a jaunty Nepalese cap and double-breasted tunic—they were all received by India's President and vice-president, and entertained to dinner by Swaran Singh, who toasted his visitors as 'the founder-members of the democratic set-up'. They presented khadas and a carpet to Mrs Gandhi. In return, she talked of India's diversity (which should have been warning enough of her intention of adding to the variety) and pledged that 'our sympathies will be with you always'. There were promises of aid from the planning minister, Durga Prasad Dhar, and cosy fraternal chats with Shankar Dayal Sharma, the Congress party president. But the government suddenly cancelled an invitation to tea with Socialist Party leaders. The Sikkimese were to be allowed no truck with the opposition.

They did not care. For many it was their first visit to the Indian capital. Just eating, drinking, and sleeping in a five-star hotel, all expenses paid by an indulgent host, was an exciting enough experience. And when it was over, they jetted off to Agra to see the Taj Mahal by moonlight and then to tour Varanasi's medieval kaleidoscope. Dizzy from their round of heady adventures, the politicians returned to Gangtok with no suspicion of what they would have to do next.

Even Kazi, resting in Kalimpong after the ordeals of his triumph, claimed that 'a constituent body with advisory capacity' was soon to be set up. He expected another Indian lawyer to draw up a final document incorporating the main features of the 8 May agreement and the 1974 Act. He also told Poudyal that the ultimate constitution would provide an elected speaker, increase the assembly's powers, give a higher status to the leader of the house, and whittle down the chief executive's authority. Little did Kazi know that an inspired article in the obliging *Times of India* had already predicted 'a quiet burial to the anachronism of a "protectorate,"' through a Sikkimese member of the Indian Parliament and '"a set of measures to maintain Sikkim's distinctiveness and cultural identity"'. The so-called 'discussions' on constitutional changes seemed to have bypassed Kazi. But reflecting the government's thinking, the *Times* drew parallels with Kashmir, Nagas and even Tamils, who were unquestionably Indian even if some of their leaders had once flirted with the notion of secession.

The portent was lost on Kazi who did not—could not—read newspapers. He did not look beyond the immediate prospect which was certainly gratifying. He consented to go to the palace on 23 July to be sworn in as chief minister. With ten out of fourteen portfolios tucked in his kho, he had overnight become the most important Sikkimese in Sikkim, enjoying far greater patronage than the Chogyal against whom his resentment still smouldered. Krishna Chandra Pradhan became minister for agriculture and animal husbandry; Bhuwani Prasad Dahal received the food and civil supplies portfolios; and the two former National Party men, Rinzing Tongden Lepcha and Dorjee Tsering Bhutia, were placed in charge of public works and health, respectively. Chatur Singh Roy's ambitions were realised when he became deputy speaker. Das was, of course, speaker. That crucial position could not be entrusted to any Sikkimese.

The anomaly of a chief executive supervising the chief minister worried Kazi as little as did prophetic newspaper articles about more drastic impending changes. He basked in the warmth of Mrs Gandhi's congratulations; she had even written to the Chogyal demanding that the new ministry receive his 'cooperation and goodwill in working purposefully for the development and well-being of the people of Sikkim'. For the first time in his life, Kazi had a house to live in at Gangtok. That satisfying sense of consequence was reinforced when K.M. Lal was formally installed as secretary to both the cabinet and chief minister, and Khatiawara became the new chief minister's honorary personal secretary. A great-niece was added to the staff to discharge family obligations and buttress Kazi's sense of importance. Life had never seemed more rosy. Being able to spurn a luncheon party in his honour at the palace was one of the minor delights of political success.

But if the new chief minister was naively bemused, Crown Prince Tenzing in London was not. At once grasping the new constitution's ominous significance, he told a British reporter that 'India has exploited Sikkim's troubles to take over the kingdom'.

REFERENCES

1. 'Time for Moderation', the *Hindustan Times* (3 July 1974).
2. 'The Himalayan Knife-edge', Cheng Huan, *Far Eastern Economic Review* (27 September 1974).
3. Khara Nanda Uprety, letter to the editor, *The Statesman* (5 September 1974).
4. Nar Bahadur Khatiawara and nine others. 'Sikkim's Merger—A Brief Resume', memorandum to Prime Minister Morarji Desai.
5. V. Gopakumar, 'An Illusion of Power', *Far Eastern Economic Review* (20 September 1974).
6. Ibid.
7. Dilip Mukherjee, 'End of a Chapter in Sikkim', the *Times of India* (6 July 1974).

CHAPTER

14

AGAINST THE LAW

'Elsewhere, protectorates are graduating to independence and colonies are marching to freedom. In Sikkim, a protectorate is moving to "freedom within India" by annexation through constitutional legerdemain.'

Hindustan Times,
30 August 1974.

'Sikkim is not a part of India, and the Indian constitution cannot be twisted to give its people representation in our parliament.'

SHYAM NANDAN MISHRA,
Lok Sabha, 2 September 1974.

Armed with the Indian government's permit to reside permanently within the inner line (a concession granted to only a very few privileged foreigners), Kazini bustled into Gangtok in late July, chuckling there had never been a dull moment in Kalimpong for twenty years. She told everyone how much she had enjoyed 'midnight cooking assignments for the dear old Kazi's people'.

With Hope gone, Kazini was looking forward to being the sole purveyor of Western wisdom in a rustic backwater. The two women had barely ever met, but the Gyalmo's established background, high-level international connections and superior rank as queen had always rankled with the sergeant's daughter and fuelled her enmity. Kazini's dislike of Coo Coo La was even more the product of jealousy. But the Chogyal's beautiful and sophisticated sister had withdrawn into a shell, and the chief minister's wife did not any longer need to fear being upstaged by either woman. She was determined to assert her position as the first lady of Sikkim. The PO and the chief executive both had wives, but they were Indian whereas Kazini, blissfully disregarding the British passport to which she clung, saw herself as the foremost member of the Bhutiya-Lepcha aristocracy.

She was soon to be disillusioned in her expectations. Gangtok boasted none of Kalimpong's raffish cosmopolitanism. There were no sprigs of foreign royalty, no mysterious European travellers or swashbuckling Tibetan aristocrats to animate her salon. Society was homely beyond endurance. Such social activity as once existed had revolved round the palace; there was no substitute for that focus even if the unpolished Sikkimese were looking for a replacement. They were not. Most viewed Kazini with mingled fear and mistrust. Sometimes, even her husband seemed to share that view. 'She'll say the wrong things and everything will be "garbar"!' he muttered in his broken Hindi when I asked why she wasn't living in Gangtok. With her heavy make-up and exotic attire—furs draped over brocade bakus—Kazini was a strange apparition from another world. Her meddling was best avoided. The dak bungalow with its unimaginative departmental furniture that had been allotted to her husband was humble compared to the palace, India House or even Mintokgang. To add to her chagrin, K.M. Lal was housed in an identical bungalow next door, able to keep an eye on every little flutter in her modest domain.

It was a disappointing homecoming. Worse was the discovery of the narrow field of her husband's operations, fenced in as it was by the chief executive's overriding powers.

Even within his own enclosure, Kazi dared not take a single step without clearance from India House or Mintokgang. The chief minister cut a sorry figure as he waited on Bajpai and Das for orders. Kazini was excluded from their confabulations, and was convinced that the Indian security men posted day and night outside her doors were really spying on Kazi and her.

Alert to undercurrents, she suspected that bigger plans were in the air. Khatiawara talked of repealing Revenue Order Number One of 1917 which forbade alienation of Bhutiya-Lepcha land. The eight-member Land Reforms Committee, of which he was chairman, promised to parcel out estates, including Kazi's, among Nepalese peasants. Their zeal was beginning to provoke a reaction. Some legislators complained that the Constitution Act had been 'bulldozed through the assembly with undue haste'. Others objected that the chief minister made no attempt to stand up for even minimum rights. Santosh Kumar Rai, who had become Congress general secretary, told reporters that he knew very little of what went on in the party.

Neither did Kazini. She got the first hint of moves for closer ties with India when Swaran Singh told the Lok Sabha on 25 July that Sikkim had not yet asked to take part in New Delhi's political institutions. His announcement—'If and when such a request is received, it will be for this Parliament to decide'—seemed to suggest some annoyance at the delay in asking. If Kazini was kept in the dark, Sikkim's head of state, who had a constitutional right to be informed of developments and whose concurrence was necessary for any measures affecting Sikkim's status, was even more so: he did not hear a word of approaches to the Indian government until more than a month later. The bomb burst then, and it was impossible to say whether the Chogyal had deliberately been denied information or whether Kazi's supposed overtures were a back-dated invention.

Apparently, Sikkim's five ministers resolved at their very first meeting, with the chief executive holding the ring, the day after they were sworn in, to ask the Indian government to 'confirm their willingness to discharge the rights, responsibilities and powers to accept the request set out in the Government of Sikkim Act and resolutions' of 20 and 28 June. Das sent a copy of this resolution to the palace 'for the Chogyal's perusal'. The latter acknowledged receipt on 27 July asking: 'May I know exactly what is being requested of the government of India? Any letters addressed to the government of India on important matters must have my approval as it naturally involves Indo-Sikkim relations.' The Chogyal also wrote to Mrs Gandhi on 29 July emphasising his strong objections to any step that might damage Sikkim's international identity and affect relations with India. Das did not reply, probably because neither he, nor the chief minister, knew the answer to the Chogyal's question. It was for New Delhi to decide what the Sikkimese should ask for. Das was also waiting for India's response to Kazi's letter which he had forwarded on 26 July. This was done behind the Chogyal's back. Das allowed the ruler to think no steps had been taken since he had not approved of any.

It was a clandestine move, also an illegal one, as Justice Hidayatullah commented. Under clause 29(1)(b) of the Act, the chief executive was bound to 'submit all important matters to the Chogyal for his information and for his approval of the action proposed to be taken'. Under clause 5 'all executive action of the government of Sikkim taken in accordance with the provisions of this Act shall be expressed to be taken in the name of the Chogyal'. But the ruler had no idea of what Das was up to. In any case, the 20 and 28 June resolutions had no force, which is why Das did not incorporate them in the Act. The resolutions were permissible only under the Act, which did not become operative until 6 July; indeed, this was the justified argument advanced by the PO when the Chogyal objected to the 20 June proceedings. Similarly, the assembly could not exercise its right to 'seek participation and representation for the people of Sikkim in the political institutions of India' under clause 30(c) of the Act until the Act had become law. Under no circumstances, therefore, could Das have regarded Kazi's letter as a valid request to India. Yet, he had no compunctions about sending it to New Delhi, and and that, too, without consulting the Chogyal. The Indian government should have ignored such improper communications.

It was not until the afternoon of 27 August that Das at last sent a peon to the palace with a letter from Kazi dated 12 August and a covering note to say: 'I am enclosing a copy of a letter received from the chief minister while I was ill. I am sorry I did not forward it to you earlier.' Kazi's letter reminded the chief executive that New Delhi had not yet responded to his 24 July message.

This belated action seemed fishy to the Chogyal because even if the chief executive had been indisposed, he was not bedridden for the fifteen days between 12 August and 27 August. There was no reason for not sending a piece of paper a few hundred yards up the road from Mintokgang. It was also curious that Kazi's letter did not carry the usual reference number which would have been sure evidence of its authenticity. A backdated letter often gives expression to an afterthought, but serial notations cannot be inserted later: a point that is frequently made in the law courts to repudiate tampered or forged records. As a member of the IAS, K.M. Lal, who handled Kazi's correspondence, would not have overlooked this rigid bureaucratic practice if the letter had, in fact, been written on 12 August. The Sikkimese were convinced Lal wrote all the letters under instructions from Das or Bajpai, and that Kazi signed them blindly without understanding their contents.

There was another surprise in store for the Chogyal. Just after noon the following day, Bajpai sent him a letter dated

22 August from Swaran Singh, belatedly acknowledging the Chogyal's letter of 29 July to Mrs Gandhi. The PO pleaded 'forgetfulness' for this extraordinary delay of six days in a matter of such vital concern. The Sardar admitted that his government had received Kazi's requests of 24 July and 12 August and was looking into the legal and constitutional implications, adding that 'if it is found feasible to respond, we shall be happy to do so'. The illegality of the action, the conspiratorial manner in which it was being conducted, and the fraud that had been practised on the Chogyal did not in the least disturb India's external affairs minister. With no hint of apology, he wrote in terms of expansive benevolence:

> The role that you can play at the present juncture is an important one and the recognition of it by the government and the people will contribute greatly to the stability of Sikkim. You can rest assured of government of India's continued interest, which we have often reiterated, in the position that you occupy in Sikkim's life.
>
> We will do everything in our power to ensure that Sikkim's cultural heritage, rich traditions, and distinct personality are not diluted or eroded in any way as a result of the progressive democratisation and development of closer links with India. Indeed, the Chogyal's position as head of the state, and his functioning within the new Sikkim constitution, are guarantees that the personality of Sikkim shall remain unchanged.

This was the first intimation the Chogyal had of a letter from Kazi being surreptitiously sent to New Delhi and of the chief minister, chief executive, and Indian external affairs minister being in league to violate even the loaded constitution they had foisted on the kingdom. Describing the Sikkimese 'request' as 'an act of collusion' between Das and Kazi, Khatiawara says: 'The so-called request for participation in the political institutions of India and the resolution upon which the 35th amendment of the constitution of India was enacted by the Indian parliament, making Sikkim an associate state of India, was never passed in the Sikkim assembly. This fact, we as members of the Sikkim assembly, can vouch for fearlessly.'[1] The Chogyal also noted that Swaran Singh made no reference to the treaty which was the rockbase of Sikkim's constitutional position and connection with India, and that his invocation of culture, traditions and personality did not guarantee the protectorate's international status, juridical rights and separate political identity.

While the Chogyal and Jigdal Densapa were still wondering how to avert the realisation of their worst fears, as presaged in Swaran Singh's letter, they heard on All-India Radio's late-night news bulletin on 29 August that Mrs Gandhi had decided on a constitution amendment bill to at last achieve her old ambition of converting the kingdom into an associate state. Sikkim would send a member each to the Lok Sabha and Rajya Sabha. The two Sikkimese MPs would enjoy all parliamentary rights, except the power to vote for India's President and vice-president. Opposition politicians had already been told of the government's decision.

The Chogyal at once telexed Mrs Gandhi, objecting that he should have to learn of such vital decisions from the media. Her promise to respect Sikkim's treaty rights was being negated, he said, without the knowledge and genuine consent of the Sikkimese, 'distinct personality not being synonymous with separate identity'. He pointed out that 'present steps will amount to unilateral abrogation of 1950 treaty and integration of Sikkim' in India. Another message the following day pleaded that the Indian legislation be postponed until Mrs Gandhi could send a personal representative or a parliamentary delegation to ascertain opinion in the kingdom.

These and other messages were handed over to Bajpai for transmission on the India House teleprinter. Since so few of them were acknowledged, the palace often wondered whether the PO perhaps had instructions to exercise discretion in what he passed on. His was a two-way channel, and on 31 August Bajpai gave the Chogyal a copy of India's Constitution (35th Amendment) Bill whose statement of objects and reasons cited the 8 May agreement, the 11 May motion of thanks, the 1974 Act with special mention of clause 30, the 28 June resolution, and Kazi's formal request 'to provide for terms and conditions of association of Sikkim with the [Indian] union'. India's treaty with Sikkim might as well not have existed. Nor did the measure explain how and why New Delhi had twisted 'association' to mean inclusion in the Indian Parliament.

Introducing the bill in the Lok Sabha on 2 September, Swaran Singh almost apologised for it not being more drastic. 'At the present we are going up to the point to which Sikkim is prepared to go' suggested further legal aggression to come. 'After the amendment is approved by the two houses, the status of the protectorate will not be there.' In other words, the external affairs minister was saying that a treaty between India and Sikkim (to say nothing of the Anglo-Chinese convention of 1890) could be abrogated by domestic legislation in India. This was an absurdity. The Sardar, himself a lawyer, must have been well aware of that. But seemingly, there was no end to the preposterous claims he was prepared to make to a tame audience. Singh's argument that the amendment was 'a political matter and not a question of legal niceties' implied that since a political decision had already been taken, a semblance of legitimacy might as well be created. Continuing this specious reasoning, he announced that the bill flowed from the 1974 Act to which the Chogyal had assented (thereby suggesting that the Chogyal was a party to this deception!) and that the Sikkim assembly's unanimous request had been pending for some time. That was another travesty of the truth.

Apart from obedient Congressmen, only the Jana Sangh, dreaming of Hindu control of a greater India, approved of this blatant expansionism. Communist MPs accused the prime minister of acting 'in a very peremptory fashion in utter contempt of the opinion of the house'. They rightly pointed out that neither the Indian nor the Sikkimese public had been consulted. Niren Ghosh and Dasaratha Deb, two Marxist members, warned that the amendment 'would cause serious international complications and spoil the existing friendly relations between the peoples of India and Sikkim' since it was 'making a farce of the elected [Sikkim] assembly'. More pointedly, they added: 'It means absorption of Sikkim with India, it makes Sikkim part of India.' Ghosh accused the Congress government of 'national chauvinism'. Jyotirmoy Bosu, also Marxist but a wartime captain in the British—not British Indian—army, said such subversion of democracy would invite charges of Hitlerism.

Mrs Gandhi's hopes of an all-party consensus were dashed when other politicians realised that the consultations she had asked for were only intended to secure unquestioning compliance. She would accept no modification. Madhu Limaye, the Socialist leader, felt the bill should first be examined by a select committee. Madhu Dandavate, an independent MP, demanded a referendum in Sikkim. P.V. Mavlankar thought that since the Indian constitution was being rewritten, there should be a referendum in India too. G.G. Swell cautioned against playing the 'Big Brother'. And, in Frank Anthony's opinion, associate statehood was 'an invitation to the balkanisation of this country'. Only Jana Sangh members turned up on 3 September for a briefing at which the Sardar and H.R. Gokhale, India's law minister, in effect extolled their holy grail of *Akhand Bharat*, undivided India. As Dipankar Chakrabarti argued in the small Bengali journal, *Aneek*, 'if we go by the logic of buccaneers that Sikkim was a "protectorate" of India, then Burma, Sri Lanka, Afghanistan (and also Pakistan and Bangladesh) may also be claimed to be "inseparable parts of India"'.

Probably the most outspoken critic was the Organisation Congress's Shyam Nandan Mishra who denounced the measure as 'a constitutional monstrosity', and the move as 'politically unwise and constitutionally absurd'. He sent furious letters to the prime minister and did not mince words in Parliament: 'Only territories of India come under our constitutional jurisdiction, and only our people have the right to elect representatives who can shape our policy. Those to whom our laws do not apply cannot be among our legislators, and our laws cannot be extended beyond our territory....'

But he was battling against the ingrained Hindu conviction that not only the entire territory under the rule of British viceroys, but even far-flung lands in the east and west, over which Indic princes had established some sway in the mists of history, should rightly be governed from New Delhi. This psychological craving for wider jurisdiction and for the grandeur of size had suffered a sharp setback when Congress politicians accepted Partition as the price of Independence. Many Indians didn't understand why Nepal, Bhutan and Sikkim should not have gone the way of Mysore or Travancore. Hope flared up briefly when the Indian armed forces piled victory upon victory in 1971. But it was soon clear that Bangladesh was determined to guard its sovereignty as jealously as Pakistan. The Jana Sangh alone was honest enough to articulate this thinking, but to many others India meant all those South Asian lands that used to be painted red in school maps and more. The constitution amendment bill gave them an opportunity of getting back a small sliver of what had been given up as lost. Even those who did not fully share in this imperial euphoria were afraid of appearing unpatriotic or, since Sikkim's contrived crisis had artfully been presented as a conflict between popular aspiration and a repressive monarchy, as undemocratic. In any case, Mrs Gandhi's crushing majority ruled out free choice. And so the Lok Sabha agreed to introduce the bill by 140 votes to seventeen.

• • •

The Chogyal reached Calcutta on 4 September, the day of the bill's second reading. He had planned to go on to New Delhi with his three youngest children who would catch a flight there for New York. But Bajpai ordered him not to venture beyond Calcutta. Mrs Gandhi's government was not at all anxious that he attract foreign diplomatic attention in the capital, or that his views be placed before MPs whose senses had been dulled by the treacle of Swaran Singh's oratory. The Chogyal had not even been able to talk to anyone in New Delhi for Gangtok's telephone lines to the outside world had been inoperative for more than thirty-six hours. To muzzle him further, Bajpai warned that the prime minister would be most displeased if he spoke to newspapermen.

It was a confused and unhappy wait at Dum Dum where the Chogyal, his children, Jigdal Densapa and other advisers gloomily sat around in the VIP suite, wondering what to do. The PO, whom the Chogyal called, refused to relax his order. Kewal Singh was equally brusque over the telephone, bluntly telling the Sikkimese king that he was not wanted in New Delhi. Reporters and cameramen milled round the suite, hordes of security men listened to every word in ostentatious nonchalance, and a band of Sikkimese students chaperoned by Karma Topden waited anxiously for a decision. They promised support for whatever the Chogyal did. But outright defiance was never his style and he still hoped to salvage something by appeasing Mrs Gandhi. So it was agreed that his secretary would escort the children to New Delhi while he stayed back in his flat in Calcutta's Wood Street until the Indian government relented. Emerging from the airport, the Chogyal found it impossible to fight his way through a battery of newspapermen, many of whom he had already met, and paused for a moment to explain that he was not giving interviews. That amounted to speaking to newspapermen! When he reached the flat about forty-five minutes later, Bajpai was on the line to reprimand him for disobeying instructions not to talk to the press.

His presence in New Delhi would not have averted disaster. Mrs Gandhi's control of the Lok Sabha, a three-line whip, the incipient national urge for territorial glory, and a press that had been conditioned to view the Chogyal as a monster and his objections to the bill as only a device to perpetuate royal absolutism at the expense of a suffering populace, ensured failure. But the Chogyal might have been able to focus attention on the illegality of the manoeuvre and explain that the Sikkimese as a whole knew nothing of what was being done to them and their country... and how. Foreign diplomats and some journalists in New Delhi would have been glad to hear his point of view. Instead, he had to wait in Calcutta for the *coup de grace*. There was to be no grand battle and heroic stand; only an abject surrender to superior strategy.

He remained cooped up in the flat while Nar Bahadur Bhandari and Sherab Palden Lepcha left Gangtok with a ten-man delegation to plead with the Indian authorities. They were badly organised, had hardly any money, and no contacts at all in New Delhi where the official reaction to their mission was undisguisedly hostile. But they met Jyotirmoy Bosu, who seemed to understand that the team represented the people and not the throne, and Mrs Gandhi, who solemnly promised that Sikkim's distinctive personality and identity would remain intact. Bhandari was convinced that the prime minister was playing with words. He told a press conference that the Sikkimese were unhappy and suspicious about New Delhi's intentions, and could only be reassured through a referendum on Sikkim–India ties. Jigdal Densapa was separately busy, addressing press conferences in Delhi's

Sikkim House, issuing a stream of statements criticising the bill, and lobbying MPs. Back in Gangtok, an enraged Kazi threatened to sack him as well as Karma Topden who had blossomed into a prolific writer of letters to newspaper editors. From Calcutta, the Chogyal also asked for a free and fair referendum, pleading with India's President not to give his assent to the constitution amendment bill until Sikkim's true views had been verified.

But the juggernaut of Mrs Gandhi's imperialism was not to be halted. The Lok Sabha adopted the bill by 310 votes to seven and the Rajya Sabha on 7 September by 175 to eight. Swaran Singh took off for Moscow the same day, after sending off an effusive letter of congratulations to Kazi in which he conveyed the prime minister's 'heartfelt felicitations' and spoke warmly of the 'history of friendship and cooperation between the peoples of Sikkim and India'. He still would not see the Chogyal who was languishing in Calcutta. Neither would Mrs Gandhi before leaving for Madras on 9 September.

The final formalities of ratification by state governments took another six months before India's complaisant President approved of the measure, predictably taking no notice of the Chogyal's appeal to exercise his right under article 111 of India's constitution to return the bill to Parliament with his recommendations. A new article 2a was inserted in the constitution's first part reading: 'Sikkim, which comprises the territories in the tenth schedule, shall be associated with the union on the terms and conditions set out in that schedule.' The schedule was new, so were changes in articles 80 and 81 which defined membership of the Lok Sabha and Rajya Sabha. As predicted, Sikkim was provided with a member in each, New Delhi unilaterally deciding the form and extent of Gangtok's participation. It was noted too that the Indian Parliament determined, then changed, the mode of choosing the two new MPs without bothering on either occasion to consult the Sikkim assembly which it was supposed to be obliging.

An additional anomaly was the exclusion of Sikkimese MPs from voting for India's President and vice-president. That indicated that though Sikkim sent representatives to the Indian legislature, the titular jurisdiction of India's head of state did not extend to the kingdom. While this could mean indirect confirmation of the Chogyal's status, it also introduced a constitutional contradiction that no one expected would long be permitted to continue.

• • •

The only real criticism at home came from the *Hindustan Times*, but it could not have been more devastating. 'If it is not outright annexation, it comes close to it,' thundered an editorial. 'To suggest anything else would be self-deception and compound dishonesty with folly. Sikkim is to be reduced from a protectorate to a colony through nominal representation in the Indian Parliament. To what end? What deep-seated urge of the Sikkimese people is this intended to satisfy?' The *Hindustan Times* argued that the move was impermissible since the kingdom was not territorially part of India and the Chogyal's subjects were not Indian citizens. If the presence of two of them in the Indian Parliament enabled the house to discuss Sikkimese affairs, that would be in violation of another country's rights. 'The worst suspicions about the manner in which the protector has seduced its helpless and inoffensive ward, with some genuine and much synthetic drama, will now find confirmation. No country or people voluntarily choose self-effacement, and the Indian government is not going to be able to persuade the world that Sikkim's "annexation" to India represents the will of the Sikkimese people. Indeed this issue has never been placed before them.'[2]

Warning that this 'thin cover for genteel annexation' would be followed by outright acquisition, the newspaper argued that at no time had the agitation in Sikkim espoused a merger which was not even an election plank. Swaran Singh's plea of responding to Sikkimese wishes was ridiculed since an Indian draftsman had written in the provision for closer political association, and New Delhi had deliberately distorted history to rush through legislation. Chauvinistic expansion would not only frighten Nepal and Bhutan, but it was also totally unnecessary since the 1950 treaty already adequately protected Indian security in Sikkim. As the newspaper put it:

> The country has a right to know whether the 'annexation' of Sikkim is part of a larger frontier policy proposed to be spelt out, or whether it is an isolated aberration.
>
> Far from doing any good, this decision—and the underlying tendency it represents—is going to bring India insecurity, unrest and international opprobrium. Congressmen, as much as members of the opposition, have a duty to question and oppose the betrayal of the true long-term interest and ideals of the nation for illusory gain. Only the most blind or cynical will derive any satisfaction over the sorry progression of the Indian presence in Sikkim from that of friend to master. The crusading zeal and decisiveness that the government displays over Sikkim has not been available for tackling the far more urgent problems and mounting crises at home. Perhaps there is no need for the common man to ask for bread. He's getting Sikkim.[3]

In addition to laying bare the hypocrisy of New Delhi's shoddy manoeuvre, the *Hindustan Times* published a telling drawing by Sudhir Dhar, showing Mrs Gandhi in a flowered kho labelled 'Sikkim', coyly preening under the arc-lights of a fashion show. It was called 'The Autumn Collection'. The paper's forthrightness may not have succeeded in influencing public opinion, but George Verghese, the editor, lost his job not long afterwards. The proprietor of the *Hindustan Times* was grumbling even six years later of Verghese's 'deep prejudices'.

Other countries sat up in alarm. Pakistan's Zulfiqar Ali Bhutto accused India of swallowing up Sikkim. Landlocked, vulnerable, and entirely dependent Bhutan, which had already repealed a law whereby the monarchy needed a three-yearly vote of confidence from an assembly that might be susceptible to pressure, also let it be known it would like Indian advisers to be gradually phased out. Nepal, being more confident, rumbled in less indirect protest. 'It is natural for us as close neighbours to feel concerned at the events of the past one year in Sikkim,' announced the foreign minister, Gyanendra Bahadur Karki. Dwelling on historical ties between the two kingdoms, he added: 'As Sikkim is Nepal's closest neighbour, we would naturally like it to retain its traditional entity (*sic*).' A calling attention motion by a member of Nepal's Rashtriya Panchayat (Parliament) complained that 'a small state being swallowed by a big country in the present epoch is a matter of concern to us.' There were public meetings to protest against 'India's policy of colonialism and imperialism'; 500 students demonstrated outside the Indian embassy in Kathmandu and its library was stormed. Several Indian shops were looted as anti-India riots spread.

In China, the *People's Daily* denounced the move as a 'flagrant act of colonial expansion,' while Hsinhua, the Chinese news agency, compared Indian actions with Russia's 1968 invasion of Czechoslovakia. 'One is a super-power and the other is a sub-superpower. One takes over the mantle of the old czars while the other steps into the boots of colonialism. One carries out expansion in all parts of the world while the other expands in South Asia. This is the root cause for India's annexation of Sikkim.'[4] The dispute spilled over into the UN where Rikhi Jaipal, India's representative, tried to rebut

Chinese accusations with the bland lie that 'in the days of British rule over India, Sikkim was a princely state under British protection exactly like the other five hundred-odd princely states that were protected by Great Britain.' According to him, New Delhi had merely acceded to Gangtok's request to accommodate two Sikkimese MPs:

> This is all that has happened. It is a natural and free political evolution of the people of Sikkim in the direction of internal democracy and closer links with neighbouring India. This is entirely in accordance with the wishes of the people of Sikkim as expressed in their elections.
>
> It goes without saying that India has not annexed Sikkim. The plain fact is that Sikkim is still outside the territory of the union of India. The Chinese allegation that India has annexed Sikkim is, therefore, clearly mistaken.[5]

Mrs Gandhi thought otherwise. Desperately groping for justification, shedding all sense of history or logic, even caution, she compared associate statehood for Sikkim with Pakistan's seizure of the two tiny principalities of Hunza and Swat, and with China's absorption of Tibet. The prime minister further damned herself by gloating: 'China has not even been able to establish complete control over Tibet!' It was evidence of her view of realpolitik, unblemished by any considerations of law or morality. When she again repeated that with a British gun salute and as a member of Narendra Mahal, Sir Tashi was just another Indian prince, the Chogyal wrote to point out the discrepancy between her views and those of her government's UN representative:

> If your excellency's statement on Sikkim is correctly reported, it confirms my worst fears which I placed before you with regard to the comments on the Government of Sikkim Act 1974, and my views on the effect and interpretation of the

> 35th amendment to the Indian constitution. It would also confirm that India's action in the past two years had as its main object the destruction of Sikkim as a country and the unilateral and arbitrary integration of our country with India, disregarding the true wishes of our people which can be ascertained only through a direct reference to them, and the Indo-Sikkim treaty.

He need not have worried. For though India might believe it had attained the old status of permanent association through seemingly constitutional means, Hidayatullah's twenty-three-page note explained that the process was so flagrantly illegal as not to affect the kingdom's juridical position at all:

> In the opinion of counsel the status of Sikkim in international law before and after the constitutional amendment in India remains exactly the same. Sikkim's international distinct personality is unaffected, and it is a protectorate as before. In the discussion the expression 'associate state' has been used. It will be noticed that Sikkim has not become an Indian state or union territory. Sikkim is not included in the first schedule of the constitution where the states and union territories are named.[6]

Describing the constitutional changes that had been effected, the eminent Indian lawyer continued:

> But the collocation of the [Indian constitutional] articles has no bearing on Sikkim. In any event the Indian constitution cannot be relied upon to alter Sikkim's status. Another treaty can only change the treaty of 1950. Schedule 10 cannot be cited for Sikkim in view of what I have said above because no law of one state can affect the status of an agreeing state, a party to a treaty. This is an accepted international position. The constitution binds India and NOT Sikkim. What binds

> Sikkim is the Government of Sikkim Act alone and the deliberations and resolutions of the assembly if they can be regarded as valid under the constitution of Sikkim, and the request of the Sikkim chief minister if valid... In the opinion of counsel the status of Sikkim is that of a protectorate with internal autonomy curtailed only as far as the treaty speaks, and this denotes a distinct international personality as before. The expression 'associate state' does not figure in the constitutional amendment which uses the expression 'associated with the union'. The expression 'associate state' is a recognised international expression.[7]

There was more in this vein. Hidayatullah discussed various forms of protectorship and association, none of which required either party to surrender or submerge its sovereignty. But the India–Sikkim link was different. 'The "association" here is not of this character but is an attempt to unify legislative and executive administration by affording legislative participation to Sikkim and to increase executive control of India over Sikkim.' This was a 'journey towards becoming a colony,' he said, while 'India made its journey the other way when it became an original member of the League of Nations, just as Bhutan has done.'

International authorities on the rights and responsibilities of associated states, and of protecting and protected powers were not, he said, of the opinion that one country's subjection to the general protecting power of another country destroyed or extinguished the first country's own juridical personality. Legal experts, the Hague court and the UN had upheld this view as Waldock had earlier done in his brief to the Chogyal:

> To conclude, therefore, Sikkim enjoyed an international personality and still does so, although sovereignty is shared. This is as a result of historical association with India even prior to the Indo-Sikkim treaty of 1950. This still continues

> in spite of the events of 1973 and the amendment of the Indian constitution.[8]

Hidayatullah did not think Kazi's request had any force because the Chogyal's prior approval had not been obtained. No request could be made except in the ruler's name. But even if it were genuine, the Indian Parliament could not prescribe MPs from Sikkim since the 1974 Act said nothing about parliamentary representation. The Indian amendment could not, therefore, apply to Sikkim. The two countries had distinct and separate constitutions, and no MP could swear allegiance to both. The only way in which Sikkim could be associated with India was for the assembly in Gangtok to amend the 1974 Act with another law providing for parliamentary representation in New Delhi.

He added:

> The Indo-Sikkim treaty is not being observed in its spirit and letter. India has unilaterally accepted additional responsibilities and opened the door to two Sikkimese in its parliament, and this is not in the treaty. Similarly there is no provision for election of such members to parliament in the Government of Sikkim Act 1974. The 10th schedule to the constitution cannot replace the treaty in the matter of relations between India and Sikkim.[9]

It must be stressed that the author of this authoritative and lucid exposure of an act of brigandage was no malign American or devious Chinese. He was a former chief justice of India's own Supreme Court who had also been the country's vice-president. Hidayatullah held that recent Indian actions sought to destroy the treaty which alone governed bilateral relations and could not be abrogated except by mutual consent, certainly not through irrelevant domestic legislation in India. But where was the court of law in which the Chogyal could cite Hidayatullah's views? India's campaign relied for its success on the country's strength, Sikkim's weakness, and on the indifference, ignorance and prejudice of the Indian public. Having marked out this populist arena for the battle, Mrs Gandhi was at liberty to choose those weapons that she could wield best, and which were beyond the Chogyal's capacity. He could not mobilise mobs. He could not deploy soldiers. He had no crushing administrative machinery. He had no diplomatic voice. Right was of little account without the supporting attribute of might.

The early part of the second week of September saw the Chogyal still forced to linger in Calcutta but engaged in an acrimonious telegraphic correspondence with the chief minister. It was a futile exercise since the constitutional points he made were beyond Kazi's interest or understanding. In any case, the chief minister was as little responsible for his replies as he had been for the political action taken in his name. But determined not to overlook any possibility of rescue, the Chogyal telephoned Das on 10 September to suggest that all the ministers and their advisers accompany him to New Delhi for talks with the Indian government. The invitation was repeated the next day in a message to the chief minister. It was rewarded with lengthy vituperation.

The Chogyal made this offer when, secure in her parliamentary coup, Mrs Gandhi at last allowed him to leave Calcutta. On 12 September, after eight days of waiting, he flew to New Delhi, where Swaran Singh, just back from Moscow, again confirmed that it was precisely because Sikkim enjoyed some element of an international personality that its defence and foreign affairs had been handed over to India in 1950. Such a transfer was not necessary for Indian states like Punjab or West Bengal. The minister also assured the Chogyal that the two new MPs would sit in Parliament as Sikkim subjects and not as Indians. He would like to discuss these matters further, he said, but was pressed for time as he was going abroad again, this time to the UN. But the Chogyal was asked to visit New Delhi in the first week of October.

Menon called the next day, taking with him a stately white-haired Sikh with courtly manners. This was Gurbachan Singh, who had been appointed political officer. Bajpai was going to The Hague—seat of the International Court of Justice—as India's ambassador, and Singh would assume his duties in Gangtok on 19 September. Nothing was said about the PO-designate's connection with RAW. His own airy explanation was that he had been in the prime minister's secretariat. Nor was the Chogyal aware that Singh was destined to be the last incumbent, and that the post created for Claude White would soon be wound up. Gurbachan Singh was in attendance when the Chogyal again met Swaran Singh on 14 September. There were equally unsatisfactory meetings with Mrs Gandhi and Kewal Singh. When John Lall, Bahadur Singh and Baleswar Prasad—all three had served in Gangtok—called in turn, advising him to accept New Delhi's fait accompli and go abroad for the time being, the Chogyal was convinced they had been sent by the Indian government. But he was not the man to run away. Recalling their intervention he fumed in earthy rage: 'It's like saying your wife will still be your legal wife, but she'll sleep with me!' To his visitors, however, the Chogyal politely explained that his duty lay in Gangtok. He returned home on 18 September, having accomplished nothing.

The scenario had changed. India House was about to receive a new tenant, but a new man had already been installed in Mintokgang. B.S. Das had been transferred elsewhere on 16 September while the Chogyal was still in India. Many in the durbar like to believe that, in the end, Das could not bring himself to go through with Mrs Gandhi's plans. They were taken in by Das's gentlemanly ways; he in turn, interpreted their friendliness to mean the Sikkimese 'always switch over to the winning side'.

In a memorable note submitted just seven months after his arrival in Gangtok, the chief executive warned the Chogyal not to expect independence and advised him to come to terms with India's permanent supremacy. 'The interests of small countries have never been protected except in the context of a geopolitical situation,' he wrote, reminding the Chogyal of Tibet, Hungary, Czechoslovakia and Panama. China had 'explicitly accepted India's special interest in the Himalayan kingdoms,' Das wrote, adding 'if Indian interests in any of the Himalayan kingdoms are ever affected, it can safely be assumed that she (India) will effectively intervene.' He pointed to the campaign in Nagaland and to two wars over Kashmir (despite UN resolutions and Western and Chinese support for Pakistan) as evidence of New Delhi's often underestimated determination to defend its rights. Das attributed the continued existence of the Himalayan kingdoms only to Nehru's idealism. 'India will never again be ruled by an idealist and whoever may be the prime minister of India, he or she will never allow morality or idealism to override India's national interests...'

The note warned that in spite of legal rights, the situation gave 'very little choice or manoeuvrability to Sikkim. She has, therefore, to derive the maximum benefit out of a bad bargain because wisdom lies in this course alone.' There was no alternative to closer association with New Delhi which would offer the Sikkimese wider economic and professional opportunities in India. It would also mean a system of frequent mutual consultations on matters of common interest. But he insisted the Chogyal should grant more political powers to the Nepalese so that they did not resent Sikkim's Bhutiya-Lepcha ethos and were not tempted to look south.

Das did not think the monarchy would, or should, be disturbed. But he predicted that the Indian army would remain in Sikkim 'for a very, very long time to come.' Also, even the exercise of the kingdom's guaranteed internal autonomy would 'be related to India's economic, political or security interests'.[10] Neither internal autonomy nor the status of a protectorate should be taken for granted, because both depended on New Delhi's perception of Indian requirements. In short, integration in India was a distinct possibility.

It was honest but not an encouraging analysis. It explained Das's acquiescence in the motion of thanks, the 20 June and 28 June proceedings, the passage of the 1974 Act and phoney request for participation, as well as his concurrence in Kazi's populist pressures and the activities of the three Indian OSDs. But his manner was always pleasant, which once prompted the Chogyal to remark that only his personality distinguished the chief executive from more abrasive Indian officials. 'He thinks the Chogyal's not such a bad fellow after all, and poor chap, he's suffered a lot already, so let's make him unconscious before we cut off his head so that it doesn't hurt too much!' It was a perspicacious comment on a man whose smooth tongue and kindly ways persuaded many Sikkimese that he had been recalled because he had proved to be that impossible creature, a reluctant executioner.

No one in Gangtok had heard of his successor. Even the Chogyal, with his intimate knowledge of the upper echelons of India's administrative hierarchy, wondered who Bipin Bihari Lal might be. Rustomji reminded him that Lal had been a colleague at the ICS training camp and produced a snapshot to prove they had been together in 1942. The Chogyal recognised him then as Bipin Bihari Lal Mathur. The caste suffix had been discarded during his career in Uttar Pradesh.

The new chief executive could not have been more unlike B.S. Das. He was an elderly widower, nagging, fault-finding, inclined to be rude even to the Chogyal, bullying in his attitude to Kazi and other politicians, and offensively domineering with civil service subordinates. He lived frugally and did not entertain unless he had to; but demanded that Sikkimese officials run domestic errands not only for him but also for his son and daughter in India. Such servitude would have been unthinkable under the durbar. Gangtok was too dazed to protest. The Sikkimese were also awed, for Mrs Gandhi's hatchet man had been commerce and industries secretary in New Delhi, and then secretary to the Planning Commission. Sikkim had never before had an administrator of such exalted rank. Mintokgang's previous occupants had all stood several rungs below the PO who was indisputably the senior Indian in the kingdom and gave all the orders. The pecking order was about to be reversed. Gurbachan Singh, a joint secretary in New Delhi's official hierarchy, might still enjoy social precedence by virtue of his diplomatic status, but, as a secretary in the union government, Lal ranked higher and was by far the more important personage.

'I should have twigged...' mused the Chogyal, looking back. He was ordinarily extremely sensitive to the finer nuances of bureaucratic etiquette, but his antennae failed him then. 'Something major was obviously afoot... they wouldn't have sent a secretary otherwise....'

REFERENCES

1. Nar Bahadur Khatiawara and nine others, 'Sikkim's Merger—A Brief Resume' (unpublished).
2. 'Kanchenjunga, Here We Come', *Hindustan Times* (30 August 1974).
3. Ibid.
4. *People's Daily* (Beijing, 3 September 1974).
5. Rikhi Jaipal, United Nations General Assembly (2 October 1974).
6. Mohammed Hidayatullah, 'Opinion in the Matter of the Chogyal of Sikkim and the 35th Amendment of the Constitution of India' (unpublished).

7. Ibid.
8. Ibid.
9. Ibid.
10. B.S. Das, 'Note on Sikkim–India Relations' (unpublished, Gangtok, 20 November 1973).

CHAPTER

15

WINNER TAKES ALL

'The monarchy being a sacred and binding institution, its protection and continuance should be the guiding factor, and India should ensure it.'

B.S. DAS,
'Note on Sikkim–India Relations',
20 November 1973 (unpublished).

'I am proud of my nationality. But does it mean that my Indian nationality should have ever come in the way of giving an honest opinion? Should nationality create, cause or justify hurdles in the discharge of the legal and moral duties of a judge?'

TARACHAND HARIOMAL,
chief judge of the Central Court of Sikkim.
'Note to Morarji Desai, Charan Singh and Shanti Bhusan',
15 April 1977 (unpublished).

Seven days after Lal moved into Mintokgang, he received a letter from the Chogyal inviting the cabinet to a meeting on 25 September. The new chief executive at once replied that Kazi and his colleagues wished to have no truck with the palace. To drive home the boycott, ministers were advised to stay away from the Chogyal's receptions in honour of the PO and chief executive.

Lal was creating an ominous situation. Since the government was carried out in the Chogyal's name by his ministers and by a chief executive formally appointed by him, it could be presumed that he was not altogether unconcerned in its business. Moreover, the chief executive was under a direct obligation to keep him informed of all that happened and to obtain his consent for decisions taken. But the ruler was not allowed to discuss anything at all with assembly members: Lal was determined to carry the strategy well beyond the limits observed by Das. Rebuff followed rebuff. When Densapa sent the Chogyal's customary Dussehra message to be printed in the *Sikkim Herald*, Gangtok's official publication, Lal promptly returned it as being offensive. The Chogyal offered to rewrite the short text, but after hesitating for a day or two, Lal apparently decided that a public snub would serve his purpose better. The offer was rejected.

Eventually, in early October, the Chogyal wrote to Kewal Singh protesting that he had not once met the chief minister and that the government could not operate if ministers were to remain incommunicado:

> The ministers as well as the Chogyal have constitutional roles and responsibilities to discharge and there has to be some solution to the present impasse.
>
> Differences there are bound to be, but to avoid any dialogue and display such utter disregard for mutual regard and courtesy is a ludicrous way of functioning, unless, unfortunately, the intention is to carry this stage of confrontation to a bitter conclusion.

Evading the heart of the matter, the foreign secretary went off at a tangent to accuse the Chogyal of instigating violence and spreading anti-Indian propaganda. He spoke of reports, presumably received from Lal and Gurbachan Singh, of the crown prince's provocative attitude, warned that people had lost all faith in the ruler, and added, on a threatening note, that Khatiawara could any day drum up a mob of 10,000 to overwhelm the palace if India withdrew the CRP. The Chogyal's reply did not lack dignity:

> With regard to your warning that if all opposition does not cease in Sikkim, the government of India would withdraw all CRP force units and that Mr Khatiawara is in a position to produce ten thousand anti-Chogyal demonstrators at any time, my only comment is that it is a possible contingency I must face, and I can assure you that I shall face it with fortitude, courage and a firm conviction that such demonstrators would not consist of Sikkimese.

A combination of circumstances explained New Delhi's intensified intimidatory tactics. There was an uncomfortable awareness that associate statehood had been illegally imposed, and that Indian control was founded only in force. Also worrying was the campaign abroad spearheaded by two groups, the International League of the Rights of Man and the Friends of Sikkim, who had sent complaints to the UN secretary-general, Dr Kurt Waldheim, and to the UN Decolonisation Committee. Senator Claiborne Pell's vigorous championship was equally disturbing. In India, the *Hindustan Times* continued annoyingly to speak of 'the institution of the Chogyal which reflects the separate personality of Sikkim', and to object that 'the seeming transfer of power from the Chogyal to the chief minister or the assembly means little since the Indian chief executive is vested with supreme authority and is also the speaker of the legislature. Neither the legislature nor the cabinet has any real power and it is understandable that the Sikkim Congress should chafe at this situation.'[1]

This was the long and the short of it. More and more Sikkimese seemed ready to overlook their differences with the durbar in the national interest. If the Chogyal was still unpopular with some people, overt manifestations of Indian arbitrariness were even more so. Under Lal and the three OSDs, who had become much more assertive with Das's departure, Sikkim 'witnessed the epitome of the worst aspects of the British Raj in India', as Khatiawara's memorandum was to put it, adding that their 'callous attitude towards us Sikkimese recalls to our mind the humiliating, snobbish and brutal attitude of the civil servants of the British Raj in India'. He spoke of 'misrule and tyranny'. Nar Bahadur Bhandari deplored the administration's 'authoritarian style of functioning'. Senior Sikkimese civil servants complained of having to buy crockery for Lal's table and seedlings for his garden, find accommodation for his children in Calcutta, and to being sharply berated, with sarcastic strictures entered in their personal files, for the least delay or flaw in service. The chief executive had acquired the hauteur of some British members of the ICS without any of their social polish or sense of service. As commerce and industries secretary in New Delhi, he had become accustomed to being courted by important businessmen whose hospitality he continued to enjoy whenever he visited Calcutta. Not surprisingly, perhaps, he expected even greater ingratiation in Gangtok.

Lal was an irascible man. His temper didn't improve when the Sikkimese proved unresponsive to allurements. The 1975–'76 aid figure was a handsome ₹ 131.5 million; after years of cheeseparing, the Indian government also sanctioned an unprecedentedly lavish ₹ 400-million plan. Several of the durbar's old development schemes, which India had refused to countenance before, were dragged out, the dust brushed off, and presented as evidence of Lal's imaginative generosity. The intention was not to encourage growth since no one paid the least attention to execution, but to find an excuse to distribute money. The result was that Marwari traders flocked to Sikkim, paying fortunes for permits and licences. Many of the thirty-two assembly members—the batisey chor, thirty-two thieves, as Bhandari called them—waxed rich on the proceeds. Their undisguised venality, drunken sprees and periodic weekends in the fleshpots of Calcutta added to discontent.

The Sikkim Students' Association in Darjeeling, formed by Hem Lal Bhandari, who was studying at the Jesuit college there, was one of several symptoms of resentment. It organised school boycotts and rallies against associate statehood, criticised politicians for submitting to bullying, and demanded restoration of the Chogyal's powers. When the association called a public meeting in Gangtok on 10 October, P.R. Khorana, a Madhya Pradesh policeman who had succeeded Dutta Chowdhury as commissioner, refused to allow the speakers to use microphones. The meeting was held all the same, and under Khorana's supervision, the CRP lashed into the crowd with more than usual ferocity.

'They were beating the students like anything,' recalls Nar Bahadur Bhandari, the future chief minister who was no relation of Hem Lal's. 'When I intervened, I too was badly beaten up in the Daronga sweet shop. About 500 CRP men gheraoed me. They said I would be killed if I didn't write a letter supporting Kazi. When I became unconscious they took me to the Thutob Namgyal hospital.' This was around seven in the evening. Bhandari did not regain consciousness until the following afternoon when the Gangtok doctors, fearing the chief executive's reprisal for sheltering such an outspoken critic, turned him out. Friends eventually took Bhandari to the Planters' Hospital in Darjeeling where he was admitted. But he still complains of pains in the chest as a result of the thrashing he received. 'I can't easily walk uphill. I need regular hot packs and massages.' Two younger members of the association, Namygal Tsering and Prakash Basnet, were kidnapped, also beaten up, and taken to Singtam where they were kept in captivity for several days.

It was beginning to dawn on India that Sikkimese nationalists would continue to affirm loyalty to king and country so long as they had a focal point for resistance. The Chogyal did not have to do anything to be a national and international lodestar. He symbolised Sikkim just by being on the throne. Also, while kingly problems evoke little sympathy, a king in difficulties is instant fodder for European and American newspaper columnists. More stringent measures were called for, especially since young people—the two Bhandaris, Sherab Palden, the Youth Pioneers, and others—were beginning to look on the Chogyal as the symbol of their struggle. Civil servants who had to bow and scrape before Gurbachan Singh, Lal and Kazi also regularly paid their respects at the palace, pouring out tales of the humiliations they were made to suffer. In fact, more people called on the Chogyal than ever before.

The campaign to demolish this growing appeal began in earnest in the autumn of 1974 when a Sikkim Congress meeting, with the chief minister presiding, accused the head of state and the crown prince of 'instigating and supporting anti-social and anti-democratic elements'. Kazi also claimed that the Chogyal's brother, Jigmed Tenzing Namgyal, had been sent abroad to canvass Western support though everyone knew that the Oxford-educated prince was virtually an invalid. His Tibetan wife, the exquisitely beautiful Soyang-la, nailed the lie with a press statement giving details of the medical treatment he was receiving in Calcutta. Two weeks later, Kazi and Kazini (accompanied by Khatiawara, Krishna Chandra and Rinzing) set out for New Delhi at Mrs Gandhi's invitation, the chief minister promising to ask their hostess to deal 'speedily and firmly with the Chogyal'. Kazi also announced that the administration would not pay for the upkeep of the palace and the Sikkim Guards, and that he was going to seize about 20,000 acres of the royal estates in the Lepcha reserve around Dzongu. But Mrs Gandhi and Yeshwantrao Chavan, who had taken over from Swaran Singh in October, pleaded with the chief minister to be patient with his king. Responding magnanimously, Kazi even admitted to reporters that the

Chogyal was not 'in the hands of Chinese'. The purport of this piece of playacting was to indicate that it was only at India's instance that Sikkim tolerated its monarch.

The November visit was for only two days. Before its dust had settled, Lal's administration accused the Chogyal and Tenzing of plotting to assassinate Kazi. Lal announced that a large quantity of explosives had been unearthed at a spot on the Siliguri road, about four miles from Gangtok. It was said that Kazi travelled that way. So did the Chogyal and hundreds of other people, pointed out sceptics, adding that the explosives allegedly recovered were of a kind available only to the Indian army. But inconsistencies passed unnoticed as Indian newspapers printed outraged articles. Kazi was congratulated on his miraculous escape, and the palace depicted as the nerve-centre of murderous conspiracies. Emboldened, the Sikkim Congress demanded on 25 November that the Chogyal should be expelled at once. Lal darkly hinted a week later that he had further evidence of the palace's involvement in a second plot. The evidence was never produced, but it was becoming very clear as the psychological pressure mounted that if his opponents could not eliminate the Chogyal politically, they would kill him through calumny.

The chief executive was meanwhile steadily hacking away at the throne's constitutional foundations. When he began to issue the government's official *Sikkim Durbar Gazette* entirely on his own, insisting that the term durbar meant only the chief executive, the Chogyal protested that no definition of the government could exclude the head of state. The difference was referred to New Delhi in terms of article 29(2), but the PO announced the very next day that the Indian government agreed with Lal. The latter's right unilaterally to appoint, post, promote, transfer and dismiss civil servants of whatever seniority, without reference to the ruler, was similarly upheld within twelve hours. In fact, the speed with which Gurbachan Singh produced these overnight verdicts in the chief executive's favour prompted some Sikkimese to wonder whether disputes were at all referred to New Delhi. It seemed to them that India House and Mintokgang had been empowered in advance to dismiss all the Chogyal's pleas and make a mockery of article 29(2). The upshot was that Lal told the ruler nothing at all of what was being done in his name.

About this time a systematic campaign began to strike out all references to the man who was still head of state. Lal replaced the Chogyal with Kazi as chairman of the Tashi Namgyal Academy, an educational institution that had been created and built up by the ruler to express his vision of the kingdom's further education. Lal also converted the Palden Thondup Institute, which had revived and popularised traditional handicrafts, into the Cottage Industries Institute. He then dropped 'Namgyal' from the formal description of the Institute of Tibetology, a unique repository of all the literature, arts, science and religion of a vanished culture that the Chogyal had set up in 1958. People close to the throne were not spared either. At the chief executive's bidding, Keshab Chandra Pradhan, the chief conservator of forests and Krishna Chandra's elder brother, sent the CRP to evict Coo Coo La from the forest department bungalow she had been allotted because her own property had been taken over by the army. The Gyalum was asked to vacate Thakse palace. Athing-La was removed from chairmanship of the State Bank of Sikkim. These were petty moves designed to demonstrate that the royal family and its friends were not to be allowed even courtesy privileges, and that all authority vested only in the chief executive. Lal must have been disconcerted when officials and ordinary people ignored his diktat and turned up in even greater numbers for the 1974 Phanglabsol, Kagyet, and Losoong dances and measured the ground with their bodies in the Chogyal's presence.

Disapproval had to be expressed. An opportunity presented itself in March 1975, some weeks before the Chogyal's official birthday. Following the 1973 birthday riots, 4 April 1974 had passed quietly without ceremony. But the Chogyal felt that resumption of the traditional durbar and presentation of the chief secretary's report would help to restore confidence. While the participation of the chief executive and chief minister would emphasise their corporate functions, it would also show to the people that the throne, though still occupying a public position, was reconciled to its diminished role. The PO's presence would underline amity with India. But Lal and Kazi quickly declared 4 April 'martyrs' day' instead. Lal then brusquely rebuked the Chogyal that 'after the enactment of the Government of Sikkim Act 1974 the holding of a durbar by the Chogyal and the reading there of the annual administrative report would be quite an anachronism completely out of place at this juncture'.

Carrying the war a stage farther, the administration ruled that civil servants 'should be directed not to visit the palace whether for social, official or semi-official functions or purposes, without taking prior approval from the ministers under whose control they are working'. Such permission was never granted. Officials were also individually summoned to Mintokgang or Kazi's bungalow and told not to appear at the Tsuk-la-khang even for religious festivals. They were to look away if they happened to encounter the Chogyal. Henceforth, the king was to be a non-person in his own kingdom. He was to be shunned and ostracised by his subjects under strict instructions from the foreigner who ruled in his name. Clearly, Lal was enjoying himself.

Still naïvely looking to New Delhi for justice, the Chogyal telegraphed Mrs Gandhi on 1 April that 'the chief executive has lately been arrogating to himself dictatorial powers and has been acting in a manner as if he were not responsible to any authority in Sikkim... he has consistently and deliberately violated all provisions of the Act pertaining to submitting of all important matters to the Chogyal for information and approval for the action proposed to be taken, as is incumbent upon him under the Act... Further, he has conducted his correspondence with me in terms which are grossly discourteous and insubordinate.'

A mulish streak in his psyche refused to give in. Even some sympathetic Indians believed that but for this trait, the Chogyal would have been able to benefit from an opportunity to reign though not rule. He threw away that chance, they regretted, because he would not be reconciled to the authority vested in elected leaders. He displayed his recalcitrance at every turn by challenging the administration and repaid with ingratitude an India that had rescued his throne and saved his dynasty. He should have secluded himself in the palace, it was said, emerging only for ceremonial events to which he was invited, leaving governance to Kazi, which meant the two Lals—B.B. and K.M.

But the Chogyal was first a Sikkimese and then a king. If he seemed less amenable than anyone else, it was because he was in a stronger position to voice misgivings shared by many other Sikkimese and to take action that was beyond the courage and capacity of humbler folk. Understandably, he did not entertain too high an opinion of Kazi and his colleagues; like many others, he had few illusions about the 1974 elections. But the basic issue, as he rightly saw it, was no longer between palace and politicians. The dispute was between Sikkim and India which had installed a tame ministry in Gangtok to fight its battles by proxy. The Chogyal would no longer have cavilled at sharing power with a truly representative chief minister. But he was not going to surrender to an Indian chief executive the responsibilities that vested in him under the constitution, responsibilities moreover that New Delhi had repeatedly stressed he should discharge in the interests of democratic progress and Indo-Sikkimese harmony.

This assertiveness made a temporary, not long-term, difference. If the Chogyal had been content with an empty title and a pension, whiling his time away in drinking and at the mah-jong table, India might have tolerated the monarchy to the end of his life, while pointing to his lifestyle to show how useless and irrelevant it had become. After that, some means would doubtless have been devised to debar the vigorous and popular young Tenzing from ascending a throne which would by then have become redundant in any case.

The monarchy remained the only serious obstacle to Sikkim's absorption. If a republic with a protectorate tied to its apron-strings was a political oddity, a kingdom in association with a republic was even more of a constitutional monstrosity. But there was no way in which Mrs Gandhi's government could wipe out this anomaly so long as the Chogyal existed. His office was sanctified by an Act that also guaranteed Sikkim's exclusion from India's territory. The plan, therefore, was to make it impossible for the Chogyal to function even within the narrow limits India had prescribed, and to continue to whip up political animosity against him. India could then plead that the throne had made itself utterly repugnant to the people. It was a tantalising game of patience; but being aware of the Chogyal's disposition, the PO and chief executive expected sooner or later to wear down his flexibility and provoke him into taking a false step that Kazi would then be able to advance as justification for repealing the constitution and abolishing the monarchy. With the Chogyal gone, nothing need prevent India from annexing the kingdom.

• • •

An excuse for a confrontation had been brewing since January 1975 when Nepal's King Birendra invited the Chogyal to his coronation scheduled for 24 February. Since Sikkim's traditional relations with Tibet, Nepal, and Bhutan were outside India's purview, Kathmandu sent the letter direct to Gangtok. But India, already aggrieved by the previous year's protests in the

Nepalese capital, was again displeased. As a snub to Birendra, Mrs Gandhi decided to send India's vice-president to Kathmandu, though the President himself had attended the coronation of King Jigme Singye Wangchuck of Bhutan the previous June. Piling insult on injury, the external affairs ministry told the Nepalese ambassador, K.B. Malla, that under no circumstances should sovereign courtesies be extended to the Chogyal. India's ambassador, Maharaj Krishna Rasgotra, repeated the warning in Kathmandu. Indian obduracy on this point of protocol had prevented the Chogyal from attending Birendra's wedding. Bhutanese ingenuity alone had avoided similar controversy at the Thimpu coronation. While agreeing not to offend Indian susceptibilities by treating the Chogyal to modern Western honours like a gun salute, the Bhutanese received him instead with all the traditional Himalayan honours due to a reigning monarch—pennants, outriders, lamas, and dancers with a musical accompaniment of conch shells, trumpets, and other instruments reserved for royalty.

But the palace was hesitant, informing the Nepalese on 16 January that the crown prince might represent his father. Then, Jigdal Densapa wrote again on 6 February, confirming the Chogyal's acceptance and expressing the hope that he would receive the courtesies due to a head of state. A telegram followed on 15 February, and the Nepalese ambassador telexed back the same day—by way of the external affairs ministry in New Delhi and India House in Gangtok—that though the Chogyal would 'be received and honoured in Nepal as a special personal guest [of the king],' he would be 'accorded such status as is advised by the government of India'. Ranjit Gupta, one of India House's political secretaries, sent on the reply to the palace. Gurbachan Singh was also provided with copies of all the correspondence with the embassy, and of a letter that the Chogyal wrote (16 February) to King Birendra, accepting his invitation. The PO acknowledged receipt the following day, thanked the Chogyal for keeping him informed, and concluded by writing, 'I trust that your Highness will have a good trip.'

The local administration was also kept fully informed. Though Lal did not allow the Chogyal to communicate with his ministers and officials, the palace followed its usual practice of circulating typed copies of the tour programme as soon as it was finalised on 15 February. The same day, Densapa asked the chief executive to make the necessary travel arrangements and to see to it that Khorana provided an appropriate police escort. Lal had already been informed that Densapa, Rasaily (press, publicity, and culture secretary in addition to being auditor-general and familiar with Nepalese customs and protocol), the two Guards captains, Yongda and Chhetri, and a personal servant would accompany the Chogyal. A subsequent message advised him that the party would set out on 21 February.

No objections were voiced until the morning of 21 February when the chief executive suddenly appeared at the palace, as the luggage and presents were being carried down to be loaded into vehicles, and a stream of relatives and retainers waited in the verandah with their khadas to say goodbye. Lal's initial demand was that Rasaily should not go since he was needed in Gangtok. When the Chogyal demurred at this unexpected order, Lal sprang another surprise: the cabinet objected to the trip which would have to be cancelled altogether. The Chogyal pointed out that there had been ample time earlier to raise objections. It was too late now. His acceptance had been announced and he could not abruptly call off the visit at the last moment without inconveniencing the court of Kathmandu and himself losing face. Roughly warning him that if he insisted on going he would have to face the consequences, Lal strode out of the palace. What these consequences were began to emerge when the royal party set out, Khorana in uniform sitting beside the Chogyal in his white Mercedes.

Small knots of half-hearted demonstrators along the way spoke of hasty efforts to organise protests, but what struck the

Chogyal was that Khorana quickly donned his hat whenever they approached habitation. 'You seem to be afraid of bombs or something,' the Chogyal remarked, only half in jest. 'That hat isn't armour-plated by any chance, is it?' The police commissioner smiled weakly without saying anything. But something hurtled through the air just then to explode on the windscreen with an ear-splitting bang as the car slid over the Singtam bridge. Amidst the noise and the confusion, the driver stepped on the accelerator and kept up speed until people and houses had been left far behind. They stopped then to inspect the damage and found that the glass had cracked, and its metal frame melted and twisted under the impact. Khorana claimed to be at a loss, but warned that a broken-down tractor blocked the road at Rongpu. They made a wide detour to Kalimpong, and again took a longer route through Lava because the police commissioner feared hostile demonstrators at Teesta, well within West Bengal.

These irritations were nothing compared to the storm that broke out while the Chogyal was in Kathmandu. An hour-long audience with King Birendra, private conversations with Senator Charles Percy and Lord Mountbatten, and accidental encounters at social functions with China's vice-premier, Chen Hsi-lien, gave rise to wild charges of conspiracy. They seemed to be confirmed when the Chogyal told a press conference that he 'would not leave any stone unturned' to preserve his country's identity. Advised by its mentors that the Chogyal had left Gangtok clandestinely, India's 'free' media at once screamed that with the USA, Britain, China and Nepal behind him, he was going to appeal to the UN. All-India Radio, an arm of the government mockingly called 'All Indira Radio', led the attack. The sinister aim, they said, was to convert Sikkim into a beachhead of Western imperialism. Reporters covering the Kathmandu press conference speculated that the Chogyal might not return to Gangtok. Some of his Sikkimese friends also felt it might be tactically advisable to stay on in Nepal, ostensibly on pilgrimage visiting Buddhist shrines. That would obliquely proclaim his objection to New Delhi's manoeuvres, and also make it impossible for Lal and Kazi to run a headless government. But prevarication was not in his nature. 'My country is Sikkim,' he told questioners. 'I certainly want to live and die there.'

That should have set at rest doubts about his seeking redress beyond India. But briefed by the external affairs ministry, hysterical Indian newspapers were not to be mollified. It was paradoxical, though, that the point most vehemently made was that any international approach would violate the treaty which gave India exclusive control of the kingdom's foreign relations. It did not seem to occur to anyone that Mrs Gandhi had gleefully driven coach and horses through that agreement.

In Gangtok, Kazi burst into ferocious anger. Accusing the Chogyal of slipping away without the government's knowledge or permission, he presided over vengeful meetings and regaled visitors with blood-curdling descriptions of the punishment he would inflict on his king. Chavan received two letters above Kazi's signature demanding the throne's abolition. Poudyal and Santosh Kumar Rai, speaking for the Youth Congress, also wanted the monarchy liquidated. While Gangtok bubbled, officials in New Delhi wrung their hands in simulated anxiety to explain they might no longer be able to protect the Chogyal from his people's fury. A dramatic finale was expected as he flew back to Calcutta on 1 March to rest in Wood Street for a while and repeat everything that he had said in Kathmandu, again calling for a referendum in Sikkim.

He had planned to return on 3 March but was obliged to stay on an extra day for an appointment with his doctor. The delay upset carefully made arrangements for the 'spontaneous' outburst of popular rage that was to have greeted him. Rangpo was deserted when the Chogyal arrived on 4 March, escorted by a pilot car, four jeeps laden with West Bengal policemen, and twelve Sikkim Guards soldiers under Yongda and Chhetri.

They had met the flight at Bagdogra but Khorana had pleaded illness for not being at the airport, as custom decreed he should have been. He hadn't sent any Sikkim police, or CRP either, to receive the ruler at the border. Instead, the Rangpo checkpost had been vacated so that a police presence did not inhibit the demonstrators Lal's administration had mobilised. Like Kazi, Khorana also reported to the chief executive. But the men who had collected on 3 March had tired of waiting and drifted away.

However, a truck and a jeep still blocked the bridge over the Rangpo river between the two countries. Logs and boulders had been piled across the road at the Sikkim end. Since West Bengal policemen could not cross into the kingdom, Yongda and Chhetri climbed out to clear the way. They were busily at work when Poudyal and Subeidi, leading a crowd of about forty young Nepalese, all brandishing lathis and kukris, suddenly materialised and began stoning the guardsmen. The latter tried to defend themselves and Poudyal's arm was slashed in the free-for-all that inevitably followed. The fracas provoked Chavan to address the Indian Parliament in sombre tones:

> The government of Sikkim and the government of India have been particularly shocked in recent weeks to know of efforts to intimidate, terrorise, threaten and even physically harm political leaders and common people in Sikkim in a bid to disrupt law and order, obstruct the functioning of the government and subvert the democratic process. There have been assassination attempts on the chief minister by the use of explosives, there was the stabbing of an unarmed member of the Sikkim assembly by a member of the Chogyal's entourage in the Chogyal's presence, and some other distressing information have come to light only a few days ago of elaborate plans to use violence against elected representatives.[2]

Poudyal's injury could not have been inflicted by a Sikkim Guardsmen, and certainly not by Yongda or Chhetri, for none of them carried kukris, the traditional Nepalese weapon, when in uniform. However, every man jack of the Nepalese demonstrators had his kukri. Even if the Chogyal's peaceable disposition were discounted, he was aware that murdering or wounding a legislator, even Kazi, would solve nothing for him, since other equally malleable politicians would be induced to continue New Delhi's work. He knew too that India could extract a rich dividend from the propaganda effect of such folly. One explanation of Poudyal's undoubted injury is that it was accidentally inflicted in the mêlée. Another is that he was a martyr, not to the Chogyal's cruelty, but to the machinations of those who needed just such a crime to pin on the palace and, more specifically, on the Sikkim Guards. No one thought it necessary to ask who benefitted most from Ram Chandra Poudyal's bleeding wrist.

When the royal party reached Gangtok, there was Khorana, supposedly confined to bed, waiting in the bazaar to flag down the escort jeep. 'You're supposed to be so ill you couldn't even come to receive me,' exploded the Chogyal. 'How dare you stop my escort!' The police commissioner retorted that the Guards had attempted to murder a legislator; he had been commanded by the chief executive to stop and search all the royal vehicles for a bloodstained weapon or other incriminating evidence.

India and Sikkim were both in tumult. Everybody was baying for the Chogyal's head. Kazi and his party shrieked that the Guards would at once have to be disbanded, and the Chogyal deposed. Lal would not go quite so far as yet—he could not—but he ordered Captain Yongda's arrest. This was striking directly at the palace: the Chogyal could feel the net closing in.

• • •

The chief executive had already launched another personal attack. He had suspended Rasaily, who was in favour at court, from service on the grounds that he had defied orders in accompanying the Chogyal to Kathmandu. This being a weak charge, the auditor-general was simultaneously accused of corruption while serving as food commissioner from 1966 to 1970. Keshab Chandra Pradhan also obligingly filed a petition charging Rasaily with embezzling ₹ 557,000 when he was chief conservator of forests in 1961–'62. Rasaily had gone to the palace with the Chogyal and refused to emerge to be arrested. The policemen Khorana sent had no authority over the Chogyal's household and had to return without their quarry. Disappointed, Lal told newspapermen that a man who abetted absconding thieves was not fit to remain head of state.

Unfortunately for the chief executive, Yongda's arrest embroiled him in a legal dispute. Tarachand Hariomal, chief judge of the central court, refused to sanctify Lal's calculated vindictiveness. Hariomal had earlier fought off pressure to do the chief executive's bidding. He now examined the charge-sheet and evidence, and instructed the police to release the captain on bail. He again incurred Lal's anger by granting bail to Rasaily when he surrendered in court. 'I sent for the police commissioner with all the relevant papers,' says the chief judge of the central court. 'Again, there were pressures for not releasing him on bail. Beyond the first information report which contained no details, no other papers were produced. Without going deep into the merits of the charge at such an early stage and in the absence of proper material, the accused was ordered to be released on bail on execution of a personal bond of ₹ 100,000 with two sureties each in the like amount, in view of the unexplained spell of inaction during the long period of about twelve years and non-production of papers, if any, relating to the alleged charge. All this seems to have angered the chief executive.'

None of these clearly fabricated charges against Yongda and Rasaily were ever put to the test. Though Yongda was again imprisoned on the eve of the army offensive, nothing was said about the Poudyal stabbing. Even the complaints then cited were not pursued. Nor was the auditor-general prosecuted. A district and sessions judge dismissed the charges against him in 1980. Rasaily was reinstated in service without blemish. Keshab Chandra Pradhan made no attempt to substantiate his petition. The brains in the agency who planned the operation so meticulously knew their men.

• • •

Hariomal passionately believed in the separation of powers. 'It has to be conceded that no nation can prosper or progess without an independent judiciary with the rule of law as a basic and fundamental feature,'[4] he argued in a long memorandum to Charan Singh when the latter was home minister in Morarji Desai's Janata government. Copies were also sent to the prime minister and Shanti Bhushan, who held the law portfolio. 'The time-honoured doctrine of separation of powers and independence of the judiciary from the corrupting influences of individuals and political parties has remained a source of inspiration for all civilised nations of the world.'[5]

When Hariomal first arrived in Gangtok, the kingdom had four district magistrates and a munsif magistrate, all of whom enjoyed civil and criminal jurisdiction. Anxious to effect reforms, Hariomal appointed an additional munsif, the two law officers being entrusted with civil cases, so that district magistrates were gradually relieved of many judicial duties. An extensive scheme to reorganise the system, finalised in 1972, was to have been announced at the 1973 birthday durbar; the Chogyal implemented it some months later and courts and judges were firmly established by the time Lal took over.

The chief executive at once tried to circumvent the reforms by conferring magisterial powers on deputy development officers who were his subordinates. To the chief judge this was setting the clock back. Citing the Indian constitution's directive principles, India's Code of Criminal Procedure, and Sikkim's healthily evolving trend toward a judiciary that was independent of the executive, Hariomal told the chief executive that administrative officers could, at most, try motor vehicle cases. Incensed, Lal hit back by putting bureaucratic spokes in the judicial wheel. The judge learnt that Sanyal, the Namche OSD, had refused to provide the usual court accommodation, residence and transport facilities for Tsewing Dorjee Rinzing, the munsif magistrate, who had to spend two weeks every month touring the south. When a frightened Rinzing sought a transfer to some more innocuous job, Hariomal again provoked Lal's anger by insisting that the munsif should be allowed to continue with his duties.

The chief executive had not forgotten that Hariomal had resisted Das's relatively mild probings, granted bail to Yongda and Rasaily and also stayed the order evicting Princess Coo Coo La from the forest department bungalow. He had further cause to feel thwarted five days after the police and CRP broke up the Sikkim Students' Association rally. Santosh Kumar Rai had sent a confidential note to P.S. Subba, magistrate of east Sikkim, complaining that seventeen members of the association (including Rasaily's younger brother, Tejendra) were creating 'mischief' and were expected to commit arson. Subba capped this by announcing he had private knowledge of earlier incidents in which some of the boys were allegedly involved, and at once ordered their arrest, rejecting bail applications and petitions to be bound over for good behaviour. It was improper for a magistrate to act on the Congress general secretary's nebulous allegations against political opponents, without a shred of supporting evidence. His reliance on private information was as irregular. Hariomal also felt that Subba should have considered how badly the students had been beaten up by the police and that many of them were still in hospital.

The case was transferred to the Gangtok district court where an appeal was upheld. Neither Rai nor the administration made any attempt to prove their charges.

Lal suffered yet another setback when S.K. Prasad, chief judge of the high court, also an Indian on secondment like Hariomal, allowed the first ever habeas corpus writ since the court had been created in 1955, to release six young men who had been jailed on 6 December in connection with the explosives said to have been buried to blow up Kazi. When the case came up for hearing, Prasad roundly admonished the administration for abusing power. The general law gave the government of a small and peaceful country ample authority, he said, to prevent crime and uphold public order without invoking the extraordinary security regulation under which the six youths had been imprisoned.[6]

It had become clear to Lal that the judiciary would never acquiesce in his lawless rule. He, therefore, set out to take over the judiciary. Hariomal was asked on 21 January why judicial files should not be sent to the chief executive who was head of the department. The judge replied that the practice was to send all papers to the Chogyal as head of state. Any other course would impede the course of justice since the chief executive was head of the administration and he, too, had to submit all important matters to the ruler. Not only did the 1974 Act guarantee an independent judiciary, but the assembly over which Lal presided could not discuss or ask questions about matters before the courts or the appointment and emoluments of law officers:

> Clearly and neatly, therefore, the judicial set-up was contemplated to continue as already in existence, unless altered or amended by the head of state himself.
>
> Designated as the chief executive was, he could not have under the Act any control, much less overriding powers, over the judiciary. But however unfortunate it may have been, the

> judiciary too appeared to have been destined to receive rude shocks and come under great strain....[7]

This was an altogether new experience for the judge since the Chogyal had never interfered with his department. Nor had he placed any strains on the judiciary. Hariomal, therefore, refused to heed warnings of reprisals. 'Well, I, with all humility, have remained firm in my opinion and conviction that in no civilised country should the judiciary be allowed to be under the executive, stoutly opposed the suggestion as the same would have been disastrous and detrimental to any civilised society.'[8]

The judge's understanding of civilised norms was not shared by Lal who wrote to the Chogyal on 4 March to claim that 'the chief executive is the head of the administration in Sikkim—and that covers all departments and organisations under the government without any exception'. Arguing that the Act 'nowhere lays down that the judicial department will function directly under the Chogyal', he complained of 'the irregular practice followed' by Hariomal and demanded that 'all files of the judicial department, as all other departments of the government, in which higher orders are needed, have to be submitted to the chief executive'. In his fourteen-page note to the Janata regime's home and law ministers in New Delhi two years later, on 15 April 1977, Hariomal described what followed as 'the complete collapse of the administration of justice, in a way most humiliating and distressing'.

The Chogyal explained to Gurbachan Singh on 9 March 1975 why the judiciary and executive should remain separate in Sikkim as in India. He then replied to Lal eighteen days later with a four-page letter invoking the tripartite agreement and the 1974 Act, both of which guaranteed independent judges and judicial functions. These necessary safeguards would be destroyed if an official who headed the administration as well as presided over the legislature were also to control the courts. The

Act's clear enunciation of the chief executive's powers, which left nothing to implication or imagination, did not directly or indirectly include judicial supervision. 'I am irrevocably committed to a full, responsible government for my people, and it would be my sacred duty to ensure that the judiciary remains truly independent. I am not averse to any essential changes in order to strengthen, but not to reduce, the independence of the judiciary.' Lal did not answer, but apparently referred the Chogyal's resistance to New Delhi. Though the PO forwarded his complaint on 28 March, the palace was not told of it until three days later.

There were many reasons for the chief executive to act quickly. Judges who refused to support trumped-up charges or to help in the administration's vendetta against Sikkimese nationalists understandably annoyed someone of his autocratic temperament. But of more serious concern were efforts to prevent India's thirty-fifth constitutional amendment from being enforced in the kingdom. Rasaily had petitioned the courts that since the 1974 Act did not envisage parliamentary representation in India, or any change in the 1950 treaty, associate statehood had no validity. It would, therefore, be illegal for the kingdom to send MPs to New Delhi. He asked that the chief executive, chief minister, assembly members, and administration be restrained from taking any action under the Indian constitutional amendment making Sikkim an associate state. In a second petition, Rasaily argued for a preventive injunction against the assembly, as there was reason to fear it might violate article 23(20)(a) of the Act which forbade legislators to discuss or ask questions about the Chogyal and royal family.

The first hearing of these two cases was on 29 March. Hariomal had not had time to study the constitutional points raised in Rasaily's eighteen-page application. Ananda Bhattacharyya, the government advocate representing Lal, Kazi, and the other defendants, also said he would like some more time. He, therefore, agreed to the judge's plan for an interim order to maintain the status quo until both men had been able to examine the submission. But Bhattacharyya was suddenly called out of the courtroom just as the order was about to be issued. He returned a few minutes later with an application signed by some of the defendants, opposing an interim injunction and requesting adjournment.

Hariomal ignored the advocate's second thoughts, and dictated an order restraining the assembly for the time being from sending MPs to New Delhi or discussing the Chogyal and his relatives. 'In that order I had merely referred to some of the pleas raised by the plaintiff, as, for instance, according to the plaintiff, in the absence of any specific provision in the Sikkim constitution itself, the provision as amended in the constitution of India could not be imposed on Sikkim and any discussion on the Chogyal in the assembly would constitute violation of the specific provision of the Sikkim constitution. I did not and could not legally and legitimately give any opinion on any such pleas which required serious thought and consideration, and at that stage.'[9] So he asked Lal, Kazi and the rest to file their objections by 28 April, promising a final verdict after considering them.

This was the last straw. On 1 April, the PO told the Chogyal that New Delhi had decreed that 'the head of the judicial department shall submit to the chief executive all cases pertaining to the judicial department which requires high-level orders'. The reason: 'The chief executive, as the head of administration in Sikkim, had full control over this department.'

As it happened, the Chogyal had sent yet another appeal to Mrs Gandhi that day though India House had not yet relayed the message. He followed it up by pointing out that such ex parte judgments did not allow the opposing point of view even to be heard. The effect of the Indian government's unilateral decisions on interpretations and interpolations of the law in another country was to bypass and undermine the authority of

Sikkimese courts through executive orders. He also suggested that he was perfectly ready to hand over his powers as head of the judiciary to a three-member judicial committee under Sikkim's chief justice. But as before, the arguments fell on stony ground. The intention was to subvert and cripple, not strengthen, the kingdom's judiciary.

Lal sent a clerk round to Hariomal's office late on 2 April with a copy of the order. He himself telephoned the judge next day to remind him that members of the judiciary were now also forbidden to visit the palace. On no account were they to call there on the Chogyal's official birthday. The judicial department was at the chief executive's mercy for appointments, emoluments, transfer, promotion, reversion, dismissal, accommodation, office facilities, transport, staff, and for everything, in fact, that was necessary for comfort, convenience and confidence. Hariomal reacted with despair:

> The lighthouse was damaged and demolished with contempt which it never deserved. About two days later, I was called by the chief executive on the pretext of discussing and drawing up a scheme for the appointment of some civil judicial officers. But his main target was the ad interim order dated March 29 in the civil suit [Rasaily's two petitions]. In a tone arrogant and insulting, he asked me why I had passed even such an apparently innocuous order and not adjourned the matter. Little did he know that it was a judicial order and not an administrative one. Any such interference could entail serious consequences. But the judiciary is powerless if ignored by the executive. It was the most humiliating experience in my life as a judge. Little did he realise that it was not an insult to me but that he was trying to debase the institution and its value. I must admit that I could not stand it. I told the chief executive that I would not continue in office and would submit my resignation immediately. But it appeared he did not want that. He intended to humiliate the judiciary further.

> My resignation could have possibly created some public stir there or in India. The chief executive abruptly changed his mood and spoke a few kind words and persuaded me not to put in my resignation.[10]

Lal had changed only his tactics, not intention. Two days later he sent K.V. Natarajan, the development commissioner, also Indian, a man whom Hariomal liked and trusted, to persuade him to go away for a while. The judge had exhausted all the leave due to him, but Natarajan had been assured that would present no difficulty. Hariomal eventually reluctantly applied for ten days' absence, which Lal granted with alacrity. Hariomal left for New Delhi on 10 April, unaware that the chief executive had summoned the assembly for that very day to defy and disobey the injunction he had issued on 29 March.

Another legal conundrum was pending in Delhi High Court where a local lawyer, Som Dutt Sharma, had filed a writ petition on 8 November 1974, challenging the thirty-fifth amendment on the grounds that the admission of a foreign monarchy as an 'associate state' destroyed the unitary basis of India's constitution. Sharma claimed that Sikkim was at liberty to disregard Indian directives and that New Delhi's laws could not automatically apply there. Yet, India would have to bear the cost of Sikkimese elections and election hearings, as well as pay salaries and allowances to the two MPs. India would not even enjoy the reciprocal benefit of free trade and commerce. Each time Sharma's petition was due to be heard, however, the Delhi judge postponed the case until it was overtaken by more decisive happenings. But before Mrs Gandhi deployed her army, the Sikkimese made one last bid to rally to their flag. They lived up to the verdict of a former PO, V.H. Coelho, in his book, *Sikkim and Bhutan*, 'The people of Sikkim, however, remain calm and undisturbed but proudly determined to fight any intruder and to protect their homeland even with their native weapons, the kukris.'

REFERENCES

1. 'Avoid More Folly,' *Hindustan Times* editorial (10 April 1975).
2. Lok Sabha proceedings (11 April 1975).
3. Tarachand Hariomal, 'Now It Can Be Told', note to Morarji Desai, Charan Singh and Shanti Bhusan (15 April 1977, unpublished).
4. Ibid.
5. Ibid.
6. *Hindustan Standard* (Calcutta, 3 January 1975).
7. Hariomal, *op. cit.*
8. Ibid.
9. Ibid.
10. Ibid.

CHAPTER

16

LAST-DITCH STAND

'In Sikkim, three and a half battalions of CRPF were kept ready, all administrative powers were concentrated in the hands of the Indian Chief Executive officer, the voice of patriotic youth and students protesting against Indian expansionism was throttled, foreign journalists were barred entry three days prior to the so-called referendum, and only Goebbelsian propaganda from India was allowed.'

'India Swallows Sikkim', *Aneek*,
April–May 1975 (Translated from Bengali
by SOUMYA GUHA THAKURTA).

'We the people of Sikkim declare that the Sikkimese people do not recognise the right of any external power or authority to dictate the political and economic structure of Sikkim.'

Declaration of Independence,
Sikkim Students' Association,
Gangtok, 26 January 1975.

If the revolt was delayed, it was mainly because many Sikkimese still believed in New Delhi's professions. Those who did not were intimidated by the Indian soldiers and CRP men who had taken over Gangtok, and by the spectacle of Gurbachan Singh and Lal lording it over the Chogyal and the chief minister. They had established an effective network of control as well as espionage, and very little happened in the countryside without the three OSDs at once reporting it to Mintokgang or India House.

The only satisfied Sikkimese were in the tight circle that directly benefited from subservience, the leaders of the 'batisey chor'. Kazi was not personally accused of making money, but he had drifted out on a limb and was easily petrified into obedience. 'My husband is in a daze,' wailed Kazini, seeing in his nervous bewilderment the crumbling of all her grand designs. 'He is a tortured man... he signs whatever they place before him!' To be just a provincial chief minister's spouse was a disappointment for a spirited woman who had climbed so far and took such pride in her worldly adventures. She had desperately schemed and intrigued for many decades. Now she found that Kazi had far less power even than the chief ministers of Indian states. The unfrocked lama, nursing his hatred of the Namgyals, whom she had groomed and goaded, had failed her. The rustic young Nepalese she had fashioned into a revolutionary had become her most bitter foe. Kazini had, moreover, to put up with virtually round-the-clock surveillance. Apart from the CRP at the door, her bungalow was plainly visible from Khorana's verandah. Not only did K.M. Lal also keep a close watch on visitors, he was himself frequently in the house. His appearances brought on the sulky silences that had replaced her bubbling garrulity, while the chief minister hurriedly drove away callers lest his wife's nagging indiscretions be overheard. The precaution was probably unnecessary. Recognising the danger of the times, very few people dared to compromise themselves by calling on her. If Kazini had earlier been shunned for what she had done to Sikkim, she was now avoided for what she was suspected of plotting for Sikkim.

But there were murmurs all the same, echoes of tokens of resistance. Two Sikkimese men, Dilkumar Khati and Shyam

Sundar Rasaily, another brother of the controversial auditor-general, had fled to Nepal where their Sikkim Bill Protest Committee was attracting considerable sympathy. Three of the eight members of Khatiawara's land reforms committee (Loden Tshering Lepcha, Passang Tsering Bhutia, and Dharma Gompo Lama) had refused to sign the report whose drastic recommendations would have destroyed the economic basis of Sikkimese society. Passang Tsering's house promptly became the target of hostile demonstrations. Bhutiya-Lepchas lived in fear of violence and dispossession. The administration harassed them in many small ways, and even the more responsible Nepalese were beginning to resent the influx of Marwaris and immigrants from Darjeeling. The kingdom's tranquillity, unbroken between 1949 and 1973, was shattered by formidable displays of governmental force and constant sniping at people who were not sufficiently fervent in India's cause or subservient to New Delhi's men on the spot.

The spirit of resistance found expression in the Sikkim Students' Association's Declaration of Independence on 26 January 1975, the twenty-fifth anniversary of India's Republic Day. It was a fanciful document, more idealistic than practical, but it emphatically captured all that more timid people would have liked to proclaim. Condemning the 1974 Act as 'designed to perpetuate the subjection and exploitation of the Sikkimese people and to strengthen the hold of Indian imperialism on Sikkim', the six-paragraph declaration asked: 'Would the people of India have foregone their independence for two seats in the British Parliament?' Hem Lal Bhandari, a cherubic youth with some understanding of law but innocent of politics, was arrested in Darjeeling while distributing copies of the declaration. Complaining that the Indian police had no right to imprison a Sikkimese for speaking out in his country's defence, Gangtok commented that even the British did not inhibit the many Indian nationalists who used to freely advocate their cause in Britain.

The palace could not hope to escape being penalised for such flashes of resistance. Gurbachan Singh ordered the Chogyal to confine the Sikkim Guards to his own compound. They were not to be posted at the homes of the Gyalum, Prince Jigmed Tenzing or Princess Coo Coo La because, he wrote, their presence was an affront to the people. Lal then turned his attention to preventing the crown prince from attending the Bhumchu festival at Tashiding where the oracle of sanctified water annually predicts Sikkim's future: his presence was expected to encourage nationalists. Warned not to go, Tenzing retorted that if the chief executive had inside information of any danger, he should share it with the palace. The prince then set out, but had to return from Kewsing when he learnt of plans to gherao him in the Rawang guest-house.

Good-looking, clean-limbed, and fresh from Cambridge, combining the English public schoolboy's suave charm with the graciousness of an Oriental prince, Tenzing was then twenty-three years old. Unusual in a sturdy young Sikkimese of wealth and position, he did not drink, smoke or philander. An occasional thumba of chhang was the extent of his indulgence. The crown prince also provided a lively contrast to his father, reduced to a greying vision of shyness and stammering, his features marked by repeated disappointment. The Chogyal was increasingly a victim of deep melancholy. He spent hours in solitary puja either in his bedroom or in the small upstairs chapel in the palace, and talked often of retiring to a monastery. There was little bitterness in his conversation but always a sense of pain at the deception of friends like T.N. Kaul whom he had trusted, at the mockery of Kewal Singh's promises, and at his betrayal by Mrs Gandhi whom he continued to admire and respect. Their machinations left him bewildered and unhappy for he could not understand what powers India did not already have and hoped to gain by annexing his kingdom.

Nor was the heavy irony of New Delhi's attentions lost on the ruler who suddenly found he was treated to elaborate honours whenever he went to India. Before 1973, his visits, except when a state guest in New Delhi, were private occasions, meriting no more than a single plainclothes security guard. But after the riots, and especially after the passage of the 1974 Act, he could not stir even in Calcutta without an embarrassingly lavish escort. Much to the consternation of everyone else in the building, he once casually dropped in at my tiny rooftop flat with pilot jeep, motorcycle outriders, the Indian and Sikkimese flags fluttering on his limousine, and two Ambassador cars and a black maria, all packed with policemen. West Bengal, apparently, had strict instructions to hedge him in with overpowering ceremony. It might have pleased the Chogyal once when he still entertained hopes of sovereignty. After 1973, he saw it only as gilding on the bars of his prison.

At home, the chief executive hunted for excuses to further insult and humiliate the king. No charge was too grotesque. He was accused of stealing nearly ₹ 2 million that had allegedly been sanctioned many years earlier for a new palace, and of complicity when a Sindhi employee of the Sikkim State Trading Corporation's Calcutta office was apparently caught trying to export an eleventh-century bronze Chola Nataraja. Tipped off by the authorities, Calcutta newspapers suggested that the Chogyal was 'trying to raise funds either for planned retirement in the United States or to prepare for counter-insurgency operations in Sikkim.' The palace budget, which had been cut from ₹ 3.6 million in 1971–'72 to ₹ 2.9 million in 1973–'74, was slashed by 75 per cent the following year. Being in sole control of finance, Lal also refused to allot a penny of the ₹ 2.5 million annually required for the Sikkim Guards. The Gyalum's modest pension (₹ 500 a month) was cut off, and the chief executive would not allow anything either for the education of the three younger Namgyals in the United States. With many dependent relatives, a large staff to support, and obliged as head of state to keep up some style, the Chogyal was at his wits' end for money. The monastic peace he had known as a youth seemed to offer an escape from the torture of political, financial, and personal anxieties. He wanted to have as little as possible to do with the politicians and officials who had eroded his faith in humanity. He yearned to opt out.

Tenzing would not hear of it. He was the crown prince. Sikkim and the throne would one day be his. He was determined to salvage his inheritance. The prince, therefore, took pains to understand and respond to Sikkimese sensitivities. He listened with deferential attention to older politicians, even those who opposed his father, conducted himself with affable dignity among Indian civil servants and military officers, and was able to establish immediate rapport with young Sikkimese. His easy simplicity and attractive, outward-going nature made an instant appeal. Kazini spoke fondly of him, and even Kazi was reputed to have remarked that things might have been different if Tenzing has been on the throne. The Raniphul incident seemed to have been forgotten. A spell of training with Indian Administrative Service probationers, followed by a short stint in Mrs Gandhi's secretariat, had made him many friends in India and also taught him the rudiments of paper work. When not helping his father with files, the athletic young prince merrily kicked a football with Indian soldiers or practised archery with Sikkimese village lads, without the slightest trace of condescension. Observing him at work or play, so full of vigorous promise, no one remembered the curse of the Namgyals that first-borns came to an untimely end. He was the hope of Denzong's future.

Tenzing had heard from his friends that Lal had made an abortive bid to annex Sikkim on 4 March, the day Poudyal and Subeidi ambushed the Chogyal at Rangpo. Hoping to cash in on the public mood, the chief executive asked the cabinet to adopt resolutions dissolving the Guards and deposing the ruler. A frightened Kazi was ready to oblige, but Krishna Chandra Pradhan confirms that the rest tried to bargain for their rights. 'The demand was dropped only when we asked if we would then be allowed to elect our own head of state as in India, and for guarantees that the end of the monarchy would not mean the end of a separate Sikkim.' When he heard of this untypical display of ministerial acumen, Tenzing persuaded his father to make another overture to the Sikkim Congress. They were invited to discuss their grievances with the palace and advise the Chogyal on how he could best adjust to new circumstances. 'My doors are always open,' he announced. 'Unless a dialogue starts, how can we proceed?' The crown prince was even more forthright when he told a foreign correspondent: 'The people of my country are capable of being governed by themselves; they do not want to be governed by India.'

He had listened to public grievances, noted the complaints of officials, heard of Kazini's bitter tirades, and deduced from the 4 March episode that at least some legislators might be prepared to take a stand against Indian encroachment. Encouraged by all he saw and heard, Tenzing decided to act on his own initiative, and, without discussing his plans with anyone in the palace, drove down to Kazi's bungalow on 10 March. It was an exploratory sortie. The two men talked and argued for three hours. Tenzing pleaded for Sikkimese unity in the face of a national crisis, the chief minister brooded on his old grouses against the durbar or contemplated in dread India's reprisal if he responded to the prince.

The wheel had turned full circle, and Kazini now fervently begged for a truce with the palace, and a joint effort to save the kingdom. Between her and the prince they ultimately wore down Kazi's timid hesitation. He would close ranks, he promised, if the Chogyal validated the 1974 elections, recognised the Sikkim Congress as the party in power, and confirmed him in office. In addition, the chief minister demanded control of the portfolios that had been retained in Indian hands in violation of the tripartite agreement. Tenzing at once assured him that he personally was prepared to accept all the terms. He was convinced his father would too, but promised to return next evening with the Chogyal's formal approval. They would then discuss a strategy for confronting New Delhi.

The visit must have been reported. Gurbachan Singh sent for the chief minister on 11 March, accused him of deceit and treachery, and paraded other members of the assembly who had signified their willingness to oust Kazi. He was told that the only way of averting punishment was to endorse the proposals made by Lal on 4 March. Kazi's nerves gave way, and he agreed to do everything that was asked of him. He also consented to stay on in India House to avoid another encounter with Tenzing. The PO's wife invited Kazini to join her husband. Mrs Khorana pressed her to spend the evening at her house. A spate of seemingly fortuitous social invitations flooded in from other even more unexpected sources. The intention was to ensure there was no one in the chief minister's bungalow save the CRP when the prince kept his tryst. But Kazini would not budge. She stayed at home, in the small back room that was her study and whose most noticeable feature, unexpected in a woman's boudoir, was a rusty typewriter. She watched with dismay as the CRP guards were reinforced, and the gates securely locked.

That was how Tenzing found the bungalow when he drove up in his Austrian Halflinger, a light mini-jeep, with three guardsmen, two of whom carried revolvers, crammed into the space behind his driver's seat. The Indian soldiers surrounding the house refused him admission because the chief minister was away and his wife, they said, did not wish to be disturbed. But Kazini saw the vehicle with its four occupants, heard the exchange, and came out to invite Tenzing in. The CRP refused to open the gates but with her love of the dramatic, Kazini urged him to jump over the low bars. Tenzing, who was wearing a sports shirt and tight black jeans, did so with an easy leap, to be at once rushed by the soldiers. 'They levelled their rifles at him, at least a dozen bayonets pointed at the poor boy, and I was so frightened of what they might do to dear Tenzing that I flung my arms round him and refused to let go!' Kazini recalls. She embraced him in a tight hug until the rifles had been withdrawn, whereupon she explained all that had happened and apologised for her absent husband's vacillation. She would send word to Tenzing, she promised, as soon as she had been able again to persuade the chief minister to stand firm. The prince drove back, discovering when he reached the palace that a felt-tipped pen was missing from his jeans pocket. It must have dropped out when he jumped the gate.

The trivial loss was soon forgotten for Gangtok was buzzing with rumours of fierce and acrimonious rows in the chief minister's bungalow. Some said Kazini had pitched into her husband with more than usual ferocity when he got back from the PO. Others, that both had been summoned to India House and given a dressing-down by Gurbachan Singh and Lal, the chief minister silently listening while his wife was berated. There were further rumbustious scenes when they returned home. Whatever transpired, Kazini afterwards bitterly lamented that Sikkimese men were too feeble even to protect their wives.

It was not enough to put down Kazi and Kazini. The palace had also to be disciplined. Gurbachan Singh, therefore, wrote ominously to the Chogyal on 13 March:

> It has been brought to my notice that, as Maharajkumar Tenzing was leaving the chief minister's residence at about 9 pm on 11 March, an object dropped from his baku which was picked up by the chief minister's bodyguard. The object could conceivably be a type of explosive device. There have, as you know, been two earlier occasions when explosives have been found buried in roads along which the chief minister was expected to travel.

> This incident, especially following upon the earlier two, is indeed most serious, and I cannot express strongly enough my concern and, needless to add, disapproval of this evident resort to violence as a method to overcome political problems.
>
> Public opinion in the state is incensed enough, particularly over the Rangpo incident last week. Now we have a direct indication of your son's intentions which will, if remaining unchecked, most certainly lead to consequences which the government of India does not desire. Nor, I am sure, does the government of Sikkim and, I should sincerely like to hope, that it is not your desire either. However, one cannot conclude otherwise judging by the actions and activities I assume on your behalf, if not under your direction or at least with your knowledge, of those close to you.

He then added:

> A further very disturbing report came to me last night which, again, concerns a visit to the chief minister's residence by the Maharajkumar. He is reported to have been accompanied by three vehicles containing personnel of Sikkim Guards. As I have pointed out earlier, both in conversation and in writing, the function of the Sikkim Guards is essentially for palace duties. They are not meant to be used as a show of strength on any occasion that your son chooses to go visiting around town. Even if it were considered necessary for him to be accompanied by a bodyguard, surely one person should suffice. Three vehicle-loads can hardly be termed as a bodyguard.
>
> The path you appear to have chosen to follow is a path which, I fear, will surely lead to a collision. In this case, the sole responsibility for the serious consequences which would inevitably result would be yours. I say this in all earnestness and with all the emphasis at my command.

> I regret to have to write this letter but developments over the last several days leave me no option and I should be failing in my duty if I were not to communicate to you my grave concern and serious misgivings.

It was an outrageous letter by any reckoning. That the PO was actively intervening in the kingdom's internal affairs was a minor point; nor did his blunt threats or impertinent language any longer occasion surprise. But the disregard and distortion of simple facts showed that in its campaign of calumny, India House felt it could dispense with the truth because it did not fear contradiction. Tenzing was wearing jeans and not a kho or baku. No one had heard of the earlier two incidents cited. An escort of three men in a small vehicle had been inflated into three vehicles loaded with guardsmen. The harmless little felt pen that had presumably dropped out of Tenzing's pocket had been transformed into a bomb. Ever afterwards, Kazini shudderingly described her husband's security man, who had apparently pounced on the pen when Tenzing bounded over the gate, as Gangtok's most notorious picker-up of non-exploding explosives.

The most sinister feature of Gurbachan Singh's letter was the attempt to implicate the Chogyal and his son in three attempts at murder. 'I would have ignored the false allegations,' replied the ruler, 'if it were not for the fact that I am now convinced that a plot is being laid to somehow remove the Chogyal from Sikkim, and what could be a better excuse than to somehow involve me or the crown prince in an attempt to violently do away with the chief minister.' He wrote angry and sorrowful letters of protest on 15 March, 23 March and 25 March, firmly denying all allegations and demanding substantiation. But the PO did not think it necessary to reply to any of them. It was enough to cast suspicion. Two months later, Tenzing was still corresponding with the chief executive over the 'explosive device' that he was supposed to have sent to an Indian forensic institute to be analysed:

> I presume all the necessary tests have been made and the political officer has no doubt informed you of the real nature of this so-called 'explosive device'. Therefore, I should be extremely grateful if you could return my pen at your earliest convenience.

Tenzing never did get it back. It would have been far too humiliating for high Indian officials to return a felt-tipped pen that had been invested with such dynamic qualities.

Tenzing did not give up. He was looking for some other means of reopening negotiations, when Krishna Chandra, hearing rumours of his adventures, went to see him. Tenzing told the agriculture minister all that had happened, and it was decided that Krishna Chandra should undertake the next step. He found Kazi surprisingly receptive to the idea of closing ranks against India. 'The chief minister himself asked me to draw up some kind of manifesto and to get at least two-thirds of the assembly members to sign it. He said he would present the document to the chief executive as representing the wishes of the majority.' True to his cautious nature, Kazi was not sticking out his neck more than necessary; for him, the safe shield of more daring colleagues. His critics later suggested that Kazi did not at any time intend to present India with an ultimatum. Knowing his nature, they speculated that the reason for readily falling in with the agriculture minister's proposal was to obtain the proof needed to betray him in the end.

Krishna Chandra was an uncomfortable colleague. Often irresponsible and always disconcertingly erratic, he did not fit in with the emerging pattern. He had denounced Khatiawara's extremism, accused Poudyal of violence against the head of state, and declined discussions with a team of official Indian planners on the grounds that the Sikkimese did not have enough say in their economic affairs. The PO and the chief executive were suspicious of him. But Krishna Chandra could not easily be removed. He had been president of the ruling party, held an important portfolio, and after all, it was his arrest that sparked off the 1973 riots and everything that followed. It is not impossible, therefore, that the chief minister was luring him into a trap. On the other hand, it isn't unlikely either that if the gamble paid off, Kazi would be only too happy to throw off India's yoke. His wife's reasoning was far less complex. Smarting from insults, she wanted to clear the stage. If Krishna Chandra is to be believed, the draft manifesto was typed out on the ageing machine in her boudoir.

Dated 12 March, it was in the form of a letter to Mrs Gandhi, routed through the chief minister, chief executive, and the PO. The names of twenty-nine legislators were typed for them to sign against; a point of incidental interest being that each carried the suffix MSA (Member, Sikkim Assembly) instead of the Indian MLA (Member, Legislative Assembly) that India House and Mintokgang used for them. Kazi's name was left out because, he explained, he was the recipient. Also, he would have a better chance of success if he could plead that the party had forced the document on him. He may still have been playing safe, or this may have been another aspect of his deviousness. Khatiawara did not figure because he was too close to the Indian establishment, while Kalzang Bhutia, the National Party member, was excluded from what was planned as a Sikkim Congress exercise. The approved text read:

> We, the undersigned cabinet ministers of the government of Sikkim, and members of the Sikkim assembly, having met to discuss the unhappy prevailing situation in our country, have come to certain conclusions, and we have accordingly passed the following resolutions with immediate effect:
>
> Resolution Number One: That the three portfolios, viz., home, finance and establishment, that are at the moment

being enjoyed by the chief executive should, in accordance with 8 May agreement of 1973, be immediately handed over to the chief minister of Sikkim.

Resolution Number Two: That the chief executive, in the interest of the smooth running of the administration and consonant with the dignity and prestige of the Sikkimese people, shall act as adviser to the government of Sikkim, and in that capacity only.

Resolution Number Three: That this meeting demands the immediate removal of the three OSDs who were brought to Sikkim before the last election, namely, Shri Sanyal, Shri K.M. Lal and Shri Manavalam. Now that there is a popular government in Sikkim, their presence is redundant.

Resolution Number Four: Those officers who are at present on deputation to the government of Sikkim shall not have any further extension. They shall not also be replaced by other deputationists.

The text went on:

Resolution Number Five: That the high court judge and the central court judge should be sent on deputation from the government of India, and the present incumbents should be relieved of their appointments with immediate effect.

Resolution Number Six: That the Sikkim Congress welcomes the Chogyal's reported statement for a dialogue with the chief minister.

A number of Congress members trickled into Kazi's bungalow as word spread of what was going on. Soon there were enough present to permit a full-fledged party meeting. The six resolutions were formally moved, seconded and unanimously adopted; all the eighteen legislators who had turned up signed the letter. Among them were four ministers—Krishna

Chandra, Rinzing, Kharel and Nayan Tsering Lepcha—as well as Subeidi, Shebchung Bhutia, Badri Nath Pradhan and Bhim Bahadur Gurung. Several copies were typed, of which Krishna Chandra took away four. They would suffice, he said, to collect the eleven remaining signatures.

With Indian soldiers all round, eighteen legislators could not gather under Kazi's roof without word reaching India House and Mintokgang. Except for the chief minister, none of those present was noted for his discretion. The air of suppressed excitement in the ruling party would have given the game away even if the CRP had not reported in detail on the lengthy proceedings. Therefore, when Lal summoned the agriculture minister two days later, Krishna Chandra at once concluded that his house would be searched, and handed over the copies to Rinzing. Whether the public works minister voluntarily betrayed his colleagues or was coerced into doing so must rank with Lloyd's acquisition of the Darjeeling deed as one of many shadowy episodes in the kingdom's history. But Lal had the document before anyone else had signed it.

He realised how explosive it could be. The men who were constantly being lauded in India as Sikkim's first freely elected representatives, and as the Chogyal's implacable enemies, the very leaders New Delhi was using as a human battering-ram against the palace, had given notice of their intention of going their own way. They did not want the chief executive or his lieutenants. They wanted full governing powers. They were even prepared to come to terms with the Chogyal. If their demands reached the press or parliament, Mrs Gandhi's government would stand indicted by the very process it had fostered, and rejected by the men it was sponsoring.

The conspiracy would have to be nipped in the bud if New Delhi were to save the achievements of the previous two years. More, the possibility of recurrence would firmly have to be ruled out. That could only be done by removing the totems of

Sikkim's separate identity: flag, coat of arms, distinctive number plates, freedom from Indian taxes, PO, chief executive, and—most vital—the Chogyal. Everything that remained of an independent kingdom protected by treaty, even if it was called an associate state, would have to go.

It was first necessary to compel the authors to repudiate their handiwork. Kazi was summoned again, and threatened once more with the loss of his job. He was warned, too, that his wife's inner line and residence permits would be revoked. Without them she would not be able to set foot in Kalimpong, leave alone play at being first lady in Gangtok. She could even be deported. All the signatories were individually interviewed. Some were similarly warned of New Delhi's severe displeasure. Others were promised rewards. They looked to the chief minister for a lead. The politicians would have stood firm if Kazi had. But he quickly capitulated and called a Congress working committee meeting on 16 March to retract all that had been agreed to four days earlier.

Three new resolutions declared the 12 March meeting illegal and unauthorised, denounced its organisers, and nullified the decisions taken then. The main fusillade was reserved for Resolution Number Six on the Chogyal:

> Opening a parley and negotiations with the Chogyal, whose anti-democratic and anti-people policies are totally against the interest of the Sikkimese people is, in itself, an act of grave breach of party discipline. The whole world knows that it is the Chogyal who has, throughout his life, been the greatest obstacle in the smooth functioning of the democratic government, and his latest actions have proved beyond a shadow of doubt that the Chogyal is unable to reconcile himself to the loss of his absolute powers and the changes brought about by the mass upsurge of April-May 1973. He and his agents have been doing everything in their powers to discredit and weaken the party and the government led by it

> so that they may regain their lost powers. With this end in view, they have sent their agents into the ranks of the party to carry out their subversive activities, and it is these infiltrators who have succeeded in misleading some party members and ministers in attending an illegally constituted meeting called without the knowledge and consent of the party leader and president.

Grinning sheepishly at Kazini as he lounged at her dining-table, Subeidi claimed he had signed the second set of resolutions only because everyone else had done so. He still stood by the first move, which he described as neither pro-Chogyal, nor anti-India, but just nationalist. Bhim Bahadur Gurung more candidly admitted he had been promised a job. 'There will be something for me either in the ministry or as member of Parliament in New Delhi.' All the others were equally equivocal. They had gone along because they feared for their skins or looked greedily to rewards. Such men were ideally suited to India's purpose. But Krishna Chandra Pradhan's lead role in throwing down the gauntlet to India on 12 March could not be glossed over. Though no names were mentioned, the 16 March resolutions clearly had him in mind when they demanded punishment for anyone whose conduct was 'not befitting a responsible minister' because 'such a person is not worthy of remaining in the post'. Kazi was authorised 'to take immediate appropriate disciplinary action against those party leaders and ministers who have so far failed to dissociate themselves with the said illegal meeting held on 12 March 1975 and the resolutions adopted therein'.

Krishna Chandra signed this document, too, with the rest. But instead of waiting for the axe to fall, he upstaged Kazi and pre-empted Lal in a last defiant fling. He sent off a letter of resignation to the palace. Ceremonially addressing the ruler as Mewang Chogyal Chempo, he wrote:

> I wish to inform you that in view of the aspirations of the Sikkimese people, I have time and again requested that the reserved subjects, namely, finance, home and establishment, which were transferred to the assembly and, therefore, to the council of ministers under the May 8 agreement, should be made over to the council of ministers. This is very vital in bringing harmony and responsible government to Sikkim.
>
> However, there has been no such progress or any sign towards this direction, and the condition in the country is deteriorating.
>
> In the circumstances, it is with the greatest regret that I am constrained to submit my resignation to the council of ministers.

It was a mischievous move, for Krishna Chandra knew that Lal was putting pressure on the Chogyal to dismiss him. The Chogyal, too, somewhat quizzically decided to probe the chief executive's reasons rather than end the matter by accepting the resignation. Possibly, he hoped to use the agriculture minister's letter to persuade the chief executive to part with the disputed portfolios. But when he asked what Krishna Chandra had done to merit dismissal, Lal retorted with habitual brusqueness that 'no reasons need be given either for appointment or removal of a minister'.

The refusal only provoked the Chogyal to further stubbornness. Several terse letters were exchanged between the palace and Mintokgang on 17 March and 18 March, the chief executive eventually giving the Chogyal half an hour to issue the order of dismissal. At the same time, he sought, through the PO, and predictably obtained, New Delhi's almost instantaneous approval of his view that the monarch was not allowed to question anything he had been ordered to sign. But just in case the Chogyal still persisted in being difficult, the chief executive sent for K.M. Lal and instructed him to draft a letter of dismissal in Kazi's name.

Having gone to all this trouble, Lal was beside himself with anger when the palace sent him the resignation letter, two days after it had been submitted. He was even more enraged by the Chogyal's acknowledgement, in which the king told Krishna Chandra of Lal's demand, and persistent refusal to enlighten him as to the reason—'despite my request, no reason has been given by the chief executive, nor the chief minister, for your removal, and as such, I presume the reason could be differences over what you have stated in your resignation letter'. Lal had relished the notion of sacking the agriculture minister. He would have savoured even more the pleasure of again bending the Chogyal to his will. Deprived of two preys, he fell back on using his old cat's paw to write to the palace with more than his usual offensiveness. Kazi was convinced, he said, 'that this so-called letter of resignation was an afterthought and that the whole plan was cooked up between you and Mr K.C. Pradhan.' The chief minister was also supposed to have 'taken serious objection' to the manner in which the Chogyal had 'so obviously meddled with local politics and, instead of acting as an objective and constitutional head, had shown such a clear partisan bias'. Poor Kazi might have been written off by most Sikkimese, but he still had his uses.

Indians, too, were taken in by this strategy because the 12 March manifesto was rigorously suppressed. Newspapers happily distorted facts to suggest that the chief minister had been faced with a party revolt which he had quelled. Hardly anyone realised that far from attacking Kazi, Resolution Number One would have greatly enhanced his powers. The offence was to India. Resolution Number Two sought to drastically whittle down Lal's authority, while the third and fourth clauses compounded the effect by trying to weaken New Delhi's general administrative control. The fifth aimed at ensuring that the judiciary retained its independence. In sum, the letter would have circumscribed India's authority, vested far more power in Sikkimese hands, and provided a bridge between the Chogyal and legislators. This could never be countenanced. The episode could not just be ignored either. Krishna Chandra Pradhan, the principal architect, was still a person of some consequence. He had to be politically eliminated.

And so the strategy that was born in Tenzing's mind failed. But the support it drew, even if fleeting and quickly crushed, warned Gurbachan Singh and Lal that the Sikkimese could not be taken for granted. The Chogyal had to be removed and union with India made irrevocable. The army struck twenty-six days later. The crown prince's attempted coup may, in fact, have hastened the end.

CHAPTER

17

THUMB IMPRESSION

'I think you know that there was no referendum in Sikkim either to decide its international status or for any other purpose.'

BISHWESWAR PRASAD KOIRALA,
former prime minister of Nepal,
The Weekly Mirror, Kathmandu, 20 July 1979.

'We have always said and still say that the manner of Sikkim's merger with India was not legal and constitutional.'

LAL BAHADUR BASNET,
Times of India, 15 October 1979.

It was teatime in the English village of Tanyard, near Frittenden. John Eric Clarke, an elderly solicitor and county coroner for Kent, with a lifelong interest in the mysteries of wireless communication, was initiating the young son of a law partner in his own passion. They had just made contact with an Australian, when another party came up on frequency to say that someone higher up the 20-metre band was 'going on about something'. Clarke, G8KA and FC6FPHd to other radio buffs, moved up, logged the station, and said, 'I heard a high-pitched voice speaking very good English at a very high speed from which I gathered he was being invaded.'

The signal was weak but quite intelligible, and he identified the speaker as AC3PT, the code name for 'P.T. Namgyal' who had been listed since 1951 in the *Radio Amateur Call Book*, address: 'The Palace, Gangtok, Sikkim'. But the solicitor did not realise he was the Chogyal, of whom he had only dimly heard. 'It did not fully dawn on us what was happening. I knew more about plants sent back from Sikkim by some of the great plant collectors than I did about its ruler.' Clarke heard AC3PT, with whom he had never worked before, say something about a military attack, and ask his contact to report the aggression to the International League for Human Rights. The signal suddenly ceased and though he called AC3PT several times, there was no response. 'I sat back in amazement and wondered what it was all about!'

The Chogyal's SOS was also picked up by several stations in Sweden. Naoki Akiyama heard it in Japan and later complained to *Radio Communication*, the ham's journal, that AC3PT had broken off abruptly and not responded to the postcard that was customarily mailed after making contact with a new party. Akiyama sounded quite put out, in fact, with this most discourteous amateur in Gangtok. Another Japanese contact, Nobuyasu Itoh, heard and taped the full message, sending copies to Tokyo and Yokohama newspapers and to the League in New York. Clarke says he did not at first know what to do as he had missed the first part of AC3PT's broadcast. Later, he telephoned a neighbour in Kent, Major-General Sir Alec Bishop, who had been British deputy high commissioner in Calcutta in the early '60s. Bishop suggested the infallible remedy of his class—a letter to the *Times*.

This was on 9 April. It was late evening in Gangtok, the Chogyal and Tenzing discussing the day's shattering events. The telephones were dead, the gates under heavy guard, the palace cut off from the world. The bloody corpse in the sentry box had completely unnerved the Chogyal. He did not know what the next offensive would be and wondered if they were all to be massacred. The Indian army's incomprehensible betrayal, as he saw it, persuaded him to expect the worst. Tenzing then remembered that they had an easy means of communication in the spare room downstairs, long ago used by Sir Tashi as his studio. Father and son sat down at their transmitter, put on their earphones and tried to notify the world of their plight. It was probably against club rules to use a ham facility for serious purposes, though Clarke doubts this. In any case, men who knew they had lost their country, who had been attacked in force and strength, and feared for their lives, could not afford to be fastidious. The breach of regulations was washed out in young Basant Kumar Chhetri's blood. 'If my country was being invaded, I would not hesitate to go on the air,' says the Kent coroner.

The Chogyal was an experienced amateur broadcaster. His trans-continental conversations were regularly recorded in radio buffs' journals in many countries. He had talked to kindred spirits in places as far apart as Iran and Argentina. The International Amateur Radio Union's coveted Worked All Continents certificate, awarded to him in 1970, was prominently framed in his study. The Collins S/Line De Luxe model he used—receiver, transmitter, linear amplifier, and other ancillary equipment, four pieces in all—may not have been the best, but it had been imported in 1964 through India, with New Delhi's knowledge and permission. K.B. Nair of the external affairs ministry had sanctioned the purchase. The crown prince had inherited some of his father's interest in things mechanical, and was almost as enthusiastic about amateur broadcasting. Neither made any secret of the hobby.

But communication was not good that night. The invasion noticed by Clarke was from Khorana's wireless station: the police had picked up the frequency and was doing its best to jam the palace. It was not, therefore, surprising that Gurdip Singh Bedi, the India House first secretary, should bluster into the palace next morning, with ten policemen in tow, to accuse the Chogyal of operating a clandestine radio. He seized every single piece of equipment. The records and log-books were also confiscated and taken away.

The Chogyal's isolation was now complete. The palace was under heavy guard. Visitors were turned away with the stock excuse that the Chogyal was too ill to receive anyone, and that Jigdal Densapa would get in touch with callers. The Ridge crawled with soldiers. Indian troops occupied the Guards lines below. The CRP also stood sentry outside Thakse palace and Rhenock House above the bazaar where Lhanzin-La lived. Both buildings had been ransacked from top to bottom, and the Gyalum, then seventy-three years old, roughly pushed aside as soldiers strode into her bedchamber. All their telephones had been disconnected at the junction box; people who asked the operator for the palace, Thakse or Rhenock House were told the numbers were unobtainable because of a cable fault. The Densapa bungalow was similarly cut off. But the connections were briefly restored from time to time to enable the PO to call the palace. Gurbachan Singh would then cite his own privileged conversation to scoff at the idea of any restriction on the Chogyal's freedom.

Khatiawara was to describe the parallel drama at the legislature. 'On 9 April 1975, the Indian army was deployed to annex Sikkim,' he wrote. 'All the assembly members of Sikkim were once again rounded up and under threat were escorted to the assembly on April 10 and made to sign on the dotted line...' Actually, only twenty-nine were present. Poudyal was nursing his injured wrist in hospital, and Passang Tsering Bhutia and Tasa Tengay Lepcha were nowhere to be found when soldiers were sent to bring in the people's representatives. Marshalled like criminals under Lal's stern eye, the rest well knew that the chief judge of the central court had forbidden the assembly to violate the constitution's express prohibition of any discussion of the Chogyal or of Sikkim's relations with India. But the few members who ventured to point this out were roughly silenced. 'We were told to "shut up" and "not to be too clever" by the president of the assembly, Shri B.B. Lal.'[1]

The chief executive inaugurated the session with a measured condemnation of Hariomal's 29 March injunction. He claimed that the court had not only acted illegally but had also transgressed against the people's majesty. Lal played on the vanity of immature politicians:

> The service of notices by the court on the president and members of the house amounts to service of notices on this august house itself, and the question arises whether this august house, which represents the will of the people and is the legislative organ of government, having its own powers and privileges, is subject to the process of a court, and whether a court can direct this august house and its members, along with its president, to do certain things or not to do certain things, and whether the issue of any such directions by a court to this august house does not constitute a breach of privilege of this house. There are many who think that a legislative body which is supreme in its own sphere and which has its own powers, and can lay down its own procedure which alone is binding on it, is not subject to the processes of court.[2]

If this were so, the Sikkim assembly would have been a sovereign parliament. Lal fostered that misconception by recalling that erring civil servants had been summoned to the bar of the Lok Sabha and reprimanded. He also tossed them the prize of a privileges committee, naming six members to uphold the legislature's dignity and punish offenders. But Lal's 'august house' was 'supreme' only to the extent permitted by the Act creating it. It could not, for instance, declare Sikkim's independence or dismiss the chief executive appointed by India. Neither could it violate any of the restrictions imposed by article 23 (2) of the 1974 Act. Hariomal had done no more than point out these inherent disabilities, that too, when his judicial opinion was directly sought. To have done otherwise would have been a grave dereliction of duty, and manifest disrespect for the constitution.

But in a political speech that appealed to emotion with half-truths and misleading analogies, Lal suggested that the chief judge had gone out of his way to give gratuitous offence to the sovereign people because he was in league with a feudal monarchy. Lal was confident that his naïve listeners would not know that the chief judge of the central court could not be dragged to the assembly and scolded like any petty bureaucrat. Nor were they aware that even the Lok Sabha is not entirely sovereign since India's Supreme Court holds that its enactments must respect the basic features of the constitution which are superior to Parliament.

The limits of their knowledge were exposed by the questions they asked and the suggestions they made. Kazi thought that Rasaily had to be punished because he had 'filed a case challenging the authority of this assembly to pass the Government of Sikkim Act 1974'. Bhim Bahadur Gurung, too, believed that 'the court has challenged the authority of this house for passing the 1974 Act and this is beyond the jurisdiction of the court'. The misconception was shared by three ministers (Bhuwani Prasad Dahal, Rinzing Tongden Lepcha and Nayan Tsering Lepcha) who similarly accused Hariomal of impugning the constitution.

Only Krishna Chandra Pradhan acknowledged that far from questioning the Act—as Lal made out—the court had underlined the inviolability of provisions that the assembly was being egged on to flout. Being well aware of Lal's intention, he pleaded that members 'should not discuss more than what has been promised to the people at the time of election'. It was a pointed reminder that the Sikkim Congress had no mandate to tamper with the monarchy or wipe out the kingdom's special status. But his was a lone voice, easily silenced after the abortive political coup had been suppressed.

Instead, Rinzing read out from a prepared Nepalese text (Bhim Bahadur Gurung doing likewise in English) to move two resolutions accusing the Chogyal of 'persistent harmful activities... designed to restore his autocratic rule in Sikkim, stifle democracy, frustrate the establishment of responsible government in Sikkim and impede the orderly political and economic progress of the people of Sikkim'. The first motion declared that 'the institution of the Chogyal is hereby abolished and Sikkim shall henceforth be a constituent unit of India, enjoying a democratic and fully responsible government'. The second proposed that the decision 'shall be submitted to the people forthwith for their approval' and that India would then be asked 'to take such measures as may be necessary and appropriate to implement this resolution as early as possible'.

Krishna Chandra again tried to intervene. The government already exercised all the Chogyal's powers, he said, and should, therefore, first have to explain how far it had 'fulfilled the wishes and aspirations of the people'. But the chief executive would only allow speeches for or against Rinzing's two resolutions. That at once brought several members to their feet, anxious to curry favour by vociferously supporting the motions. Trying to atone for his recent waywardness, Kazi lavished praise on Lal for his management of the very departments he had been deprived of. Vast sums of money had been released for public welfare projects only because the chief executive had sole control of finance, he declared. The law and order situation was improving only because Lal still managed home and establishment. Kazi was at his servile and sycophantic best:

> There has never been an occasion since the installation of the popular ministry for difference of opinion between the cabinet and the chief executive, and the cabinet is associated with the works of the departments under the chief executive...

> Similarly, the government of India has never interfered with the internal administration of Sikkim after the installation of the popular ministry.'[3]

It was an astounding exhibition of obsequiousness, compounded by the chief minister's claim that the proposed changes would fulfil his party's election promises. Kazi did not have to be asked to eat humble pie; any other diet would have given him indigestion. He rounded off the peroration by accusing the Chogyal of not cooperating with the administration and by saying that the Nepal visit and Rasaily's petition were intended 'to overthrow the popularly constituted government'. Dipankar Chakrabarti's *Aneek* sarcastically called Kazi 'a "great democrat" with New Delhi stamped all over'. He was 'an unashamed front of the Indian expansionist establishment'.

Rinzing's two motions naturally received unanimous support. But this did not make them any more valid. There was no way in which the 29 March injunction could be vacated except by Hariomal's final order, or by a superior court striking it down on appeal. But even without this inhibition, the assembly could have taken no decision on the throne or merger with India without first repealing article 23(2) of the 1974 Act. Finally, all decisions by the assembly still had to be ratified by the Chogyal before they could acquire the force of law. He had the option of assenting to resolutions or withholding assent and returning them to the assembly. If again adopted within three months, he would have no option but to agree if they were otherwise valid—in this case they were not. His delaying power could be compared with the right of Britain's House of Lords which can hold up, but not prevent, legislation to abolish it. But the third paragraph of article 21 of the 1974 Act introduced a distinctive element in Sikkim. The Chogyal was obliged to seek New Delhi's views on any measure affecting the responsibilities of the Indian government or of the chief executive, and was bound to act accordingly. But New Delhi could not bypass him and directly endorse the Gangtok assembly's illegal actions.

Gurbachan Singh only shrugged in grand seigniorial dismissal when these crippling drawbacks were pointed out to him. 'Revolutions evolve their own constitutionality,' he declared.

No revolution could have been more phoney. The violence and bloodshed of 9 April was still fresh in people's minds, as Khatiawara's storm-troopers whipped up public support for Lal's manipulations. The mood in Gangtok was of anxiety, not elation. So many armed men in uniform did not make for peace of mind. News filtered in of arson, looting, and murder in outlying townships, adding to the tension. Since no one knew what was happening in the palace, its closed gates bristling with guns, rumour fed on speculation. Some said the Chogyal had been bundled off to exile in Ootacamund in the Nilgiri Hills of south India. According to another version, he had fled to Bhutan by way of Buxar camp. Yet others speculated he might have crossed one of Sikkim's northern passes on foot to escape into ancestral Tibet. There were rumours of a surreptitious journey into Nepal, like Thutob Namgyal's. A corollary to all these themes was that he had, indeed, attempted flight, but had been caught and brought back. It was whispered that the king was being held incommunicado, and under constant severe interrogation, until he agreed to sign an instrument of accession like India's own princes.

Manuel in his rusty black was glimpsed occasionally, the only stirring of life within the sealed-off palace. He would emerge clutching his shopping bag as if it might be snatched away at any moment and walk dolefully down to the bazaar in a circle of rifle-slung Indian soldiers. Gloomy at the best of times, the old housekeeper looked like a convicted man on his way to the scaffold, his lugubrious countenance drawn even longer. The vision was not reassuring.

There were plenty of other reasons for disquiet. Shops that did not close in time were looted. Private vehicles that ventured into the streets were promptly commandeered in the name of the people. Kangaroo courts in Singtam and Melli set elderly citizens to chop wood and fetch water for Sikkim Congress leaders, as in 1973. Young stalwarts armed with kukris and knuckledusters swaggered in the bazaar, gorged themselves in restaurants, and airily waved away the bills. About a dozen of Khatiawara's Youth Congress toughs muscled into the Nor-Khill hotel one night to demand service. Told that the dining-room was closed, they peremptorily ordered the steward to open it or explain his refusal to Santosh Kumar Rai, the party secretary.

Others stormed into Martam House, determined to lynch Karma Topden's ill and ageing father. They withdrew only when they saw the paralytic old man lying helplessly in bed. But Netuk Tsering and Man Kumar Basnet, the other two National Party leaders, were not spared. Their clothes were torn off, and they were paraded through the bazaar with ropes tied round their necks and filth from the gutters spattered on their faces. Athing-La, the venerable Barmiok Kazi, was also hauled out of his house while four CRP men, ostensibly looking after his safety, watched placidly. 'They made me carry a Sikkim Congress flag, punched me and said I would be taken to Gyalzing and killed,' says the patriarch. He was too embarrassed to describe in detail that nightmare ride through a jeering mob. What appears to have saved him from worse was Kazini's angry intervention. Rushing out, she dragged the old man from his persecutors and bundled him into the dak bungalow screaming virulent abuse at Khatiawara and his comrades. 'This is not what I fought for,' she wailed while, outside, rumbled another procession chanting 'Death to Kazini'. Sonam Gyatso paid for opposing the Sikkim Congress in the 1974 elections by being kidnapped and taken prisoner to Kewsing.

The mob held the country to ransom. In spite of Khorana's 450 constables, the 2,000 CRP men under Lal, and about 25,000 regular soldiers, Sikkim lay at the mercy of rowdy hooligans. 'The boys are angry... I can't control them,' mumbled Kazi, wringing his hands, while the chief executive received news of each assault with hoots of laughter. Gurbachan Singh talked more ponderously of ancient vendettas among the nobility. But there was little spontaneity about this officially organised show of force by about 3,000 demonstrators. Sikkim Nationalised Transport trucks packed with Nepalese workers wound their way through the streets, their chant of 'Palden Namgyal, Sikkim *chhor*!' (Palden Namgyal, leave Sikkim) clearly audible from the palace. Watching on the Ridge, I counted fifty-four of these trucks in a convoy. The Sikkimese claimed that the rhythm and accent of the cheerleaders indicated they were professional trade union organisers from the Darjeeling tea gardens and road repair gangs. RAW's rent-a-mob agents had been busy. But the PO seized on this evidence of engineered wrath to inform the Chogyal that the mob might storm the palace, and that it would be safer for him to move out to Thakse. 'I was born in this house and I will die here,' was all the reply he got. Then, as Gurbachan Singh was leaving in a huff, the Chogyal shook him by the hand and, with a sparkle of his old humour, added: 'And do let the mob in, Your Excellency!'

The implied accusation seemed to be confirmed when Kazi told reporters that India would withdraw the CRP 'and send the people into the palace... let's see what he does then!'

Meticulous as ever with his paperwork, the Chogyal wrote to the PO after the latter's second visit urging him to vacate the palace:

> This morning when you came to the palace at 11 am, you had suggested that I should move out to Thakse palace for a few days as a security measure because of the likely danger from the mob. Tonight when you came again at 7.39 pm you had repeated the same suggestion.
>
> I had informed you on both occasions that I cannot leave my ancestral residence, and since you had removed the Sikkim

> Guards who were responsible for palace security, the responsibility for the palace security now rests squarely with the chief executive who is at the head of the administration. In the event he feels that he is unable to control the situation, I would suggest that he seeks the assistance of the army through you.
>
> It is strange that the chief executive has not met me for the past few weeks despite the fact that I am still the Chogyal and the constitutional head of government.

Coo Coo La, meanwhile, faced almost as much harassment in New Delhi where she occupied a suite of rooms in Sikkim House. She had intended to return to Gangtok on 7 April, well in time for the following week's hearing of her objections against the forest department's eviction order which Hariomal had temporarily stayed. Having no suspicion of the impending crisis in Sikkim, the princess was somewhat surprised when Kewal Singh, who was not a particular friend, invited her to his home. S.K. Singh, the ministry's tubby little official spokesman, whom she found pompous and obstructive, was there with several other officials with the same surname—'There seemed to be a lot of Singhs floating around,' she recalls. The invitation was for interrogation. They grilled the princess for more than two hours on the Chogyal's supposed Chinese contacts, whom she had met in Hong Kong two years previously and about American interest in Sikkim. Unaware of the offensive about to be launched, Coo Coo La nevertheless felt that her hosts were trying to find out what obstacles they might expect to encounter. In turn, she told them of her long-held suspicion of Indian incitement of the durbar's opponents, especially of covert action by intelligence bureau personnel. She did not mention RAW.

Returning to Chanakyapuri, Coo Coo La found that several truck-loads of CRP men had pitched tents in the Sikkim House lawns. Guards toting rifles with bayonets fixed had orders to keep out visitors, and keep her in. Sikkim House's eleven telephone lines were all dead. The water and electricity connections had been cut off. The princess was alone with two or three servants. 'We didn't have candles, but luckily, two bath tubs were full so I could, at least, wash. I slept on the roof where it was cooler.' Her imprisonment lasted fourteen days. Later she learnt that the police raided her flat in Calcutta during that time. After ransacking every one of its cupboards and almirahs, they sealed the doors with little round discs of red wax, rather like Mao buttons. Coo Coo La eventually had to go down to Calcutta to be present during a further inspection, and to answer endless questions. Armed guards accompanied her, and two plainclothes men with revolvers kept permanent watch on the landing outside the flat.

But the princess was nothing if not resourceful. She managed to smuggle her trusted steward out of Sikkim House, sending him to Gangtok with messages for the Chogyal and to find out what was happening. He took her court papers so that the eviction case did not go by default. Thupten Geley was a Tibetan refugee in his early forties, tall, rapier-thin, with aristocratic aquiline features, both debonair and dignified. He had been an acolyte in the Bare Labrang monastery when Tibet revolted in 1959, escaping to India in the Dalai Lama's train. Accustomed to danger, Thupten Geley knew how to cover his tracks. But he was a distinctive-looking man and someone recognised him on the bus just past Raniphul. He was arrested and searched. All the princess's papers were taken away. They took him to Rhenock jail late that night, and after two days there, to prison in Gangtok. No magistrate's orders authorised his arrest and incarceration. No charges were levelled to justify uninterrupted nocturnal questioning. These were just features of the official lawlessness that instilled fear in people. Ordinary peasants could expect no mercy if the proud princess's steward could be so roughly treated.

• • •

Sikkim's vote for constitutional suicide was held in an atmosphere of mounting terror. Even so, the chief executive took pains to ensure that the outcome did not disappoint him. He was taking no chances with judges who might find it difficult to discard a lifetime's tradition of uprightness. The gazette extraordinary of 11 April ordained that 'the special poll shall not be called in question in any civil court of law'. It also stipulated that 'an appeal shall lie in respect of any matter relating to the special poll from the orders of the additional election commissioner to the chief executive whose decision shall be final'.

As assembly president, Lal summoned the emergency session and pushed through resolutions that no member admitted to drafting. As head of the administration, he appointed the polling officer, supervised the setting up of booths and ballot-boxes, and made all other arrangements for voting. Security and secrecy were in his hands. Lal would also be sole and final arbiter of the verdict. Prosecutor, counsel, judge, jury and executioner were all rolled in one. Never before or since in the subcontinent's history has so much arbitrary authority formally been vested in a single person.

The morning of 14 April dawned crisp and clear. Two battalions of armed CRP troops, as well as Khorana's 450 policemen, manned fifty-seven polling booths for an estimated 97,000 voters. All the walls in Gangtok were plastered with Sikkim Congress posters. Its tricolour flew over every roof and balustrade. Government jeeps laden with Youth Congress volunteers sped in all directions. The resolution was printed in English, Nepalese and Sikkimese on slips of pink paper. There were two boxes in each polling booth. The white box was labelled 'Against'. The box in exactly the same shade of pink as the ballot paper was marked 'For'.

Inevitably, people objected that the same colour had deliberately been chosen to mislead the simple into believing that since ballot papers were pink, they were meant for the pink boxes. The Sikkimese were not allowed any opportunity to discuss the procedure or digest what was being perpetrated in their name. The opposing point of view was not heard at all. The Chogyal was locked up in his palace. Captain Yongda languished in Namche jail. Krishna Chandra Pradhan had gone to ground in Kaiser Bahadur Thapa's house below the bazaar—though the hiding place was then a secret—and refused to see anyone or answer the telephone. The National Party did not dare appear abroad after the public assault on its leaders. Loyal civil servants were just as frightened. Khatiawara's boys, with the police and CRP behind them, saw to it that only the merger lobby voiced its views. It did so with arrogant confidence.

The resolution's wording was also loaded. The simpler Sikkimese believed that an opinion survey was being conducted to decide whether power should be wielded by the palace or politicians. Some believed they were being asked to choose between the Chogyal and Kazi. Others admitted they did not want the Chogyal but wanted even less to be a part of India. They were allowed no choice. 'There are two separate issues with no necessary connection,' the *Hindustan Times* pointed out editorially. 'In the Sikkim poll they were linked, almost as cause and consequence.' Commenting on flaws, the paper faulted New Delhi's premises and criticised Lal's management of what it called a 'mock referendum'.

> If anything has discredited Sikkim's demand for merger with India, it is the so-called referendum which demonstrably could not have been held and completed in a fair or reasonable manner within 72 hours... The fact that the referendum was conducted with such incredible speed must produce scepticism... The procedures followed were of questionable constitutional validity. The only justification for all this can be the argument for revolutionary legality. But if the will of the people had to find expression outside and beyond the assembly, there was no need to diminish its sanctity by staging a mock referendum. And this in the India of Gandhi and Nehru.' [4]

The paper went on to argue that the 'fait accompli casts a good deal of doubt on just how popular these decisions are'. Its warning against expansionism—'Security depends on people, not territory'—might directly have been addressed to RAW.

The conduct of the operation fully justified these strictures. There was no secrecy about this ballot. Some booths had a strip of curtain across the door. But it was pushed aside, with Indian soldiers and Youth Congress volunteers firmly planted inside, breathing down the necks of voters, ordering them what to do. Only in a few scattered places did this unwarranted intervention provoke angry exchanges and fisticuffs (a fight broke out in Leeyoeng bustee) for the majority of Sikkimese were by then too inured to being pushed around by Lal and the forces at his command to put up any resistance. The most they dared was to stay away, and this they did in massive numbers all over the country. Only a thin trickle of voters could be seen in Gangtok where the presiding officer told me at the end of the day that a mere 453 out of 2,200 registered voters—not even 20.6 per cent—had bothered to turn up.

Attendance must have been considerably lower in the distant countryside which had scarcely been touched by controversy. The complicated resolution would have been unintelligible in remote villages where Kazi's party had no base. It was doubtful, in fact, if the administration had taken the trouble to set up polling stations at all in the mountainous interior. It took at least two days by jeep, the fastest mode of transport, to reach some of these inaccessible habitations, and it just would not have been physically possible to complete arrangements, hold the polls, and count votes between 11 and 15 April.

Yet, Lal announced an unbelievable 63-per-cent turnout. Even less credible was the gazette proclamation that, of the 61,133 votes cast, 59,637 favoured the resolution and only 1,496 opposed it. The chief minister's victory manifesto was prepared in advance in certain knowledge of the outcome: the official claim of 97-per-cent support being typed in later on a different machine. In thus banking on the effectiveness of the administrative machinery, Kazi took his cue from Gurbachan Singh who regaled the press early in the afternoon of 15 April with a message from Nar Bahadur Bhandari, acknowledging defeat. According to the PO, Bhandari congratulated the Sikkim Congress and dissolved his own Prajatantra Party. Bhandari vehemently denies sending any such message. In any case, all the results had not come in then. In fact, counting was still going on in some places. Yet, Singh, with his RAW background, had no compunction about announcing the outcome.

Khatiawara wrote devastatingly about the farce of the referendum.

> The events of the 1973 uprising were fresh in the minds of the people when elections to the Sikkim assembly in April 1974 were announced. After months of electioneering, the elections were held on 15 April, but barely 37 per cent of the total electorate exercised their franchise. Yet when the 'special poll' was held within 72 hours of announcement, surprisingly enough it was claimed that over 65 per cent of the voters voted.
>
> It is an open secret that in a difficult and hilly terrain like ours, it would be next to impossible to even reach some of the polling booths in the interior in such a short time. Yet even in the far-flung areas, voting is said to have taken place. The results of the poll were indeed fantastic, because the whole affair had been so very well stage-managed that even though ballot boxes did not reach some of the polling booths, there was no difficulty in announcing the results.
>
> All polling booths were managed by Indian personnel assisted by the CRP. The polling for the few that turned up at the booths was done by the CRP on duty. Those of the voters who tried to be smart and tried to cast their votes themselves were beaten up in the booth itself, and ordered to cast the vote in the 'red box'—the so-called box of the people!' [5]

His memorandum to Morarji Desai added:

> The 'special poll' took place under the auspices of the Sikkim election commission which had not been vested with any authority to conduct such polls under the Government of Sikkim Act 1974, or under any other law of Sikkim. The 'special poll' was, therefore, unconstitutional and illegal, and forcibly imposed on the Sikkimese people. In fact, it was conducted merely to hoodwink some of the hon'ble members of (India's) Parliament who had demanded for a 'referendum' in Sikkim in course of the debate on the thirty-fifth amendment Bill in Parliament in September 1974.
>
> At the time of the 'special poll' the authorities informed the people that the poll was being held to find out the people's wishes as to whether they still wanted the autocratic role of the Chogyal or full democracy under Kazi. At no stage were the people told that the 'opinion poll' was taking place to settle the merger issue. The Sikkimese were thus befooled and deceived, and so were the hon'ble members of Parliament and the people of India as a whole.[6]

Nevertheless, Kazi, the ideal ventriloquist's dummy, issued an impressively vigorous statement on 15 April in which he asserted that the poll results were only to be expected. He then coyly took Mrs Gandhi's government to task for not gobbling up the kingdom quickly enough.

> I must say in frankness that in the past there have been occasions when the government of India, while fully and genuinely sympathising with the aspirations of the Sikkimese people, have not moved rapidly or far enough in implementing the demands voiced by us. After yesterday's poll there is now no basis for either delay or hesitation on the part of the government of India. Indeed, I would say that the government of India have the unshakable responsibility of

> urgently implementing the will expressed by the Sikkimese people.
>
> I would like to mention that I have already proposed to the Prime Minister that some of us should immediately visit New Delhi in order to impress upon the central government the urgency and unanimity of our demand that the resolution of 10 April be implemented in toto and at the earliest.

Strong words from a man with little thought and no language. But New Delhi avidly sustained this theatre of the absurd. Not only did Mrs Gandhi's ministers affect the utmost surprise, and even consternation, at Kazi's simulated annoyance, but external affairs ministry officials ponderously told reporters that the Sikkimese had never before described New Delhi as 'the central government'. The usage was pregnant with significance, said the very men who had drafted the letter and foisted it on Kazi via Singh and the two Lals. The embarrassingly contrived duet was intended once again to convey the impression that the insistent Sikkimese were forcing a reluctant India to swallow their country.

• • •

Gangtok was crawling with journalists. Foreign correspondents had not been allowed in, but the Indian media were generously represented, most chaperoned by Gurdip Singh Bedi and Ranjit Gupta, who provided jeeps and arranged accommodation. I was on my own in the Nor-Khill hotel, finding it almost as difficult to see Kazini as the Chogyal. When I telephoned the old dak bungalow late in the evening of my first day, Kazi said his wife was out. Early the next morning he claimed she was ill. The charade continued until eventually Kazi whispered over the wires that it would be better not to see her. Martam House had raised its barricades in fear of another invasion. Kaiser Bahadur Thapa was never at home. But at Rhenock house, Lhanzin-la wheedled a kindly CRP guard into allowing her to give me tea in the servants' shed on the ledge below the bungalow. 'I'll lose my job if anyone gets to know that I let you out of the house and even to meet someone!' the guard muttered, while apologising profusely for having to force the princess to receive a guest in the road.

The Chogyal seemed to have retreated into hermetic seclusion. Gurbachan Singh had been warmly welcoming when I telephoned him from Calcutta, assuring me that an audience at the palace would present no problems. I could see the Chogyal as often as I wished and for as long as I wanted to. But turned away from the gates like everyone else, I went to the chief minister who advised against having anything to do with the fallen monarch. *'Chogyal khatam ho gaya,'* (The Chogyal is finished) he warned, adding that permission to see him could only be given by the chief executive. Lal was evasive. 'If Thondup wishes to see you, he will. He does exactly what he wants to, proper or improper. Look at him now, harbouring a wanted criminal!' But when I told him what he knew already, that there was no way of sending word to the Chogyal, the chief executive let out one of his long hoots of raucous laughter. Ranjit Gupta in India House, to whom the PO directed me, was more specific. My request, as well as similar applications from several other journalists, had been forwarded to the palace. The Chogyal had a cold and temperature, but his secretary, Jigdal Densapa, who was with him in the palace, had promised to let us know as soon as he was feeling up to receiving visitors. It did not sound plausible, but had to be accepted.

There the matter stood until I bumped into Gupta around five one evening coming out of Green's Hotel in the bazaar. Almost as an after-thought, he told me to be at the palace gates in forty-five minutes; apparently, the Chogyal had agreed to see me at six o'clock. When I reached the gates at the appointed time, it was to find all the reporters in Gangtok waiting there. They had all been given the same time so that instead of the promised private interviews, we were gathered for an organised press conference under the Indian government's eagle eye. Gupta was there, so were several men in uniform. They let us in through the gates and trooped us up the long drive and round the bend by the chorten across the crunching gravel like schoolboys on an outing. Just to make sure that we did not linger too long in the pernicious atmosphere within, we were all expected at India House for drinks with the PO at seven. About fifty minutes was thought to be reasonably safe in the Chogyal's company.

It was a dismal abode that we entered. The first person I saw was black-garbed Manuel, dark and solemn in the shadows of the gloomy hall, the servants massed behind him with frightened faces. The meeting was to be in the drawing-room, but I slipped away down the zigzag passage and hearing voices, turned right into the long dining-room. It was a double room really, with folding doors, dominated by a carved Burmese sideboard, used only for rare banquets. Now it had been converted into a working room. Piles of paper rose on the table, Densapa and Rasaily conferred in anxious tones, Sodeun-La, Coo Coo La's eldest daughter, was fluttering about, and Bhuvanesh Kumari in her habitual, faded denim, corrected drafts. Only the Chogyal and his son were formally attired in black khos with gleaming white cuffs. They sat in two of the lacquered dining chairs, reading through a long document. The Chogyal looked up at my entrance and stared for an endless moment in the disconcerting way he sometimes had, over the top of his spectacles—a long, silent look eloquent with hurt, disappointment, and bewilderment. For all that he was royal keeper of the sacred chhos, it was the look of a dumb creature in pain.

The press conference was a fiasco. Movie and television lights suddenly blazed in the drawing-room, illuminating its pale tangerine walls, ceiling patterned in squares of gold and white with gold fretwork discs, and a carpet specially woven in grey and orange. It was a sparsely furnished room, the only furniture, apart from the bodens and chokseys lining the walls, an elaborately carved dwarf bookcase and two small gilt tables, one supported by three allegorical figures, the other by three skeletons. There was also a little writing-desk in one corner. The feeling usually was of space. Now it was cluttered with rows of tubular steel chairs facing the high choksey where the Chogyal received visitors on happier occasions. Cameras on their stands and trailing yards of wire added to the congestion. The lights fused because the load was more than the supply could stand, and the room plunged in darkness. Then the connection was restored and the Chogyal and Tenzing took their seats under the thankas. No one stood up as they entered. No one stopped chattering or even bothered to stub out cigarettes.

Our army escort at once produced notebook and pencil (which is more than most of the reporters did) but he need not have bothered for nothing substantive was mentioned. The Chogyal rambled through an interminably long legal statement, the one he was checking in the dining-room, that still prudently avoided levelling any direct accusations against New Delhi about how the Sikkimese had been deceived. It could hardly have been a more faltering defence. The audience was listless. The few token questions were entirely devoid of serious interest in investigation. Everybody already knew from Lal and Gurbachan Singh all that it was thought necessary to know. Sikkim's obituary had been written under New Delhi's firmly persuasive guidelines. The story was dead and the Chogyal's listeners, indifferent or unsympathetic to start with, soon showed how bored they were by his stammering recital.

But the meeting served a propaganda purpose. It was pointed out next morning that the monarch obviously enjoyed full liberty since he had entertained so many journalists at home. 'Did he hold his press conference in prison or his palace?' asked Santosh Kumar Rai, while the chief executive pealed with merriment. India's free press at once assured the Congress general secretary that his victorious party was truly magnanimous to allow the tyrant not only to continue to live in such sumptuous style, but every opportunity to disseminate his lies to the world. Those who had thought up the idea of the palace press conference had cleverly banked on the Chogyal's indecisiveness and fear of India. They felt certain that even in extremity, he would baulk at publicly charging RAW with inciting treason in his country or Mrs Gandhi's government with military aggression. They were proved right. Sikkim's trusting ruler had again walked into a trap.

What did emerge from that last public appearance of the twelfth consecrated Denzong Chogyal was that he had not called the meeting at all. India House had telephoned the palace a bare half hour earlier to announce that a press conference had been arranged, and that the Chogyal should be ready to receive journalists. None of our individual requests to see him had been communicated to the Chogyal, to Jigdal Densapa or anyone else on the staff. Gurbachan Singh, B.B. Lal, Ranjit Gupta and the rest had unblushingly lied to the media. The palace had been entirely ignorant of our presence in Gangtok.

Later that evening and to my considerable surprise, Gurbachan Singh allowed me to leave his party and return to the palace. I told the PO that the Chogyal had invited me to stay on to dine and that I had accepted but couldn't stay on because of the India House party. He was expecting me to return. Possibly because an outright refusal would have contradicted official boasts that the Chogyal was at complete liberty, Gurbachan Singh telephoned the army to let me in. The beleaguered household seemed different then, exuding an air of cheerful battle as Densapa opened tins and scrambled eggs, while the Chogyal hunted for a bottle of wine. 'Have some Tavel!' he said. As a connoisseur of fine wines, the Chogyal felt that the robust rosé from the Rhone didn't compare with a vintage burgundy.

Although he would not embarrass New Delhi before the press, he did not mince words in private. Earlier that day he had sent another message to Mrs Gandhi pointing out that he had not been informed of the assembly resolution and special poll. Such acts, he stressed, were 'all illegal, unconstitutional and brought about under force of arms and permissive hooliganism against canons of democratic and constitutional practice'. They were also in flagrant breach of the 1974 Act which he had tried to adhere to while 'the council of ministers and most of the assembly members have flouted it with impunity, and instead accused (him) of obstructing popular aspirations although they never state where and how except through grossly concocted allegations of assassination attempts said to have been inspired and masterminded by the palace'. This was a fighting protest contrary to his dejected performance before journalists:

> In the absence of conditions for fair and free polling, the result of such referendum in any case was a foregone conclusion with the Sikkim Congress hooligans on the rampage, backed by CRP, leaving the supporters of the Chogyal or any other opposition, and the youth and students, completely cowed down without opportunity of canvassing, etc.
>
> Such a referendum should be held under neutral authority, and all parties given a fair opportunity for canvassing freely with their representatives at polling booths, etc.
>
> Regret even Indian election commission not competent to conduct such referendum as its outcome affects vital issue of whether Sikkim should form a territorial part of India as said to have been demanded by the Sikkim Congress, nor has it any authority under our constitution or any agreements.
>
> In view of this unconstitutional and undemocratic and illegal action by those who have assumed all powers arbitrarily,

> particularly the chief executive, a civil servant appointee acting as if he were the head of state and the head of government, would request being released from house arrest and immediate meeting with your Excellency.[7]

There was no meeting. If India House forwarded the message, Mrs Gandhi did not deign to reply. What could she have said, anyway?

Gurbachan Singh allowed me to call at the palace once more to say goodbye. He did so making plain his reluctance, but at least he did not refuse. His authority seemed to have ended by the weekend for Sikkim's merger with India meant the end of the PO and India House which were both diplomatic institutions under the external affairs ministry. Lal, to whom the last PO suggested I apply for permission to see the Chogyal again before returning to Calcutta, shot out a curt 'No' and banged down the receiver.

• • •

An Indian air force helicopter waited at Libing helipad on 16 April to take the chief minister to Bagdogra where he would emplane for New Delhi. Chatur Singh Roy, Nar Bahadur Khatiawara and Santosh Kumar Rai were accompanying him. Mrs Gandhi was said to have invited them in response to Kazi's statement of the previous day. He would also meet Chavan, the home minister, the Lok Sabha speaker, and India's President. Kazini watched almost in tears as her husband was given a formal send-off from the dak bungalow. He ceremonially inspected a guard of honour and took the salute under the kingdom's still fluttering red and white flag. Glowing like a little boy who has won a prize as he received honours that were pleasantly reminiscent of the palace, Kazi beckoned me out to the backyard—about the only place that was free from eavesdroppers—for a hurriedly whispered few words.

I had witnessed (and participated in) an unedifying domestic upheaval late the previous night when, instead of being sated with their ballot-box victory, Kazi and Kazini had squabbled viciously. Breaking under the strain of failure and disappointment, Kazini shrieked at her husband in a shrill volley of kitchen Hindustani. Frustration, memories of Tenzing's foiled venture and of Krishan Chandra Pradhan's arrested coup momentarily turned her into the kingdom's most fanatical monarchist. She accused her spouse of betraying his country and earning posterity's obloquy. 'What will people say of you afterwards, Kazi? Answer me that, answer, answer, answer!' she screamed, lurching about the sitting-room. 'They will say that Kazi sold his country, *sold* it, Kazi!' If the throne could not be saved, he should, at least, insist that the Chogyal be installed as governor. Even in her dementia, Kazini was aware that the two men shared a common culture and might yet be able to save something of the future.

The chief minister did not seriously defend himself. He was desperately afraid that the CRP, lounging sleepless outside the door, would hear his wife's frantically dangerous ravings. 'What will they say?' he moaned. 'What will people think if they hear you?' He asked me to leave the house. *'Ap jayiye!* Please go!' he implored. I had brought on the paroxysm. *'Bahar sab baat soona jata!'* (They can hear everything outside!) Virtually pushing me out, he dragged the exhausted woman, still weeping hysterically, into an inner room and banged the door.

Kazi did not refer to that unnerving scene. But its memory obviously impelled him to explain his helplessness. 'How can the Chogyal became governor?' he asked rhetorically. 'He's opposed statehood all along. He is still fighting it. But I tell you he is finished. *Chogyal khatam ho gya.* You should listen to me and forget him. He's nobody now. They will set up a vigilance commission and get him.' But what of Sikkim? I asked, and at once the confidence flowed back into his innocuously amiable face. In spite of what he had said about statehood a moment earlier, Kazi did not seem to believe it was imminent. The country was safe, he assured me. '*Yeh* palace *log* propaganda *karta hai jo hamara* flag *leh leyga*...' (The palace propaganda is that our flag will be taken away...) '*Kahan* flag *leh liya?*' (Where have they taken away the flag?) He pointed to the standard flapping above the narrow strip of grass. Kazi was sure too that some formula would be invented to protect Sikkim's special status. '*Abhi-baat-chit hoyega.* Merger *me* India *ka bahut bad-naam hoyega!*' (There will have to be talks now. Merger would give India a very bad name!)

And with that fond prophecy, the chief minister of Sikkim, resplendent in silken kho, climbed into his jeep and drove off to the helipad in an impressive convoy. Did he believe himself, I wondered. In the years that followed, when Kazi and Kazini were ensconced in Mintokgang, making the most of their eminence, I was repeatedly turned away from their door. The chief minister and his lady wanted no reminders of the past, especially of an episode that was personally painful and could be politically embarrassing.

The Sikkimese delegates were received in New Delhi like conquering heroes. Mrs Gandhi graciously promised that their application would be 'seriously and sympathetically considered'. There was nothing to consider, really, for the application and its elaborate support of resolutions and referendum had been mirrored in advance on 11 April when Chavan made a long speech in Parliament recounting the Chogyal's misdeeds, and again talked of 'evidence of possible conspiracy against the chief minister and his colleagues indicating complicity of some Sikkim Guards'. India's external affairs minister reminded MPs how his government had resisted many earlier invitations to take over the kingdom, leaving them in no doubt that such an opportunity would not again be missed. He blamed the crisis squarely on the duplicity of the Chogyal who had approved the 1973 tripartite agreement and the 1974 Act, but had not displayed 'sincerity' in making the arrangements work. He had not accepted the democratic system under which he ceased to 'have the overriding powers he had exercised for more than two decades'.

Kazi returned from New Delhi on 17 April. Four days later, Chavan introduced the Constitution (36th Amendment) Bill to convert the kingdom from an 'associate state' into India's twenty-second state. Few measures could have been completed in such desperate hurry. The Lok Sabha adopted the bill by 299 votes to eleven on 23 April and the Rajya Sabha by 158 to three on 26 April. It was then quickly rushed through the process of ratification by thirteen states to receive presidential assent on 18 May. The kingdom had securely been knotted up in the ends of Mrs Gandhi's saree before the Sikkimese could say Denzong Chogyal. Clearly, legal preparations had been completed long before the prearranged drama of Kazi's appeal.

• • •

Lal obviously enjoyed being master of ceremonies at a gathering in his sitting room the morning after the dismal command performance in the palace. There were no military escorts, shorthand writers or compulsory parties immediately afterwards to limit duration. The sunlight flowed in through Mintokgang's open windows as the peoples' representatives were supposed to speak freely to the people's chroniclers. Questions were as consciously sympathetic as they had been hostile or contemptuous the night before. But if the Chogyal's press conference had worn a forlorn air, the Sikkim Congress exercise was tense and tight-lipped.

Huddled in a bay window, the triumphant ministers might have been a bunch of very raw actors nervously waiting for an audition. Eyes swivelled round to seek Lal's approval before replying to the simplest questions. The chief executive hooted and chuckled with laughter, and the OSDs, who were in discreet attendance, noted every single glance and expression.

Kazi might have been Kanchendzonga enthroned at the Kagyet dances, an immobile presiding deity wrapped in silence. None of his Bhutiya-Lepcha colleagues uttered a word. The floor belonged to Khatiawara and Santosh Kumar Rai who, basking in the warmth of official approbation, lustily held forth on the sacred principles of democracy. I asked where Sikkim stood in relation to the 1974 Act and Khatiawara at once replied: 'Our April 10 resolution and referendum of April 14 have done away with the Act.' Chavan possibly had in mind this planned repudiation of legislation through populist assertiveness when he told Parliament that 'What is operating there is the will of the people.' It was an interesting essay in law-making (or -breaking) by the mob; a dangerous process that New Delhi would not have promoted if it were not also sure of controlling the logical conclusion. For if 'the will of the people', Gurbachan Singh's 'revolutionary constitutionality', could wipe out one set of laws, it could also reject others, India's constitutional amendments, for instance.

None of this worried Lal as he moved forward to take full advantage of his now unbridled powers. His first task was to get rid of Rasaily. None of the charges levelled earlier would stick, so the auditor-general was dismissed on 24 April, allegedly for embezzling ₹ 2,500 from the Sikkim Lottery. Next to go was Tarachand Hariomal who was still on enforced holiday in Delhi. A junior foreign office employee, A.S. Bhasin, told the chief judge that he was expected to apply for an extension of absence. Then Lal himself, visiting New Delhi, confirmed that in spite of having used up all the leave due to him, Hariomal should ask for more. The judge was still in New Delhi on 9 May when he received a telegram: 'Have to confirm termination of your services as judge, Central Court of Sikkim, from ninth May forenoon.'

S.K. Prasad of Sikkim High Court was served with a similar peremptory order of dismissal on the same day. As Hariomal later commented:

> My only regret has been that such an esteemed institution, built after years of labour and based on moral and ethical values, respected and recognised under national and international charters and codes of conduct, had been so ruthlessly crushed, humiliated and debased with no regard for propriety and human values. Can any civilised society be a mute witness to such gross encroachments and insults? Can society accept foul means for even fair ends and allow such an all-important edifice to be pulled down in a way so immoral, illegal and unethical?[8]

Society could and would, when it served the government's political interests to do so and more.

As reward for having made this culmination possible, B.B. Lal was made governor of Sikkim the very day the amending bill received the President's assent. The national flag was unceremoniously hauled down on 18 May though the ancient royal standard continued to be flown in the palace and in the flat in Calcutta when the Chogyal was in residence.

India House, formerly the Residency, became Raj Bhavan, and even more the burra kothi when Lal moved in as governor. But it was a sadly denuded mansion that Gurbachan Singh left, grumbling, to everyone's astonishment, that the Chogyal had not given him a parting present. The external affairs ministry handed over the building to the home ministry stripped of its deep carpets, fine china and gleaming silver, old prints and the library of rare volumes on Tibet, Bhutan and Sikkim. The absence of elegance did not trouble Lal. His Excellency—as the new governor loved to be called—was soon down in Calcutta, buying curtain material and haggling over the price of thick pottery bowls in the cheaper wholesale markets. He found more congenial consolation in Sikkimese obsequiousness. Even durbar officials and some of the Chogyal's relatives tried to appease the governor with gifts of fruit, flowers, momos and cakes baked by the palace chef. The reality of power was so readily acknowledged because the monarchical tradition had been reinforced in the popular mind. Lal was not just 'another little Chogyal,' as an Indian opposition MP derisively put it. He was far more an absolute ruler than the Chogyal had ever been.

'There are about twenty-seven sentry boxes around the palace, and it looks as if the Chogyal is going to stay put for the whole summer,' wrote Lhanzin-La from Gangtok. It was a lonely incarceration, for his staff deserted him in adversity. Since they were all on the government's payroll, they were asked to decide whether or not they wished to remain in official service. However the question was camouflaged, it meant: did they wish to be transferred to the general administration or continue as private employees of the palace? The only person (except, possibly, one or two of the servants) to place loyalty above career was Mrs Ongkit Targain, a bubbling little woman with iron-grey hair who had been the Chogyal's stenographer and typist since the mid-'50s. Karma Topden had already left for Calcutta. Manuel went to the new government guest house, and the three ADCs were found official berths. Paljor Tashi, Lhanzin-La's husband, joined the tourism department. His boss, Jigdal Densapa, the most trusted and seniormost of the Chogyal's aides, drew his salary and enjoyed his official jeep without formal duties, since Lal did not trust him enough to place him in an appropriately senior post. But he preferred this limbo to serving his ruler. 'I must confess I was a little surprised at Jigdal,' was all the Chogyal could bring himself to say by way of criticism. 'The ADCs wouldn't have gone if he hadn't.' Being already in Calcutta, Karma Topden was spared an uncomfortable choice. He flirted with the idea of returning to the palace and talked of launching a new nationalist party but shied away when the Chogyal took him at his word and made an offer.

Apart from the faithful Mrs Targain, the Chogyal also had the services of Roland Chhetri, the Guards captain who returned to the palace to serve as ADC, staff officer, and general factotum, when his army career petered out in the Sirwani prison camp. An old woman and a young man, both of Lepcha descent, were all the retainers left to the brooding king. Everyone else, including politicians, civil servants and close relations—all of whom had benefited enormously from his patronage—was far too busy securing private interests under the new dispensation to bother with a dethroned and dispossessed monarch.

What was Sikkim left with?

Justice Hidayatullah's view was that Indian constitutional amendments had no force in Sikkim because 'no law of one state can affect the status of an agreeing state, a party to a treaty'. Only another treaty—not the Indian constitution—could alter the kingdom's position. Even in 1974, he foresaw the possibility that New Delhi would sooner or later invoke the principle of *clausula rebus sic stantibus* (treaties will be observed only while things thus stand), pleading catastrophic changes that violated the intentions of the signatories. Examining the earlier amendment's wording, Hidayatullah had warned:

> It will be noticed that the expression 'treaty' is sedulously avoided. The only intention can be that at some future occasion, it may be said that the treaty cannot now operate because of the events that have taken place. It will be noticed that the Chogyal was the signatory, and he has had no share in the resolutions and requests which have completely avoided him. If such a claim for application of the doctrine is made, it will amount to *abus de droit* (abuse of rights) of the signatory of the treaty.[9]

Anticipating changes, India's lawyer-vice-president stressed that no enactment in New Delhi could convert the kingdom into an Indian state. It was bound by the still extant 1974 Act. If that Act had ceased to apply, as claimed by Khatiawara and Chavan, Sikkim reverted to being a protected monarchy.

That is, the status quo ante. If the resolutions and referendum were acknowledged to have swept away the 1974 Act, then they also restored the rightful position under earlier laws, agreements and institutions. Sikkim's traditional monarchy enthroned in customary law, deriving sanctity from Buddhist belief, solemnised by the oath of Kabi between the Namgyal ancestor, Khye-Bumsa, and Thekong-tek, the Lepcha chief from whom the Densapas claimed descent, in the mists of the thirteenth century, and legitimised by centuries of recognition by China, Tibet, Nepal, Bhutan, Britain and India remained, shorn of the restrictions imposed in 1974 when a new office was created for the existing incumbent. So did the 1953 constitutional proclamation and the entire system of political, administrative and judicial management that had been in force until the intervention. The 1950 treaty also came into its own again as the only binding compact between India and Sikkim, clearly defining the former's rights and establishing the latter's status as a protected kingdom with an unambiguous international identity.

India tried to evade problems arising out of this de jure return to the past through carefully worded legislative precautions. Clause 3(m) of the Constitution (38th Amendment) Act read:

> Neither the Supreme Court nor any other court shall have jurisdiction in respect of any dispute or other matter arising out of any treaty, agreement, engagement or other similar instrument relating to Sikkim which was entered into or executed before the appointed day and to which the government of India or any of its predecessor governments was a party...

Som Dutt Sharma's petition in the Delhi High Court, Rasaily's in the Gangtok central court, and Hariomal's interim injunction were thus sought to be nullified by a stroke of the legislative pen. So, in effect, was the treaty. It was like a criminal empowering himself with immunity against prosecution. Instead of protecting rights, the law seemed to defend lawlessness. Another clause in the Act reserved for New Delhi more direct authority than it enjoyed in any Indian state. Clause 3(g) vested the governor with 'special responsibility for peace and for an equitable arrangement for ensuring the social and economic advancement of different sections of the population of Sikkim...' In theory, this was supposed to mean that the governor should protect Bhutiya-Lepchas from being overrun by the Nepalese. In practice, it concentrated the powers of Chogyal, PO, chief executive and chief minister in a single nominated functionary whose 'special responsibility' became a magic formula to justify every conceivable kind of political and administrative intervention.

• • •

Abroad, the coup invited universal public censure. Even Britain's *Guardian* newspaper, always supportive of India, accused Mrs Gandhi's government of 'proceeding with a mixture of charade and ruthlessness once the goal of annexation had been set'. Its editorial was titled 'The Swallowing of Sikkim'. Predictably, *The Observer*, with its tradition of sympathy for small countries and subject peoples, was far more scathing. Under the heading 'Imperial India' it warned that the 'piece of political fraud presented as democracy' would increase the suspicions of all the frontier peoples. 'The high democratic principles used to defend the take-over of Sikkim sound no more convincing in Indian mouths than they did in an earlier age when used by the British Raj.' The media around the world was equally critical.

Governments abroad were not as outspoken though an official statement in Beijing vehemently denounced India's action. Five years later, the completely apolitical Princess

Soyang-La, who had applied for a visa at the Chinese embassy in Kathmandu to visit her mother in Tibet, was told that the Chogyal's sister-in-law could not travel on an Indian passport. She was welcome to go to Lhasa but the Chinese gave her a laissez-passer recognising her Sikkimese nationality and enabling her to enter Tibet as a subject of the Chogyal's. New Delhi raised no objection.

Nar Bahadur Khatiawara was not aware of diplomatic and legal niceties. Nor did any great concern for moral principle inspire his postures. He was just a young man on the make who campaigned against the durbar and rendered service to those who promised to further his personal interests and radical cause. When those promises were not kept, he decided to reveal what he had done and why, and to rip off the mask from all that led to the annexation. The anguished torrent of the covering letter with his memorandum to Morarji Desai explained his deep disenchantment:

> Sikkim is a small country and its people, regardless of their origin, are gentle and peace-loving. We have, however, been consistently branded as being anti-Indian merely because of our aspirations to be Sikkimese, and to govern ourselves. In these efforts, we have unquestionably looked to India for assistance and guidance, and will continue to do so. We have reposed complete trust and confidence in India, fully expecting that she would extend to us honest, wholehearted and unflinching support in this regard, but all our hopes have been belied.
>
> We regret that under pretext of ushering in democracy to fulfil 'the wishes of the people', India's action in Sikkim seems to have been motivated solely with the object of annexing it, and making it a part and parcel of India. We were also some of the many Sikkimese who had taken very active part in the 1973 uprising expecting fully that our hopes and aspirations for democracy and people's rule in Sikkim under the principle of

'one-man-one-vote' and our demands for a written constitution, so far denied, would be fulfilled.[10]

The letter went on to say:

> In this regard it is our party's considered belief that the people of Sikkim always treated every Indian as our guardian who would look after the interests of the Sikkimese people in all respects. Never at any moment did we realise, nor did we ever doubt the sincerity of our well-wishers and the high-ups, in the government of India, including Srimati Indira Gandhi, Sardar Swaran Singh, Shri Y.B. Chavan, foreign secretary Sri Kewal Singh, political officer in Sikkim, Sri K.S. Bajpai, Sri B.S. Das, chief executive of Sikkim, and lastly, Sri B.B. Lal, at present the governor of Sikkim, that we were being completely duped, and that our demand for full-fledged democracy in Sikkim would be a far cry.
>
> The methods used by them were the age-old methods of the imperialistic and expansionist nations of divide and rule, propagating false propaganda, creating an illusion that democracy was being introduced and democratic institutions were being strengthened for the benefit of the Sikkimese people, whereas, in reality, the trust of the simple and innocent people was being deceived, exploited and betrayed.[11]

The people's majesty could be as gullible as any anointed sovereign.

REFERENCES:

1. Nar Bahadur Khatiawara and nine others, 'Sikkim's Merger—A Brief Resume', (unpublished memorandum to Morarji Desai).
2. Sikkim Assembly (10 April 1975).
3. Ibid.

4. 'A Merger is Arranged', *Hindustan Times* (15 April 1975).
5. Khatiawara. *op. cit.*
6. Ibid.
7. The Chogyal to Mrs Indira Gandhi (15 April 1975).
8. Tarachand Hariomal, 'Now it can be Told' (Unpublished manuscript).
9. Mohammed Hidayatullah, 'Opinion in the Matter of the Chogyal of Sikkim and the 35th Amendment of the Constitution of India' (unpublished).
10. Khatiawara, *op cit.*
11. Ibid.

APPENDICES

PUBLIC APOLOGY

This is to inform that Sunanda K. Datta-Ray, author of the book SMASH AND GRAB subtitled 'Annexation of Sikkim', and Vikas Publishing House Pvt. Ltd., had at no time intended to cast any aspersions on the reputation and integrity of Mr. Gurbachan Singh, Political Officer in Sikkim in 1974–75, nor did they at any time intend to suggest or insinuate that Mr. Gurbachan Singh was in any way responsible for removing valuable antiquities from India House in Gangtok in which he had resided as Political Officer. The publishers and author express unqualified regret in case such an impression has been created. Consequently, Mr. Gurbachan Singh has agreed to withdraw Suit No. 1236 of 1986 filed against the publishers and author in the Delhi High Court.

(The *Times of India, Indian Express* and *The Statesman* printed the double-column box announcement free of charge for the author.)

VIKAS PUBLISHING HOUSE PVT LTD

576, Masjid Road, Jangpura, New Delhi - 110 014
Tel: 4314605, 4315313, 4314902 Cable: VIKASBOOKS, New Delhi
Fax: (91) 11-4310879 Email: *orders@vikas.gobookshopping.com*
Website: *www.gobookshopping.com*

16 February 2000

Mr Sunanda K.Datta-Ray
39 Friends Colony East
New Delhi 110 065.

Fax No. 631 8645

Dear Mr Datta-Ray,

This is with reference to your fax message dated 14 February 2000.

Since we are not interested in publishing another edition of your book, **SMASH AND GRAB: ANNEXATION OF SIKKIM**, we are returning the rights to you.

This may be treated as *NO OBJECTION CERTIFICATE* from our side.

With kind regards,

Yours sincerely,

PIYUSH CHAWLA
DIRECTOR, PUBLISHING & MARKETING

OBSERVER'S FICTION

"The OBSERVER correspondent in Calcutta, Sunanda Datta-Ray, on assignment to report the strained relationship between India and Sikkim, was prevented from leaving the country and from filing his report of the latest developments to London."

THE OBSERVER, Sunday, June 23

FACT

"If this complaint refers to me, I must repudiate it as utterly unfounded and disclaim all responsibility for a travesty of fact. I have been in Gangtok since 20 June on assignment for the STATESMAN; I have been entertained several times by both the Indian political officer and the chief executive of Sikkim; and have had no difficulty at all in meeting and talking to leaders of the various political groups, including the Sikkim Congress President, Mr Kendhup Dorji Kazi...The only reason why I did not send you an account of happenings in Sikkim is because there was no reply from THE OBSERVER — at least until the time of my leaving Calcutta — to the message of inquiry I sent you earlier the previous week. But this silence is certainly not to be attributed to any official restraints (of which there was none whatsoever) on my journalistic activities. . ."

Sunanda K. Datta-Ray in a letter from Gangtok to THE OBSERVER, June 30.

INDIA WEEKLY, LONDON

Index

Abu Dhabi, 43
Acharya, Tanka Prasad, 65
Adow, Chumbi, 110
Afghanistan, 38, 42, 314
Aitchison, Sir Charles, 51
Aitchison's Treaties, 51, 105
Akhand Bharat, 193, 314
Akiyama, Naoki, 380
Aksai Chin, 107, 116
All India Radio (AIR), 162–63, 246, 267, 312, 345
Alley, Reshmi Prasad, 72
All-India State People's Conference, 60, 69–70
Amanullah, King, 141
Anglo–Chinese convention (1890), 37–38, 53, 55, 103–04, 110, 112–13, 116, 188, 313
Anglo–Gorkha war, 29
Anti-Bill agitation, 285, 289
Arunachal Pradesh, 51, 106
Asia Society, 187
Assam, 24, 53, 88, 95, 105, 232
Ataturk, Kemal, 145
Athing-La Rai Bahadur Tashi Dahdul of Barmiok, 26, 60, 91, 144, 165, 204, 209, 224, 234, 388
birthday celebrations of, 217–49, 340, 350, 356
Australia, 93, 167, 191, 379
Azad, Maulana Abul Kalam, 61

Bagdogra, 5, 7, 84, 107, 273, 294, 303, 347, 403
Bahadur, Jung, 33
Bailey, F.M, 62
Bajpai, Kayatyani Shankar, 90, 99–100, 179, 181, 192, 195, 204, 209–10, 217, 219, 225–26, 232, 235–36, 239–42, 244, 250–51, 255, 261, 274–77, 279, 280, 283–84, 286, 290, 298, 301, 308, 310, 312–13, 316–17, 327, 414
Barfungpa, 26, 60
Barmiok kazi, 26, 49, 54, 388
Basnet, Harka Bahadur, 173, 202, 211, 213
  Lal Bahadur, 151, 205
  Man Bahadur, 202, 227, 291
  Man Kumar, 241, 388
  Prakash, 336
Bedi, Gurdip Singh, 226, 232, 275, 276, 381, 397

Beijing, 83, 87, 136, 143, 173, 175, 412
Bell, Sir Charles, 38, 55, 143, 166
Bengal Eastern Frontier Regulation, 94
Bentinck, Lord William, 30
Bhandari, Hem Lal, 336–37, 361
 Nar Bahadur, 247–48, 265–67, 283, 317, 335–37, 395
Bhattacharyya, Ananda, 224, 354–55
Bhushan, Shanti, 350
Bhutan, 24, 26, 43, 45, 54, 59, 60, 87, 89, 106, 109, 124, 131, 141, 143, 162, 164–67, 169, 193, 197, 211, 254, 324, 387, 408, 411
 and, Britain, 32, 103, 184
  India, 40 -42, 52, 61–64, 77, 83, 86–87, 94, 109–11, 188, 249–51, 315, 320–21, 343
  Sikkim, 28, 64, 77, 127, 142, 201, 342
  Tibet, 28–29
Bhutia, Dorjee Tsering, 304
 Kalzang Gyatso, 266, 278, 294, 299, 371
 Passang Tsering, 361, 382
 Shebchung, 252, 266, 373
Bhutto, Zulfiqar Ali, 100, 321
Bosu, Jyotirmoy, 314, 317
Bowles, Chester, 164
Britain, 4, 7, 25–53, 58, 62, 73–74, 76, 78–79, 81, 89–90, 100–01, 104–06, 110–12, 120, 123, 126, 131, 141, 145, 153, 165–67, 169, 175, 180, 185, 188–89, 191–92, 195, 204, 257, 261, 271, 273, 305, 307, 314–15, 335, 345, 380, 386, 411–12
 and, Bhutan, 32, 103, 184
  Sikkim, 23, 29–30, 37, 52, 55, 57, 103, 142, 184, 322, 361
Bulletin Number Two, 202, 204, 205
Bunau–Varilla, Philipe, 190–91
Burma, 141, 145, 314

Calcutta, 5, 7, 30, 37, 60, 67, 89, 111, 137, 143, 147, 152, 179, 184, 232, 235, 246, 253, 259, 287, 288, 290, 302, 316–18, 326, 335–37, 346, 363, 380, 391, 398, 403, 408–09
Campbell, Dr A., 32–33
Caroe, Sir Olaf, 50
Carter administration, 192
Central Bureau of Investigation, 133
Chagla, M.C., 88
Chakrabarti, Dipankar, 314, 386
Chakung, 26, 49, 66, 141, 147–48, 179, 204, 212–13, 244, 247, 254, 266, 269
Chang Kua–hua, General, 109
Chang–Tin Tang, 106
Chankapa, Katuk Lama, 46
Chapin, Seldon, 91
Chavan, Yeshwantrao B., 337, 346–47, 403, 405–07, 410, 414
Chempo, Lhatsun, 27
Chempo, Rigdsin, 27
Chempo, Sempah, 27
Chen Hsi-lien, 345
Chen, Ivan, 104, 105
Chhetri, Basant Kumar, 13, 21, 381
Captain Roland Christopher, 4, 13, 231, 263, 409

Chhatra Bahadur, 211, 212, 213, 215, 265
Hemlata, 266
L. B., 261
Maya Devi, 146
Chhoden, Rai Bahadur Lobzang, 26
Chiang Kai-shek, 64, 105
China, 23, 27–28, 45, 52, 83, 89, 102, 103–17, 119, 123, 133, 136–37, 141–43, 145, 148, 153, 161–62, 164, 166, 168, 175–76, 178, 185–86, 188, 190, 198, 201, 219, 236–37, 302, 313, 321–22, 325, 328, 338, 345, 390, 411, 413
and, Britain, 3638, 53, 77, 103
India, 8, 28, 65, 73, 87, 119
Sikkim, 1, 24, 33, 87
Communist, 52, 64, 87, 116, 141
Chinese People's Liberation Army, 73
Chogyal, Chempo, 202, 205, 208, 375
Chopra, I.S., 97, 99, 169, 209, 214, 250
Chou En-lai, 4, 111, 145, 151
Chowdhury, S. Dutta, 223–24, 229–30, 232–33, 241, 244, 336
Chu Shi-kuei, General, 109
Chumbi, 24–25, 32–34, 36–38, 54, 65, 67, 107, 112–13, 116, 120, 198
Chumthang, 90, 95, 96
Churchill, Lord Randolph, 35
Clarke, John Eric, 379
Coelho, Vincent, 188
Colombo Plan, 136, 164–65, 193
committee, people's consultative, 112, 153
Connaught, Duke of, 43
Coo Coo La (Pema Tseuden Yapshi Pheunkhang), Princess, 87, 91, 160, 198, 212, 261, 285, 302, 351, 362
Cooke, Hope, *see* Gyalmo of Sikkim
Cornwallis, Lord, 42
Curzon, Lord, 142

Dahal, Bhuwani Prasad, 211, 213, 215, 227, 304, 384
Roop Narain, 220, 243, 266
Dahdul, Dorji, 72, 160
Dr Lekhi, 285
Dalai Lama, 21, 27–28, 31, 35, 52–54, 65, 83, 104–07, 109, 122, 141, 143, 155, 219, 392
Dalam Athing, 49
Dalimkote; Damsang, ruins of, 142
Dandavate, Madhu, 314
Darjeeling, 9, 28, 30–36, 38, 40, 45, 47–48, 50, 57–59, 90–91, 104, 108–09, 123, 160, 162, 174–75, 215, 220, 224, 237, 247, 250, 252, 294, 336, 361, 373, 389
Sikkim's claim of, 31, 51, 57–58, 175
Das, B. S., 249–52, 254, 262–65, 267–68, 271, 274–79, 281–88, 291–301, 304, 308–11, 326–29, 333, 414
Das, Kusu, 115–16
Daschowdhury, B.K., 161
Dayal, Harishwar, 62, 65, 70–75, 77–78, 81, 135, 193, 195, 222, 236, 256
Deb Raja, 28

Deb, Dasaratha, 314
Debgong, 29, 30, 31
Deki, Sangey, 58, 91, 158
Densapa, Jigdal, 5–6, 12, 24, 26, 47, 91, 160, 161, 165, 167, 168, 207, 209, 218–19, 224, 227, 234, 236, 240, 252, 283, 287, 289, 312, 316, 317, 333, 343–44, 382, 398–99, 401, 409, 411
Dentam, 125, 265
Denzong Rong Sezum, 252
Desai, Morarji, 117, 138, 178, 187, 189, 238, 279, 350, 396, 413
Desai, N.J., 88
Desideri, Ippolito, 24, 27
Devanagri, 40, 181
Devare, Sudhir, 226
Dewan, Khangsa, 45, 48, 49
Dhar, Durga Prasad, 303
Dhar, Sudhir, 320
Dharma Gompo Lama, 361
Dolma, Yishey, 36–37
Dorji, Jigmie, 59, 62, 64, 89, 143, 166
  Kunzang, 211, 213, 227
  Raja Sonam Tobgye, 62, 64, 165
  Rani Chuni Wangmo, 62, 141, 143, 165–66
  Tashi Ashi, 167
Douglas-Home, Sir Alec, 151
Doyle, Denis Conan, 141–42
Durand, Sir Mortimer, 37
Durbar Gazette, 338, 392
Dutt, Subimal, 86, 108, 162

East India Company, 29, 35, 58, 109
Eden, Ashley, 45, 49, 103
Edgar, John Ware, 28, 29, 34, 44, 45, 48
Eisenhower, President Dwight, 76
Elgin, Lord, 53
France, 75, 76, 191

Gandhi, Indira, 1, 5–7, 82, 85, 88, 138, 150–51, 174, 177–80, 184, 189–91, 193, 195–97, 199, 223, 230–31, 233, 236–37, 239, 245–46, 250, 253, 258, 267, 270, 281–82, 285, 289, 292–94, 298–99, 302–03, 305, 309, 311–12, 314–18, 320, 322, 326–27, 330, 337, 340, 343, 346, 355, 357, 362, 364, 371, 393, 402–03, 405–06, 414
  government of, 1, 189, 196, 237, 316, 342, 373, 396, 397, 401, 412
Gandhi, Mahatma, 152, 191
Gangtok Central Court, 9–10, 263, 349, 372, 382, 384, 407, 411
Gawler, Lt-Col J.C., 33
Gazetteer of India, 26
George V, King, 60
Ghosh, Niren, 314
Giri, V.V., 201
Goa, 12, 43, 77
Gokhale, H.R., 314
Gorkhas, 29, 49, 215, 220
Gould, Sir Basil, 64
Government of Sikkim Act 1974, 279, 297, 304, 313, 322, 325, 329, 340, 352–54, 361, 363, 383–84, 386, 396, 402, 405, 407, 410–11
Government of Sikkim Bill 1974, 297, 299, 301–02
Grant, J.W., 30

Grey, Sir Edward, 166
Griffin, George and Chrissie, 179
Gupta, Ranjit, 343, 397, 398–99, 401
Guru Rimpoche, 27
Gurung, Bhim Bahadur, 153, 169–70, 176, 207, 209, 210, 221, 228, 266. 272, 296, 373, 375, 384, 385
  D.B., 204–06, 212
  Ganja Bahadur, 232–33
  Indra Bahadur, 265
  Lt–Col Kishen Singh, 8, 10, 15–16
Gurungs, 287, 297
Gyalmo of Sikkim (Hope Cooke), 12, 36, 90, 92–94, 97, 100, 117, 138, 150, 155, 158–60, 164, 168, 173–74, 177, 198, 241, 259, 306
Gyaltsen, Sherab, 224, 227, 283
Gyalum of Sikkim, 8, 24, 47, 53, 90, 122, 219, 339, 362, 363, 383
Gyalzing, 9, 10, 71, 12324, 138, 151, 212, 251, 263, 265, 266, 388
Gyantse, 54, 58, 83, 89, 141, 203
Gyatso, Sonam, 265, 388

Haidar, Salman, 249
Haldipur, R.N., 185, 264
Halim, Ruth Karthak Lepchani, 152–53, 155
Hariomal, Tarachand, 263, 349, 407
Hart, J.H., 37
Herrera, General Omar Torrijos, 191
Hidayatullah, Mohammed, 40, 52, 75, 79, 195, 309, 323–26, 410
Himalayan federation, 64, 70
Himalayan Mountaineering Institute, 237
Hooker, Joseph, 32, 45, 67, 120
Hoon, Brigadier A., 225, 279
Hope Leezum, Princess, 169, 259
Hopkinson, A.J., 63, 65
Hussain, Dr Zakir, 177

Iggulden, Captain H.A., 24
Imperial Gazetteer, 42
India, Constitution (36th Amendment) bill, 406
  Constitution (38th Amendment) Act, 411
  Memorandum of Government of India's Views on Constitutional Scheme of Sikkim (25 October 1951), 222
  and, Bhutan, 40 –42, 52, 61–64, 77, 83, 86–87, 94, 109–11, 188, 249–51, 315, 320–21, 343
    Sikkim, 40, 52, 61–64, 77, 109–11, 188, 320–21
  Constituent Assembly of, 52, 61, 72
  Opposition parties (political) of, 193, 314–16
Indian Central Reserve Police, 8, 241, 251
Indian Military Academy (IMA), 59
Indian States, Memorandum on, 166
Indian Statutory Commission, 40
Indo–Sikkim treaty of 1950, 77, 79, 82, 110, 123, 169, 174–75, 187–88, 193, 196, 244–45, 253, 257, 260, 281, 283, 312, 320, 323–26, 354, 411

Indo–Bhutanese treaty, 61
Indo–Nepalese treaty, 61
Indrabodhi, King, 25
International Court of Justice, 58, 165, 192, 327
International League for the Rights of Man, 334
Iyengar, C.S., 60

Jacob, Lt-Gen J.F.R., 19
Jagota, Major R.K., 8
Jaipal, Rikhi, 321
Jana Sangh, 193, 314–15
Janata Congress, 207–13, 215, 219, 221, 223, 246, 255
Janata Parishad, 267
Janata Party (India), 238, 279
Janata Party (Sikkim), 153, 169, 170, 206
Janata Raj Day, 298
Japan, 39, 96, 122, 135, 380
Jelap la, 35, 36, 53, 104, 115
Joint Action Committee, 223, 255

Kabi, 22, 266, 411
Kagyet, 157, 159, 167, 17981, 219, 339, 407
Kali Chakra, 158
Kalimpong, 28, 45, 49, 58, 62, 89, 99, 141–42, 144–45, 147, 149–52, 165, 168, 198, 203–04, 206, 212, 220, 226, 228, 232, 235–38, 244, 252, 259, 262, 266, 268, 303, 306, 345, 374
Kamath, H.V., 113, 144
Kanchenjunga, 66, 83, 180–81
Karki, Gyanendra Bahadur, 321
Karki, Tarak Kumar, 220
Karmapa Lama, 59, 139, 223
Kashmir, 4, 41, 63, 65, 86, 103, 136, 196, 304, 328
Kathmandu, 29, 144, 167, 321, 342–46, 349, 413
Katoch, Major Arjun, 19
Kaul, T.N., 8791, 100, 117, 159, 164, 175, 178, 185, 189–90, 192–99, 362
Kaur, Rajkumar Amrit, 144
Kazi Lendhup Dorji Khangsarpa of Chakung, 7, 26, 45–46, 58, 66, 69, 87, 129, 138, 141, 148, 154, 269, 280
Kazini, Elisa Maria Langford–Rae of Chakung, 144, 146–47
Keating, Kenneth, 94
Kerensky, Alexander Feodorevitch, 203
Keskar, Dr B.V., 41, 72, 73, 162
Kewsing, 108, 139, 212, 362, 388
Khangsarpas, 45, 49, 154
Kharel, Bhuwani Prasad, 266, 278, 373
Khati, Dilkumar, 361
  Purna Bahadur, 210
Khatiawara, Nar Bahadur, 9, 151, 204–06, 208, 212–13, 219–21, 223–24, 228–29, 235, 238, 242, 247, 252–55, 262, 265–66, 271–72, 278, 280, 286, 296–97, 303, 305, 308, 311, 334–35, 337, 361, 370–71, 382, 387–88, 393, 395, 403, 407, 410, 413
Khorana, P.R, 336, 344–45, 347–49, 360, 366, 381, 388, 392
Khye–Bumsa, 22, 25, 219, 266, 411
Kissinger, Dr Henry, 191
Kowcher, General, 225
Kula, Princess, 53
Kullar, Maj-Gen Harbhajan Singh, 5, 14, 18, 19, 21

Kumari, Maharajkumari
Bhuvanesh, 5, 19, 399
Kuomintang, 52, 105
Kutch, 115–16
Kwei Huan, 53

Ladakh, 25, 53, 65, 103, 106–07, 109
Lal, Bipin Bihari, 3, 59, 267, 329
Lal, K.M., 251, 262, 271, 305, 307, 310, 360, 372, 376
Lall, John, 74, 97, 100, 121, 128, 131, 327
Land Reforms Committee, 308, 361
Lansdowne, Lord, 37
Lasso, Athing, 48
Lee-Warner, Sir William, 39
Lepcha, Man Bahadur, 14
  Nayan Tsering, 373, 384
  Rinzing Tongden, 252, 265, 304, 384
  Sherab Palden, 317, 337
  Tasa Tengay, 278, 294, 299, 382
Letters of Exchange, 78
Lhadi Medi, 49, 67, 91
Lhanzin-La, Tashi, 26, 93, 149, 243, 258–59, 382, 398, 409
Lhasa, 24, 27–29, 31–32, 35, 37, 46–47, 53–55, 65, 71, 83, 88–89, 104–07, 109–10, 126, 142–43, 175, 413
Lho-Mon-Tsong-sum, 48, 107, 127, 287
Limaye, Madhu, 314
Linlithgow, Lord, 41
Liu Shao Chi, 114
Lloyd, Captain George W.A., 30–31, 373
Lok Sabha, 109, 161, 184, 284, 308, 312–13, 316–18, 383–84, 403, 406
Lukshyama, 34, 90
Lusaka declaration, 76
Luxembourg, 76, 185

Macaulay, Colman, 29, 35, 120
Macdonald family, 141, 145
maharajas, 5, 34, 40, 42, 43, 57, 78, 103, 114, 145, 166, 172, 184
Maila, Phurba, 153
Malla, K.B., 343
Manavalam, Davy, 251, 263, 285, 372
Manchu theory, 106
Maneckshaw, Field Marshal Sam, 6–7
Manipur, 4
Mannerheim, Marshal Carl Gustaf, 146
Manuel, Emil, 12, 242, 387, 399, 409
Mao Tse-tung, 28
Marwari businessmen, 67, 137, 223, 239, 276, 335, 361
Mathur, J.C., 163
Mauritania, 75, 165
Mavlankar, P.V., 314
McGovern, William Montgomery, 39
McMahon Line, 105, 107, 112, 116
McMahon, Sir Henry, 104 –05
media reports, 71, 93, 96, 152, 161, 233, 243, 245, 259, 287, 288, 293, 304, 316–17, 318, 337, 338, 346, 349, 363, 377, 380
  Daily Telegraph, 50, 93
  Far Eastern Economic Review, 289, 300
  Hindustan Standard, 302
  Hindustan Times, 284, 319–21, 334, 393
  Hsinhua News Agency, 111, 321

- *Le Monde*, 288
- *Manchester Guardian*, 144, 312
- *Newsweek*, 262
- *Now*, 152
- *Observer*, 412
- *Onlooker*, 148
- *People's Daily*, 321
- Press Trust of India, 288
- *Sikkim*, 175, 187
- *Statesman*, 246, 252
- *Times of India*, 304
- *Washington Post*, 93

Mehta, Jagat, 101, 115
Mehta, K.L, 88
Memorandum on Indian States, 166
Menon, N.B., 88, 281–82, 292, 327
Menon, V.P., 42, 62–64
- *The Story of the Integration of the Indian States*, 42

Metcalfe, Sir Charles, 30–31
Minto, Lord, 102, 104
Minyak dynasty, 25
Mipon Rab, 25
Mishra, Shyam Nandan, 315
Mitter, Sir Brojendra Lal, 60
Monaco, 76, 93, 165, 185
monasteries, 3, 9, 44, 46, 49, 58, 65, 121, 138, 201, 362, 391
Montez, Lola (Mrs James), 154
Morley, John, 102
Morocco, 75
Moscow, 88, 134, 198, 249, 318, 326
Mountbatten, Lord Louis, 51, 62–63
Mysore, 39, 315

Nagas, 65, 175, 304
Nair, K.B., 381
Namguay, Dunya, 32–35
Namgyal Institute of Tibetology, 122, 174–75, 234
Namgyal, Chador, 181
- Crown Prince Tenzing, 12, 17, 20, 21, 39, 91, 92, 168, 226, 231–35, 245, 264, 293, 305, 333, 337, 342, 343, 362, 364–67, 369–70, 378, 380–81, 400, 404
- dynasty, 10, 108, 193, 197, 282
- Gyurmed, 28
- Palden Thondup, 2, 91
- Phuntsog, 25, 26, 44, 138
- Prince Jigmed Tenzing, 337, 362
- Prince Wangchuck, 91, 168, 177
- Princess Yangchen, 91
- Sidkeong, 34
- Sir Tashi, 2, 37, 39, 62, 243, 339
- Tchoda, 36, 38, 45, 54
- Thutob, 27–28, 35–38, 40, 45, 49, 60, 82, 165, 222, 285, 336, 387
- Tsering, 132, 186
- Tsugphud, 27, 30–33, 35, 48, 57, 174

Namgyals, 26, 53, 87, 88, 154, 165, 219, 360, 363, 364
Namphong hill, 163
Narayan, Roop, 60, 62
Narendra Mahal, 42, 43, 61, 322
Natarajan, K.V., 357
Nathu-la, 1, 83, 96, 107, 112, 113, 115–17
nawabs, 42, 43, 60
Naxalbari, 24
Nehru, Jawaharlal, 4, 41, 52, 55, 58, 61, 63, 65, 69, 70, 72, 73, 83, 85, 86–87, 89–90, 91, 103, 105, 106, 108, 109–12, 114, 115, 121, 123, 134, 136, 141, 161–63, 166, 188, 189, 190, 328, 393
Neh-Thi-Tsenpo, 25

Nepal, 12, 23–25, 28–30, 32, 36, 42, 61, 65, 77, 90, 98, 103, 106, 108, 122, 131, 141, 144, 146, 160, 161, 167, 175, 179, 193, 211, 215, 221, 230, 233, 243, 252, 254, 269, 315, 320–21, 342–45, 361, 386–87, 411
Nepalese in Sikkim, 2, 7, 10, 21, 39, 44, 48–50, 55, 64, 66, 70, 72, 84, 86, 93, 127, 129, 133–34, 139, 151, 157, 172, 201–02, 204, 206, 208–10, 220, 224, 227, 229, 231, 242, 247–48, 253–55, 257, 262–66, 288, 303, 308, 328, 347–48, 360, 385, 389, 392, 412
Netuk Lama, 201
New Zealand and Cook Islands, 195
Non-aligned Nations Movement, 191
North Vietnam, 165
Noyes, Winchester, 91

O'Malley, L.S.S., 67

Pakistan, 17, 42, 52, 77, 79, 100, 111, 115, 116, 190, 236, 249, 315, 321, 322, 328
Palden, Prince, 239
Paljor Stadium, 71, 225, 232, 240
Paljor, Tendook, 45, 59
Palkhivala, Nani A., 192, 194
Panama, 190–91, 328
Panchen Lama, 60
Pant, Apa Saheb, 90, 100
Pant, K.C., 179–80
Patel, Sardar Vallabhbhai, 60, 63, 154
Patterson, George, 41, 237
Pechying Lama, 210
Pell, Senator Claiborne, 334
Percy, Senator Charles, 94, 345
Peter, Prince of Greece, 141
Phari Kutsap, 54
Phodang Lama, 45, 48, 49, 154
Phodrang, Yapshi Samdup, 54
Planning Commission, 261, 270, 330
political officers (POs), role of, 3–6, 8, 14, 18–19, 21, 36–39, 46, 48, 55, 62–65, 70–72, 77, 82–88, 90, 92–95, 97–101, 107, 117, 126–27, 129–30, 135, 152, 161, 164, 166–67, 172–73, 176–77, 183–84, 188, 198, 209, 215, 218–19, 223, 226–28, 230, 233, 235–36, 239–42, 245, 250, 252, 255–57, 261, 275–76, 278, 280–81, 284, 288, 290–91, 295, 298–99, 301, 307, 309, 311, 313, 316, 327, 330, 332, 338, 342–43, 354–55, 357, 367, 369–71, 374, 376, 382, 389, 395, 398–99, 401, 403, 412
Portugal, 77
Poudyal, Ram Chandra, 8, 222, 232, 266, 269, 278, 283, 288, 296, 297, 304, 346, 347–48, 350, 364, 370, 382
Pradhan, Adhik Lal, 227
  Badri Nath, 253, 266, 373
  Kashi Raj, 112, 129, 132, 153, 221
  Krishna Chandra, 131, 151, 186, 206–07, 209–10, 213, 220–21, 228, 235, 247, 266, 272, 304, 364, 375, 378, 384, 393

Laxmidas, 40
Nahakul, 131, 153, 169, 172, 176, 206–08, 210, 213, 221, 227, 228–29, 243–44, 252
Prasad, Baleshwar, 100
Dr Rajendra, 61
Raghubir, 70, 130
S.K., 352, 407
Puerto Rico, 76, 195

Quit Sikkim movement, 184

Rabdentse, 29, 36, 120
Radhakrishnan, Sarvepalli, 145
Radio Amateur Call Book, 380
Ragashars, 53
Rai, Chandra Das, 72, 132–34, 161, 224, 227, 232, 287
Rai, Deo Prakash, 220
Rai, Kaloo, 172, 209, 210, 221, 223, 224, 227, 229, 245, 252
Rai, Santosh Kumar, 209, 213, 220, 308, 346, 351–52, 388, 401, 403, 407
Raina, Asoka, 236, 238
Rajagopaul, G.R., 271, 277–78, 280–82, 284, 286, 289, 296
Rajya Sabha, 109, 284, 312, 318, 406
Ram, Govind, 275–76
Rana, Maharajah Mohan Shumshere Jang Bahadur, 145
Rangpo, 42, 71, 125, 175, 198, 207, 235, 241, 261, 346–47, 364, 368
Raniphul, 231–33, 235, 364, 391
Rasaily, Madan Mohan, 9, 12, 136, 137, 160–61, 218–19, 224, 227, 228–29, 232, 283, 344, 348–51, 354, 356, 384, 386, 399, 407, 411
Shyam Sundar, 360–61
Tejendra, 351
Rasgotra, Maharaj Krishna, 343
Rashtrapati Bhavan, 173, 177, 199, 250, 408
Rashtriya Swayamsevak Sangh, 193
Rau, Sir Benegal Narsing, 60, 166
Rawang, 211, 362
Razalim, Durga Prasad, 211, 212
Reading, Lord, 43
Research and Analysis Wing (RAW), 100, 143, 197, 218, 226, 236–38, 251, 254, 262, 270, 289, 327, 389, 390, 394, 395, 401
Reserve Bank of India, 137
Revenue Order Number One, 308
Rhenock, 26, 49, 54, 142, 235, 391
Rhenock House, 382, 398
Rhenock, Kazi Tse–ten Tashi, 26
Rhenock, Kazi Paljor Tashi (Penjola), 26, 47, 49
Ridge, 3–4, 10–12, 116, 163, 241, 277, 382, 389
Rinchinpong, 33
Rinzing, Tsewing Dorjee, 351
Risley, H.H., 38, 49
Roerich, Svetoslav and Devika Rani, 141
Rowland, John, 116
Roy, Chatur Singh, 220, 227, 228, 266, 269, 272, 286, 301, 304, 403
Rusk, Dean, 191
Rustomji, Nari, 59, 88, 98, 100, 121, 159, 251, 329

Sakya, Sanu, 187
Samyukta Socialist Party, 220

San Marino, 164–65
Sanyal, Jayanta, 251, 263, 351, 372
Security Act, 220
Sen, Sirdar D. K., 57
Shah, Prithvi Narayan, 29
Shape, Tsarong, 104
Sharma, Shankar Dayal, 303
  Som Dutt, 357
  Tulsi, 224, 227
Shastri, Lal Bahadur, 115–16, 173–74
Sheng Tai, 37
Sherab, Kunzang, 160, 224, 227
Sherpa, Nima, 13
Shukla, Satyendra R., *Sikkim: The Story of integration*, 150
Sikkim Gazette, 92
Sikkim through Figures, 126
Sikkim, 1948 agreement of, 70
  1961 agreement of, 121
  1973 agreement of, 8, 240, 255, 257, 260, 263, 268–69, 271 –72, 281, 286, 292, 295, 298, 304, 313, 346, 353, 365, 372, 376, 405
  and, Bhutan, 28, 64, 77, 127, 142, 201, 342
    Britain, 23, 29–30, 37, 43, 51, 52, 55, 57, 76, 103, 105, 142, 184, 322, 361
    India, 40, 52, 61–64, 77, 109–11, 188, 320–21
  associate statehood for, 194, 288, 312, 314, 322–24, 334, 336, 354, 357, 374, 404–06, 411
    India's views on, 4, 40–42, 52, 73–75, 101, 128, 201, 208, 283–84, 324, 410,
  Bill Protest Committee, 361
  coinage, 40, 64, 122
  Congress, 74, 246, 253–54, 262, 265–68, 276, 281–85, 289, 291, 292, 298, 301–02, 334, 337–38, 365, 371, 372, 384, 388, 392, 395, 402, 406
  Constitution Bill Protest Committee, 283
  constitution drawn up (1951), 129, 221–22, 260
  constitutional position of, 197, 210, 288, 301, 312
  councillors, 129–32, 153, 167, 202, 210, 212, 214, 216, 221, 256, 272
  economic plans for, 123
  emergency in, 112, 153, 224
  Executive Council, 129–32, 170–71, 204, 212, 256, 258, 270
  executive councillors, 112, 132, 153 –54, 171–72, 176–77, 199, 203, 209–14, 257, 265
  festivals of, 25, 158, 180, 339, 340, 362
  Field Force, 36
  flag of, 2, 21, 85, 88, 173, 177, 184, 218, 267, 284, 291, 357, 363, 403, 405, 408
  Friends of, 334
  general elections in, 131–32, 134, 153, 169, 200, 202, 204, 206, 209–10, 212, 216, 219, 221, 246, 264, 267, 341, 365, 388, 395
  Guards, 3, 4, 6–10, 13, 16–20, 33, 95, 108, 120–21, 134, 138, 181, 223–24, 233, 241, 256, 286, 337, 346, 347–48, 362, 363, 368, 389–90, 405

Guards Prison Camp (Sirwani), 17, 410
House, 163, 189, 318, 390–91
independence for, 60, 114, 143–44, 159, 161, 170, 173, 176, 183–84, 186, 187, 193–95, 198, 210, 216, 229, 328, 361, 383
independence of judiciary, 168, 202, 255, 263–64, 350–54, 356, 377
membership to international agencies, 164, 185, 193, 195, 197
memorandum to New Delhi, 57–58, 134, 175, 238, 279, 335, 350, 396, 413
national anthem of, 16
Nationalised Transport, 125, 273, 298, 389
panchayat elections in, 128
political parties, demands of, 69
  Denzong Rong Sezum, 252
  Janata Parishad, 267
  Janata Party, 170
  National Party, 15, 46, 127–31, 133, 137, 153, 169–70, 172, 173, 201–03, 210, 211, 213–16, 221, 227, 234, 241, 245, 252, 254, 255, 257, 265, 266, 291, 304, 371, 388, 393
  Praja Mandal, 66, 69
  Praja Sudharak Samaj, 66, 69
  Prajatantra Party, 265, 266, 283, 287, 395
  Rajya Praja Sammelan, 66, 69, 72, 128, 133, 207
  Sikkim National Congress (SNC), 133–35, 148, 152, 153, 155, 169–71, 172, 202–07, 210, 211–16, 219–21, 223, 228, 246, 247, 255
  State Congress, 69–73, 112, 127–29, 131–32, 153, 170, 173, 201, 207–08, 210, 252
  Swatantra Dal, 132–33, 186
prime minister of, 72–73, 129, 131, 209, 214, 288, 296
State Council, 59, 69, 129
students of, 270, 287, 316
Students' Association, 336, 351
Declaration of Independence (1975) by, 361
Subjects Regulations (1961), 134
subjects, 86, 91, 108, 203, 230, 326
topography of, 29, 66–68, 96, 138, 180, 395
treaties, *see* under treaty
Simla conference, 51, 55, 105, 116
Singh, Avtar, 85, 219, 235, 240
  Brigadier Dipender, 18
  Captain Dimik, 70, 72, 129, 221
  Charan, 350
  Colonel Sudharshan, 18
  Gurbachan, 4–6, 8, 13–14, 18–20, 21, 81, 100, 251, 327, 330, 333, 337, 338, 343, 353, 359, 362, 366, 367, 369, 378, 382, 387, 389, 395, 398, 400–01, 403, 407, 408
  Inderjit Bahadur, 88, 100, 101, 327
  Kewal, 242, 245, 250, 255, 259–60, 282, 292, 301–03, 316, 327, 333, 362, 390, 414

Maharaja Gulab, 103
Raja Dinesh, 185, 193
S.K., 390
Swaran, 193, 197, 280, 282, 292, 303, 308, 311–13, 316, 318, 320, 326, 327, 337, 414
Tejpal, 239
Singtam, 16, 71, 133–34, 220, 223, 231, 233–35, 251–53, 261, 273–77, 336, 345, 388
Sitaramayya, Pt B. Pattabhi, 60
South Block, 163, 164
Soviet Union and Czechoslovakia, 188, 321, 328
Soyang-La, Princess, 337, 413
State Bank of India, 142
State Council and Executive Council Proclamation of 1953, 129, 134, 172, 208, 215, 256, 257, 411
Subba, Mrs Kalavati, 283
Subba, P.S., 351
Subeidi, N.K., 151, 223, 224, 262, 266, 278, 283, 288, 296–97, 347, 364, 373, 375
Surita, Ivan, 85
Surpa, Dzasa Surkhang, 65
Swell, G.G., 314

Tagore, Rabindranath, 141
Tarching Lama, 49
Targain, Ongkit, 409
Taring Raja, 54, 155
Tashi, Guru, 25
Paljor, 26, 47, 409
Tasho, E.T., 124, 139
Tawang, 65, 102, 106, 112
Teesta river, 29, 32, 68, 96, 142, 259, 294, 345
Temple, Sir Richard, 35, 45
Tenzing, Nima, 211, 227
Thakse palace, 219, 339, 382, 389
Thapa, Kaiser Bahadur, 126, 160, 175, 187, 393, 398
Theebaw, King of Burma, 141
Thekong–tek, 22, 26, 153, 219, 266, 411
Thimpu, 166–67, 249, 343
Third World, 191
Thondup, Gyalo, 109
Thupten Geley, 391
Tibet, 1, 2–4, 21–29, 31–33, 35–38, 42, 45, 47, 49–58, 61, 63–65, 67–68, 71, 77, 85, 87, 89, 90, 92, 97, 99, 102–10, 112–13, 115, 121–22, 128, 138, 141–44, 148, 154, 158, 162, 165, 167, 169, 174–75, 181, 193, 198, 201, 208, 230, 232, 234, 237, 244, 259, 262, 302, 307, 322, 328, 337, 339, 342, 387, 391, 408, 411, 413
Tonga, and Britain, 42, 76
Tongsa Penlop, 165
Topden, Karma, 47, 93, 95, 149, 155, 198, 212, 218, 224–25, 227, 230, 232, 234, 255, 258, 263, 287, 316, 318, 388, 409
Kunga, 254
Martam, 46–47, 130, 133, 153, 170, 171, 172, 201, 227
Mrs, 47
Topkhani, 274–77, 280
treaties, unequal, 75–77, 188, 191–92
treaty, 1842 treaty between the ruler of Kashmir and Tibet, 65
between US and Philipe Banau–Varilla, 190–92